MARK C

The Retailing Book

We work with leading authors to develop the
strongest educational materials in retailing, bringing
cutting-edge thinking and best learning practice to
a global market.

Under a range of well-known imprints, including
Financial Times Prentice Hall, we craft high quality print and
electronic publications which help readers to understand
and apply their content, whether studying or at work.

To find out more about the complete range of our
publishing, please visit us on the World Wide Web at:
www.pearsoned.co.uk

The Retailing Book

Principles and Applications

Edited by Paul Freathy

 Prentice Hall
FINANCIAL TIMES

An imprint of **Pearson Education**

Harlow, England • London • New York • Boston • San Francisco • Toronto • Sydney • Singapore • Hong Kong
Tokyo • Seoul • Taipei • New Delhi • Cape Town • Madrid • Mexico City • Amsterdam • Munich • Paris • Milan

Pearson Education Limited
Edinburgh Gate
Harlow
Essex CM20 2JE
England

and Associated Companies around the world

Visit us on the World Wide Web at:
www.pearsoned.co.uk

ISBN 0273-65548-5

British Library Cataloguing-in-Publication Data
A catalogue record for this book is available from the British Library.

Library of Congress Cataloging-in-Publication Data

The retailing book : principles and applications / edited by Paul Freathy.
    p. cm.
  Includes bibliographical references and index.
  ISBN 0-273-65548-5
   1. Retail trade. I. Freathy, Paul

  HF5429.R4787 2003
  658.8'7--dc21   2003048265

10 9 8 7 6 5 4 3 2 1
06 05 04 03

Typeset in 9.5/12pt Stone Sans by 30
Printed by Ashford Colour Press Ltd, Gosport.

To Iris, Iestyn and Gethin

Contents

Preface

I start this book with a confession – I am an eclectic. The idea for *The Retailing Book* was not wholly my own. Rather it stemmed from a series of discussions with colleagues concerning the provision of retail texts for students. Whilst it was acknowledged that there are a number of competent retail works available, these are often quite advanced and rely upon the reader having a basic understanding of the subject area. The majority of introductory texts that are available tend to be focused on the United States and have only limited relevance for students elsewhere. Given the increased popularity of retailing as an academic subject we felt that a gap in the market currently existed.

The Retailing Book has therefore been written as an introductory text for individuals wishing to understand more about the complexities of the retail sector. It is designed to provide readers with a broad overview of contemporary retailing and to link these developments to a series of theoretical frameworks. The book is divided into eight parts. Each part begins with a core chapter that provides a conceptual understanding of the subject area. In developing these chapters I have unashamedly drawn on my experiences with distance learning teaching and included self-assessment questions (SAQs), numerous examples and suggestions for further reading. Each of the core chapters are followed by in-depth case studies that apply practical examples to the topic area.

Key features

- **Concise presentation** that provides students with a broad understanding of retail management. The principles that are learnt can be built on by other, more advanced texts.
- **Combined core and case study chapters** help create a balance between theory and practice.
- **Use of international companies** to illustrate best practice, thus allowing students to understand the global and dynamic nature of retailing.

- **Self-assessment questions** reinforce the learning objectives of each chapter, stimulating students to think more deeply about the subject whilst confirming their understanding of the material.

Web site

The Institute for Retail Studies has a web site dedicated to retailing. Students may find the materials and information contained on the site useful to their studies. There are research papers that can be downloaded free of charge and other supplementary information for *The Retailing Book*. Visitors will also find details of the Market Reports and Statistical Series that the Institute publishes. Moreover the site gives a number of useful links to retailers' web pages, research journals and other academic and commercial research centres. The site addresss is www.stir.ac.uk/marketing/irs.

Introduction

I am thankful that *The Retailing Book* has moved from an idea scribbled on a single piece of paper to the edited tome you have in front of you. Behind its conception was considerable discussion as to what form and format it should take – there already exist many solid, competent retail texts on the market and there was a strong desire not to replicate these.

I have therefore attempted to position *The Retailing Book* as an introductory text to the subject of retailing and retail management. Drawing upon both retail academics and retail practitioners, *The Retailing Book* offers an overview of the main strategic functions within retailing and illustrates their operation through a series of 'real life' case studies. It aims to provide the foundation for understanding the concept of retailing, and is designed to complement – rather than compete with – many of the texts currently available.

As this book is an introductory text, it attempts to cover a wide range of retail topics. However, by its very nature, *The Retailing Book* will be limited in what it can include. Retailing remains a complex, diverse and constantly changing subject area and, despite having twenty-four chapters, there are numerous topics that remain unexamined. Despite this, the aim is to provide a basic understanding of the subject of retailing. It does this by dividing the book into eight Parts, each with an introductory chapter to the subject area. This conceptual chapter is then followed by two case study chapters. which provide practical examples in a retail setting. If, having read the theoretical chapter and studied the cases, you are enthusiastic enough to investigate the subject further, a series of additional readings are provided for you.

While reading through the main theoretical chapters you will come across self-assessment questions (SAQs). SAQs are included in the text and allow you to recap on what you have read so far. It is all too easy to read through a chapter without pausing to consider any of the issues under discussion. SAQs will ask you to reflect on what you have learned and ask you questions directly related to the material you have read. Answers to the SAQs are provided at the end of *The Retailing Book*.

As has already been mentioned, then, the book is divided into eight Parts. These are:

Part 1: The retail context. The first Part of the book provides an overview of the retail environment. The retail sector has undergone significant structural change with the growth of the large multiple retailers, the concentration of market power, the growth of out-of-town retailing and increased competition from overseas retailers. Chapter 1 provides an overview of these events and provides a framework and context for the other chapters in the book, while the two case studies that follow it illustrate the dynamic nature of the retail environment.

Chapter 2 demonstrates how a number of the developments discussed in the previous chapter have manifested themselves in practice. Burt and Sparks detail the experiences of four grocery multiples and highlight how retailing has moved beyond national boundaries to operate in an international arena. Similarly, in Chapter 3, a study of airport retailing demonstrates how changes in the external environment can reconfigure an entire retail sector.

Part 2: Strategic planning in retailing. Having provided a basic framework for understanding the retail environment, *The Retailing Book* looks at how companies strategically plan for the future. Chapter 4 provides an overview of the planning process and discusses the methods used by retailers to develop and grow their businesses. This chapter aims to provide a basic description of the methods that retailers use to take their businesses forward in the medium and long term.

The two case studies illustrate the parameters that are placed upon retailers when planning strategically. Focusing upon the issues of retail ethics and retail finance, these chapters aim to show that strategic planning does not operate in a vacuum and is subject to a series of constraints that may limit the direction or the success of an individual firm.

Part 3: Retail development. This considers the importance of retail location. You will undoubtedly come across the saying that the three most important things in retailing are 'location, location, location'. Chapter 7 explains the thinking behind this old saying and considers the issues of land-use planning and shopping centre development. Chapter 8 illustrates how the planning system can influence the movement of retailers to an out-of-town location and highlights the consequent impact that this can have upon the city centre.

Chapter 9 focuses on the role of the Town Centre Manager (TCM). In order to promote town centres in the face of increased competition from retail parks, a range of initiatives have been undertaken. This chapter provides examples of how TCMs have sought to counter the threat of out-of-town retail parks and discusses their continued role in the marketing of town centre locations.

Part 4: Retail marketing. Marketing was once described as 'the best fun you can have with your clothes on'. Certainly, those who study and teach marketing develop a passion for the subject. Chapter 10 provides a brief introduction to the marketing concept and attempts to explain the reasons behind this enthusiasm. Central to the concept of marketing is an understanding of the consumer. Chapter 11 demonstrates how the first stage in satisfying customer demand is to gather detailed and relevant information that allows you to better plan your marketing strategy. Having taken the opportunity to understand your customers, the next stage is to create the goods and services they require. Chapter 12, therefore, considers the role of branding and the benefits that can be derived from the development of a brand strategy.

Part 5: Human resource management. You will often hear the saying that 'retailing is a people business'. Certainly, it is true that individuals *can* make a significant difference to the fortunes of a retail company. In this fifth Part we consider the role of people in retailing. Chapter 13 provides an overview of the retail labour market and details the composition of retail employment. The case studies examine two issues that are of constant concern to many retailers. Reducing labour turnover and improving customer service are issues that require proactive HRM strategies: both authors are experienced retail practitioners who are involved in the management of people.

Part 6: Buying and merchandising. This represents a relatively under-researched area of academic study. In many texts the subject receives little or no attention and the majority of published works (with certain exceptions) tend to be US based. The intention of Chapter 16 is to provide an introduction to the area of buying and merchandising. This in itself is not an easy task, as there is no single approach that characterises the role of a buyer or merchandiser. The chapter therefore seeks to provide a series of generic principles that may or may not be exercised by retail businesses. Chapter 17 provides an applied example and details the buying and merchandising process in a fashion retailer. By way of contrast, Chapter 18 takes a supply-side perspective and considers the issues surrounding international sourcing and relationship development within the fresh goods market.

Part 7: Retail logistics. The seventh section of *The Retailing Book* draws upon acknowledged experts in the field of retail logistics. The aim of Chapter 19 is to highlight developments in logistics and provide you with a basic introduction to the factors driving change in distribution. In Chapter 20, the focus is upon the logistics challenges that derive from new channels of distribution and, in particular, the supply-side implications of e-commerce. In Chapter 21, we consider the wider role of cooperation and provide a detailed case study on strategic alliances in the Swedish grocery market.

Part 8: Retail futures. Having provided a reflection on contemporary retailing, the final Part of *The Retailing Book* speculates on the future of retailing. Despite the protestations of *X-files* devotees, the truth is *not* out there. There is no pre-determined path which retailing will follow. Chapter 22 provides a framework for conceptualising future retail outcomes while the two case studies examine areas of significant retail development. Chapter 23 broadens the previous debate on e-commerce and considers the range of issues that stem from the implementation of an e-tailing strategy. In the final chapter, retail payment systems are examined and we consider whether, in the future, we are likely to see the emergence of a cashless society.

While *The Retailing Book* is aimed at providing an understanding of the main issues and themes that occur within contemporary retailing, it is also designed to stimulate your interest in this creative, innovative and exciting market sector. Whether, you decide to read the book from cover to cover, or choose chapters selectively, your knowledge of retailing will hopefully be both broadened and enhanced. Therefore, on behalf of all the contributing authors, I trust you will enjoy *The Retailing Book*.

Paul Freathy
December 2002

List of contributors

Nicholas Alexander is Professor of Services Management at the University of Ulster. He has served as a member of the Retail and Consumer Services Foresight Panel, the Foresight Task Force on E-Commerce, the Retail and Distribution Social Context Subgroup and the Retail Export Group at the Department of Trade and Industry (DTI). He has led DTI Scoping Missions to Brazil and Poland. Nicholas is an editor of *The Service Industries Journal* and has been guest editor of the *International Marketing Review* and *Business History*. He is the author of *International Retailing* and has edited a number of retail texts. Nick is also the author of numerous academic articles and commercial reports.

Grete Birtwistle is Head of the Division of Marketing in the Caledonian Business School, Glasgow Caledonian University. Her PhD explored the market positioning and consumer perception of store image of UK fashion retailers. Her current research is within the area of supply chain management with a particular focus on quick response. Before joining the University she spent a number of years working in fashion retailing. She is a visiting lecturer at the Department of Textiles and Consumer Sciences, Florida State University, Tallahassee.

Adelina Broadbridge is a Senior Lecturer in the Department of Marketing at the University of Stirling. She joined the University after spending several years working in the retail sector for Barkers of Kensington and Harrods. She teaches across a variety of undergraduate and postgraduate programmes and is currently Director of the MBA in Retailing by distance learning programme. Her research interests are in the field of human resource management, primarily within the retail sector. These interests have focused on gender in management, the career development of managers, stress and perceptions of retailing as a graduate career. Her current research projects include continuing work on the career progression of retail managers, the human resource implications of the professionalisation of charity shops and the implications for students' well-being of combining employment with university life.

Steve Burt is Professor of Retail Marketing at the Institute for Retail Studies in the Department of Marketing, University of Stirling. He is President of the European Association for Education and Research in Commercial Distribution. His research interests have focused on the area of comparative and international retailing and structural change in retailing. Recent research activity has looked at the international transfer of retail image, retail grocery branding in the United Kingdom and takeover and merger activity.

Eric Calderwood is a management consultant specialising in retail development and undertaking consultancy projects for a range of retail and public sector clients. Eric has over 25 years' practical retail experience in buying, marketing, retail operations and store development, largely within the consumer co-operative movement of the United Kingdom. His main research and consultancy activities concentrate on the relationship of retailers and their customers. He has an MBA from the University of Stirling and has published research into the shopping behaviour of rural communities.

Keri Davies is a Senior Lecturer in the Department of Marketing, University of Stirling. Before joining the Department in 1987 Keri worked in Manchester in the Northern Office of the Town and Country Planning Association and as a research assistant at Sheffield Polytechnic and in the Department of Computing Science at the University of Stirling. His research interests include retail change in the Pacific Asia region, land use planning, marketing and retail education.

John Fernie is Professor of Retail Marketing and Head of the School of Management and Languages at Heriot-Watt University, Edinburgh. He has written and contributed to numerous textbooks and papers on retail management, especially in the field of retail logistics and the internationalisation of retail formats. He is editor of the *International Journal of Retail and Distribution Management* and received the award of Editor of the Year in 1997 in addition to Leading Editor awards in 1994, 1998 and 2000. He is on the editorial board of the *Journal of Product and Brand Management*. He is an active member of the Institute of Logistics and Transport and the Chartered Institute of Marketing in the United Kingdom as well as holding office in the American Collegiate Retail Association. In 2001 he became a member of the Logistics Directors Forum, a group of leading professionals in supply chain management and logistics in the United Kingdom.

Susan S. Fiorito is an Associate Professor of Merchandising at Florida State University, Tallahassee. Her areas of research interest include retail technologies, retail buying processes and strategies and family-owned businesses. Susan completed a sabbatical year researching at the Institute for Retail Studies at the University of Stirling. Amongst other things she has learnt the meaning of the word 'driech'.

Paul Freathy is Professor of Retail Management at the University of Stirling. He is responsible for developing management education for the retail sector and has taught senior managers in Europe, Africa and the West Indies. His teaching specialisms include strategic management and marketing. He has been a member of the Department of Trade and Industry Retail Strategy Task Force and has undertaken applied research for a number of private sector and not-for-profit organisations. His current research focuses on retail developments in the airport sector and he collaborates closely with members of the air transport industry.

Cliff Guy is a Professor at the Department of City and Regional Planning at Cardiff University. His research interests include retail development and its interaction with land use planning and with property investment trends, impacts of retail change on town centres and local shops, international comparisons in retail development and town planning policy. In 2000 he was a member of the advisory panel on Research into Secondary Retailing to the National Retail Planning Forum. Cliff is a member of the Royal Town Planning Institute and Fellow of the Royal Society of Arts.

Alan Hallsworth is Professor of Retailing at the Manchester Metropolitan University Business School (MMUBS). In the 1970s his retail research involved assessing the impact of food superstores on their trading rivals – a topic he is currently revisiting with the assistance of an Economic and Social Research Council grant in order to study such change over time. He has also researched the factors behind retail internationalisation. A particular interest is retail change in Canada and he is a past President of the British Association for Canadian Studies. With colleagues at MMUBS he is involved in promoting diversity on the high street and in the small shop sector.

Jim Hendrie has been involved in retailing for 25 years, in shop, area and regional management. He has worked in many different fast-moving consumer goods (FMCG) sectors, with companies such as Spar, Martin Retail Group, Thorntons and Hallmark Cards. Having studied business and management in the late 1970s and early 1980s, he embarked upon an MBA in Retailing by distance learning at Stirling University in May 2000, which he completed in October 2002. Jim currently works for a national high street retailer.

Ulf Johansson is Associate Professor in Business Administration at Lund University, Sweden and is responsible for the retail management programme at Campus Helsingborg (part of Lund University). His research interests include retail marketing, strategy and leadership as well as buyer–seller relationships, strategic alliances, networks and internationalisation. Empirically, most of his research is focused upon retail and manufacturing relationships in the European food industry. Ulf has published several books (in Swedish) as well as numerous articles in academic journals. Ulf also works as a consultant to companies both inside and outside the retail industry.

Alan McKinnon is Professor of Logistics and Director of the Logistics Research Centre at Heriot-Watt University, Edinburgh. Alan has been researching and teaching in the field of logistics for 25 years and has published widely on the subject. He has undertaken several studies for the European Commission and been an adviser to several UK government departments and parliamentary committees. He was chairman of the UK government's Retail Logistics Task Force and has recently been appointed to its Freight and Logistics Research Group. Alan is a Fellow of the Institute of Logistics and Transport and a founder member of its Logistics Research Network set up to promote research on logistics and freight transport in UK universities and colleges.

Frank O'Connell is Retail Director for the Aer Rianta Group. He is also Chairman of the Travel Value Association and on the board of the International Travel Retail Confederation. Frank has an MBA from the University of Stirling and has published in a number of academic journals. In 1998 he was co-author of a retail text on *European Airport Retailing*.

Gordon O'Connor is a Store Manager for the Irish grocery retailer Superquinn. Gordon joined the company as a part-time employee while still at school and became a full-time colleague in 1982. In 1984 he joined the company's retail training programme and was appointed to a Junior Management position in 1986. In 1997 he gained an MBA in Retailing and Wholesaling from the University of Stirling. In 1998 he was appointed Store Manager in the Bray Branch. In 2001 he was seconded to Superquinn's support office where he oversaw several diversification projects, including the development of in-store banking. In 2002 he returned to store management once again in the Bray Branch where he continues to enjoy the challenge!

Andrew Paddison is a Lecturer in Marketing at the University of Stirling. Prior to this he held academic posts at Middlesex University and the University of Paisley. His main teaching responsibilities are in retailing and marketing strategy. Currently he is involved in teaching undergraduate courses on retail operations, postgraduate courses on marketing strategy and management development programmes in retailing. His research interests are in town centre management and small shops. Recent articles have been published on charity shops and ethnic minority enterprises, whilst a number of consultancy projects have been undertaken for local authorities.

Mike Pretious is a Lecturer in Retailing and Marketing at the Institute for Retail Studies, University of Stirling. His teaching focuses primarily on retail marketing, buying and merchandising. Mike teaches on the University's MSc degree in Retail Management and the MBA in Retailing by distance learning. His current research interests are in the areas of retail buying and business crime.

Jonathan Reynolds is Director of the Oxford Institute of Retail Management (OXIRM) and Fellow in Retail Marketing at Templeton College. He first joined the College to work with UK food retailer Tesco on the application of new information technology. A geographer, urban planner and retailer by turn, he has published and spoken widely on retailing and technology and retail and services marketing. He works with a wide range of retailing and consumer service businesses on both executive education and applied research projects. As a faculty member of Oxford University's Saïd Business School, he teaches e-commerce on Oxford's MBA programme. He has recently completed a period of sabbatical leave as Visiting Professor at the Amos Tuck Business School at Dartmouth College.

Jill Ritchie graduated with an MBA from the University of Stirling in 2001. She is currently employed by a leading international management consultancy firm.

Leigh Sparks is Professor of Retail Studies at the University of Stirling, where his research concentrates on aspects of retailing, with particular emphasis on structural and spatial change. His research has been funded by major businesses, research councils and governments, and he has published widely in leading retailing and marketing journals. He was previously Head of the Department of Marketing, Director of the Institute for Retail Studies and Dean of the Faculty of Management. He is currently Director of the Scottish Higher Education Funding Council-funded Centre for the Study of Retailing in Scotland (CSRS) and co-editor of *The International Review of Retail, Distribution and Consumer Research.*

Ian Spencer is a Teaching Fellow in the Department of Marketing at the University of Stirling. He holds a Bachelor's degree from Stirling. Prior to joining the

Department Ian worked as a financial auditor for a major consultancy company. He currently teaches on the undergraduate Marketing degree, the MBA in Retailing by distance learning as well as on management development programmes. His teaching specialisms include finance and capital budgeting.

Paul Whysall is Professor of Retailing at Nottingham Business School, Nottingham Trent University and currently is academic leader of the Marketing Group within the Department of Strategic Management and Marketing. In the past his main research interest was focused around aspects of retail location and retail planning, but in recent years he has been developing an interest in ethical aspects of retailing and marketing ethics in general, as well as having written about ethics and e-commerce. His main teaching is now in the area of business ethics.

Steve Worthington is Professor of Marketing at Monash University. He specialises in the issues surrounding the distribution of financial services particularly via plastic cards and in the organisation and control of the payment systems through which these cards are used. Steve has published widely, both in academic journals and in more practitioner-focused publications. He has also written a number of case studies concerning both bank and retailer provision of financial services. A frequent presenter/chairman at industry conferences, Steve has also been used by the media as an independent commentator on the delivery of financial services by plastic cards. He has also authored a major report entitled 'Branding and Relationships in Plastic Cards', which has been published by the *Financial Times*.

Acknowledgements

The Retailing Book has drawn on the competencies and expertise of numerous academics and practitioners from the United Kingdom, Europe and beyond. The key learning points can be easily understood, as 'real-life' examples help place the various theories in context. I would like to thank the following individuals for their willingness to participate, their ability to meet my deadlines and their speed in responding to my queries. The potentially difficult task of editing *The Retailing Book* was made easier by their cooperation.

Nicholas Alexander – University of Ulster
Grete Birtwisle – Glasgow Caledonian University
Adelina Broadbridge – University of Stirling
Steve Burt – University of Stirling
Eric Calderwood – Eric Calderwood Associates
Keri Davies – University of Stirling
John Fernie – Heriot-Watt University
Susan Fiorito – Florida State University
Cliff Guy – University of Cardiff
Alan Hallsworth – Manchester Metropolitan University
Jim Hendrie – Hibernian Stores
Ulf Johansson – Lund University
Alan McKinnon – Heriot-Watt University
Frank O'Connor – Aer Rianta
Gordon O'Connor – Superquinn
Andrew Paddison – University of Stirling
Mike Pretious – University of Stirling
Jill Ritchie – Consultant
Jonathan Reynolds – OXIRM, Templeton College, University of Oxford
Leigh Sparks – University of Stirling
Ian Spencer – University of Stirling
Paul Whysall – Nottingham Business School
Steve Worthington – Monash University

I would also like to thank the following for their input into the original proposal. The suggestions they provided were both useful and constructive.

Ray Wright – Anglia Polytechnic University
David Bennison – Manchester Metropolitan University
Margaret-Anne Lawler – Dublin Institute of Technology
Gary Warnaby – University of Salford

Finally, I would like to thank the entire team at Pearson Education: Thomas Sigel, Senior Acquisitions Editor; Ernestine Weller, Editorial Assistant; Richard Whitbread, Desk Editor; and Sarah Phillipson, Marketing Manager, for all their efforts in making this book a reality.

Paul Freathy
University of Stirling

Publisher's Acknowledgements

We are grateful to the following for permission to reproduce copyright material:

Table 1.7 from Corporate Branding, Retailing & Retail Internationalisation, in *Corporate Reputation Review* 5(2/3), 194–212 (Burt, S. and Sparks, L. 2002); Table 1.9 from *Future patterns of retailing in Scotland*, Chief Researcher, The Scottish Executive Central Research Unit, Edinburgh (Dawson, J. 2000); Table 1.10 from *Supermarkets*, Vol. 2, Table 5.12, p. 54, Deputy Information Centre Manager, Competition Commission (Competition Commission, 2000); Table 1.11 from Dawson, J. and Burt, S. (1998) European Retailing: dynamics, restructuring & development issues, in D. Pinder, (ed.), *The New Europe: economy, society and environment*. Reproduced by permission of John Wiley & Sons Limited; Tables 2.1 & 2.2 from Grocery retailing in Europe, M+M Planet Retail, www.planetretail.net (Planet Retail, 2002); Table 2.3 from Ahold Annual Reports 1992, 1996 and 2001, Ahold Corporate Communications; Table 2.5 from Delhaize Group Annual Reports 1992, 1996 and 2001, Investor Relations Manager, Delhaize Group; Table 2.6 from Tesco Annual Reports 1992, 1996 and 2001, Tesco PLC; Table 7.1 from *Planning Policy Wales*, Publications Centre (National Assembly for Wales, 2002); Figure 10.4 from Customer care: the ultimate marketing tool, in R. Wensley (ed.), *Marketing Proceedings* (Thomas, M. 1987), Warwick University Marketing Group 20th annual Conference – Reviewing Effective Research and Good Practice; Table 11.7 from Office for National Statistics, www. statistics. gov. (HMSO, 2000); Table 13.1 from *Labour Market Trends*, 110(10): S26, HMSO (Office for National Statistics, 2002); Table 16.2 from *Retailing Management*, 4th edition, McGraw Hill Irwin (Levy, M. and Weitz, B. © 2001). Reproduced with permission of The McGraw-Hill Companies; Table 19.1 from Cooper, J., Browne, M. and Peters, M. (1991) *European Logistics*, reproduced by permission of Blackwell Publishing Ltd., Oxford; Figure 19.7 from Reverse Logistics: a review of the literature & framework for future investigation, *Journal of Business Logistics*, 19(1), 85–102 (Carter, C. R. and Ellram, L. M. 1998), reproduced by permission of the Council of Logistics Management; Figure 21.1 from AMS Marketing Service AG, Action Alliance (Powerpoint handout), AMSWebmaster @USDA.gov.; Table 23.1 from Food Marketing Newsletter, January – special supplement by CIES, The Food Business Forum (CIES, 2002); Figure 23.2 from Consumers use of the Internet, Q 10, August 2002, www.oftel.gov.uk/publications/research/2002/q10intr1002.htm (OFTEL, 2002);

xxx **Publisher's Acknowledgements**

Figure 23.3 from Households with Internet access 1998/99, 1999/2000, Regional
Trends, HMSO (National Statistics, 2001); Tables 23.2 and 23.4 from *The quiet rev-
olution. A report on the state of eBusiness in the UK,* CBI. (KPMG Consulting, 2001);
Table 23.3 from 'Top UK retail sites, December 2001' (HMSO, 2001); Table 24.1
from APACS 'Payment trends 1990–2000', reproduced by permission of Corporate
Communications, APACS.

The Body Shop International PLC for an extract from 'The Body Shop Values', pub-
lished on www.bodyshop.com; Guardian Newspapers Limited for an extract from
'Carelessness at Mothercare leaves cupboard bare' by Helen Slingsby, published in
The Guardian, 9th October, 2001; IKEA for an extract from 'IKEA and the
Environment', published on www.ikea.co.uk; and Pearson Education Limited for
an extract from *Logistics and Supply Chain Management* by M. Christopher.

We are grateful to the Financial Times Limited for permission to reprint the following material:

Out of town but much in mind – approval of a new shopping centre for
Manchester has refuelled an old debate, © *Financial Times*, 12 March, 1993.

In some instances we have been unable to trace the owners of copyright material,
and we would appreciate any information that would enable us to do so.

The retail context

CHAPTER 1

The retail context: An overview

Steve Burt and Leigh Sparks

Aim

The aim of this chapter is to introduce students to the retail sector and to provide a context or framework for the remainder of the book.

Learning objectives

By the end of this chapter you should:

- understand the nature of, and activities involved in, retailing, and how these have changed and continue to change;

- comprehend the fundamental importance to retailing of consumers and consumer change;

- be able to identify the importance and effects of the changing patterns and structures in retailing;

- demonstrate an awareness of the activities involved in retail management;

- be aware of the possible challenges facing retailing in the future.

Introduction

Retailing is a distinct, diverse and dynamic sector of many economies. The ubiquitous presence and organisational structure of many retail outlets – large numbers of small, local, independent shops – has however for a long time blinded many to the challenges and opportunities in retailing. With the emergence of modern techniques of retailing and the rise of large retail companies and new retail forms and formats, retailing has become much more visible and central to consumers' and governments' concerns. Reflecting as it does cultures and consumers, retailing is the primary conduit for production and consumption linkages in economies.

The pace of change in retailing and in the various environments with which it interacts, together with the complex and distinct features of modern retailing, make it an exciting and challenging sector to work in, as well as a fascinating topic for study. The diversity of retailing, both within and amongst countries, adds further to the richness of the subject.

Retailing is a huge part of many economies. Perhaps 25 per cent of all enterprises in the European Union (EU) are involved in retailing, engaging about 12 per cent of the total working population. There are well over 3.5 million shops in the EU. Within these totals however are massive dichotomies (Dawson 1995). There are many single-shop businesses, but also some of the largest companies in Europe. There are large and small fixed shops, mobile shops and even virtual shops. Retailing is a local affair with local demands, but Euro-brands are rising and indeed global brands are important. Retail sales are rising but the number of shops is falling and their format is changing. Low pay characterises much of the sector, but managerial pay is above average and for the most successful executives rewards are considerable. Retailing is a business sector of contrasts, undergoing considerable change. It is therefore rewarding to study, and contains unique issues and opportunities for research and practice.

Retailing is traditionally defined as the sale of articles, either individually or in small numbers, directly to the consumer. Whilst this might sound straightforward it is but a simplistic statement about a complex set of processes and relationships. This chapter takes the key components of the practice of retailing (Figure 1.1) and seeks to show the distinctive and changing nature of the retail sector. It moves from consideration of aspects of the retail environment to the places and locations where retailing takes place. It examines the interrelationships linking retail businesses with other organisations and considers the internal operations of retailers themselves. The people who take on the running of retail businesses and individual shops, the nature of the selling and retailing processes, and the supply and sale of goods are all introduced and discussed.

As with any introduction to a subject, it is recognised that other elements might have been introduced, but it is believed that this structure is both explanatory and pedagogically useful and provides a suitable context for the more detailed chapters that follow. The chapter concludes by summarising the state of the retail industry today and considering briefly some of the challenges for the future.

Figure 1.1 The retail industry

Culture and retail consumers

Any consideration of retailing has to begin with the country or local environment in which retailing takes place. In terms of the distinctiveness of the sector the very specific relationships retailing has with culture and consumers are crucial. Retailing must be responsive to the culture within which it operates. Internationally, this creates a great diversity in terms of regulatory and shopping environments, service standards and store format and layout. For example, Japanese culture and societal behaviours are fundamentally different to the cultural norms and values of countries such as Saudi Arabia or the southern United States. Whilst we might suggest that some aspects of a global culture are emerging, and certainly it is clear that cultures evolve, in reality retailing mainly adapts to the *local or national* situation and norms.

These cultural norms are derived from societal and economic situations. Retailing is an economic transaction, but also in many cases fundamentally a social interaction. The norms of economic and social behaviour permeate, inform and, on occasions, constrain the retail operations. The restrictive shop opening hours in much of Germany are a legal recognition of cultural dimensions to the organisation of society, and have long-standing roots. The restriction of alcohol sales to government-owned shops in Sweden and Canada reflects societal concerns. The persistence of fresh produce markets in Mediterranean Europe and wet markets in East Asia derives from traditional patterns of food preparation and consumption. The advertising of retail products through weekly newspaper 'fliers' or inserts in Denmark or the United States have different origins and obligations, but nonetheless inform and constrain the retailer and retail practice. Such advertising and promotional offers would be deemed wasteful, inappropriate or ineffective in other societies and economies. Limits on what can be advertised or sold in Islamic countries, or what advertisements or catalogues can contain, reflect cultural and religious norms of these societies.

It is tempting to use these national examples to suggest that there are uniform national cultures and thus retailers' responses to culture work best on the national level. But culture is a complex, multi-dimensional concept that derives from a range of personal and group values and attitudes. There are local and international aspects of culture. But culture is also a social phenomenon, which may be learnt and can be passed from generation to generation. It is also adaptive in that culture can change to meet circumstances or outside stimuli.

For retailers, there are a number of implications of culture and its component aspects. First, as culture is absorbed, learnt and transmitted from generation to generation, certain aspects of it may become deep-rooted and thus hard to change. There are therefore boundaries on what can be sold or how or when it can be sold. What is acceptable within societies varies. Secondly, a shared culture binds some groups together and thus can provide the basis for identifying markets or market segments. We might for example point to the presence of immigrant communities and particular consumer behaviour patterns in large cities across the world. Or we might point to aspects of 'youth culture' or even 'counter-culture' to which retailers have tried to respond. Thirdly however, we have to be careful not to over-emphasise the responsive nature of retailing. Whilst retailing operates mainly within cultural norms and thus reflects these, retailers can also shape these cultural norms in many ways. Retail operations and environments are not neutral entities, but rather can condition and structure consumer moods and behaviours and in some cases can over the long term influence cultural norms. The manufactured environments of many stores develop consumers by requiring them, implicitly or explicitly, to rethink aspects of their beliefs and attitudes.

Examples of this in the United Kingdom include the design revolution sparked by Terence Conran's Habitat stores from the 1960s, the critical and unique importance (until recently) of Marks & Spencer to British clothing manufacturing and retailing and the campaigning and ethical sensibilities overtly used by Anita Roddick and The Body Shop. These three retailers changed British society and aspects of British culture. We might suggest that IKEA, McDonald's or Starbucks are doing the same thing today, albeit in different ways and on an international basis.

This emphasis on culture demands that retailers be embedded in the culture of the economy and society in which they operate. This may best be achieved by being part of that economy and society, or at least understanding it, and is thus mainly accomplished through an understanding of local consumers. Knowledge of what drives local consumers and what they need and want (in product and service terms) is fundamental to the operation of retailing. This embeddedness may be derived from the local operations, companies or managers, or may be achieved by a thoroughly researched knowledge of the local consumer base. Whichever, there is a radical difference for retailing here when compared to most other management activities and industrial sectors. In retailing the issues of consumer knowledge intrude directly into the business, day in and day out. Retailing is dependent on people, both because it employs a lot of staff to serve customers in stores and because an understanding of people's behaviours, attitudes and psychology are important.

One basic constraint on the development of retailing is the demographic structure of the market. At its most simple, demographic change relates to features such as the number, age structure and location of individuals and households. For retailers, changes in these dimensions are fundamental as they affect the size and location of their target markets. An examination of some demographic aspects in Europe immediately identifies far-reaching changes in recent decades.

First (Table 1.1), whilst population growth continues in most countries, the *rate* of growth has reduced substantially over the last half-century. We can attribute this to lower birth rates, fertility levels and socio-economic changes such as the full participation of women in the paid labour force. For retailers this means that they can no longer rely on previous assumptions of 'natural' population growth to increase market size. The battle for market share is thus much harder.

Secondly (Table 1.2), whilst the population may (just) still be growing, there has been a fundamental shift in its age composition. The decline in the birth rate, coupled with reduction in child mortality, longer life expectancy and improved medical care have resulted in a much more 'elderly' population structure than before. Even though large numbers of this elderly population are more affluent and active than previous generations, retailers still have to consider how they respond to this and other population segments. The retail offer has to be adjusted to meet the changing numbers in different target markets. These different age segments have of course very different attitudes. Retailers have to understand these generations and their behaviours and attitudes, as in Generation X or Y or the MTV generation.

Table 1.1 Population change in Europe 1950–2010

| | Change in total population (%) | | | | | |
	1950–59	1960–69	1970–79	1980–89	1990–99e	2000–2010e
Austria	N/A	+5.4	+1.1	+0.9	+0.7	+1.6
Belgium	+5.9	+5.6	+1.7	+0.5	+0.8	+0.9
Denmark	+7.3	+8.1	+4.2	−1.2	−2.4	+3.1
Finland	+10.8	+4.1	+3.7	+3.8	0.0	+1.5
France	+9.4	+11.1	+6.8	+3.4	+0.4	+3.9
Germany	+10.9	+9.5	+2.5	−1.5	−2.5	−0.4
Greece	+10.3	+5.5	+9.6	+2.5	+5.7	+2.0
Ireland	−4.7	+3.9	+14.6	+10.7	+9.5	+2.3
Italy	+6.6	+6.9	+5.8	+0.8	+1.1	0.0
Luxembourg	+6.9	+9.7	+4.7	+3.9	+0.8	+7.7
The Netherlands	+13.6	+13.5	+8.5	+5.9	+4.5	+5.1
Norway	+9.5	+8.4	+5.4	+3.4	+2.4	+4.4
Portugal	+5.1	+2.4	+9.8	+6.5	+4.4	+1.2
Spain	+8.8	+10.9	+10.8	+5.9	+3.7	+0.9
Sweden	+6.1	+7.5	+3.4	−2.4	−0.1	+1.6
Switzerland	+14.3	+15.5	+2.9	−3.1	−4.5	+2.7
UK	+3.5	+5.8	+1.0	+0.8	+1.9	+1.5
Europe	N/A	+8.4	+4.8	+2.0	+1.7	+1.4

e = projected

N/A = not available

Source: Derived from National Statistics (http://www.statistics.gov.uk); Eurostat (http://www.europa.en.int/comm/eurostat/Public/datashop/print-catalogue/EN?catalogue/Eurostat); United Nations Statistics (http://www.unstats.un.org/unsd/default.htm)

Thirdly (Table 1.3), we can consider households as well as individuals. Demographic changes have been allied with socio-economic and lifestyle changes (such as later age of marriage and higher divorce rates) to radically restructure both the number and composition of households in most countries. We have far more households now in Europe than before, but there are fewer people (often only one person) in each of them. For retailers this can provide opportunities and market growth (for example in furnishings), but also requires them to adapt their product sizes and ranges, say by introducing packet sizes suitable for individual consumption.

How people live their lives has changed dramatically. Your behaviour as a teenager bears little resemblance to many activities carried out by your parents as teenagers. There are more opportunities, more choices and in many cases more affluence to enable satisfaction of needs. These needs themselves have of course altered fundamentally.

Table 1.2 The ageing of the European population 1950–2020

	Proportion of population over 65 years of age (%)							
	1950	1960	1970	1980	1990	2000	2010e	2020e
Austria	10.5	12.2	14.2	15.5	14.0	15.3	17.5	20.0
Belgium	11.0	12.0	13.4	13.9	13.3	16.7	17.3	19.8
Denmark	9.0	10.6	12.3	14.1	14.7	14.7	15.4	17.8
Finland	6.6	7.3	9.1	11.5	11.9	14.9	17.4	22.2
France	11.4	11.6	12.9	13.9	13.4	15.9	16.8	20.6
Germany	9.3	10.8	13.2	15.4	14.4	16.2	19.3	20.8
Greece	6.8	8.1	11.1	13.0	12.9	16.9	18.9	20.9
Ireland	10.7	11.1	11.2	10.8	10.0	11.6	12.6	15.9
Italy	8.0	9.3	10.7	13.0	13.1	17.4	19.4	21.5
Luxembourg	9.5	10.8	12.7	13.4	12.6	15.2	16.4	19.3
The Netherlands	7.7	9.0	10.2	11.5	12.8	13.6	14.9	18.4
Norway	9.6	10.9	12.9	14.6	15.9	15.3	15.2	N/A
Portugal	7.0	8.0	9.2	10.3	10.5	15.3	15.9	17.2
Spain	7.2	8.2	9.7	10.6	10.9	16.8	17.9	19.9
Sweden	10.2	10.9	12.7	16.2	17.5	16.9	18.1	N/A
Switzerland	9.6	10.2	12.2	13.6	14.4	15.3	17.4	20.5
UK	10.7	11.7	13.0	14.9	15.0	15.5	16.4	19.2

e = estimate

N/A = not available

Derived from National Statistics (http://www.statistics.gov.uk);

Eurostat (http://www.europa.en.int/comm/eurostat/Public/datashop/print-catalogue/EN?cata-logue/Eurostat); United Nations Statistics (http://www.unstats.un.org/unsd/default.htm)

These basic demographic considerations can be combined with other changes. The occupational structure of economies has changed, together with the gender balance of the workforce. The distribution of income has altered generally and between the sexes. More women are now in paid employment than before and many have much greater economic power and freedom. Consumers are more educated and informed than ever before. These changing situational factors naturally have implications for attitudes and values and affect life cycles and stages. The traditional certainty of marriage by 21, children by 25, the housewife staying at home and the male breadwinner has gone. Holidays are more likely to be in Spain than Blackpool. Curry is more commonly eaten than fish and chips. Such behaviours reflect the changed realities of living in the twenty-first century.

One particular certainty that has disappeared is the idea that whole swathes of the country would be doing the same things at the same times. Meal times previously were common. Television programmes were watched in huge numbers. People all dressed the same. Football matches took place at 3pm on a Saturday. Telephone calls were made from home or a phone box (for which we queued). Holidays were taken at the same time. Now, families eat together far less often.

Table 1.3 The growth of one-person households in Europe 1970–2001

	Proportion of total households that are one-person households (%)			
	1970/71	1980/81	1990/91	2000/01
Sweden	25.3	32.8	39.6	N/A
Denmark	23.4	29.5	34.0	37.1
Finland	23.9	29.5	32.4	36.9***
Germany	21.1	30.8	34.8	36.0
Norway	21.2	27.9	34.3	N/A
Switzerland	19.6	28.9	29.1	34.0
Netherlands	17.1	22.1	32.4	32.4*
Belgium	18.8	23.2	25.3	31.1
France	20.8	24.6	26.1	31.5
Austria	24.6	26.0	27.9	30.5
UK	17.9	21.7	25.5	31.0
Italy	12.9	20.7	22.2	22.8
Ireland	14.2	17.1	21.6	22.9
Greece	11.9	14.6	18.3	20.7**
Portugal	N/A	N/A	13.7	14.2
Spain	N/A	N/A	10.9	11.5

* 1993
** 1995
*** 1999

N/A = not available

Derived from Eurostat (http://www.europa.en.int/comm/eurostat/Public/datashop/print-catalogue/EN?catalogue/Eurostat); National Statistics (http://www.statistics.gov.uk)

Satellite TV has multiplied the choice of programmes to watch. Other media bombard the marketplace with choice and options. Football occurs anytime, anyday, and is broadcast live. Phones ring on trains (and in lectures!). We are a fragmented, sectionalised and highly differentiated country though increasingly a mobile but connected society. Retailers have to work much harder to identify the group commonalities that do exist and to react quickly to changing patterns.

Consumers are a dynamic grouping. Consumers change and consumer behaviour alters over time. Norms of consumer behaviour that were once thought to be inviolate or immutable have altered considerably. As economies and societies have developed so consumer desires have changed. What is important to the society or to groups of consumers has evolved. The way in which time and money are interrelated is one illustration of the process. Consumers in many economies use time very differently to previous generations. We are increasingly a '24/7' economy. Equally consumers have a different potential for and perception of travel, both generally and for shopping. The implications of this for retailing are fundamental. Consumers' needs, and their ability to satisfy those needs, have altered dramatically, giving rise to retailing concepts such as organic superstores, lifestyle shopping, outlet malls, convenience stores and fast food. At the product level, changing attitudes towards vegetarianism, meat consumption, microwaveable meals or the acceptability of fur or products based on animal testing are equivalent examples.

We can identify a range of implications for retailing from these various cultural and consumer changes (see also Bowlby 2000; Dawson 1995; Miller *et al* 1998). First there are trends in *consumption*, that is the general structure of demand and the amount of specific goods consumed. A good example is the modern supermarket. Here the increased product ranges in areas of ready meals and prepared foods reflect changing demand patterns. The segmentation of products by price or by other attributes, such as organic, gluten-free, healthy living or children's meals, is a reaction to wider trends in the market. The extension of retailing into banking, insurance, health care and services such as mobile phones and top-up phone cards also illustrates the shift in consumption towards services.

There are then implications for *consumer behaviour*, that is consumer decisions as to which of their wants they wish to satisfy, and how, when and where they are going to obtain satisfaction. The most obvious change for retailers in this area has been the increasing demand for convenience. Convenience in terms of time and location has become increasingly important, giving rise to 24-hour trading, petrol station convenience stores, home and workplace delivery and supermarket retailers at railway stations amongst a range of options.

Thirdly, there are changes in *shopping behaviour*, that is the consumer process during the shopping activity itself. As consumers have changed so the elements of the retail offer that attract them and encourage them to purchase or consume has changed. Much more attention has had to be paid by retailers to elements of store design, ambience and smell as well as issues to do with the balance between price, service and quality. For many people going shopping has become more of a leisure activity. Consumers expect to be more in control of the trip and to be on occasions entertained. So we see the development of cafés in bookshops such as Borders, or a total redesign of the selling of a product as in Sephora, or involvement in production as in The Bear Factory.

Combining these various strands of consumer change, we can suggest that there are now different reasons behind different shopping trips and that consumers satisfy their desires in different ways and at different times (Table 1.4). Sometimes consumers need to replenish basic items and the trip is a highly functional one. At other times similar items may be purchased from a different format, for example the same consumer might buy the same goods from a Tesco superstore, a Tesco Metro or Tesco.com. Other shopping trips are focused more on the trip itself. Leisure in its broadest sense is critical to the experience of the trip and of the shopping. In considering Table 1.4 retailers have to be able to focus on consumers and their changing behaviours. This is much more complex than it has been in the past.

Self-assessment Question 1 *Think of your own shopping trips over the past week or month. Where did you shop? What did you buy? Why? Can you apply the list of shopping trips in Table 1.4 to your own experiences?*

Table 1.4 Types of shopping trips

Purpose	Reason	Product example	Retailer and format example
Essential	Replenishment of stock items; primary shopping trip	Food and household items	Food superstore (Tesco)
Purposive	Clear purpose to trip; major item purchase	Electrical items	Retail park (B&Q, Comet, etc.), shopping centre with department stores (House of Fraser)
Leisure (or fun)	Social activity, occasionally ancillary to visit	General purchases, gifts	Town centre, shopping centre or mall (e.g. Bluewater), leisure activity focus (museum shop, HMV, JJB Sports, Manchester United Superstore)
Convenience	Time constrained, top-up trip, everyday purchases	Ready meals, milk, newspapers	Convenience store (Alldays) or petrol station store (Shell)
Experimental	Unusual product or innovative method	Tickets, home delivery of large items, local produce	Ticketmaster.com, Argos, farm shop

We have spent some time on the changes taking place in consumption as this underpins much of the activity that we describe as retailing. We now turn to other aspects of the retail operation (Figure 1.1).

Retail locations and outlets

This emphasis on culture and consumers is reflected in the importance afforded by retailers to the places where retailing takes place – its location. This is in itself a distinctive dimension of the retail industry, as few industries involve such a diverse and dispersed type of outlet network. There are for example over 23,300 7-Eleven convenience stores across the world, with almost 9,200 in Japan alone. The Body Shop operates over 1,800 outlets in 49 countries and trades in 25 languages. Ahold has over 9,000 stores in 28 countries on four continents. It is hard to conceive of businesses outside retailing having such extensive branch networks to control. Whilst the old adage 'location, location, location' has probably been overplayed it retains some truth, and above all is an identifying characteristic of the retail trade. Retailers must understand the spaces within which consumers operate and try to match these in terms of their locational and operational decisions. Retailers thus manage the macro-location (the country, region or city) and the micro-location (the store location and internal environment). In this section we consider mainly the macro-locational issues, leaving store design and other internal store-based issues to a later section.

Retailing not only has a distinctive locational dimension but is also further distinguished by its diversity of location. Furthermore, locations are dynamic.

Some shop locations seem fixed in the most visible of ways, as with Harrods in London, Galeries Lafayette and Printemps in Paris or Bloomingdales in New York. Others are more transient, such as wet or night markets, car-boot sales, farmers markets and other similar activities. Whilst some street locations clearly have a premium for retail activity, such as Ginza in Tokyo, Oxford Street in London or Fifth Avenue in New York, others come and go. Town centres and city centres are for many economies the main place of concentration of retailing – market spaces in historic cities such as Carlisle and York in the United Kingdom illustrate this well. Neighbourhood stores or corner shops have a similar function on a different scale. In some economies this central emphasis has been disturbed by the decentralisation of much retail activity (Longstreth 1997; 1999).

The most developed car-borne and thus decentralised retail economy is the United States. In many town and city centres the central area ('downtown') is a desolate, retail-free zone. The retail activity mainly occurs in suburban malls and strip centres along important highways or at key road intersections. The location for retailing has thus been fundamentally altered over time and has had important implications for the form of much of the retail infrastructure. Large hypermarkets, power centres, strip malls and covered shopping centres with huge car parks are a result. The internalisation and privatisation of retail space in a mall is a further outcome of this transformation.

If we consider the United Kingdom we can see this process of decentralisation quite clearly, though it is not as extensive as in the United States. Retailing was for a long time a city or town centre activity, but since the Second World War, and the latter part of the twentieth century in particular, it has become more decentralised. When people 'go shopping' now they are as likely to be thinking of an off-centre superstore, a retail warehouse park, a regional shopping centre or a factory outlet centre as they are of the high street in the local town.

This movement away from central locations has been encouraged by a number of factors, including the following:

• the growth of an affluent and mobile population in suburban areas in contrast to a declining, less affluent and less mobile town and city centre population;
• the development of strong corporate chains with fewer ties to a locality and more willingness and need to move shops to areas of demand and opportunity;
• changes in the methods of selling, which have seen a demand for larger stores and associated parking; such stores are harder to accommodate in built-up areas and have been cheaper to build and operate in decentralised locations.

This decentralisation has been controversial as it utilises greenfield land in many instances, often has an adverse aesthetic impact and expands the reliance on private transport. (Consumers have however embraced it.) As a consequence, some locations in both urban and rural situations have seen a huge reduction in retail outlets and consequent problems of accessibility and choice for consumers who are not mobile (economically or physically). Land-use planners have therefore been increasingly concerned to integrate retail development within existing towns and cities (Guy 1994a; Davies 1995). Nonetheless the policies of the 1980s and 1990s have resulted in large numbers of decentralised food and non-food superstores.

We might also want to draw a distinction between managed and unmanaged shopping locations. Individual shops are obviously managed. A shopping street however is basically a loose, unmanaged collection of individual stores and thus provides a general node for shopping. Town centres are often amalgams of several such streets. However we also have managed shopping environments. Some of these, for example arcades in city centres or town markets, are long-standing, albeit relatively small components of the shopping panorama. Others however (such as regional shopping centres), and particularly those built in the 1980s and 1990s, are major retail destinations in their own right.

Many cities have various forms of planned shopping centre within their boundaries (Table 1.5) – Buchanan Galleries in the centre of Glasgow is a major retail attraction. But there are also decentralised locations containing shopping centres, which can draw people from large distances, and other planned environments serving a variety of functions. Gateshead's Metro Centre is an early UK off-centre regional example. The Mall at Cribbs Causeway in Bristol or Cheshire Oaks Factory Outlet Centre in the north-west of England are other recent examples of planned decentralised retail environments. These centres are designed, planned and managed as distinctive retail locations. In some cases, for example Bluewater in Kent, they are marketed as a brand in their own right.

Table 1.5 Types of shopping centre development

Type of shopping centre	Provision	Example (from Glasgow)
Major city-centre renewal schemes	Provide a wide range of shopping facilities adding to the provision of the existing town or city centre	Buchanan Galleries
Small in-town schemes	Usually provide specialist shopping facilities	Princes Square
Non-central-city centres (district and neighbourhood centres)	Comprise several stores and sometimes a superstore or hypermarket targeted at everyday consumption needs	Bearsden Shopping Centre
Edge-of-town and out-of-town centres (retail parks, factory outlet centres)	Typically based around one or two large superstores and containing retailers in a variety of product areas	The Forge
Large out-of-town regional shopping centres	Create the equivalent of a new city centre outside the city	Braehead Shopping Centre
Centres associated with transport nodes	Built, for example, at sites such as railway stations (often within the urban area) and airports (outside it)	Central Station Concourse; Glasgow Airport

Across many western countries the twin processes of decentralisation and managed environments have transformed the retail landscape (Dawson and Burt 1998; Ruston 1999), with considerable impact on existing locations. As a consequence there is increasing interest in whether management techniques from planned shopping centres can be applied to unplanned town centres. Many UK towns now have town centre managers who engage in active place marketing to attract and retain consumers. Locations rather than individual shops are thus also in competition.

Whilst much retailing prioritises micro-locational factors in the location selection process, in that we are locating one shop and looking for the best possible market, this is not always the case. Some retailers or locations have an international reputation and attract visitors in very different ways (for example Mall of America, the largest shopping centre in the United States, has fly-drive holidays to attract visitors). Selected forms of retailing such as mail-order are to some extent location-free. It could be argued that virtual or Internet retailing has the potential to release retailing from its various locational strait jackets, and to expand the market place globally. Location in that sense perhaps matters less.

By contrast, some retailers have become clear destinations in their own right and as a result transform the local landscape wherever they appear; for example Wal-Mart Supercenters have become destination stores in the United States. The company has such a reputation that consumers will travel to it almost no matter where in a town or city it is located. The store becomes a destination. IKEA's arrival has had the same impact in many countries. The location of individual stores does not however remain static. The hundreds of Wal-Mart stores in the United States that have been closed as the company's locational demand has evolved bear silent witness to their extensive construction and deconstruction of local landscapes. These closed stores illustrate the volatility of retail demand and supply, but also the way in which some retailers can manipulate demand and consumer decision making. In the United Kingdom it used to be the case that towns fought hard to get a Marks & Spencer store because of the spin-off benefit in increased consumer visits and prestige it brought. Marks & Spencer would receive favourable rental agreements to participate in a shopping centre scheme, whilst other retailers would then pay higher rents to locate next to the Marks & Spencer store.

Shopkeepers and retail managers

The nature of retail business is also distinctive and diverse in terms of those who take on the management and operation of retail businesses – the shopkeepers and retail managers. The organisation or firm type has implications for resources, the scope of operation and decision-making roles and capabilities. Retailing remains numerically dominated in almost every country by independent retailers, that is shopkeepers who are the owner and/or manager of a single store and retail almost anything, from the generalist corner store to the specialist selling second-hand wedding dresses. This form of retailing has been central to retail operations throughout history. Retailing has low entry and exit barriers. However, the independent retailer is but one form of business organisation, five forms are generally identified (Table 1.6). As we have just noted, the local shop run as an independent business is the mainstay in numerical terms of most retailing.

Table 1.6 Retail organisational types

Type	Examples
Independent retailing	Single local shop
Government shops	LCBO (Liquor Control Board of Ontario Stores), Royal Mail
Corporate retailers	Marks & Spencer (public)
	Littlewoods (private)
Consumer co-operatives	Co-operative Group
Contractual chains	Body Shop (franchise)
	Spar (affiliated group)
	NISA (buying group)

In some countries the government has been a major retailer, controlling and operating many stores (as in the past in communist Poland) or reserving control for particular product lines (such as government liquor stores in Ontario, Canada).

More commonly, there are corporate or multiple retailers. These are businesses operating several (or 'multiple') shops as a company entity. Such companies dominate the trading component of retailing in many countries and can be enormous businesses (such as Wal-Mart), sometimes with operations in many countries (for example Carrefour, Ahold or IKEA). Corporate retailers operate large retail outlets such as superstores, small stores in town centres and shopping malls and even concessions within department stores. They are often focused on particular lines of trade, for example JJB Sports or New Look.

Historically, consumer cooperatives have been strong in many countries and remain so in, for example, Finland, Denmark, Switzerland and Japan. These businesses are owned by members and typically are run for mutual benefit, not shareholder profit. The Co-operative Group with thousands of shops dominates this form in the United Kingdom, although some smaller single-shop societies do still exist, such as Grosmont in the Lake District. In some local communities residents have grouped together to run a community cooperative shop.

Finally, many previously independent retailers have given up some degree of independence by becoming part of a contractual chain or a franchise, that is they are independent businesses but are supplied by or legally linked to a larger 'umbrella' organisation. The contractual forms vary from operation to operation (as with Spar, 7-Eleven Japan, The Body Shop). All attempt to collectively maximise buying, marketing and other activities to improve overall performance, in the belief that working together, combined with independent shop ownership and its local knowledge, enhances their competitive position. In essence they seek the organisational benefits of the larger corporate chains alongside the flexibility and entrepreneurial flair of the independent trader.

The balance of power amongst these business organisational forms varies from country to country and has altered over time. As a general rule centrally controlled, large organisations (running chains of large and small stores) have gained power and market share from other forms, particularly from independent and cooperative retailers (Figure 1.2), and have become the dominant commercial form in many countries. This power has been gained through the cost and

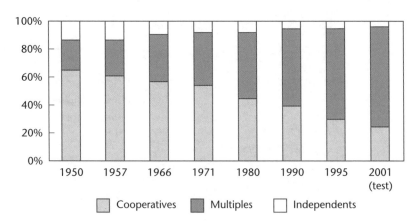

Figure 1.2 Market share by organisational type in the UK (1950–2001)

efficiency advantages of operating larger businesses under central control. This illustrates the economies of scale and scope available to retailers, but also suggests more distancing of the business from the local situation if retailers are not careful. The role and function of store management in a chain organisation has consequently become more critical over time, though the boundaries of central versus local control remain flexible and variable amongst companies. Local retailers with local knowledge and an ability to satisfy local needs and wants can be successful over a long period. However, succession is often a long-term problem for such retailers. The combination of central economies and standardisation with local management knowledge, as in franchises, has also been successful in recent years and certain circumstances.

It should be clear from the discussion thus far that retailing has been transformed in many ways. This transformation necessarily extends to the management of retail businesses. As the scale of the retail store has increased, and as the scale of the retail business has grown, so too has the need for professional, well-trained management. The types of skills and demands that a store manager in any organisational type has to exhibit are now very different from the shopkeepers of old. Current local shopkeepers work in a massively competitive industry, where store management and control principles and techniques have developed strongly.

A large food superstore could take up to £100 million a year in sales. The store could be open 24 hours a day, 7 days a week. There might be over 600 employees on the site working a variety of shift patterns and employed at many different grades. The amount of product and number of consumers passing in and out of the store in a day is huge. The technology in the store is highly advanced and sophisticated. Yet this store is one part of a business that could have £20 billion worth of sales in a year, employ over 150,000 people and have most of its main board earning over £1 million per annum. It stores, marketing, buying and logistics operations are all professional and dynamic environments. Retailing has some of the most exacting, exciting and well-paid jobs in the country and has become increasingly reliant on professional, graduate-level staff.

The picture painted above of corporate management is but one aspect of the business. Other people find their role in retailing by setting up companies, running small selective stores or small chains and thus satisfying their own entrepreneurial and personal drive. Companies such as Sock Shop, The Body Shop, JJB Sports, Carphone Warehouse and Lush have come from personal ambitions and drive to produce a better retail offer in a field that interests the founders. Retailing can accommodate, and indeed needs, a variety of forms of 'management' and operation.

Product sourcing and distribution

The growth of large retail companies such as Wal-Mart, Tesco, Kingfisher or Carrefour also illustrates another fundamental difference between retailing and other forms of business. To a much greater extent than, for example, manufacturing, retailers have to build structures for managing multi-plant operations with much greater variety and variability in concept and transactions. Retail management at the highest level is very different to other production-based businesses and is at the local level much more open to demand vicissitudes. The role of technology in data capture and transmission and in chain control has therefore increased substantially.

The business of retailing involves the selection and assembly of goods for sale, that is the process of product sourcing and distribution. This process is dominated by variety – of types of good, sourcing strategy and product mix. Retailers sell a wide variety of items. Some are concentrated in a narrow line of business (specialist stores such as Lush, Sephora, New Look, Claire's Accessories) whereas others are much wider in their scope (general stores such as Asda/Wal-Mart Supercentre). The balance amongst items may change over time but retailers have to source their product range. This involves the retailers themselves dealing with particular suppliers (perhaps local suppliers), with a wholesaler or with some other form of intermediary.

The products themselves have changed over time. Whilst there has always been a market for exotic and non-local product, the expectations of many consumers and the abilities of many retailers have transformed the supply position. A reliance on local (that is immediate area) sourcing is now not the normal relationship. For many retailers products from around the world are standard elements to be included in the product mix. Some would question the economic, cultural and environmental benefits of this to both the origin and the destination countries (see Klein 1999).

As retailers have become larger and as their abilities have increased they have been better able to exploit international product sourcing and buying opportunities. For many products the costs of production are much lower in countries outside the developed world and it therefore makes economic sense to manufacture abroad and transport the product. Thus many clothing manufacturers have relocated factories to the Far East or elsewhere. The management and logistics problems this creates are resolvable by retailers, but there has been a consumer backlash over exploitation of cheap labour in some locations and the loss of indigenous jobs. Retailers are therefore under pressure to make sure they act appropriately.

Clothing production is the obvious example of products being sourced from far afield, but the same is also true of food. Any British supermarket contains many non-UK or non-EU products. Control of the supply chain is thus vital to get products to the stores in good condition. This process of retailer control of supply systems and the use of computer technology for control of central distribution have been key features of recent years. British logistics systems are amongst the most efficient in the world as a consequence (Fernie and Sparks 1998).

In addition to control over the range and location of products, retailers have extended their influence over the contents of the product. Claims for organic production, sustainable forests and fair trade origins require control, often extending to audited codes of conduct for supplier inputs and methods of production. As societal and consumer concerns change the retailer needs to source, manage and guarantee products that meet these concerns.

Table 1.7 Tesco corporate brand relationship extension

Activity	Example	Tesco example
Building transaction and information linkages	POS, loyalty cards	Tesco Clubcard, Tesco personal finance, cashback, location maps
Extending and deepening infrastructure links	In-store branding, new store formats, new infrastructure	Tesco Extra, Metro, Express etc. formats, Tesco.net, Tesco Direct, Tesco.com
Operational links for customers	Consistency of high service performance	'One in front' campaign, 'Every little helps', first-class service
Personal/face-to-face links	Staff interaction with customers	Service areas, e.g. butchers, customer service desks, customer panels and question time
Service or expertise links	0800 lines, development of clubs	Baby Club, Wine Club, pharmacy, recipe cards
Cementing financial links	Direct financial services	Tesco personal finance, including insurance, pensions, credit cards, Tesco banking
Building emotional links	Lifestyle advertising, customer information, trust	Television advertising, Finest products, healthy eating leaflets, Computers for Schools, championing 'grey' market goods and reduced brand prices, bag for life
Searching for event links	In-store activities, sponsorship of events, local charity activity	Collection schemes, for sale wall, local event details in store, Millennium Dome sponsorship
Have usage links	Convenience products	'Grab and Go' areas, newspaper and lottery areas, 24 hour opening
Media communications links	Traditional and Internet	Corporate affairs activities
Distribution and availability links	Format development, home delivery, catalogues	Tesco Direct, Tesco clothing catalogue, Tesco specialist magazines, e.g. vegetarian, Internet cafés in store, Tesco ISP

Source: Burt and Sparks (2002)

Self-assessment Question 2 *Have a look at the labels of 5–10 articles of your clothing. In which countries were they manufactured? Does this surprise you or not? Do you make purchases based on criteria such as country of manufacture or on brand, price, or doesn't it matter? What do you expect from a retailer in this regard?*

Retailers have a choice over what products to sell, but also under what name to sell them. This might simply be the choice of the name of the store, but retailers have themselves become names or brands of note. The approach to retailer branding varies across the globe, but large retailers are becoming much more concerned in managing their own names or brand, particularly in clothing – think of Next, Mango, Gap, Zara, Benetton and H&M. Retail branding is now becoming more extensive in other retail product sectors.

In the United Kingdom retailers such as Tesco have developed a very extensive and sophisticated branding strategy that has allowed them to leverage their name and reputation into sectors other than their core business. Table 1.7 shows how Tesco has used its corporate name to extend its own brand offer. In food retailing in the United Kingdom retailer brands (also known as own label or private label) have become increasingly dominant. Product supply is thus even more within the retailers' control and advertising and promotion is constantly reinforcing the corporate brand. The retailer has become the brand and is trusted by the consumer. In addition to the brand extension into services shown in Table 1.7 this has also allowed brand disaggregation in the core food business (Table 1.8). Most food retailers now have a structured branding approach targeting specific consumer segments.

Table 1.8 Grocery retail branding price segmentation in the late 1990s

	Exclusive	Standard	Value
Tesco	Finest	Tesco	Value
Safeway	The Best	Safeway	Saver
Sainsbury	Taste the Difference	Sainsbury's	Economy
Asda	Extra Special	Asda	Smart Price

Note: This table is constructed on the basis of product price points. It excludes alternative branding concepts based on other product attributes such as health (e.g. Sainsbury's Be Good to Yourself, Tesco Healthy Eating and Safeway Healthy Choice), organic origin (e.g. all company retailer organic brands) or other segments (e.g. Sainsbury's Blue Parrot Café brand of healthy eating products for children).

Business relationships

As has been emphasised, retailing involves relationships with other businesses and groups. These too have their own distinctive characteristics arising from the nature of retailing. The requirement to source products, combined as we have seen with issues over branding, inevitably means that retailers are concerned with relationships with business partners as well as relationships with staff and consumers. These business relationships can take many forms, but essentially retailers can choose either collaborative or transactional (sometimes conflictual) relationships. In short, retailers can either work with partners to achieve shared objectives or they can use their position alone simply to operate the business to achieve their own ends.

For example, product sourcing involves a number of elements, but retailers are attempting to purchase and obtain product at a given price and quality. For some retailers price is the overriding concern and they will always seek the lowest price for products they know their customers will purchase. This inevitably means that the relationships they have with individual suppliers are transient and focus on transactional price components alone. The relationship in that sense is straightforward, but often comes down to a conflict about price.

More complex, but of importance to many retailers, is the notion of a collaborative relationship with suppliers that involves all parties in something more than simply a transaction based on price. The relationship might be to secure a source of supply or to obtain a given quality and quantity of a product. It might be to develop a product line or to ensure product consistency and quality, or to allow access to a unique product. If a retailer is branding the product then the collaborative arrangement may be about ensuring certain standards. For many retailers, therefore, whilst price may well be very important, there could equally be other aspects of the business relationship that need to be in place. Some of these relationships or partnerships are of long-standing and have involved extensive product development and consequent growth of both partners. Thus in food retailing manufacturing companies such as Northern Foods have become highly significant and large businesses in their own right, primarily though their collaborative arrangement for retailer brand production over a long period.

Retailers of course have business relationships beyond product sourcing. Relationships exist with an array of service providers depending on the operation. Finance is one example of such relationships, with independent retailers seeking bank finance and multiple or corporate retailers searching for institutional finance to enable them to develop their store portfolios. One of the most important relationships occurs in the physical supply of products to the retailer. Product sourcing in a transactional sense has been identified above, but products have also to be delivered to the retail store for merchandising. Logistics systems and logistics providers therefore may be key components of another set of business relationships. Whilst we may see many vehicles on the motorway carrying retailer logos and livery most are owned and operated by contractual logistics services partners such as Exel or Tibbet & Britten.

As might be imagined, with product sourcing complexities, expansion in the number of stores and spatial breadth in many companies and the increased expectations of consumers with respect to product quality and availability, logistics supply systems have become more and more important. For many retailers being in retailing is sufficient, and logistics systems are often out-sourced to these logistics services providers. This requires another set of relationships to be managed. Further relationships (for example, store fitting, legal, property) could also be considered.

Customer relationships have become of increased importance to retailers. Historically, whilst retailers were in competition with each other on a local level customers were less mobile and less volatile or promiscuous in their patronage. As a result there was a degree of certainty or relationship with the local store or cooperative.

As consumers changed behaviours and utilised their increased mobility and choice so retailers have been less able to depend on certainty of demand. In such circumstances large retailers have tried to identify, brand and get to know their customers.

The main mechanism for the development of this relationship has been the 'loyalty' card. These plastic cards have been enormously popular with many retailers and attempt to build a relationship with individual customers. The depth of this relationship may often be exaggerated, but retailers hope that by owning a loyalty card the customer will practise more loyalty and shop around less. For this change in behaviour retailers give customers some reward, usually a small dividend on purchase volume, but occasionally rights to buy products from a catalogue. The modern loyalty card is a product both of consumer change and technology development. In essence large retailers are using systems to identify customers. This is a practice or advantage that the best local retailers have almost instinctively. But the advent of cheap but large computer systems has enabled large retailers to try to replicate these advantages.

Self-assessment Question 3 *Do you have any retailer loyalty cards? Which are they and why did you enrol? Has possession affected your behaviour? Are you concerned about the knowledge the retailer has about you or do you feel sufficiently 'rewarded' by them? If you do not have any such cards, why not? Was this a positive decision or could you simply not be bothered?*

Whilst the loyalty card is an overt manifestation of the customer–retailer relationship, unique (only available in my store) retail brands, payment or credit facilities, customer service activities and employee–customer interaction in general are all employed ultimately to develop long-standing relationships (and loyalty) with customers.

Merchandising and selling

For many people outside retailing selling is often viewed as the same as retailing, but selling is only one component of the retail operation. Selling itself varies of course, with the move to self-service in many product categories and retailers reducing the sales role in the store. In other retailers the skills of the sales staff are critical in the delivery of customer service and the repeat patronage of consumers. The art and science of selling and the quality of the sales staff are of fundamental importance for much business success. In other situations the lack of quality or knowledge of the staff acts as a negative influence on consumers.

Store and selling design varies enormously by situation (Underhill 1999). The emphasis on design, staff knowledge and staff competency may be vital in some situations but of no consequence in others. The retail offer has become more disparate overall as retailers have attempted to match their offer to the demands of the customer. Some stores are dramatic (such as Sephora, Girl Heaven), some are functional (for example Aldi or Lidl), others playful (for example Bear Factory, Disney or REI). Some have many staff selling; others simply have takers of money. All, however, are based on retailers' understanding of what works with their customers.

Store-based selling has its own distinctive characteristics. How the product is merchandised and the ways in which design and display interact are important in attracting consumers and obtaining their custom. As a result much effort is expended in laying out the store and in ensuring that products are presented appropriately. This presentation includes aspects of visual display as well as essential product information. Depending on the product lines involved and the approach of the retailer, such merchandising may be of lesser or greater importance. Even in supposedly simple retailer situations such as markets, product display can be sophisticated and help consumers make choices amongst 'stores' and products. Mail-order retailers (for example Argos) have similar selling objectives but a different set of tasks and expectations to manage, through a one-dimensional page in a catalogue (although the Internet opens up some other possibilities for them).

Store merchandising and display techniques condition the retail environment in every store. Some of the techniques are rather obvious and relatively easy to identify; others are far more subtle and difficult to discern (Underhill 1999). Visual merchandising and design direct your attention and your direction by leading you around and through the merchandise. 'Hot Spots' in the store are created to drag you through the shop and grab your attention. Lighting and music are used in some stores to alter the mood of their various parts. Colour is used to create an environment or an image. Touch is encouraged to exploit the tactile senses. Even smells are use to evoke responses, whether it be perfume, cosmetics or coffee and fresh bread. Some designs and displays are organised to recreate remembered activities or past situations. In short, stores are not abstract collections of products but managed selling environments, designed to stimulate customer reactions and purchase.

Self-assessment Question 4 *On your next trip to a supermarket think about how you normally shop in the store. Do you follow a set path or go to particular products? Why? Why are the products you want where they are? What influences you in terms of lighting, noise, smells or taste?*

The state of the retail world

The description so far of the process of retailing has pointed both to the major functional areas of retail business activity and to some of the changes that have been taking place in the sector. Any analysis of recent trends (Table 1.9) quickly produces quite an extensive list of transformations and issues in the retail sector. The listing in Table 1.9 is readily recognisable from the recent history of retailing in the United Kingdom. Similar trends are found in many western economies (Dawson and Burt 1998). We can however condense this listing into a number of key areas.

First, it is clear that we have in recent decades lived through an enormous change in the location of retailing. We have already discussed the broad trends of decentralisation of retail location and the rise of superstores and shopping centres. Other emerging retail locations include sports stadia (for example Manchester United Superstore), hospitals, airports and museums or heritage sites (for example the Britannia shop at Ocean Terminal, Leith). Less planned activities occur in open-air markets, car-boot sales, some charity shops (Horne and Maddrell 2002) and other transient events, which can pop up almost anywhere.

Table 1.9 Major retail trends of the 1990s

A decrease in the total number of shops

An increase in the number of large food and non-food superstores

New shopping centres

Growth of retail sales and floor space

Low levels of inflation

Increase in small store formats

Concentration in retail sales

Extensions of product ranges in superstores

Strengthening of primary locations and weakening of tertiary ones

Large retailers taking control of the supply chain

Changes in accessibility to retail provision

Increased use of sophisticated technologies by retailers

More variety of potential locations

Wider use of town centre management

More awareness of retailer activity

Source: after Dawson (2000a)

Table 1.10 Sainsbury supermarket formats

Format	Sales area and layout (m²)	Product range	Car parking	Additional facilities
Savacentre	5,500–10,000	Full grocery range plus clothing, electrical goods, household, toys, etc. 40,000 lines	Large car parks. 800+ spaces, generally free	Restaurant, baker, deli, fish counter, meat counter, hot foods, salad bar, optician, travel agent, bank/building society
Supermarket	2,800–5,000. Standard supermarket	Full grocery range plus some additional lines. 18,000–25,000 lines	Associated parking. 400+ spaces, usually surface and free	Coffee shop, bakery, deli, fish counter. *Large stores*: Meat counter, hot food, salad bar, pharmacy, dry cleaner
Infill	1,900–2,400. Small supermarket for walk-in and local trade	Slightly restricted grocery range concentrating on core range. 15,000–18,000 lines	Associated parking. 150+ spaces, usually surface and free	Bakery, deli
Country town store	900–1,900. Small supermarket for country areas	Restricted grocery range. 10,000 lines	Associated parking. 200+ spaces, surface and free	Bakery, deli
Central	700–1,100. City centre store	Range concentrated on needs of lunchtime shoppers. 8,000 lines	No car parking or public car park	Salad bar, coffee bar
Local	300 or below. Convenience store	Range oriented towards fresh foods and meal solutions for top-up shoppers. 2,500–3,000 lines	No parking in town centres, but a few spaces for suburban or rural stores	None, other than long-trading hours with all day Sunday opening

Source: Competition Commission (2000) Volume 2, Table 5.12, p 54

Table 1.11 Characteristics of targeted small store formats

Store format	Target consumer requirements	Good/product elements	Store/environment elements	Examples
Discount stores	Low prices	Discount prices; relatively wide product range with few lines; variable to low quality	Relatively large size; located in suburban/ secondary high streets; decor sparse, providing frugal ambience.	Aldi; Ed; Poundstretcher
Convenience stores	Time/ convenience	Premium prices; wide range but few lines; high quality products, usually leading brands	Typically 100–200 m^2; located in suburban sites or traffic routes; design and decor stress efficiency	7-Eleven; Shell
Specialist stores	Choice	Premium or competitive prices; narrow or very narrow range of products but depth of lines; product quality variable to high	Can be very small if ultra-specialist; high visibility sites in shopping centres/on high street/in store; decor and design stress the specialist nature of the offer	Athletes Foot; Tie Rack; Oddbins
Style shops	Design/ originality/ exclusivity	Premium/high prices; very narrow product ranges with very few lines; product quality is high	Size range around 50– 200 m^2; high street/ targeted shopping centre locations; design stresses quality and exclusivity	Benetton; Next; Bally; Laura Ashley
Branded goods shops	Assurance/ reputation	Premium prices; very limited product range; narrow with few lines; high quality merchandise	In-store locations, or very small stores, 50–100 m^2; ambiance created by store design is quality based	Yves Rocher; Estée Lauder
Service shops	Added-value service	Premium or competitive prices; limited service offer quality variable but often intangible	Small outlets; high street and in-store locations; decor and design are functional	FNAC Service; Mr Minit; Supa-Snaps; Sketchley
Locality-specific shops	Impulse/ Emotion	Prices are variable, as is quality of products but usually either high or low; product range is narrow and activity or theme related, but choice provided	Location related to theme; as are design and decor, which often provide a 'bazaar'- type ambience.	Tourist shops; National Trust shops

Source: Dawson and Burt (1998)

Secondly, there has been an alteration in the format through which retailing takes place. Shops today are not like shops of previous times and retailer strategies have become more segmented. Table 1.10 shows how Sainsbury has reacted to consumer change by developing and operating a range of format/locational store types. They differ in scale, design, technique and approach. This is obvious in terms of the larger store formats, but is equally true for smaller formats. Much effort has been expended by retailers to develop and transform the small shop as part of their corporate approach to retailing (Table 1.11). Even in catalogue retailing we can see this format change with the decline of the huge, agency Grattans-style catalogue and its replacement by narrowly targeted 'specialogues', for example Artigiano, Toast, Cotton Traders or retailer brand channels such as Next Directory.

Thirdly, it should be clear from the discussion in this chapter so far that retailers have increased in scale and power (Seth and Randall 1999). They have grown enormously in size and now are large businesses in their own right (Table 1.12), often being larger than the manufacturers that supply them. They can thus reorganise various relationships to suit themselves. This scale of operation brings practical and financial benefits to the business. Recently we have seen the scale increase another level with major mergers or takeovers on the international stage, for example Wal-Mart of Woolco in Canada and Asda in the United Kingdom; the merger of Carrefour and Promodes in France; the global expansion of Ahold, Delhaize and Kingfisher. The world's leading retailers are now amongst some of the biggest organisations and have an increasingly international approach (Table 1.13).

Table 1.12 The UK's largest retailers 1990/1 and 2000/1

(a) 2000/1

Rank	Name	UK sales (number)	UK stores area (million sq.ft)	UK sales	Store facias
1	Tesco	18.37	692	17.96	Tesco
2	J. Sainsbury	12.93	453	13.74	Sainsbury's, Savacentre, Homebase
3	ASDA*	9.67	240	10.20	Asda, Asda Wal-Mart
4	Safeway	8.15	477	10.19	Safeway
5	Kingfisher	7.26	2,164	29.58	B&Q, Comet, Superdrug, Woolworths, MVC
6	Marks & Spencer	6.29	303	12.39	Marks & Spencer
7	Boots	4.69	2,124	10.34	Boots, Halfords
8	Somerfield	4.61	1,319	11.08	Somerfield, Kwik Save
9	Argos**	3.92	490	N/A	Argos
10	Dixons	3.83	1,091	6.43	Currys, PC World, Dixons, The Link

* Now owned by Wal-Mart; ** Part of the GUS Group

(b) 1990/1

Rank	Name	UK sales (number)	UK stores area (million sq.ft)	UK sales	Store facias
1	J. Sainsbury	6.84	369	10.06	Sainsbury's, Savacentre, Homebase
2	Tesco	6.35	384	9.66	Tesco
3	Marks & Spencer	4.89	288	9.47	Marks & Spencer
4	Argyll Group*	4.49	1,113	8.37	Safeway, Presto. Lo-Cost, Galbraith
5	ASDA	4.34	365	10.27	Asda, Allied Maples, Allied, Maples, Waring & Gillow
6	Isosceles**	3.11	758	7.31	Somerfield, Gateway, Wellworth, Food Giant
7	Kingfisher	3.11	2.095	19.20	B&Q, Comet, Superdrug, Woolworths, Titles, Gifts and Treats, Depot, Charlie Brown's
8	Boots the Chemist	2.98	2,266	N/A	Boots, Halfords, Children's World, Fads, Do It All (50%)
9	John Lewis Partnership	1.97	116	3.51	John Lewis and other department stores, Waitrose
10	Sears	1.87	3,432	N/A	Shoe City, Freeman Hardy Willis, Dolcis, Saxone, Roland Cartier, Manfield, Cable & Co. Warehouse, Fosters, Your Price, Wallis, Miss Selfridge, Adams, Olympus, PRO Performance Shoes, Sportsave, Millets, Selfridges, Freemans, Stage One

* Argyll Group became Safeway; ** Isosceles became Somerfield
Source: calculated from Retail Intelligence/Mintel *The UK Retail Rankings*, 1992 and 2002 editions, Corporate Intelligence Group, London

Finally, there are obviously impacts of these trends, felt at different levels. International activity does affect the retail landscape at the local level. The nature of competition and availability is such that all elements of the retail sector interact and affect consumers everywhere. Thus we need to be concerned about the people who do not gain access to the newer stores or who can not travel to the shops. Their lives are affected by this reconstruction of the retail landscape. We have to be concerned about the quality of products, both in terms of what is available to consumers but also in terms of where it is made and under what conditions. Retailing has changed, and whilst there have been major benefits there are dangers and problems as well.

Table 1.13 World's top 20 retailers (2000)

Rank	Name	Country	Principal activity	Sales (billion Euros)	Stores	% foreign sales
1	Wal-Mart	US	Non-food	194.3	4,189	17.2
2	Carrefour	France	Food	65.6	8,130	47.5
3	Kroger	US	Food	52.6	3,541	0
4	Royal Ahold	Netherlands	Food	49.2	8,112	80.8
5	Home Depot	US	Non-food	49.2	1,134	19.0
6	Metro	Germany	Non-food	47.5	2,169	42.1
7	Kmart	US	Non-food	39.7	2,105	0
8	Sears	US	Non-food	39.6	3,021	11.6
9	Albertson's	US	Food	39.5	2,512	0
10	Target	US	Non-food	39.1	1,307	0
11	ITM	France	Food	36.3	7,851	36.0
12	Safeway	US	Food	34.4	1,785	10.8
13	J.C. Penney	US	Non-food	34.2	3,800	0.5
14	Costco	US	Non-food	34.0	313	18.7
15	Tesco	UK	Food	33.7	907	12.5
16	Rewe	Germany	Food	31.5	11,788	22.0
17	Aldi	Germany	Food	31.1	5605	37.0
18	Edeka	Germany	Non-food	30.0	11,000	2.0
19	Ito-Yokado	Japan	Food	27.9	21,000	33.2
20	Tengelmann	Germany	Food	27.6	6,700	48.5

Source: PriceWaterhouseCoopers (2001) Retail and Consumer Worlds, Special Insert 38-2, Food for Thought, July 2001. Downloaded from http://www.pwcglobal.com/Extweb/pwcpublications. nsf/4bd5f76b48e282738525662b00739e22/5e9bc71203859a7d852569f3000b3050/$FILE/_e8ln66 obiegp2qjj5et9narbdc5p7i83ev0pjg_.pdf on 18 October 2001

Future retailing

The increasing scale of leading retailers is a good place to start any consideration of the future of retailing (see Dawson 2000a; Dawson 2000b; Sparks and Findlay 2000). Table 1.14 lists six major trends or challenges facing retailing management, of which scale (or bigness) has a priority. Scale provides big benefits to retailers – if it is managed correctly. There are however dangers to huge scale. In particular the management of retailing across continents and businesses, some of which have been recently purchased, is not a simple task. The pursuit of scale in retailing is likely to continue, but management has to be careful of how the organisation operates.

Table 1.14 Challenges facing retail management

Bigness:
- retaining consumer responsiveness
- keeping a focus on competition
- entering new markets
- relationships with suppliers and retail buying
- relationships with other retailers
- management of mergers and acquisitions
- marketing execution
- relationships with financial institutions
- relationships with governments

Over supply of retail floor space

Turbulence in the retail environment

Brand and brand extension

Externalisation or internalisation of functions

E-retail

Source: after Dawson (2000b)

Retailing in many countries will also be challenged by an over-supply of retail floor space and by turbulence in the environment. Retailing, as we have shown, has gone through a period of major change. This change process is not complete and competition and volatility will be ever present. For retailers this is a major challenge. It is not helped by the tendency in recent decades to build more and more stores in new locations. (The retailing this 'replaces' remains to some degree.) Some of the new developments were not well sited and/or were speculative. There is thus too much retail space, though not enough high quality locations. Being in the right place at the right cost is a management headache.

Retail management is also concerned about the activities the company undertakes. A number of these have been out-sourced in recent years (such as logistics) to allow retail management to focus on retail operations, in particular in the United Kingdom on store and brand development. Developing and maintaining a retail brand position has become a major task for retailers. Retailers are also under pressure to improve their environmental and social awareness activities and to minimise adverse effects of their business. Concerns about global production and sourcing, labour practices and the need for adaptation to local situations are increasing.

Finally, any discussion of the future of retailing has to consider the issue of e-retailing or Internet shopping. We have seen the spectacular hype and the equally spectacular fall of many Internet operations, but some survive and do well and profitable Internet retailers do exist. The two most visited UK retail Internet sites are Tesco and Argos, both of which have added e-retailing to their existing channels of operations. Some specialist operators are also doing well. There seems to be an appetite for the Internet as a shopping medium, but the extent to which it challenges or complements existing retailing is open to question (Sparks and Findlay 2000; Reynolds 2000).

One of the reasons for this is that there remain issues about the form and functions which need to be performed, and their costs. Some, such as Amazon, have developed pure Internet-based operations. Others, for example Sainsbury, have developed an Internet operation on the back of existing activity, but with specialist facilities. Tesco however chose to add the Internet channel to their existing store-based operation and to focus picking of orders and delivery from local stores. These different models may be suitable in different circumstances, though concern remains about the mechanics of delivery and whether home delivery is actually economically or environmentally desirable (Foresight Retail Logistics Task Force 2000).

Summary

This chapter set out to introduce the subject and context of retailing. Retailing has undergone major changes in form and to some extent function in recent decades. Components of this include:

- growth of particular organisational types;
- dominance of the market by major multiple retailers that continue to grow;
- increasing internationalisation of retailing activity;
- a variety of responses to the changing consumer patterns of demand;
- an increasing professionalisation of management in many retail businesses.

Retailing is a major component of the economies of many countries. Individuals experience retailing every day through their shopping activity. It has come to hold a higher place in people's minds as it has been transformed from a functional sector providing necessities to one that provides a range of experiences and opportunities. With its close understanding of consumers retailing continues to change and fascinate in equal measure.

Further reading

As an introduction to retailing, the following make a good starting point:

Dawson, J.A. (2000) *Future patterns of retailing in Scotland*, Edinburgh: Scottish Executive Central Research Unit.

Seth, A. and **Randall, G.** (1999) *The Grocers: The rise and rise of the supermarket chains*, London: Kogan Page.

Underhill, P. (1999) *Why we Buy: The science of shopping*, London: Orion.

Wrigley, N. and **Lowe, M.** (2002) *Reading Retail*, London: Arnold.

In addition, there are a number of academic journals in the area:

- *International Journal of Retail and Distribution Management;*
- *International Review of Retail, Distribution and Consumer Research;*
- *Journal of Retailing;*
- *Journal of Retailing and Consumer Services;*
- *Service Industries Journal.*

University retailing web sites

A number of universities have specialisms in retailing. Examples include (correct at August 2002):

University	Web address
Manchester Metropolitan	http://www.business.mmu.ac.uk/research/retailmanagement.htm
Loughborough	http://www.lboro.ac.uk/departments/bs/research/rgmarrg.html
Oxford	http://www.templeton.ox.ac.uk/default/default.html
Stirling	http://www.marketing.stir.ac.uk/irs/
Surrey	http://www.smsss.surrey.ac.uk/Retail/default.html

CHAPTER 2

The internationalisation of grocery retailing

Steve Burt and Leigh Sparks

Introduction

Food is a basic human necessity – we all need to eat. Despite the myriad of purchasing opportunities now available in many societies, food and drink consumption remains the largest component of individual and household expenditure. Food purchasing also occurs more frequently than any other retail activity. Many of us visit a grocery store, or perhaps more accurately a store selling grocery products, on a weekly if not daily basis. It is, therefore, not surprising that the largest retail organisations in the world are found within the food or grocery sector. Owing to the size of the domestic market, most are based in the United States (Table 2.1). The sheer scale of Wal-Mart relative to any other retailer is daunting, although it should be remembered (as with Kmart) that the company has its origins in a non-food discount store format. Strictly speaking, Wal-Mart is not a grocery retailer.

Table 2.1 Largest grocery-based retailers in the world – ranked by total sales (2000)

Group	Country of origin	Net Sales	% grocery sales	% foreign sales	Number of countries operating In
Wal-Mart	US	199,096	40	17	11
Carrefour	France	64,791	71	48	32
Ahold	Netherlands	52,471	91	82	23
Kroger	US	50,990	91	0	0
Metro	Germany	48,235	48	44	27
Albertson's	US	38,999	90	0	0
Kmart	US	38,531	36	0	0
Tesco	UK	34,400	87	10	11
Safeway	US	33,275	92	11	3
Rewe	Germany	33,193e	73	20	20

e = estimate

Source: Planet Retail (2002)

As well as meeting a basic human need, food is often characterised by particular national and regional traits. There are differences in diet, taste and attitudes to food and food preparation that translate into consumption and shopping behaviour. Despite these culture-based differences the retail grocery sector is no different from any other, in that internationalisation has become a core feature. Table 2.1 shows that most of the largest grocery retailers are now well established in foreign markets, either in terms of share of turnover or market presence. There is a contrast to be drawn however between European and US grocery retailers, with the latter mainly remaining as domestic businesses.

Retail internationalisation in theory: patterns and process

The internationalisation of grocery retailing raises a number of issues. What is essentially a culture-bound product market is increasingly served by large multinational companies, seeking economies of scale, scope and replication. Amongst the most important questions is whether grocery markets in different countries can be served by a single retail strategy. Is it possible to develop and manage a global grocery chain? Central to this debate is the word 'global', which generally has two interpretations in a retail internationalisation context. First, it signifies the number of foreign markets in which an organisation operates (the spread of operations or how many parts of the globe are covered) and secondly it implies a standardised – one size fits all – approach to retailing within these markets. These two themes are common in the academic literature.

Studies of the pattern of retail internationalisation suggest that companies tend to move into geographically or culturally close markets first, as they are perceived to be most similar to the home operating environment and therefore are 'less risky' or safer. Then, over time, companies move further afield. Treadgold (1990) captured this effect in a model which suggests that retailers go through three stages: reluctance, caution and ambition. As retailers pass through these stages they move from 'safer' to more 'distant' markets and become more proactive in their response to international market opportunities. In essence, retailers gain confidence from their earlier internationalisation experiences.

Salmon and Tordjman (1989) identify three strategies for retail internationalisation, the first of which is a purely financial investment in a foreign operation. This entails little day-to-day involvement and is often a precursor to the other two options, which are as follows:

- *A global strategy*, which requires a high level of standardisation in marketing and operational activities. Central control and coordination of activities is strong and the store network is managed as a linked group of stores rather than a collection of domestic outlets. This provides for economies of scale and replication. A distinctive product range or brand, backed by a high degree of vertical integration, is a common feature.
- *A multinational strategy*, which requires stores to be adjusted to national conditions in a multi-domestic approach. Consequently, marketing activities and operational decisions are made on a country-by-country basis, tailored to local

market and competitive conditions. The internationalising retailer effectively operates as a domestic operator in each of its markets.

A range of other models and explanations of retail internationalisation exist, for example Goldman (2001) focuses upon the role of formats for store type transfer. His typology revolves around the level of managerial adaptation and market standardisation. Whilst the first two options dove-tail with the traditional global or multinational views, Goldman suggests another four options which are variations on a theme. The six strategies are as follows:

- *the global niche position strategy*, which seeks to retain a global niche in a global segment through a high level of standardisation;
- *the opportunism strategy*, requiring adaptation of formats to take advantage of host country opportunities;
- *the format pioneering opportunity strategy*, involving the development of a 'regional' format that is replicated within a specific part of the world;
- *the format extension compatible country of origin strategy*, involving the transfer of a home format with limited changes;
- *the portfolio-based format extension strategy*, involving a similar transfer but based on a non-domestic format;
- *the competitive positioning oriented strategy*, entailing a maximisation of the key strengths of the format in light of existing indigenous competition.

The various schemas and 'models' (or essentially shorthand descriptions) of the internationalisation process are based on an examination of the outcomes of many internationalisation attempts. Often they are intuitive assessments of development processes or intentions. The various schemas themselves overlap, contradict or are in competition with each other. Perhaps we need to go back to examining processes at the company level in order to understand what is actually happening.

Retail internationalisation in practice: four case studies

As stated at the start of this chapter, the internationalisation of grocery retailing is now well under way. As Wrigley (2002) notes, there is a labyrinth of interconnectivity amongst companies in Europe as consolidation takes place. Although Table 2.1 shows the largest grocery-based retailers in the world, if one considers the list by the proportion of total sales that are made outside the home country a different array of retailers comes to the head of the table (Table 2.2). On this measure of internationalisation one could argue that the 'true' leaders of retail internationalisation are the European chains. What is striking from this list is the dominance of European-based chains from France, Germany, Belgium and the Netherlands. Indeed this particular table is headed by the Delhaize Group of Belgium, which although a relatively small group in terms of total sales achieves 84 per cent of turnover from non-domestic markets. From a British perspective we have to return to Table 2.1 to find Tesco, which derives over 10 per cent of its turnover from 11 different markets.

Table 2.2 Largest international grocery-based retailers – ranked by proportion of total sales that are non-domestic 2000

Group	Country of origin	Net Sales	% grocery sales	% non domestic sales	Number of countries operating In
Delhaize 'le lion'	Belgium	18,168	93	84	12
Ahold	Netherlands	52,471	91	82	23
Tenglemann	Germany	24,432	65	49	13
Carrefour	France	64,791	71	48	32
Metro	Germany	48,235	48	44	27
Aldi	Germany	31,000e	84	41	12
ITM Entreprises	France	30,600e	82	31	7
Auchan	France	23,620e	71	30	21
Lidl & Schwarz	Germany	16,477e	83	30	16
Ito-Yokado	Japan	30,235	46	30	5

e = estimated

Source: derived from Planet Retail (2002)

The remainder of this chapter will focus on four chains, each originating from a different European country: Ahold of the Netherlands; Carrefour of France; Delhaize Group of Belgium; and Tesco of the United Kingdom. These are selected because of their international and national importance as well as their future potential. In each case we will consider the timing and geographical pattern of expansion, the approach to international markets and the general philosophy of internationalisation as recounted in company statements.

Ahold

Ahold operates on all three continents. During the 1990s it spread from a European and North American base into Latin America and Asia (Table 2.3). Although most stores are found in Europe the United States has consistently accounted for over 50 per cent of sales during the past decade and now generates nearly 60 per cent of turnover. Ahold initially internationalised in the late 1970s, through the establishment of a Spanish subsidiary (which was sold in the mid-1980s) and the acquisitions of US chains Bi-Lo (1977) and Giant Food Stores (1981). However, expansion primarily took place in the late 1980s and 1990s.

The 1992 Annual Report stated that 'both in the mature Western European markets and in other areas, Ahold is looking for expansion opportunities through acquisition, participation or co-operation'. Since that time the company has been true to its word. Further acquisitions in the United States have been matched within Europe by greenfield entry into the Czech and Slovak Republics (1991), joint ventures in Portugal (1992) and Poland (1995) and re-entry (again via joint venture) into Spain (1996).

Table 2.3 International activities of Ahold, 1992, 1996, 2001

Locations	Number of stores			Origin of sales (%)		
	1992	1996	2001	1992	1996	2001
North America	514	817	1,430	51.5	52.0	59.3
US	514	817	1,430			
Europe	1,225	1,920	6,513	48.5	47.9	32.7
Netherlands	1,169	1,649	2,331	47.5	40.9	14.8
Scandinavia	–	–	2,991			
Portugal	40	122	198			
Spain	–	11	623			
Czech Rep	16	108	205			
Poland	–	30	165			
Latin America*	–	50	608	–	–	7.4
Brazil	–	50	110			
Argentina	–	–	236			
Chile	–	–	118			
Guatemala	–	–	144			
Asia	–	65	104	–	0.1	0.6
Thailand	–	31	44			
Malaysia	–	18	39			
Indonesia	–	–	21			
Singapore	–	1	–			
China	–	15	–			

*Ahold's Latin American interests also have stores in Peru, Paraguay, El Salvador and Honduras
Source: calculated from Annual Reports

The mid-1990s also saw significant joint venture activity. The company invested in Latin America – Brazil (1996), Argentina, Chile, Peru, Paraguay, Ecuador, El Salvador and Honduras (1998) and Asia – China, Indonesia, Malaysia, Singapore and Thailand (1996). During this period Ahold did not neglect its home market, with store numbers doubling over the decade (although the domestic share of total sales has fallen sharply as the internationalisation strategy has taken hold).

Ahold defines its mission as: 'to be the best and most successful food retailer and foodservice operator in the world'. There is now a clear strategic shift to encompass foodservice businesses alongside retailing – and the phrase food 'provider' is now appearing in company literature. This goal is to be achieved: 'by integrating a close-knit network of world-class food retail and foodservice operations that make the whole of our company work more than the sum of the parts' (Annual Report 2001). The emphasis on providing support services to existing local businesses is central to the Ahold philosophy.

Historically Ahold's retail strategy has been based on the supermarket, and this is where the group's strengths and skills traditionally lie. Recent acquisitions have added hypermarkets and convenience stores to the international portfolio, so the group now sees itself as having a: 'multi-channel, multi-brand, multi-format and multi-regional approach' (Annual Report 2001).

In line with this approach the various businesses that have been added to the Ahold umbrella continue to trade under their original 'local' brand names. Consequently Ahold operates as Stop & Shop, Giant-Landover, Giant-Carlisle, Tops, Bi-Lo and Brunos on the east coast of the United States (and also operates the Peapod e-commerce business). In Europe tradenames include Albert Heijn, C100, Pingo Doce, Fiera Nova, Hiper Dino, Hiper Sol, Super Sol, ICA, Rimi, Albert and Hypernova, whilst in Latin America Bompreco, CSU, Disco, g.barosa, la Fragua and Santa Isabel are used. Only in Asia is a single brand, Tops, found. The rationale for this multi-brand approach is a belief that the local trade names have an existing customer franchise that should be maintained, whilst Ahold can bring 'behind-the-scenes' expertise. The company argues that:

> Our strength lies in helping these companies preserve their name, identity and management culture while at the same time realizing the advantages of scale. At Ahold, we effectively exchange our group know-how to keep our local operations top-of-the bill and enhance our local identity (www.ahold.com/ aboutahold/strategy)

Central to this support function is the Ahold Networking scheme formed in 1998. This network aims to disseminate best practice and knowledge throughout the group through easily accessible databases, the exchange of information and special project groups. The precursor to the Ahold Network were various benchmarking and knowledge transfer activities in the United States. In the early 1990s synergy groups across the five US chains saw the exchange of 'every day low prices' expertise within the United States and the transfer of retail brand and space management techniques from the Netherlands. A related initiative, 'Project Complete' oversaw the integration of a range of corporate functions amongst the US chains. The support function gained a more international dimension during the 1990s when the established businesses took on formal mentoring roles in the developing countries – for example, Albert Heijn supported business development in China, Central Europe and Spain. There have been attempts to standardise processes whilst allowing variation at the format, brand and facia level.

Despite the impressive record of expansion there has been some questioning of Ahold's ability to integrate so many acquisitions. In 1999, following the economic crisis in the Asia region, the group restructured its activities and withdrew from Singapore and China – the latter a market that, despite cultural and political barriers, is seen by many as offering great future potential. Similar problems arose in Latin America. Having already bought out its partner in Brazil Ahold had to acquire full control of its Argentinian business, Disco, to prevent its partner from failing.

Integration problems also occurred in Spain, where the group was rebuilding its operation. In October 2002 Ahold announced that it would consolidate its Central European businesses in Poland and the Czech and Slovak Republics. In addition to all this operational turmoil in April 2002 Ahold's financial accounts came under scrutiny. The differences in accounting procedures between the Netherlands and the United States showed a huge difference in performance. Dutch accounting methods presented an increase in net earnings of +36 per cent, but US methods (with different treatments of property deals, financial derivatives and hedging, and goodwill) recorded a fall of –85 per cent over the same period. Internationalisation is not simply a straightforward, one-way progression around the globe.

Carrefour

Of all the European-based grocery chains Carrefour boasts the most extensive international coverage (Table 2.4). The majority of sales still originate from Europe, although less than 50 per cent are now derived from the domestic French market. The group has a long international history, taking its first steps outside France in 1969 through a joint venture in Belgium with Delhaize. Other joint venture moves into Switzerland (1970), the United Kingdom (1972), Italy (1972), Spain (1973), Brazil (1974), Austria (1976) and West Germany (1977) soon followed. The late 1970s and early 1980s saw a period of retrenchment, with only the Spanish and Brazilian ventures (plus Argentina entered in 1982) remaining as significant investments. It is noticeable that in these surviving businesses Carrefour had assumed full control.

The late 1980s saw ventures developed in the United States and Taiwan, but it was during the 1990s that Carrefour spread its wings to all corners of the globe, including some of those European markets that it had previously abandoned (for example Italy, Belgium and Switzerland). The acquisition of Euromarche in 1991 not only consolidated Carrefour's position in the domestic market but also added a number of international stores in existing markets, plus a new market, Portugal. However, it was 1993, the thirtieth anniversary of the company's formation, that saw a sea change in international strategy, with clear statements on future expansion. Countries were defined as *core mature markets* (France and Spain), where the emphasis would be on raising competitiveness; *growth opportunity markets* (Brazil, Argentina, Portugal and Taiwan), where the scope existed for further expansion of established businesses; and *new markets* (Italy, Malaysia, Turkey), where entry was at its initial stages. The strategy was clear from statements made about the re-entry into Italy: 'As in any new market, the first objective is to reach the critical mass necessary for achieving significant market penetration' (Annual Report 1993). This approach led to the closure of the US operation in 1993, and plans to open 19 international stores and only 1 domestic store during 1994.

The mid-1990s saw a major expansion in Asia to supplement the existing Taiwanese business, with entry into Malaysia in 1994, China in 1995, Hong Kong, Thailand and South Korea in 1996, followed by Indonesia, Singapore and finally Japan in 2000. In Latin America the established Brazilian and Argentinian presence was complemented by Mexico in 1994, plus Chile and Colombia in 1998. In Europe expansion included Poland (1997), the Czech Republic (1998), Slovakia (1999) and a return to Switzerland (2001).

Table 2.4 International activities of Carrefour, 1992, 1996, 2001

Locations	Number of stores			Origin of sales (%)		
	1992	1996	2001	1992	1996	2001
North America	2	–	–	N/A	–	–
US	2					
Europe	527	823	4,478	88.4*	73.3	80.8
France	485	761	1,295	69.2	59.5	49.2
Spain	40	53	1,952			
Portugal	2	2	281			
Italy	–	6	305			
Turkey	–	1	99			
Poland	–	–	60			
Czech Rep	–	–	9			
Slovakia	–	–	2			
Belgium	–	–	129			
Switzerland	–	–	8			
Greece	–	–	338			
Latin America	34	72	650	8.9*	19.5*	12.9
Argentina	6	15	400			
Brazil	28	44	222			
Mexico	–	13	19			
Chile	–	–	4			
Colombia	–	–	5			
Asia	5	24	105	0.9	2.9	6.3
Taiwan	5	13	26			
Malaysia	–	2	6			
China	–	3	24			
South Korea	–	3	22			
Indonesia	–	–	8			
Singapore	–	–	1			
Hong Kong	–	1	–			
Thailand	–	2	15			
Japan	–	–	3			
Other				1.8	4.3	–

* In 1992 and 1996 Carrefour reported Europe as France and Spain; Latin America as Argentina and Brazil; Asia as Taiwan.

Source: calculated from Annual Reports

A major boost to the international portfolio came in 1999 through a merger with Promodes (another leading French chain), which itself had an extensive store network, particularly in Europe. The merger also ensured that the domestic French market continued to develop in terms of market share and store numbers. As has been the experience with other attempts by European retailers to take the hypermarket concept into the United States, Carrefour's most significant 'failure' would seem to be its US venture (Tordjman 1988). The other withdrawal over this period was from Hong Kong in 2000.

The other significant aspect of the Promodes merger was that it transformed Carrefour from essentially a hypermarket retailer into a multi-format operation, through the addition of supermarket and hard discount businesses. Carrefour had acquired the French supermarket chain, Comptoirs Modernes, the year before, but the Promodes merger was on a totally different scale and also provided an entry into franchising as an organisational mode.

The group now identifies three key formats, although there are also over 2,200 convenience stores and nearly 200 Cash & Carry outlets in France, Spain, Belgium and Italy. The primary format is the hypermarket, with over 700 in 28 countries. All the hypermarkets now trade as Carrefour, since the rebranding of Pryca in Spain and GB in Belgium. The integration of the Promodes supermarket business means that this format trades in 9 countries through four core brands: Champion in France, Spain and Brazil; Norte in Argentina; GS in Italy; and GB in Belgium. The third format, present in 7 countries, is the hard discount store based upon the Dia, Ed and Minipreco brands. The expansion of trading formats is now formally embedded in Carrefour's vision: 'As an international, multi-format retail group, Carrefour's growth is based on the expansion of powerful and complementary networks that can meet the needs of local customers worldwide' (Annual Report 2001).

In Asia the strategy is to develop hypermarkets in order to grow rapid market share, whilst in Latin America the group aims to expand supermarkets and hard discount stores to complement an existing dense hypermarket network. Finally, in mature European markets complementary formats are to be developed. All three formats are currently found in France, Spain, Turkey, Greece, Argentina and Brazil.

Central to the Carrefour approach, whether at home or overseas, is a decentralised management style. The strategy is to train local, national management teams. Historically individual hypermarket managers have had considerable autonomy over store operations (Burt 1986). Homage to this philosophy is evident in both the 1994 and 2001 Annual Reports:

> Carrefour not only exports its unique retailing expertise to the countries in which it operates, it also strives to adapt to their specific environment at every level. (1994)

> If Carrefour is now a world retailer, it is because it has succeeded in establishing itself, country by country, as a local player, close to the customer and respectful of local lifestyles and culture. (2001)

Although in 1998 the group launched its first global promotion campaign, 'unbeatable' for the Carrefour hypermarket brand in all 20 countries, coordinated management remains a support function. At an operational level the group argues that although Carrefour, Champion and Dia are global brands close to 90 per cent of inventory is local or regional, allowing for local adaptation. Similarly, where appropriate long-established supermarket trade names have been retained, the purpose is: 'not to build a global banner, but rather to maintain a strong profile for each tradename in its country of origin, highlighting the strong points, deriving maximum advantage from the exchange of know how between countries' (Annual Report 2000).

One could ask whether consumers see quite the distinctions that Carrefour believe.

Delhaize Group

Owing to its relatively small size the Delhaize Group is often forgotten when commentators refer to the leading international grocery chains. The group, however, now earns 85 per cent of its sales outside of the domestic market, with 79 per cent derived from its US chains. The contribution of international activities has been important to Delhaize for some time (Table 2.5). As early as 1980 non-domestic sales accounted for around 47 per cent of total sales (compared to figures of 28 per cent for Ahold and 15 per cent for Carrefour), reflecting the very small and more restricted Belgian home market.

The United States has always been an important market for the group since their first investment in Food Town Stores in 1974. With the exception of a short-lived investment in the Portuguese chain, Pingo Doce, expansion during the 1980s focused solely on consolidation in the United States with the addition

Table 2.5 International activities of Delhaize Group, 1992, 1996, 2001

Locations	Number of stores			Origin of sales (%)		
	1992	1996	2001	1992	1996	2001
North America	1,021	1,125	1,459	73.3	69.7	79.0
US	1,021	1,125	1,459			
Europe	432	575	899	26.7	30.3	20.1
Belgium	410	478	675	25.7	23.9	15.0
Czech Rep	7	30	94			
Slovakia	–	–	16			
Greece	15	25	104			
France	–	42	–			
Romania	–	–	10			
Latin America	–	–	–	–	–	–
Asia	–	–	86	–	–	0.9
Singapore			31			
Indonesia			29			
Thailand			26			

Source: calculated from Annual Reports

of Food Giant, Giant Food Markets and Super Discount Markets. In the past decade other southern and central European and most recently Asian markets have attracted investment. Delhaize now trades in 10 countries.

The entry methods employed in Europe and Asia tend to be joint venture or a shareholding that allows Delhaize to assume managerial control. Czechoslovakia was entered in 1991 via a 75 per cent share in a joint venture (Delvita), Greece in 1992, through a 51 per cent stake in Alpha Beta Vassilopoulos, and Romania in 2000, when Delhaize aquired 51 per cent of Mega Image. Greenfield expansion into Slovakia occurred in 1998 based on Delvita's operations. In 1994 Delhaize also took a 74 per cent share in PG, a small French regional grocery chain. This was subsequently transferred to a 50:50 joint venture with Comptoirs Modernes three years later and sold in 2000. In Asia 1997 saw entry into Indonesia through a technical assistance arrangement that became a 51 per cent share when legislation changed the following year. The company also had a 50:50 joint venture in Thailand, which fell under full control in January 2000. A 49 per cent share was acquired in Shop 'N' Save (Singapore) in 1999. Finally, further consolidation of the US operations occurred in 1999 with the acquisition of Hannaford.

In the case of the longer-established businesses and where Delhaize has management control the different international markets are integrated at the customer interface through the use of a distinctive Lion symbol – reflecting the original Delhaize trade name. Sub-branding retaining the local market name (for example Delvita and Super Indo) is used alongside the characteristic lion profile.

The goal of Delhaize Group is 'to be one of the most admired international food retailers by its customers, its employees and its shareholders'. In order to meet this aim the focus is on:

> achieving leading positions in key mature and emerging markets through strong local chains that build on success by being best at answering local consumer needs while benefiting from the Group's size and best practice. Delhaize Group goes to market with a variety of locally adapted store formats, of which the most common is the supermarket. (http://www.delhaize.com/en/gr_strategy.asp)

In its annual reports Delhaize refers to itself as a transnational retail group, and aims for its various businesses to be amongst the three leading chains in the relevant region. As with Ahold and Carrefour the approach has been to support the regional businesses with group expertise and know-how. An electronic financial reporting system to allow cross-country benchmarking was introduced in 1999 and examples of intragroup technology transfer include the implementation of central distribution in the Czech Republic, category management in Thailand and retail brand expertise in the Czech Republic and Greece. In 2001 the group was restructured around three geographic regions – the United States, Europe and Asia – supported by four group functions – finance, human resources, information technology and legal affairs. This support structure is again encapsulated in a quote from the 2001 Annual Report: 'Delhaize Group is a federation of local companies, not a centralized, monolithic structure. Therefore, the focus is on empowerment.'

Individual chains are free to devise their own operating positions based on local market knowledge. Food Lion and the Asian companies have a clear EDLP focus, while Delhaize, Hannaford, Alfa-Beta, Delvita and Mega Image offer a choice, fresh products and service at fair price positions in their respective countries.

Tesco

British-domiciled grocery retailers have had a limited impact on the world stage, although a number of chains have at various times had international operations (for example Liptons, Cavenham, Booker, BAT and Dee). Of the surviving major UK grocery chains Sainsbury has had the longest-established international investment through its Shaws subsidiary in the United States. Although a shareholding was first taken in Shaws in 1983 growth of this operation has been slow, and success has been patchy. Tesco has, particularly in the latter part of the 1990s, begun to develop a serious international business. Tesco's published strategy now has four elements: a strong UK core business, non-food development, retailing of services and internationalisation. There is a stated 'long-term goal of becoming a truly international retailer'.

Tesco now achieves 15 per cent of its turnover from outside the United Kingdom and since entry into Malaysia has a presence in five European and four Asian markets (Table 2.6). Early attempts to move overseas however were less than successful. Tesco's largest non-domestic operation is in the Republic of Ireland. The acquisition of Power Supermarkets in 1997 represents the company's second foray into the Irish market. Corporate literature and the web site make little mention of the acquisition of Three Guys in 1978 and subsequent withdrawal in 1986 (Lord *et al.* 1988). Similarly, the acquisition and operation of a French chain, Catteau, between 1993 and 1997 is overshadowed by the successful moves into Central Europe (Hungary in 1994, Poland in 1995, the Czech and Slovak Republics in 1996) and Asia (Thailand in 1997, South Korea in 1999, Taiwan in 2000 and Malaysia in 2002). According to press reports plans exist for entry into China in future years.

Table 2.6 International activities of Tesco, 1992, 1996, 2001

Locations	Number of stores			Origin of sales (%)		
	1992	1996	2001	1992	1996	2001
North America	–	–	–	–	–	–
Europe	412	758	927	100	100	94.1
UK	412	568	729	100	94.5	84.8
France	–	103	–			
Ireland	–	–	76			
Hungary	–	43	48			
Poland	–	31	46			
Czech Rep	–	6	15			
Slovakia	–	7	13			
Latin America	–	–	–	–	–	–
Asia	–	–	52	–	–	5.9
Thailand			35			
South Korea			14			
Taiwan			3			

Source: calculated from Annual Reports

Tesco's approach to internationalisation has been based primarily upon acquisition – Global TH in Hungary, Savia in Poland, the K-Mart operations in the Czech Republic and Slovakia, Power Supermarkets in the Republic of Ireland and Lotus in Thailand. Joint venturing was used in the case of South Korea (with Samsung) and Malaysia (with Sime Darby). Taiwan represents the only greenfield entry. The international stores have all been rebranded as Tesco, although on occasion sub-branding exists, as in Thailand with the 'Tesco-Lotus' name reflecting the original acquisition. In common with most international grocery chains, whilst scale may be leveraged in terms of 'backroom' knowledge and expertise, operations have a strong local influence: 'wherever in the world we operate, we stay local. The majority of store managers in Europe and Asia are local people ... local sourcing, wherever practicable, means many products are sourced from within the end national market' (Annual Report 2002).

An interesting perspective on the Tesco experience is that in most of the central European and Asian markets the company operates through a format that was not at the time used in the domestic market – the hypermarket. This illustrates that technology transfer in internationalisation is a two-way process. The international ventures into central Europe and Thailand allowed Tesco to learn about hypermarket retailing, particularly the integration of non-food products into food stores and seasonal promotional activities. This new knowledge has been imported into the domestic operation in the 'Tesco Extra' hypermarket format. Supply chain knowledge, site research skills and retail brand development have in contrast been transferred in the other direction.

Despite a relatively late start (compared to others in this chapter) Tesco has a clear strategy of entering developing markets and claimed in the 2002 Annual Report that: 'This year marks the arrival of Tesco as an international Group with market leading positions in six of our ten countries and 65,000 staff overseas.'

Plans are now afoot to develop superstores and large supermarkets in some of the overseas markets alongside existing hypermarkets – a sign of a maturing internationalisation strategy. Finally, a further dimension to international activity was developed in 2002, with an agreement with Safeway, Inc. in the United States for Tesco to provide expertise on e-commerce. The Tesco e-commerce store-based picking process, although only in the United Kingdom, has made it the largest e-commerce grocery retailer in the world. It has undergone successful trials in Safeway's operation in the United States and is to be rolled out across part of its network.

Summary

This chapter has briefly introduced some of the academic views on retail internationalisation and provided an overview of the international activities of four European grocery chains. The intention has been to illustrate some of the practical experiences of the major European grocery retailers. We have attempted to indicate similarities and differences amongst these businesses and their operations. There are different experiences and activities. Academic models of internationalisation may therefore struggle to capture all that is going on. Our questions relate to the applicability of academic theory to practice.

Discussion questions

1. Compare and contrast the different methods of international expansion used by the four companies. How do they differ?

2. Is there any pattern to the geographical expansion of these four companies? If so, can these patterns be explained?

3. What do you think is meant by the term 'global' international grocery retailer? Do any of these companies fit your definition?

4. All of these companies have withdrawn from markets at some point. What do these withdrawals tell us about retail internationalisation?

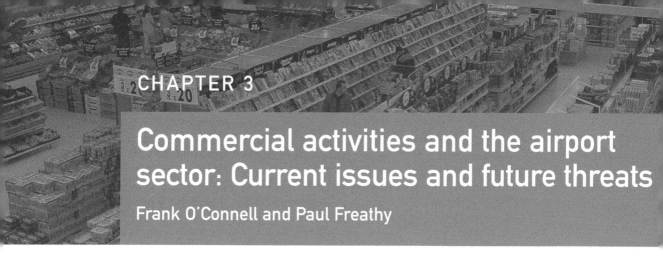

CHAPTER 3

Commercial activities and the airport sector: Current issues and future threats

Frank O'Connell and Paul Freathy

Introduction

One of the themes developed in the first chapter of this book was that change is an integral part of the retail environment. Consumers, retailers and suppliers are located within a dynamic, ever-changing environment. Flexibility and adaptation have become synonymous with long-term growth and survival. In this case study we examine the impact that environmental change can have upon one sector of the retail industry. One of the most significant (and widely publicised) changes to affect the European airport industry has been the removal of a passenger's entitlement to purchase duty and tax free goods when travelling between EU member states.

From 1 July 1999 airports within the European Union have had to limit the sale of such goods to passengers travelling outside of the EU. This has led to a situation where, for example, a passenger travelling from France to Greece cannot purchase duty free goods, whereas an individual travelling between France and Turkey can. The implications of this change are widespread and extend beyond a decline in sales towards a more fundamental reassessment of the industry's entire cost structure. The aim of this case study is to evaluate how the industry should react at a strategic level and to provide an opportunity for you to discuss the possible courses of action open to an airport retailer.[1]

Influences on the development of European airports

Over the past 30 years the air industry has undergone a radical transformation. The changes have created a series of imperatives to which the European airport authorities have been forced to respond. Whilst the influences that have prompted change are multi-causal, five factors in particular have caused the greatest reaction.

---

[1] The boundaries between retailer, wholesaler, airport operator and manufacturer have become increasingly blurred. For example, companies such as Heinemann are retailers, distributors and agents; KLM and SAS operate both airlines and retail stores, BAA and Aer Rianta are both retailers and airport managers; LVMH are retailers and manufacturers as well as suppliers to the competition.

Increases in passenger numbers

The popularity of air travel has been reflected in the increasing demand for passenger flights and the shift towards more international departures. Airports Council International (ACI) (1998) noted that passenger growth is expected to average around 3.95 per cent per annum between 1997 and 2010. While tragic incidents like 11 September 2001 will have a short- to medium-term impact upon passenger numbers the expectation is that by the year 2010 over 2 billion people will travel by air, with over 30 per cent on international flights.

The factors behind this growth are varied. Customers are more discerning in terms of the level and quality of service they expect and are increasingly willing to experience foreign travel and cultures (Humphries 1996). Aided in part by a wider choice of destination, plus the increased leisure time many now enjoy, there has been a growing propensity for tourists to expand their travel horizons beyond that of the traditional short-haul charter location.

A second factor accounting for the growth in passenger numbers has been a decline in the relative cost of travelling. An ACI (1994) survey estimated that, after accounting for inflation, air fares were approximately 70 per cent cheaper than in 1970. In addition, low cost operators such as easyJet and Ryanair have entered the market offering alternatives to the traditional state-run and state-controlled airlines.

Amongst both developed and developing nations air travel has become an increasingly important method of travel for the business community. Reinforcing the view of Schilling and Hill (1998), trade agreements have reduced barriers between the world's economic zones and increased both the propensity and incentive for international business travel. Increasingly businesses are looking to expand on an international scale rather than being confined to national boundaries.

Deregulation and liberalisation

The early 1980s witnessed the deregulation of air travel in the United States and represented a catalyst for major structural change within the industry. The development of 'wheel and spoke' and 'hubbing'[2] in the United States, established major transfer points through which the majority of flights were routed. The airports involved expanded significantly whilst others on the periphery saw traffic diminish. A similar situation was experienced in Europe when a number of airports began to emerge as hubs, drawing an increasing number of the newly created airlines to them and intensifying the pressure on established airlines to embark on a price competitive strategy. (Doganis 1992; 1995). As many of Europe's established airlines were state owned they had cost structures related to a regime of regulated air fares and route monopolies.

The structure of the air transport industry within Europe would have been considered mature, with established carriers, airport operators and an existing infrastructure. However the liberalisation of air travel within the European Union and the movement towards an 'open skies' policy within the United States led to a number of new airline operators entering the market. New point-to-point routes have opened using secondary airports and offering the consumer lower fare alternatives (Symons, Travers, Morgan 1997). Further growth potential exists as new

---

[2] Recognised methods of organising the routing and scheduling of aircraft.

markets in Asia and South America emerge, new routes open and passenger volumes increase. Whilst barriers to entry still exist and new entrants continue to find it difficult to gain slots and gate space, the anticipated growth that will stem from market liberalisation will mean an intensification of competition as airports attempt to attract new carriers (Freathy and O'Connell 1998).

Decline in state control

Traditionally airports have been administered and controlled directly by the state or by a body appointed on its behalf. A number of reasons have been put forward to account for the state's involvement in managing airports. Smith (1994) for example maintained that because many cities have only a single airport, their role becomes central to a region's economic and social development. Keogh (1994) noted that in the Irish Republic the high degree of state involvement in airport ownership was due to the relatively recent status of Ireland as an independent economy. Control over the country's airports is therefore central in ensuring not only general economic growth but also as a way of assisting in rural redevelopment and regional policy.

Whilst it remains accurate to suggest that the majority of airports throughout the world still have some form of public sector ownership, the level of operational control exercised by central government may be balanced against a greater participation from private sector interests. A reduction in the state's control and regulation of the air transport industry in favour of greater commercial sector involvement can therefore be identified (Sewell-Rutter 1995).

Smith (1994) maintains that deregulation has been prompted primarily by the state's desire to avoid the financial burdens associated with subsidising airport capital investment. Airports have traditionally had to compete with other areas of public expenditure such as education, health and defence. The increasing cost associated with operating an airport has prompted the view that airports are in an intensely competitive market and need to be run on commercial rather than state principles.

Allowing private sector organisations a financial interest in airport operations is arguably an efficient and cost-effective way for the state to maximise revenue whilst at the same time improving customer service and quality standards. The level of return is increased whilst the degree of risk is minimised as the state draws upon a specialised set of management skills (Sewell-Rutter 1995; Doganis 1995).

Increased airport congestion

One consequence of the growth in passenger numbers has been considerable terminal and airfield capacity problems. Some view congestion as the biggest challenge facing the air transport industry (ACI 1994). Although the British Airports Authority (BAA) received permission to develop a new terminal in November 2001 many airports continue to face the prospect of overcrowded transport facilities. O'Toole (1997) estimated that to cope with the growth in passenger numbers Europe's airports would have to invest in the region of $4 billion per annum in their infrastructure.

The creation of a single European market

From the above discussion we can see that airports have become a fundamental part of the European transport infrastructure. Although under constant pressure to cope with airline congestion and passenger numbers, they serve both an economic role as well as a social function. As they have grown many airports have become increasingly reliant upon the revenues generated from their commercial activities, in particular retailing. The income generated from duty free and other retail business has allowed many airports to react to the challenges identified above.

It is against this background of change that the abolition of duty and tax free goods on flights between EU member states needs to be understood. The rationale for abolishing duty free stemmed from a desire to create a single European market that encouraged the free movement of goods and services between its membership. As such, the removal of duty free can be set within the context of a wider set of initiatives designed to harmonise the trade barriers between participant countries.

The original intention was to create a single market amongst member states by December 1991; however two EU Directives (91/680 and 92/12) delayed the implementation of the provision by a further seven and a half years. The legal basis for duty and tax free allowances was the 1969 Directive 69/169/EEC, which stated that passengers can import limited quantities of products without paying VAT and excise duties when travelling. The rationale for abolition was that the movement of goods between member states should no longer be treated as 'exports' or 'imports' for tax purposes. As a consequence it was inappropriate to waive the tax and duty on purchases (Netherlands Economic Institute 1989).

European airport operators and retailers alike were united in their opposition to abolition as a significant proportion of their retail revenue was derived from intra-EU sales. In some cases it is estimated that as much as 83 per cent of retail sales could be lost (IRS 1997). It was feared that many airports would be unable to make a profit and would not have the resources to further develop their infrastructure. Gray (1994) highlighted the importance of duty free revenue for European airports. Whilst in the United States it plays a relatively insignificant role (Los Angeles 12 per cent, Seattle 11 per cent and San Francisco 5 per cent of total revenue), Schiphol derived 34 per cent of their revenue from duty free whilst at the BAA it accounted for 33 per cent. It was estimated that the abolition of duty free would cost the BAA in excess of £50 million per annum whilst in Ireland Cork airport derived over 90 per cent of its operating profit from tax and duty free sales (O'Connell 1993). Regional airports with a high percentage of intra-EU traffic would therefore appear to be most at risk.

Despite an intensive lobbying campaign from the air transport industry, which highlighted job losses, fare increases and service decline, a further extension was not forthcoming. The entitlement of passengers to purchase tax and duty free goods on intra-EU travel ended on 30 June 1999.

Strategic responses to abolition

One of the key arguments put forward by the EU Commission against a further extension of duty free was that airport retailers and operating authorities had already been provided with a seven and a half year adjustment period in order to develop alternative strategic responses. Indeed airport operators and retailers had undertaken a variety of strategic initiatives designed to offset the potential impact of abolition. In this section we discuss the responses to abolition.

One strategy has been for airports to compete more aggressively in the market and attempt to reinforce their position as the first choice for both airlines and travellers. Airports generate revenue from both commercial and aeronautical sources. By increasing the number of airlines, flights and passengers, airport authorities have sought to offset the impact of EU legislative change through volume increases. Airports such as Heathrow, Amsterdam, Paris CGD, Frankfurt and Copenhagen have positioned themselves as European hub airports and act as a consolidation point for domestic, regional and intercontinental traffic. Accompanying this strategy has been an expansion of commercial activities and an increase in retail selling space. Other airports such as Dublin and Manchester have also pursued strongly a commercial strategy and expanded their retail operations. Both airports have positioned themselves as secondary hubs and have been successful in supplementing their traditional charter traffic with a number of scheduled flights. The majority of non-charter flights operate all year round and represent an important source of revenue for the airport outside of the traditional peak summer months. European airports have not been without their problems however. For example the decline of sales per passenger in Schiphol has been attributed to the increasing levels of commercial competition between airports and airlines, the rise in passenger numbers and the enforcement of the Schengen agreement (which ended all frontier barriers between member states).

A second strategy designed to offset the impact of duty free abolition has been to expand the range of commercial activities at the airport. This has resulted in a marked increase in the amount of space dedicated to specialist shopping facilities. Many airports have attempted to develop a tenant mix that differentiates the retail offer on the basis of exclusivity rather than price. For example, in the United Kingdom, BAA increased its retail floor space (including catering) from 400,000 square feet in 1991 to 928,000 square feet in 1998 and by August 2002 had 40 different retailers at Heathrow Terminal 4 including Harrods, Hamleys, Dunhill and Escada. Similarly, Milan airport devotes 15 per cent of its total terminal space to retailing whilst Schiphol airport offers a range of over 120,000 different products.

Many airports have adopted a strategy of stocking high profile branded merchandise. In this way airport customers can recognise instantly the goods on offer. Companies such as Bally, Levi's, The Body Shop, Tie Rack and Sunglass Hut have become permanent, established features in many airports. Any dissonance related to the purchase decision can be significantly reduced by the inclusion within the tenant mix of these branded retailers. The instant recognition of branded products can lead to shorter purchase decision times, which may allow time-limited passengers the opportunity to make incremental purchases.

Retailers have attempted to further differentiate their product offer by stocking a portfolio of exclusive goods. Depending upon the volumes demanded, a brand manufacturer may develop a product and make it available only at the airport, alternatively it may offer it exclusively to an individual stockist. For example, the manufacturer Allied Domecq initially launched 'Tia Maria cream' exclusively through Allders duty free outlets.

In addition to attracting international branded retailers, the objective has been to use concessionaires to provide a flavour of the city or region that the airport serves (Klapper 1995; Bingman 1996). For example, the merchandise in the shops of the Museum Company includes artefacts that are on show in local galleries and museums. Schiphol has an outlet specialising in the sale of flower bulbs, whilst Edinburgh has a concession selling Scottish salmon and haggis. These products are often packaged as quality gifts and represent a convenient means of using any remaining local currency.

A strategy in the larger airports may also be to include a wider range of luxury and peripheral retail units that appeal to only a minority of passengers. Once an airport's traffic flow exceeds 7 million passengers a year it reaches the critical mass needed to sustain a wider range of niche retail outlets. Thus, for example, antique dealers, carpet and tapestry traders, high quality jewellers and lace makers may be found in some of the larger airports. Despite appealing to only a small segment of the travelling population large passenger volumes have made such specialised retailing a sustainable proposition.

The matching of the tenant mix to consumer demand is illustrated in a number of airports. At Heathrow the retail composition for each terminal is a reflection of the passenger profile. For example Humphries (1996) notes how half the passengers at Heathrow Terminal 1 are on business and well over half are men. Consequently branded products are sold through established quality retailers such as Austin Reed, Thomas Pink and Links of London. In Terminal 2 the high proportion of European passengers means that there is considerable demand for traditional English goods.

Passengers using Heathrow Terminals 3 and 4 are on flights to Scandinavia, the United States and the Far East and have above average levels of disposable income. Their propensity to purchase high ticket goods is consequently higher. The retail tenant mix therefore reflects this, with a variety of branded goods being sold through established retailers. In contrast, as Manchester airport has a higher proportion of charter flights, the number of retailers selling high quality, branded merchandise is reduced in favour of outlets stocking mid-range clothing, goods and accessories, for example Dixons, Our Price, Dorothy Perkins, Burtons, Warner Bros and Tie Rack.

The composition of tenants within a terminal may also change to reflect a repositioning of the airport. This is illustrated at Gatwick airport, which traditionally had a high proportion of chartered flights. As British Airways has developed its operations at Gatwick the traffic profile is becoming more typical of a main hub airport with a mixture of business, scheduled and charter flights. The retail composition, particularly in the newer North terminal, attempts to reflect this changing market.

To ensure sales revenues from retailing are maximised a number of airport operators have adopted a proactive approach to managing the tenant mix. Detailed passenger data, traffic forecasts and route profiles are provided to retail operators to help in their marketing activities. Regular review meetings, seminars and even 'away days' are arranged to analyse in detail the business performance and jointly plan for the period ahead. Many airport authorities are organising joint promotional campaigns in co-operation with the concessionaires and the leading merchandise suppliers.

In an attempt to generate additional commercial revenues airport operators have undertaken a series of other initiatives. These have included 24-hour trading, direct mail, catalogue shopping and customer loyalty schemes. More fundamentally, airports such as Schiphol International have taken the process of commercialisation further by developing landside shopping centres aimed at the non-travelling public. Schiphol Plaza is open from 07.00 to 22.00 every day, and in addition to having a selection of bars and restaurants offers a wide range of merchandise including perfume, clothing, CDs, jewellery and sports goods.

As a means of building upon their core competencies airports have also embarked on a number of joint ventures with overseas partners. Whilst not particularly new, such a strategy has become increasingly widespread. For example, the Irish airport authority Aer Rianta currently operates the three main airports in Ireland, has major shareholdings in Birmingham and Dusseldorf airports as well as having retail interests in Russia, Ukraine, Bahrain, Canada, Greece, Lebanon and Bulgaria.

Some airport authorities such as the BAA have also sought to develop interests outside of the air industry. After privatisation the company began to diversify its activities and developed hotels on its own property and opened a hotel in Belgium. In addition it jointly built and operates the high-speed rail link between London and Heathrow airport. The company has also invested in property, manages shopping facilities within a hospital and has bought a freight forwarding company. It has entered into a joint venture agreement with the US property developer McArthur Glenn and operates a series of designer outlet centres.

The skills that operators have developed in managing their airports has a commercial value and a number of authorities have established international consultancy companies through which they sell their expertise. ADP, the Paris airport operator, for example, assisted in the redesign and refurbishment of Cyprus airport whilst the Frankfurt authority helped develop a marketing strategy for the new airport at Spata in Greece.

Summary

European airport authorities operate within an expanding economic sector. With the liberalisation of the industry, the abolition of duty free and the decline of state control, environmental change has been very much in evidence. The airport industry has been forced to react to substantial macro-level changes over which it has little control. Whilst many airports have attempted to increase the breadth and variety of their retail offer emphasis is still primarily placed upon the achievement of efficiency gains through long-run cost/quality advantages.

In conclusion, therefore, the air transport sector represents a dynamic industry that has expanded significantly over the past three decades. The factors outlined above have compelled a proactive response on the part of the European airport authorities which, in an attempt to maintain a sustainable competitive advantage, have employed a variety of strategic growth methods. Moreover, there is little to suggest that the pace of change is slowing and, as a consequence, one may expect continued competitive intensity between the main firms within the industry.

Discussion questions

1. What have been the primary factors accounting for the reconfiguration of airport retailing? To what extent does the industry have control over these variables?

2. Using a simple SWOT analysis, evaluate the range of strategic initiatives undertaken by the airports since abolition.

3. What other strategic growth options could you suggest for companies in this sector of the retail industry?

4. What lessons do you feel can be drawn from this case study in terms of how retail markets operate?

PART 2

Strategic planning in retailing

CHAPTER 4

Managing the strategic environment

Paul Freathy

Aim

The aim of this chapter is to provide readers with an understanding of retail strategy and why it is important for organisations to adopt a strategic perspective.

Learning objectives

By the end of this chapter readers will be able to:

- define the concept of strategic management;

- describe how decision making occurs in theory in a retail organisation and from this define the process of strategic management;

- illustrate how strategic management operates in practice;

- address within a broad framework the strategic issues and problems faced by managers in a retail organisation.

Introduction

There is an old saying that: 'The only person who likes change is a wet baby.' This view is certainly relevant in the context of strategic management, as it is always easier to find reasons for maintaining the status quo rather than accept the need for change. Organisations are no exception. When discussing with managers the need for change a whole host of reasons are put forward to explain why companies do not undertake any form of strategic planning. Typically, responses include: 'it's too difficult', 'we haven't time' and 'we don't see the point'.

The pace of change in the business environment appears to be increasing. Many organisations are now multinational and multi-product in nature. Organisations and their managers need to know how to manage this complexity and, where possible, how to anticipate the changes that are likely to occur.

As Williams (1981) noted, 'The whole purpose of this [the strategic planning] process is to lift managers' heads up from the day-to-day, and help them take the longer term view'. It would be misleading however to suggest that business planning is the answer to all a company's woes. A well coordinated, disciplined business strategy does not guarantee success, it is only likely to reduce the risk of organisational failure.

What is strategic management?

Strategic management is not a new concept, but many companies have failed to understand its importance. Organisations have traditionally focused on operational decisions with short-run adaptation. Some 40 years ago it was noted that firms: 'devote little time to long run planning ... and rely heavily on traditional methods, general industrial practice and standard operating procedures for making decisions' (Cyert and March 1963, p 100).

There are many ways to define strategic management. Johnson and Scholes (2002) indicate that it is concerned with deciding a strategy, and planning how that strategy is to be put into effect. Ansoff (1965) approaches it by saying that it is about positioning an organisation within its environment to assure its continued success. In this chapter we will adopt the definition of strategic management as the task of *matching a company's resources and activities to the environment in which the company operates*.

From a brief look back at the last few decades it is evident that current success is no 'predictor' of future achievement. Many established businesses over the last 20 or 30 years have disappeared completely or been subsumed by other companies. For example Fine Fare, Rumbelows, Liptons, Smith's Crisps, Goldbergs and Sabena were all once household names.

Many of the problems facing companies arise from their inability to either anticipate or respond successfully to environmental change. For example, in the United Kingdom, banks traditionally operated in an environment where change took place slowly. However the entry of Marks & Spencer into financial services and the Virgin Group's development of personal equity plans sent shock waves through the established industry. As other retailers have entered the market offering everything from personal loans to pet insurance, banks have been forced to reassess their strategies for dealing with the consumer.

Strategic decision making in practice

Strategic decision making, as opposed to day-to-day operational decision making, is often a rare act for many managers. This stems from the reality that in many companies the power to make major decisions lies with only a few people. In particular the chief executive officer (CEO) is a critical influence on strategic decision making. Some CEOs take sole responsibility for making strategic decisions. Such decisions are often not based on detailed analysis but on extensive personal knowledge and intuition. Whilst this approach to decision making has often had spectacular results in the short term, few are able to sustain this form of management over many years. For those who do, the companies they leave are often weak in terms of top management as a result of inadequate management development.

We use two examples to illustrate the non-analytic approach to decision making adopted by some managers:

- *Leave well alone* – when an organisation enjoys a period of success there is an understandable temptation by managers to leave current practice untouched. This has led to many organisations failing to move with changing trends in customer preferences. One may argue that many of the problems experienced by Marks & Spencer in the late 1990s were due to complacency and a failure to understand the changing needs of the consumer.
- *Short-term perspective* – this standpoint has direct links to the leave well alone approach. An organisation facing difficulties tends to direct its energies into dealing with current short-term problems; in essence, 'fire fighting'. An additional issue which often arises for companies that adopt a short-term perspective lies in the reward structure offered to management. Evaluation, compensation and financial bonuses are all generally based on current performance levels rather than on long-term results. The same is often said of the financial institutions where analysts mark the share price up, or down, based on interim figures or on short-term considerations linked to fluctuations in interest rates or currency values.

A model for strategic management

There remains no single method for understanding the strategic management process. Each academic textbook will advocate an (albeit slightly) different method of coping and reacting to change. Generally however agreement exists over the main elements that comprise strategic planning. Typically they include the following:

- stage one: the development of a mission statement;
- stage two: undertaking a strategic analysis;
- stage three: objective setting;
- stage four: choices for growth;
- stage five: the implementation of strategy;
- stage six: the monitoring and review of the chosen strategy.

The model we will be using in this chapter is provided in Figure 4.1. Whilst at first glance the model may appear complex it remains a logical attempt to explain the different elements of the decision-making process. The remainder of this chapter will discuss each of the different stages in turn.

The relationships shown in Figure 4.1 are not linear, but iterative. A linear representation would give the impression that one stage of the process is totally distinct

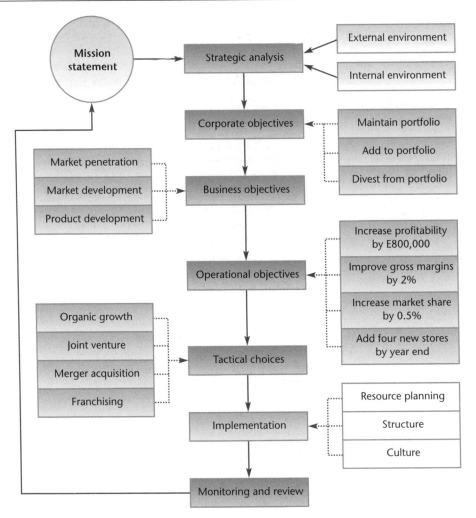

Figure 4.1 The strategic management model

from another. The process should not be thought of as a sequence of steps followed by managers, but rather stages that may be moved through and which are likely to be repeated. It is, however, worth noting again that this is only one framework available to business analysts and other strategists may advocate other approaches.

Stage one: the development of a mission statement

As can be seen from Figure 4.1, the first stage in the strategic development process is the creation of a mission statement. The justification for this is that organisations are in business to achieve something. For some it is profit, for others it may be the realisation of an ideal. Either way it is appropriate to start with the identification of the organisation's core values. The mission of an organisation therefore will be the guiding principle(s) from which everything else is derived. It sets out the purpose of the organisation to its customers and to society. For many retail businesses this means an explicit 'corporate statement', indicating the purpose of the organisation.

Whilst The Body Shop is synonymous with environmental and animal welfare (Box 4.1), other organisations may also incorporate their values into their overall philosophy. For example, the toy retailer Toys 'Я' Us states: 'We believe our business is built one customer at a time and we are committed to making each customer happy. Our goal is to be the worldwide authority on kids family and fun' (http://inc.toysrus.com 2002).

Mission statements are not however restricted purely to private sector organisations. For example, the University of Stirling's mission statement is to: 'pursue research and scholarship at an international level of excellence and to provide flexibility and innovative programmes of teaching and learning in an attractive and vibrant environment' (http://www.notices.stir.ac.uk/mission.htm 2002).

Having a clearly defined mission is no guarantee in itself that a company will remain successful in the long term. The mission may provide the strategic direction for the organisation; however, in order to be successful, it needs to be communicated to all employees. Maintaining the guiding principles of the organisation therefore depends upon senior management's commitment and ability to communicate its message.

Let us return again to the example of The Body Shop. The mission of The Body Shop reflects the views of its customers, who are concerned not only with their health but with the wish to protect the environment and avoid harming animals. To support this mission the company has developed an effective strategy which illustrates, incidentally, that a high moral stance does not preclude financial success.

Self-assessment Question 1 *Using annual reports and the Internet, identify the mission statements of three different retail organisations. Do they reflect purely profit-oriented goals or do they incorporate values of a social and ethical nature?*

Stage two: undertaking a strategic analysis

Having defined the mission of the organisation we must take the second step in the process, which is strategic analysis. This involves the appraisal of the internal and external environment of the organisation. It assists an organisation in meeting its goals and 'matching a company's resources and activities to the environment in which it operates to achieve its mission and objectives'.

Box 4.1
The Body Shop values

We consider testing products or ingredients on animals to be morally and scientifically indefensible. We support small producer communities around the world who supply us with accessories and natural ingredients. We know that you're unique, and we'll always treat you like an individual. We like you just the way you are. We believe that it is the responsibility of every individual to actively support those who have human rights denied to them. We believe that a business has the responsibility to protect the environment in which it operates, locally and globally. (Source: http://www.bodyshop.com/web/tbsgl/values.jsp 2002)

Strategic analysis at the corporate or business level places emphasis on conceptual skills and an ability to envisage not only what environmental changes might occur in the long term, but also on identifying the opportunities and threats that are likely to stem from these changes.

Environmental appraisal is often summarised in the form of a SWOT analysis and the consideration of an organisation's core skills. The SWOT summary is derived from the key strengths (S) and weaknesses (W) of the internal environment of an organisation and the major opportunities (O) and threats (T) from the external environment. Core skills are those that an organisation has developed in association with its existing product–market portfolio. Luffman *et al.* (1987: 88) noted that '... the further a company moves from its existing product–market portfolio and the resultant core skills and key resources, the greater the possibility of failure'.

External environment

An organisation's external environment is a global environment where the forces at work are based on national and international events. Kotler *et al.* (1996) identify six influential forces that can affect an organisation's operational environment.

Demographic forces: this refers to the human population in terms of size, density, location, age, gender and race. Throughout the world the composition of any nation or state is continually changing and with it will change the attitudes, beliefs and demands of the population. It is important therefore for organisations to be aware of such developments so that they can continue to offer the consumer what they require.

For example, Burt and Sparks in Chapter 1 of this book note that the number of persons in the United Kingdom over the age of 65 is estimated to double between 1950 and 2020. A shift in the age profile has consequences for a number of retailers and in some instances provides the opportunity to develop new products and services. Companies such as Mamas and Papas specifically target senior citizens and offer a range of products suited to their needs, for example needle threaders, cutlery for persons with arthritis and socks without elastic for thrombosis sufferers.

Economic forces: these are defined as all the factors that affect consumer purchasing power and spending patterns. Economic forces may operate at both the national and international level and can include inflation, exchange and interest rates as well as personal and corporate taxation levels. For example, at the national level the relative strength of sterling may make imports cheaper and exports more expensive, or vice versa. At the international level factors such as the over/under production of oil can adversely affect the price of produce or the quantities demanded.

Natural forces: this relates to factors connected to the natural environment that may affect business activities. This category covers a multitude of different issues, from natural disasters such as earthquakes, floods and crop failure to consumer movements for the protection of the natural environment. Again, whilst such factors will generally be outside of the organisation's control they will on many occasions be forced to react to them.

In examining the impact of the natural environment upon organisational strategy, the issue of time becomes important. An earthquake or a flood may influence an organisation's strategy in the short term. Whilst undoubtedly a tragic event the consequences of such a disaster may not be long term, and the organisation's strategy may not be unduly influenced.

The growth of green consciousness and the development of environmental concern has stemmed from the way in which the human population has managed its natural resources. Such movements have gained immense popularity and have had a long-term impact on the strategy of many companies. For example, companies such as The Body Shop have set new standards in transportation, purchasing, recycling and waste disposal and are a testimony to the durability of the environmental movement. Many organisations have therefore incorporated the principles of environmentalism into their overall strategy (Box 4.2).

Technological forces: these represent some of the most important influences on business today. It is difficult to think of any industry that has not been influenced by some form of technological advance. In the distributive trades the impact has been dramatic, from laser scanning and bar coding to e-commerce and the Internet. Moreover, it has provided retail organisations with a greater degree of strategic and operational control than previously. Given its central importance to the sector, systematic external analysis is crucial in order to ensure that the retailer is fully aware of the latest technological developments in the marketplace, the levels of adoption within the industry and benefits to be gained from implementation.

Political forces: the political environment consists of laws, government agencies, political parties and pressure groups. Within the context of the distributive trades such forces manifest themselves through business regulations, employment law and consumer legislation. For example, governments may decree that no overseas retailer can establish operations within a country without a local joint venture partner. Employment of non-national labour may be subjected to an extra employment tax and the addition of government tax on goods may reduce an individual's level of disposable income.

Cultural forces: these are usually defined as the factors that shape society's basic values. Obvious differences exist between different nation states. Compare for example the issue of gender equality in the United States and the Middle East. However as countries become increasingly multicultural, diversity of belief, opinion and

---

Box 4.2
IKEA and the environment

IKEA has always tried to do more with less. This goes hand in hand with our environmental work – to use resources in an economical and careful way. Three cornerstones [exist] in IKEA's environmental work:

- Our cost consciousness and resource efficiency result in less usage of raw material and less waste and discharges.
- The extensive use of wood in our products. Wood is a recyclable, biodegradable and renewable material and it is excellent from an environmental point of view.
- Training and engaging our co-workers to work with environmental issues.

(Source: http://www.ikea.co.uk/about_ikea/Social/environment.asp 2002)

attitude become inherent within individual societies. From a retail perspective this has two implications; first, one must be aware that values and beliefs are constantly developing and secondly, that such changes provide new opportunities through emerging markets. For example, the consumption of wine has become increasingly popular in Singapore over the last 10 years. Whilst previously drunk mainly by the western and Australian expatriate communities, its popularity has now spread to the younger Chinese community. This is a significantly larger market for those retailers who have been able to identify and respond early enough to the trend.

Internal environment

Understanding the developments that occur within the macro and task environments provides the first stage in a strategic analysis. Once an organisation has undertaken this it will aid them in the second stage, which is to look at internal operations. Sometimes this is referred to as a strategic audit. It attempts to identify which strengths of the company may assist in building a coherent strategy. In addition, the organisation undertakes a critical self-appraisal and identifies the weaknesses that may prevent it from achieving its mission. Typical areas of examination in a retail strategic audit may include the following.

Stores: when a retail company looks at its store portfolio there are a host of possible questions it may wish to address. For example, is the portfolio of store sizes balanced? Is there over capacity in the largest stores? Alternatively, is trading performance affected by having a set of stores that are too small to meet demand? As with many factors examined in this section, there is no right or wrong answer. It will depend on the mission and objectives of the company and what the organisation is trying to achieve.

Location: there are sophisticated assessment kits through which retailers can identify prime and non-prime locations. The question is whether the organisation's location is suitable for its purpose. Whilst this may appear rather an obvious point, locations do change over time. We can all think of once prosperous shopping streets, districts and centres that have gone into terminal decline as consumer shopping patterns change.

Buying: the trend within many retail sectors has been towards a greater centralisation of operations, that is, all the decisions over what products to purchase and how much to stock is made at head office. Removing these decision-making responsibilities from the local level has enabled store managers to focus upon customer service whilst at the same time allowing the retailer to gain a more holistic picture of company requirements. The benefits of such a strategy have been increased purchasing power, greater economies of scale and a higher degree of control over the retail offer. A company that undertook the decision to centralise its functions early on, may consider it has gained a significant advantage over its competitors through this strategy.

Product range: no retailer can provide a 100 per cent service level, that is providing all the goods and services consumers want all the time. In retail strategy, debate often centres around the correct range and level of stock to hold. This, as with many issues, is subjective and will reflect the objectives of the individual company. We would argue that the 'correct' range and level is one that reinforces the market position of the company, that is, if customers expect a broad but shallow choice of goods then this should be delivered. For example, a store may have 5,000 products, but only two or three of each product. Alternatively the retailer may choose a deep but narrow product line. For example, companies such as Tie Rack, Sock Shop and Knickerbox offer a limited number of products but an extensive number of variations.

Marketing: for many retailers marketing has been a key component in their drive towards competitive advantage. The role of marketing will be examined in more detail in Chapter 10. However a coherent marketing strategy with clearly defined aims and objectives can be regarded as a positive strength when developing a business strategy. Many retailers have become skilled at marketing their brands or services. Take, for example, Guinness's attempts to reposition itself in the Far East. Originally Guinness was perceived as a drink for older people and pregnant women because of its supposed health-giving properties. High profile marketing campaigns in Singapore and Malaysia have been successful in positioning the product as a drink for the sophisticated, intellectual consumer.

Personalities: it is often said that retailing is not about personalities. Criteria such as product, price and location are far more important. It often remains difficult however to separate the individual from the company. Because of their exposure to the media, personalities often have great influence over the fortunes of the business. Some are central to the organisation's function; for example, The Body Shop is synonymous with Anita Roddick whilst Richard Branson is associated with the Virgin Group. The importance of personalities in retailing is highlighted with the fashion designer Laura Ashley. After her untimely death many analysts argued that the company lost its focus in terms of strategy and direction.

Personnel: retailing still largely remains a labour-intensive industry and the importance of well-trained, motivated staff has never been greater. This is true for both management and shop floor workers. Unfortunately it remains a sad fact that many retailers provide little or no training for their workforce and attach little importance to staff development. Those retailers who do invest in training and are able to develop a high degree of motivation amongst their employees reduce staff turnover, lower absenteeism and improve productivity.

Systems: we have already noted how important technology is for achieving a competitive advantage and that systems provide operational efficiencies, customer service opportunities and information for strategic planning. As the use of technology has become more widespread throughout retailing and its adoption becomes the norm, its contribution to business strategy has changed. During the late 1970s and early 1980s the fact that only a few retailers were technologically proficient meant that systems could be run below their full efficiency and a competitive edge could still be maintained. Today all the large retailers have some form of system installed. 'Information overload' is a commonly heard expression amongst many retail managers who are provided daily with data on product sales, category sales, store sales, customer purchasing habits, supplier trends, etc.

Given this advance in technology it is possible to argue that retailers now need systems as a *prerequisite* to trade. It is those companies which interpret, analyse and utilise data most efficiently that are most likely to achieve their objectives.

Logistics: the contribution that this 'behind the scenes' element of retailing can make to the profitability of a business should not be underestimated. Wal-Mart have 55,000 persons employed in logistics in the United States alone and its distribution strategy is central to its success. There are a variety of methods employed for measuring the efficiency, effectiveness and consistency of the logistics function. For example, the number of items despatched on time, the accuracy of goods delivered, the number of negative complaints received are all examples of performance measures.

Many retailers now contract out their distribution functions to specialist companies such as Tibbett & Britten and Exel Logistics. These businesses take responsibility for the safe handling and movement of product throughout the supply chain. Whilst the nature of the relationship between retailer and logistics service provider will vary, a close working relationship between the two parties can be deemed a strength.

Finance: in addition to the obvious need to pay suppliers and cover staff costs and shareholder dividends, successful business planning requires resources to be allocated for specific projects and initiatives. A strong financial base is therefore of fundamental importance to a retailer. If one considers the recent problems faced by the US giant Kmart, weak sales and high debts meant that the company could not afford to revamp its stores or advertise as aggressively as it would have liked. As a result the company had to file for bankruptcy, close stores and negotiate a $2 billion loan in order to pay its creditors.

The above list of factors is by no means exhaustive. What it aims to provide is an illustration of the internal strengths and weaknesses of an organisation. Identifying the fact that their organisation may not do everything well and that there is a need for improvement is one of the biggest hurdles for managers (especially senior managers). Identifying where improvements need to be made and where strengths can be built on, provides a solid foundation upon which to take the company strategy forward.

Self-assessment Question 2 *Using examples from the trade press, newspapers and the Internet, apply the above factors to a retail company of your choice. Ensure that you identify only those factors which are genuinely perceived as a competitive advantage or represent genuine weaknesses.*

Stage three: objective setting

For one who has no objective nothing is relevant. Confucius

In many instances strategic management textbooks fail to differentiate between the types of objectives an organisation may set. In this chapter we distinguish between three types:

- corporate objectives;
- business objectives;
- operational objectives.

Theoretically, at least, each of these objectives should complement each other and be derived sequentially, that is, the business objectives being derived from the corporate and the operational from the business.

Corporate objectives: the decisions made here concern the highest level of objective setting. An organisation that has a number of separate businesses may choose to maintain its existing portfolio, that is, keep control of all its existing companies. Alternatively it may choose to acquire a new company or divest one from its portfolio. In practice such options are open mainly to medium and large organisations; for example, in 2001 the Kingfisher Group made the decision to focus upon the 'home improvements' and 'electrical' sectors. As a consequence they removed a number of strategic business units (SBUs) from their portfolio. In August 2001 the Woolworth organisation was demerged, whilst in July of the same year Kingfisher sold Superdrug to the Dutch chemist chain Kruidvat.

Business objectives: if the company decides to maintain its existing portfolio then it will have the opportunity to develop a series of business objectives. Developed by Ansoff (1965) they were initially described as growth vector components and, although more sophisticated models exist, they still serve as a useful means of conceptualising the options open to an individual organisation. For example, a company may set itself the objective of achieving greater market penetration and seek to increase its market share using its present portfolio of products. In practice today few organisations are able to trade in the long term without adding new products to their retail offer. A market penetration strategy is therefore typically used in conjunction with other strategies.

A product development strategy is commonly used within the distributive trades. Considerable time and effort goes into the process of new product development and many consumers now experience greater choice than ever before. The stages involved in new product development will be examined in greater detail in Chapter 10.

Retailing has traditionally been a nationally focused activity, but over the past decade this situation has changed radically. Increasing numbers of retailers have expanded beyond their domestic market and have ventured overseas. This market development strategy occurs for a number of reasons:

- saturation in the home market;
- underdeveloped competition in the target market;
- favourable business environment (low taxation, labour and land);
- a unique transferable product, process of patent.

An important element for any organisation when setting its business objectives is the concept of risk. Obviously no strategy remains risk free, however certain strategies carry with them greater potential risk than others. For example, a strategy of overseas market development (whilst potentially highly rewarding) often carries with it a much higher level of financial investment than attempting to further penetrate an existing market. See Box 4.3 for an illustration of these business objectives.

Operational objectives: at this stage in the strategic management process the organisation has to set a series of operational objectives that will allow it to achieve its overall mission. For clarity we have provided only four.

Over the next 12 months a company may state that it intends to achieve the following:

- increase profitability to €800,000;
- improve gross margins by 2 per cent;
- increase market share by 0.5 per cent;
- open four new stores.

Box 4.3
Tesco

Tesco stores (as opposed to Tesco plc) represent an example of how Ansoff's growth vector component operates in practice.

Product development has been a central aspect of Tesco's business strategy. In addition to selling branded products the company has three levels of own-label products (Value, Tesco and Finest). In 2000/2001 own-brand goods accounted for approximately 50 per cent of sales and the company introduced over 8,000 new food and non-food lines. The company expanded into Scotland in the early 1990s when it purchased the William Low chain (*market development*). At the same time it has pushed a strategy of *market penetration* through new store openings using a variety of different formats (Extra, superstores, Metro/high street and Express). By August 2001 the company had 702 stores in the United Kingdom with nearly 20 million square feet of floor space.

In practice these objectives will be more detailed, perhaps identifying the product groupings where margin improvements can be made or the general location for the new stores. Typically, operational objectives are short term and relate to a fixed period of time. Moreover they tend to be quantifiable and allow the organisation to have an objective measure of its business performance.

Stage four: choices for growth

Johnson and Scholes (1999: 235) preface their discussion of strategic choice with the following statement:

> one of the major criticisms which can be made of managers concerns their inability or unwillingness to consider the variety of strategic options open to the company. Rather they tend to remain bound by their recipes and resistant to change. It is for this reason that this part of the book presents a systematic way of looking at strategic choice.

Once a company has agreed its objectives a key aim will be to consider ways in which it can achieve the desired outcomes. For example, if we take the four operational objectives provided above and assume that the financial targets cannot be met through the current store portfolio a retailer may have to consider the following options.

Organic growth: this is the strategy most common to retailers. It may involve the purchase or rental of additional outlets that may then be converted into the organisation's trading format. Many single outlet retailers who plough the profits of their business into a second or subsequent retail unit may be unaware they are undertaking a strategy of organic growth.

Joint venture: as retailing has become more international, the prospect and opportunity for joint ventures have increased. Joint ventures are typically thought of as arrangements where organisations remain independent but set up a newly created organisation jointly owned by the parent companies. The benefits of undertaking a joint venture are many and varied but typically allow the organisation to obtain the following:

- materials;
- skills;
- finance;
- an understanding of cultural differences.

Joint ventures are particularly common in internationalisation, for example, Laura Ashley have had a long-term relationship with the Japanese Jusco Group. The retailer sought an overseas partner when it decided to begin trading in Japan. The skills, expertise and local knowledge that Jusco provided were seen as essential for a successful retail operation.

Acquisition and merger: in many European countries retailing has been experiencing a period of market concentration. Individual retail sectors have become dominated by a small number of large multiple retailers that have consolidated their market power through a process of organic growth and acquisition and merger. For example, in the United Kingdom Wal-Mart acquired the Asda grocery chain whilst in the United States, J. Sainsbury acquired the New England grocery retailer Shaws. The focus of these strategies has been upon enhancing the core business through the acquisition of new sites, new distribution networks and new personnel.

Franchising: this represents a form of strategic alliance. Here the franchise holder undertakes specific activities such as manufacturing, distribution or selling. As in many forms of business contract franchising places duties and responsibilities upon both parties, such as the franchiser being obliged to assist and support the relationship in technical and operational training. In return, the franchisee accepts the highly specified terms and conditions that accompany the franchiser's product or service.

Franchising has become an increasingly popular means by which an organisation can achieve its stated objectives. A number of US and European companies have successfully used this method to develop a global presence, including The Body Shop, Benetton, Burger King and KFC. McDonald's represents one of the largest franchise providers. It has 25,000 restaurants in 109 countries and opens around 500 new outlets a year. Approximately 85 per cent of all its stores are owned and operated by independent, full-time franchisers.

Stage five: the implementation of strategy

The next stage in the process of strategic decision making is that of implementation. Its importance is summed up by Bowman & Asch (1987: 195): 'Strategy implementation is crucial to effective strategic management. It is management's responsibility to ensure that an appropriate strategy is both formulated and implemented, for without the latter, precise formulation is of little use to the organisation.'

When we discuss implementation we are focusing on the parameters that are necessary in order to achieve the objectives set. Three main areas merit consideration:

- resource planning and allocation;
- structure;
- culture.

Resource planning and allocation: this usually entails allocating resources to the various organisational functions, departments or separate businesses. Companies may need to allocate resources between business functions, operating divisions, geographical areas or service departments.

When a company makes few changes in resource allocation this will often indicate that the organisation has not made significant changes to its corporate strategy and that the allocation of resources will be implemented on an historical basis. For example, those responsible for managing products, business functions or retail stores may get last year's budget plus an allowance for inflation. In some circumstances resources may be allocated by an agreed 'formula', such as a percentage of the overall budget or a per capita payment.

The first scenario of formula funding is where an organisation must allocate resources during static or declining periods. New developments or changes in strategy may involve a reallocation of existing resources rather than the assignment of any new resources. Some areas will need to be cut back in order to maintain existing areas and/or to support their development. This is frequently achieved by closing existing stores. Other ways may include labour force redundancies, the 'freezing' of posts so that individuals are not replaced on leaving the organisation or the removal of existing stores or warehouses to cheaper locations.

Allocations during growth periods often require the organisation to establish new areas of priority. For example, the development of an e-commerce strategy by companies such as Comet, Tesco and PC World requires significant resource allocation. In addition to the financial investment required, significant management time and energy will have to be spent in order to ensure that the strategy will be correctly implemented.

Some organisations will establish such priority areas centrally and approve the resource allocations from head office. Another common way in which this process takes place is through competitive bidding by various departments of the organisation for central resources. The criteria for judging successful bids must relate to the chosen strategies of the organisation. For example, a company may 'top-slice' central budgets to fund the development of new initiatives and may allow competitive bidding between departments for development funds, training budgets or other needs.

Structure: depending on the type of organisation, which in turn is influenced by contingency factors such as age, size, technical systems and the environment, each basic part of the structure differs in size and importance. To manage these parts and coordinate the tasks each part performs, organisations develop structural forms. The consideration here is whether a particular organisational structure is more capable of implementing certain strategies than another structure. This consideration introduces one of the interesting themes of business strategy – the relationship between organisation, structure and strategy.

Since the work of Chandler (1962) and Channon (1973) the relationship between strategy and structure has been the subject of a number of conceptual and empirical studies. The intention has been to show the direct or indirect links between the former and the latter. The relationship between strategy and structure is complex and is based on the interplay between strategy and a host of other variables that include culture, values, past and present functioning of the organisation, the history of success or failure and the psychological and sociological consequences of technical development. It is therefore not easy to sequence strategy and structure.

What is clear is that unless structure matches strategy inefficiency results; that is to say, a less than optimal ratio occurs between inputs and outputs. This is precisely the reason why strategists must pay close attention to structure when elaborating strategic plans; not to take structure into account is to condemn the firm to inefficiency. It is therefore important to have a grasp of the alternative structures available to organisations.

Culture: the successful implementation of strategy will require cooperation across a variety of personnel and departments within an organisation. In most organisations informal interdepartmental cooperation reduces the need for formal procedures and hastens implementation as well as improving morale. Organisations are however conservative, that is, they do not readily accept change. Schon (1969) identified this as 'dynamic' conservatism and highlighted four different means by which the status quo can be maintained. Individuals/departments/functions/(even SBUs) can behave as follows:

- ignore and take no action to implement the strategy;
- launch a counter-attack to get the decision reversed or modified;
- contain the change by not integrating it into the organisation;
- undertake the minimal action capable of meeting the undesirable intrusion.

These strategies of resistance can only be overcome by managers who are committed to change, capable of providing the leadership necessary for the situation and able to resolve the inevitable conflicts that will occur.

Stage six: the monitoring and review of the chosen strategy

Organisations in the public and private sectors are engaged in the search for success, however you choose to measure it. Common measures of commercial and business success include achieving increases in market capitalisation, sales turnover, return on capital employed, share price, pre-tax profit. A quantifiable measure of success is therefore an important element in any assessment of a particular strategic decision. In addition, time scales for measuring performance can be considered in terms of the following:

- *operations*: day to day;
- *tactics*: the short term;
- *strategy*: the long term.

It is possible to set out precise targets for operational activities, such as sales volume by day, by week, by month or by year. However, as one moves from the tactical to the strategic the factors that influence performance become less precise. It is essential for control purposes to set some interim benchmarks against which progress can be measured. Note that for control to be effective it must operate at all levels of the organisation:

- everyone is aware of the measures against which their performance is being assessed;
- everyone has an opportunity to comment as to their belief that the measures are quantifiable and achievable;
- the evaluation procedures are adequate.

The monitoring of performance against predetermined standards enables the success or failure of a particular strategy to be identified. The review of performance should be against the corporate mission and objectives that will, in turn, initiate an iteration of the whole process of strategic decision making.

Self-assessment Question 3 *In addition to the measures listed in the text, what other performance indicators might a company use to assess the efficacy of its chosen strategy. (You may wish to consider both financial and non-financial criteria.)*

Summary

In the life of an organisation many decisions are made. The strategic level at which the decisions are made can determine the future of the organisation. Business strategy, however, involves more than just decision making. For the organisation it means the development of a process that allows quantifiable goals to be formulated and considered in a systematic manner over specific time frames.

The primary benefit of undertaking a systematic approach is that it encourages managers to consider the rationale for their activities and whether alternative courses of action are more appropriate. So where managers are making choices largely by judgement a more analytical approach will at least provide an assessment of those choices and some of the opportunities that the company is forgoing in pursuing its chosen strategies. It is the adoption of an analytical approach systematised in the form of key steps that is vital. The strategic planning process is not designed to replace judgement, intuition and the experience of managers, but to support them.

Further reading

Johnson, G. and **Scholes, K.** (2002) *Exploring Corporate Strategy: Text and cases*, 6th edn, London: Prentice Hall.

McGoldrick, P. (2002) *Retail Marketing*, London: McGraw Hill.

Mintzberg, H. (2002) *The Strategy Process: Concepts, contexts, cases,* London: Prentice Hall.

Walters, D. and **Hanrahan, J.** (2000) *Retail Strategy: Planning and control*, London: Macmillan Business.

You may also find the following journals useful:

- *European Management Journal;*
- *Harvard Business Review;*
- *Journal of Management Studies;*
- *Long Range Planning;*
- *Strategic Management Journal.*

CHAPTER 5

Ethical standards in business

Paul Whysall

Introduction

In the previous chapter we considered a model for successful strategic management. One important question that needs to be addressed is the extent to which retailers are influenced by some form of 'ethical consideration' when developing their business strategy. It is therefore necessary to consider how ethical limits are placed on managerial action. This chapter is designed to provide an overview of the main issues relating to ethics before providing a case study of how an ethical dilemma may manifest itself in the retail sector.

From famine at Rhodes to modern retailing

Marcus Tullius Cicero (106 BC – 43 BC) posed a number of questions of an ethical nature, nominally to his son but more generally for society. One such question concerned a grain merchant who landed on the island of Rhodes during a famine with a cargo of corn, knowing that a large number of other vessels loaded with corn were also soon to arrive. Cicero posed the question of whether the merchant ought to inform the people of Rhodes that there were large quantities of grain about to arrive, or should he 'cash in' on his advantage? Cicero quoted other philosophers. Diogenes, for example, thought that the merchant might withhold the knowledge justifiably and sell his corn at the prevailing high price. Antipater, though, disagreed, thinking the deception here was contrary to good faith, a view which Cicero seems to accept. He felt we hold a duty to treat our fellow citizens fairly and consider the interests of others. Whilst we may conceal some things for various sound reasons we should not conceal information from those we are dealing with in order to make a profit.

However many others disagree with this view. Many argue that the seller's contractual duties only require that we represent items for sale as they are, without lying or disguising any faults, and sell at a fair market price at that time. The grain merchant does not have a responsibility to disclose 'special' information he may have (what if a storm occurs and the other ships do not arrive?). The seller does not have a duty to do a favour to buyers (many citizens of Rhodes could afford to pay the higher price). The higher price is a reward for being the first to meet a demand and for risks taken. To sell at a higher price is no more immoral than to buy at low prices speculatively, such arguments might suggest. Cicero, though, rejects such views. He can see no merit in deceiving and exploiting buyers.

Are such ancient musings at all relevant to modern commerce? Several writers have suggested they are. Thus Cordero (1988) and Koehn (1992) look to Aristotle to understand the importance and ethics of the act of exchange. Cordero sets out three conditions that constitute an unfair exchange.

- at least one party does not agree to the exchange at all;
- at least one party agrees unwittingly;
- at least one party agrees only under pressure of circumstances.

Koehn suggests the role of business is to meet people's needs, which is seen as contributing to the development of communities in which persons 'actualize their active selves', or become fulfilled and enjoy better lives. Moreover, this role of commercial activity in the development of communities gives it purpose and meaning: 'Far from being a low or crass activity, commercial exchange properly understood can be seen as the foundation for the good life of individual persons within a just community' (Koehn 1992: 354). Thus we can think perhaps both of ethics *in* retailing and the ethics *of* retailing in terms of its contribution to society.

Ethics in modern retailing

The above considerations have not gone unnoticed in the modern literature of sales and marketing. Ebejer and Morden (1988) considered what responsibilities a salesperson has to a buyer in terms of revealing information. They devised the model of 'limited paternalism'. In full paternalism, the seller would place the buyer's interests at the forefront and tell the buyer everything that would help make a sound decision. This might even include the information that a shop around the corner sells the same product more cheaply or that the product has a long history of unreliability. Ebejer and Morden contend there is some information only the seller as a specialist might know and this should be revealed if requested. However it is reasonable to expect customers to discover other aspects of the product themselves (such as comparative prices, functionality, 'street credibility'). Yet even this apparently simple resolution of the salesperson's moral duty can become quite complicated (Walters 1989; Brockway 1993).

One thing philosophers have not fully recognised, perhaps, is the complex nature of modern retailing transactions. When Aristotle discussed the idea of a fair deal he did so in terms of a farmer and a shoemaker seeking to exchange a number of melons for a pair of shoes. Both parties were undertaking a transaction using their own produce. With the exception of their families and a small number of workers few others were involved. However, the customer entering a modern retail store may be served by a junior employee of a massive international corporation. The goods purchased may well have been produced on the other side of the world, quite possibly in a location chosen because of the low wages that prevail there. The transaction may be subject to national and international (for example European Union) laws and regulations. Profits from the retailer will perhaps have implications for many other investors, including shareholders and pension fund holders. The journey to shop will probably have been made by car or bus, which has global environmental implications. Thus the implications of retail transactions are now more complex than Aristotle was able to portray them.

And what of the seller? This person may be part of a profit-sharing scheme, or be under pressure to sell in order to maintain sales targets either personally or for the store or region. How is the salesperson to judge the assumed customer's intentions? Is the customer honest? Is it a 'mystery shopper' being provocatively awkward? Is the customer simply using this store's excellent information service before making a purchase in a cheaper store or online? Knowingly or unknowingly the seller and the selling environment may put various pressures on the potential buyer. Price levels may be set in a variety of ways to entice buying. Sellers may well experience what several authors refer to as the 'boundary spanning' problem, of feeling loyalty to both the customer and their employer.

A stakeholder model

The traditional model of a retail transaction may therefore be limited and constraining. More significantly still, we may need to consider the effects across many more groups than simply the individual buyer and seller. One way this can be conceptualised is through the stakeholder model. If we define a stakeholder loosely as someone who has a legitimate interest in an activity, a 'stakeholder map' of a major retailer may look something like Figure 5.1 (see Whysall (2000a) for a fuller discussion of this model).

Figure 5.1 A stakeholder map of a retail business

Relationships between retailers and each of these stakeholder groups have prompted a number of ethical concerns in recent years. It is useful if we now consider the nature of each relationship and examples of ethical issues that may arise:

- *Customers* may be exploited by unfair pricing strategies (Kaufmann *et al.* 1994), databases and geodemographics may pose a threat to privacy (O'Malley *et al.* 1997), vulnerable groups such as so-called 'shopaholics' may need protection (Faber and O'Guinn 1988; 1992), merchandising tactics may target young children (Piacentini *et al.* 2000) and some customers may fraudulently exploit retailers' returns policies (Ward *et al.* 1998).

- *Suppliers* suffer when imported loss leaders destabilise national markets and own-label 'lookalikes' infringe copyright and reduce market share (Davies 1998). Sourcing may raise political opposition and boycotts (Smith 1990). Slotting fees may be demanded to gain shelf space (Stern 1990). Retailers' exercise of power in the supply chain has raised serious concerns and led to accusations of bullying and harassment (Brown *et al.* 1983).

- *Competitors* may act in concert, as Sainsbury, Tesco and Safeway appeared to in 1993 when seeking to prevent Costco entering the UK market. Major chains have been accused of 'blocking' rivals' entry to shopping centres, or selling at unsustainably low prices to exploit a rival's offer to 'refund twice the difference' when goods were bought more cheaply elsewhere.

- *Governments* interact with retailers on many levels. The simple view that responsible retailers would obey the law was shown to be unfounded when the grocery and DIY multiples traded illegally on Sundays and in direct contravention of the laws in England and Wales (Freathy and Sparks 1993a; 1993b). In other sectors such as dispensing pharmacies government involvement is strong, but can still be contentious (for example charging prescription costs for what might be cheaper medicines if sold over the counter).

- The *financial community* is both part of the retail system (for example high street outlets), yet also an external stakeholder in it, as through credit financing. Levels of interest charged on in-store credit have long been a focus of criticism by consumer groups. Now the situation seems to have entered a new era, with leading UK supermarket operators themselves funtioning in the banking sector.

- *Service providers* cover a wide range of businesses, each of which generate ethical concerns. For example, do store designers attempt to provide a pleasant and comfortable shopping environment or do they seek to manipulate the consumer by adopting layouts that force us to travel the entire store? Similarly, do advertising agencies develop campaigns to inform us of the latest and most up-to-date products or do they seek to hide the truth through the manipulation of marketing media? (Whysall 2000b).

- *Employees* clearly represent one of the key groups of stakeholders. Broadbridge (1995; 1996; 1997) highlighted a range of important employee issues where ethical concerns may arise, for example overall levels of pay, male/female pay differentials and equality of opportunity in promotion. Other pertinent issues include aspects of privacy and the testing of employees (McLean and Moore 1997), recruitment policies, multi-skilling, health and safety concerns, union representation and the continuing demands on retail staff from longer shop opening hours. Attempts to improve store security (such as in-store video surveillance) may also have ethical implications for employees (Kirkup and Carrigan 2000).

- *Managers'* roles raise a number of ethical issues. For example, high executive salaries in retailing have generated considerable critical press coverage. Concern has been expressed at individuals receiving 'golden handshakes' and large bonuses even when a company under performs.

- *Landlords and property interests* are important actors in the retail environment. Even national retailers have refused to honour rental agreements in times of difficult trading. Other issues include property maintenance, the policing of 'bad neighbours' and so-called 'commercial squatting', where traders illegally occupy vacant sites and can prove notoriously difficult to evict.

- The *owners* of a retail business can raise ethical considerations, for example, the founders of the business may have a philanthropic view and wish to take a long-term perspective on the direction and strategy of the company. In contrast, institutional investors may wish to take a short- to medium-term view that maximises the financial performance of the business. Such decisions will result in vastly different outcomes for other stakeholder groups.

- Retailers' relationships with *the community* also take a diversity of forms. The retailer plays various (ethical?) roles: a provider of essential community services (as dispensing chemist or post office); a guardian of heritage and tradition (maintaining the village shop; occupying historic buildings); and, through planning gain, a provider of public facilities and infrastructure. Then we see the retailer as a supporter of good causes, sponsoring computers in schools or environmental projects. Alternatively, is there an ethical issue when a retailer closes a supermarket in the inner city, thereby reducing the retail provision available for the elderly, disabled and less mobile (Burnett 1996)?

- *Activist groups* represent a sub-set within the wider society. In areas such as town planning a range of activist groups often exist, from those seeking to protect their local environments against retail development (Whysall 1999), to interest groups such as civic societies campaigning for more sensitive town centre developments, and then on to eco-warriors and more extreme groups. Animal rights protesters have, over recent decades, directly and indirectly had major impacts on such as furriers and cosmetics producers (such as Boots). Political boycotts have targeted types of produce because of their sourcing (for example French produce after nuclear tests in the South Pacific), or specific companies (for example 'clean clothes' campaigns against designer clothing produced in sweatshop conditions). For some there may even be a violent dimension to the activism – 'spiking' foodstuffs, retail terrorism, etc.

So how do we define 'ethical retailing'?

From the above discussion it would appear evident that ethical concerns in retailing are widespread. Placing such concerns in a stakeholder framework should help us appreciate the complexly interconnected and interdependent nature of those concerns. However at this point we are still no nearer knowing what is ethical behaviour in general, let alone ethical retail behaviour.

Perhaps first we need to clarify several different views of the term 'ethical retailing'. To some, ethical retailing is about good causes, so a charity shop raising funds for medical research might be seen as ethical. Another aspect of ethical retailing may be what form the business takes: are cooperatives or partnerships more ethically acceptable (Dandy 1996)? Here, neither of those rather narrow conceptualisations are adopted. The assumption is that retailing is a legitimate activity, usually seeking to make legitimate profits, and that it should be done in ways that are considered ethical. Thus the assumption is that being more or less ethical (assuming it can be that relative) is a choice faced by all retailers.

So what determines an ethical action? Utilitarians may seek the greater good for the greater number, whilst others (so called deontologists) may look to the Golden Rule of 'do as you would be done by' or Kant's notion of treating people respectfully and never using others as means to an end (such as profit). To Aristotle, there were key virtues that formed the foundation for the 'good life'. Either side of these virtues were usually excesses that were not virtuous and thus not ethical. Thus the virtuous warrior to Aristotle would be brave, but not reckless nor cowardly. The virtuous citizen would be charitable, avoiding the extremes of miserliness on the one hand, and poverty and dependence on the other. What would a virtuous retail business be like? Probably it would compete in a tough but scrupulously fair way. Tough competition would be seen as generating better customer service and better returns for investors. The retailer would support good causes, but not to an extent that this undermined other responsibilities to employees, shareholders and customers. It would offer good employment conditions and treat suppliers as well as was consistent with wider responsibilities. In short, it might be seen to be trading off the interests of the various stakeholder groups to find the best (that is the most ethical and just) overall combination.

And how might we evaluate what is a just outcome across such stakeholders, given that they often have competing objectives and needs? Rawls (1972) developed a complex conceptualisation of justice that employed the notion of a 'veil of ignorance'. This veil implies that when faced with an ethical dilemma we should imagine that we are playing a role in the problem, but do not know which role. A just solution would be one that we would accept under such terms, even if it transpires that we may be one of the 'losers' eventually. Thus, faced with a proposal to extend opening store hours to meet consumer demand, should we accept that as just? We know there may be store employees who have personal misgivings about extended hours. But if we can see that the benefits to others are great enough (customer satisfaction, greater profits, bigger orders to suppliers, more jobs for others) we may be willing to accept it as the right decision even if it is inconvenient to certain stakeholders (perhaps including ourselves).

Finally: a hypothetical case study

The following case study draws upon the retail practices of a number of different UK, European and US/Canadian retailers. It does not refer specifically to any single retail organisation.

Anchor Clothing have been a feature of Canadian retailing for nearly thirty years. They are a well known, well respected, high profile organisation located in over 200 shopping malls across the south eastern part of Canada. Over the years they have developed a strong brand image based around good quality clothing, largely Canadian made, at middle-range prices. They have a loyal (if ageing) customer base. While not a family-owned firm, many of the senior managers have worked for the company since it was established and have only limited experience of retailing outside of Anchor. The current Chief Executive Officer (CEO) joined the company at the age of sixteen and worked his way up through the organisation.

A market analysis of Anchor in the early 1990s had been very complimentary towards the company and had concluded that '....essentially Anchor have succeeded by delivering value-for-money, stylish clothes to a core of loyal consumers'.

However, over the last couple of years, Anchor's market share and profitability have slumped. Senior managers all have their own views on the causes of this decline. In an effort to halt this downturn, the company commissioned a market research company to investigate the causes. In addition to speaking to management and staff, the researchers interviewed customers and examined the competition. After an extensive data gathering exercise, a number of reasons were identified:

- The company was losing market share to competitors. This was due to the aggressive marketing and pricing strategies characteristic of modern retailing. By contrast, Anchor was seen to lack innovation in the way it merchandised and presented its product. When questioned about the range of products on offer, customers typically used the terms 'unfashionable', 'boring' and 'tired'.
- Anchor had failed to keep up with changing consumer preferences. In particular it had been slow to react to the increasing demand for designer labels and fashion brands. Historically, the company sold only its own brand of clothes. This led to a related problem concerning the company's market position. The customer market had polarised, with individuals buying either from discount retailers or up-market designer outlets. Like a number of other 'middle market' retailers, Anchor had struggled to maintain a consumer base.
- While the company had been very successful in the early 1990s, it had failed to innovate in terms of store design and layout. The view from senior management could be characterised as 'don't rock the boat' and 'if it isn't broken, don't fix it'. Its stores, while clean and tidy, were described as dull and uninteresting by target customers.
- While Anchor remains popular with older customers, these groups are spending proportionally less. The company had attempted to target a younger market segment; however, research had revealed that these people did not find Anchor an attractive shopping destination.

Unfortunately, the report came a little too late for the head of the company. After a series of poor results for the fourth consecutive year, a new CEO was brought into the business with the explicit aim of reviving the company's flagging fortunes. One of his first activities was to undertake a major management restructuring exercise. As a result, a number of the old senior management left the company and several new appointments have been made. *You* have worked for Anchor for several years and have impressed the buying director with your commitment to work and your focus upon achieving measurable outputs. Due to the restructuring exercise you find yourself promoted to the position of Buying Controller and head a team of six buyers who source and purchase menswear for the company.

The new CEO addresses his senior team. In his talk he is critical of the conservative way in which the company has done things. He notes that the company has been slow to adapt to customer change and that an 'arrogant complacency' has crept into the company. As such, there is little or no monitoring of competitor activity and little incentive to change the company strategy. One key point that is made is that the business needs to question the way in which it conducts its business. The final words from the CEO resonate in your ears: 'If we are to survive as a business we have to question what we do and how we do it. There are no sacred cows'.

To this end, the senior management team revisit every aspect of the business. One key proposal is a radical change in Anchor's buying policy. Whereas until two years ago, 90% of Anchor's merchandise was made in Canada and currently about 60% still is, they propose a major switch to overseas sources. These are seen as cheaper, possibly better quality and more responsive to fashion changes, although reducing cost is undoubtedly the main driver behind the new strategy. Several companies across the southern belt are at present almost entirely committed to supplying Anchor: these will be dropped as a result.

The company's relationship with these suppliers goes back many years. Anchor has worked closely with its suppliers and has collaborated on many aspects of the buying and merchandising process. This close working relationship has helped develop a strong feeling of trust between the company and its suppliers. You are fully aware that for many of these suppliers, the loss of Anchor's business could prove devastating and may well result in factory closures and job losses. Moreover, some suppliers are located in employment 'black-spots' where opportunities to find alternative work are limited. Factory closures in these areas will have a devastating impact upon the local economy.

You are to be sent overseas to find alternative sources of supply to make up Anchor's new ranges, which have been created by a number of leading fashion designers. One key aspect of your remit is to look for companies who can deliver at a cheaper price than you are currently paying. However, news of the proposed switch of policy has been leaked to the press and several stories have appeared in national newspapers making serious criticisms of Anchor. The main points made against the company are:

- The emphasis on cheap foreign sources will mean that Anchor will be sourcing from 'sweatshop' suppliers. In many of the countries you are to visit, young people from as low as 10 years of age are employed in clothing factories. Many major charities and religious groups have been active in opposing these practices, and several retailers have agreed not to source from these suppliers, but the new Anchor management has so far refused to take such a stance.

- Anchor have been accused of being disloyal to their own suppliers who have served them well for many years. The company is accused of creating a 'dependency culture', with suppliers wholly reliant upon Anchor for their business. Perhaps unfortunately for Anchor, the Government has also been promoting a 'buy Canadian' campaign in the media. This has been seen as a way of reducing imports and helping to rejuvenate particular sectors of the economy. Trade unions have proposed boycotts of Anchor stores in protest.

● Some large institutional investors are said to be critical of Anchor's new policy. Anchor has been seen as one of the pillars of retailing in Canada. While currently undergoing difficulties, the brand is still seen as having considerable value and long term potential. Investors are worried that such a radical set of initiatives could irreparably harm the company. As a result, some have been publicly quoted as saying they could withdraw investment from Anchor.

To compound these difficulties a number of suppliers have also stated that if Anchor go ahead and terminate the contracts, they will sue the company for a breach of contract.

Anchor's management have rejected such criticisms and dismiss such threats. They argue that Canadian consumers already buy many garments produced in such conditions unknowingly, and that it is unfair to criticise Anchor when such buying practices are quite widespread among retailers. They argue that they are merely moving with established consumer trends. Rather than seeing themselves as creating job losses through this shift, they argue that they are safeguarding their own workforce's employment prospects. They have told investors that this shift will help them become more profitable in the future, whereas without it, future dividends are likely to be disappointingly low.

On the matter of sweatshops, Anchor's spokesperson was reported to have said that what goes on in Third World countries is not a matter of concern for the company. Those countries set their own rules, and it is not Anchor's business to interfere. Moreover, Anchor's business will still generate economic growth in these developing societies and wages paid by Anchor's suppliers are 5–10% above the averages in those countries. Personally, you are unsure where these figures have come from – given that you know that the majority of suppliers have yet to be identified – and also know your brief is to find low cost suppliers whenever possible.

Discussion questions

1. Does Anchor's role as a well respected clothing retailer place any moral obligations on the company?
2. Should Anchor be more loyal to its long established suppliers and, if so, why?
3. As a senior person within the company, do you have any personal ethical issues here? Is there a case for you to 'blow the whistle' and tell the press of your concerns? If you were to 'blow the whistle', would you be willing to do so publicly, or would you try to keep the source secret?
4. What do you think an 'ethical' retailer would do in Anchor's position?

CHAPTER 6

Understanding finance

Paul Freathy and Ian Spencer

Introduction

Mention the word 'finance' and many managers will be quick to tell you how little they know about the subject, or that they do not understand how it fits in with their overall strategy. This is somewhat disconcerting, as an understanding of finance is central to an understanding of retailing.

In this case study we attempt to demystify one part of the finance area. The case examines a common problem for a retailer. That is, how to raise enough capital in order to fund future growth. The scenario is a simple one. Iestyn Morgan, founder of and the managing director of Cleddau Stores, has been successful in developing his retail business. He is now looking to develop further his portfolio of retail stores and needs advice on the best way to raise enough money to fund any expansion.

Old friends

Iestyn Morgan rose from his desk and warmly greeted his old friend and work colleague.

'Nice to see you again Gethin,' said Iestyn. 'I trust you had a pleasant trip.' Gethin Elis had worked for nearly 20 years in the retail sector and was now back in Wales to meet up with his former work mate.

'How's business?' asked Gethin.

'Business is booming. I've opened another three stores in the past month and we're due to open another two before Easter.'

'You're becoming something of a retail star,' said Gethin. 'How many stores do you have now altogether?'

'At the moment, 23–' replied Iestyn. 'But I think there's potential for at least another 20–25 in the next two years.'

Cleddau Stores had started with one shop in the early 1980s and specialised in quality foods and foodstuffs. Trading from a 300 square meter unit, the company had soon developed a reputation for providing customers with unusual products from around the world. Over the years Iestyn had developed good relations with his suppliers and was now able to offer such delicacies as ostrich pâté and smoked wild boar as well as the more traditional cooked meats, pastries and fresh vegetables.

As the retail grocery multiples had developed and expanded in the 1980s, Iestyn's own approach had been to avoid competing head on with them. Instead his stores concentrated on stocking exotic products delivered with high levels of customer service. The niche that Iestyn Morgan had found himself proved to be very successful and he had expanded Cleddau Stores by opening one or two shops every couple of years since the mid-1980s. Over the past two years Iestyn's approach had begun to change. He had increased his speed of store expansion and had opened five stores in a little over six months.

'I was worried that I was growing the business too slowly,' Iestyn said to Gethin. 'I've therefore used some of the company's reserves to expand the number of out-lets. Iestyn then revealed his idea for the future of his company.

'I've been looking at the possibility of buying a small chain of stores and con-verting them to the Cleddau format. A couple of small chains have come up in the past but I've never really looked at them seriously. I think times are changing and I need to be a little more proactive. What I need to do first, however, is consider the best way of funding any potential acquisitions.'

Gethin replied: 'I may be able to help you here. In my new position as a finan-cial analyst one of my recent roles has been to evaluate the different forms of funding that a retailer can draw upon when expanding his or her business. I will explain them to you if you wish.'

'OK', said Iestyn, 'but keep them simple and tell me about the main sources.'

Raising equity capital

Basically, there are three ways in which a firm can raise capital. These are by issu-ing ordinary share capital (sometimes known as equity capital), preference capital and debt.' 'Sounds exciting' said Iestyn jokingly. 'All firms have access to equity capital as it represents the ownership stake in the company. So for example some-one such as yourself can offer for sale a share of your business (your equity). If the company does well the shareholders will benefit. If the company does badly they will have to bear the losses. Anyone who invests in your company does so on the expectation of receiving dividends or making a capital gain. There is no contrac-tual obligation on the part of the firm to pay a dividend. Dividends are usually only paid if the firm makes a profit. However if the company is profitable the board of directors may decide not to pay dividends in order to retain the profits to finance further growth in the company. In principle however the board of direc-tors are expected to run the firm in the interests of the shareholders. Therefore they should only retain earnings if they think the funds can be employed to finance investments that will allow even larger dividends to be paid in the future.'

'What stops the board of directors taking the money from an investor and then going off and doing their own thing?' asked Iestyn.

'Various factors combine to see that the board of directors act in the interests of the stakeholders. For example shareholders have the right to vote at the annual general meeting and be responsible for electing the board of directors. Furthermore if the company is seen as not acting in the interests of its shareholders it could be difficult for the business to raise funds in the future as well as depress the existing share price of the company.'

'Does that mean I can go out and buy one share in a company and influence the way in which the business operates?' asked Iestyn.

'In theory, yes, in practice no,' replied Gethin. 'The voting rights of shareholders do not in practice provide effective constraints on the board of directors in a large corporation where there are thousands of shareholders. Generally management can call on the voting powers of the apathetic majority of shareholders plus institutional investors who may own many thousands of shares.'

'What about in the case of small firms?' asked Iestyn. 'Is it the same?'

'In small firms it is often the case that management owns a majority of the sharess, leaving the minority of shareholders virtually powerless. Fortunately the fact that the firm may need to raise funds in the future is likely to prove a more effective constraint on management, as does the threat of a take over. Unless the management owns a majority of the shares the threat of a take over is one of the most effective disciplines imposed on them.'

'OK, to get this right. I can sell a share in my company in order to fund future growth. Apart from getting to vote at the meetings what else will any shareholder be entitled to?' asked Iestyn.

'The Constitution of a company (that is the rules of what it can and can not do) is to a large extent dictated by the requirements of company law and is embodied in its Memorandum and Articles of Association. These set out the rights of the shareholders. In addition to the right to vote at shareholders meetings and the right to elect directors they also include the right to receive a copy of the annual accounts and reports of the company, the right to receive any dividend payment and the right to receive any capital that is distributed when the company is dissolved.'

'Isn't the Memorandum and Articles of Association the document that sets the limit on the number of shares a company can issue?' asked Iestyn.

'Yes,' replied Gethin, 'although this figure can be changed with the approval of the shareholders. The maximum number of shares that a company can issue is known as the "authorised share capital". Generally the directors of the company will provide themselves with some flexibility to issue additional shares by keeping the amount of authorised share capital in excess of the number of shares issued.'

What Gethin has described is the issuing of ordinary shares to interested parties. However other types of shares also exist that differ slightly from what has been described above. A retailer may wish to issue shares that do not carry the full range of rights associated with ordinary shares. For example, 'deferred shares' have their entitlement to dividends deferred until a certain date or until the company reaches a certain level of profit, but in other respects carry full rights. Alternatively, 'B' shares entitle holders to be paid in additional shares rather than in cash dividends.

Growing the business

The growth of Cleddau Stores to date has been via retained earnings. In his attempt to take the business forward Iestyn has ploughed a significant proportion of the company's profits back into the business. What Iestyn is a little unclear about is whether an organisation such as his could issue more shares once the initial capital had been raised.

'Suppose,' said Iestyn, 'that my business is doing very well and in a couple of years' time I need more money to expand, what are my options? Do I have to borrow from the bank? Do I use the profits the company has made? Can I raise additional equity capital by issuing more shares?'

Gethin replied, 'If a company wishes to issue new shares, existing shareholders have a pre-emptive right under the Companies Act to subscribe to any issue the board of directors might decide on within the limit prescribed by the authorised share capital. Basically this means that there is a law preventing the board of directors diluting the power of existing shareholders by the sale of shares to outside investors. As a result most new issues of shares in the United Kingdom are in the form of rights issues, with the new shares being offered to existing shareholders in proportion to their existing holdings.'

'Let's just see if I have got this right,' remarks Iestyn. 'In the future I may wish to raise more equity capital by selling additional shares to investors through what is described as a rights issue. If I do this I have to offer the shares at a discount rather than at the prevailing market price to my existing shareholders.'

'Correct,' said Gethin. 'Otherwise there would be no benefit to the shareholders. They could acquire additional shares directly from the stock market at the prevailing market price. The number of new shares offered to a shareholder is in direct proportion to the amount that he or she already holds in the company with a conventional discount in the region of 15–20 per cent.'

Debt finance

Feeling that he now had at least a basic understanding about equity capital, Iestyn was keen to understand what other options he had for growing and expanding his business. One thing he had prided himself on was that the company had almost zero borrowings. His business had been built on the basis of investing as much surplus as possible back into the company. His dealings with the bank were therefore limited. Iestyn knew in many ways he was fortunate to be in this position. He had heard many anecdotal stories about financial institutions lending money to small businesses and then withdrawing the loan at the last moment. He was unsure whether these stories were apocryphal or not, but they had led him to avoid approaching the banks in order to fund his earlier expansion. Iestyn realised that the situation he was now facing was slightly different – the scale of expansion he was considering was beyond his own personal means. Whilst the option of a share issue was certainly something to consider he did not wish to discount other alternatives.

Given that Iestyn has almost no bank debt, Gethin commented, 'You certainly have been fortunate not to have had to borrow any funds to finance your activities. You are however the exception rather than the rule. I think you know yourself that any large-scale expansion is going to require you to raise some additional finance. If you look to borrow from a bank you have to be quite clear on the commitments that stem from such borrowings. If I borrow money from a lender I agree to make interest payments on a regular basis and to repay the amount borrowed (the principal) according to an agreed schedule. This is different from equity where the shareholders have the right to share in dividends declared by the board of directors. Debt finance does not entitle the lender to dividends.'

'Whilst this may sound attractive these commitments have to be met whether or not the company is making a profit. Any failure by a company to meet its debt obligations can have disastrous consequences. When a company defaults on its debt payments the lender (often a bank) has the right to have a receiver appointed to administer the company's assets to protect its interests. This can result in the bankruptcy and liquidation of the company.

'The use of debt clearly implies some risk for the company but, from the standpoint of the lender, debt is a lower risk form of investment than equity capital. As a result debt usually promises a lower expected rate of return to the lender. For the company this lower expected rate of return translates into a lower cost for debt in relation to equity capital. A cheaper form of finance means more profits for the shareholders of the company but this has to be weighed against the additional risk of having outstanding debts.'

'That has clarified the situation nicely,' Iestyn replied. 'The main differences between debt and equity finance are that debt involves the borrower making explicit and specified payments to cover borrowings and interest whereas equity simply promises a residual claim on profits in the future.'

'Not only that,' Gethin added, 'debt does not provide an ownership interest in the firm in the same way as equity does, just because a bank lends you money does not give it any rights of ownership. Also it means that the debt holders have no voting power. One other thing that may be of relevance is that interest payments on any debt are generally regarded as a cost and are considered to be an expense for calculating taxable profit. This may result in a lower tax bill, whereas dividends on equity are not considered to be a cost but a distribution of income.'

'When we talk about borrowing and debt I automatically think about going to the bank. Would this be my only option or are there other forms of borrowing I could look to, in order to fund any expansion plans?' asked Iestyn.

'Borrowing can be undertaken in a large number of different ways, but two broad approaches can be identified?' replied Gethin. 'Borrowing from financial institutions such as banks and borrowing by issuing securities such as bonds or notes. Traditionally banks in the United Kingdom have provided companies with short-term finance for their working capital requirements in the form of overdrafts. An overdraft is a borrowing arrangement that allows a company to borrow on a short-term basis up to an agreed limit. It is an extremely flexible form of financing. Within the limit set, the firm can vary its borrowing according to its needs. This makes it particularly suitable for financing some part of the company's assets that vary over time with the level of its business, such as its stocks and debtors (that is, the credit it extends).'

'This seems very useful for periods of short-term debt,' commented Iestyn. 'What about funding in the longer term? In the same way as a bank lends an individual money to buy a car, is it possible to take out a loan over the longer term?'

'Banks that obtained their funds on a short-term basis were initially reluctant to commit these funds to long-term loans. But in recent years the lending policies of banks have been changing and term loans have become increasingly important.

As a company grows and develops a trading history its relationship with its bank may change. If successful, the business will be seen as less of a credit risk and hence may attract lower borrowing charges. The credit risk may be further reduced by the ability of a bank to monitor the changing financial position over time of a borrower through changes in the company's bank account.'

Gethin opened his briefcase. 'I was looking at this very issue for my company a couple of weeks ago. I had to present a set of financial recommendations to our board so I wanted to make sure I understood the main differences between overdrafts and term loans.' He pulled out a sheet of paper that highlighted the primary features of term loans. They may be summarised as follows:

- loans have maturities of more than one year: the majority of term loans are arranged on a medium-term basis (1–5 years) although longer-term loans of up to 15 years are not unusual;
- interest rates vary over the life of the loan, being tied to the bank's base rate and adjusted on a periodic basis (for example every three months);
- they are repayable according to an agreed schedule, usually instalments over the life of the loan, the start of the repayments in some cases being delayed for a number of time periods (referred to as the grace period), but it may also be possible to arrange repayment in a lump sum at the final maturity of the loan;
- term loans cannot be recalled at the discretion of the bank as is the case with overdrafts.

Iestyn read through the sheet of paper.

'Again this seems quite clear and understandable,' he said. 'What are the advantages for the borrower of taking out a term loan? Gethin had already anticipated the question and produced a second sheet of paper, entitled 'The advantages to the borrower of term loans'. The document highlights three primary advantages:

- the guaranteed availability of the funds for a specified period of time;
- the ability to negotiate a repayment schedule related to the expected cash flow of the business;
- lower transaction costs than the issue of securities (debt or equity) for smaller amounts of capital.

Having read through the document Iestyn sat back and looked at his watch. They had been talking for nearly two hours. As Gethin drank his (cold) coffee Iestyn reached across his desk, picked up a red folder and handed it to Gethin.

'What you have said makes a lot of sense. I can see I have a number of options if I wish to expand Cleddau Stores. Have a look at this and tell me what you think.' In the folder Gethin saw an offer for sale of 25 convenience stores only 20 miles from Cleddau's head office. The stores had not yet come on to the market, but Iestyn had approached the owner informally a couple of years ago and expressed an interest in purchasing the chain. Now the owner was retiring and looking to sell the business.

Having read through the folder Gethin remarked, 'This is quite a significant step for you to undertake. Do you intend to make a bid for the stores by yourself?'

'What other options do I have?' asked Iestyn.

'Well, in order to raise finance for this long-term investment the basic question you have to ask yourself is whether you are prepared to relinquish some degree of ownership. If you are, you can go into partnership with one or two individuals. This is different from raising equity capital as the majority of partners will provide finance but also want an input into the running of the business. However a partnership is useful in that you are able to offset some of the risks of developing and growing the company. Also if you choose your partners carefully they can also bring in a range of skills and expertise you may not have.'

'And the downside?' asked Iestyn

'Partnerships can sometimes bring conflict. Partners may have a different view on how the business should be run, what markets they should be trading in and what the long-term direction of the firm should be. If you have been running this business successfully since the 1980s you may have problems adjusting to working with partners.'

'You've have got me worried now. Is there any way I can reduce the risk associated with acquiring these new stores without relinquishing control of the business?' asked Iestyn.

'The other option is to set up a limited company. To be honest, I was surprised you had not explored this option earlier. The advantage of a limited company is that in law the company is seen as being distinct from the owners; that is, the company is viewed as a separate legal entity. You are limited financially to the capital you have invested in the company. However if the company fails and there are insufficient assets to meet your obligations your personal assets and savings are safe. In a partnership you are liable personally. This means that if Cleddau Stores was ever to go into receivership you would have to find the money to pay off creditors and suppliers, even if it means selling your house.'

Discussion questions

1. Why is Iestyn so keen to grow his retail business? What are the incentives and dangers behind his strategy of store expansion?

2. What are the main differences between equity and debt?

3. Why is equity less risky for the company than debt?

4. What are the advantages of limited companies over sole proprietorships and partnerships?

PART 3

Retail development

CHAPTER 7

The retail development process: An overview

Cliff Guy

Aims

The aim of this chapter is to provide an understanding of the issues involved in retail planning and development.

Learning objectives

By the end of this chapter you should understand:

- how new retail premises come into being;
- what financial and information resources are used, and why;
- why new retail space comes in 'packages' known as 'shopping centres' and what forms of shopping centre are most suited to different retail purposes;
- what influences systems of land use planning have on the volume, form and location of shopping centre development;
- what effects these outcomes have on retailers' strategies for growth and change.

Introduction

The following discussion is based mainly on the United Kingdom, but examples are also provided from other parts of western Europe and from North America. The chapter is structured as follows: the next section describes a simplified version of the retail development process, including the roles of the various actors involved, and the flows of information and finance that drive the process. Once this has been completed the third section describes the land use planning process in the United Kingdom and other countries. It explains how land use planning affects proposals for shopping centre development and redevelopment.

The fourth section of the chapter describes in more detail several common forms of 'planned' shopping centre developments ('planned' in this context means 'organised' rather than 'made subject to land use planning'). These are contrasted with the 'unplanned' clusters of shopping and personal business premises typical of the older parts of western European towns and cities, including most central areas. The attraction of planned and unplanned retail areas for different types of retail function are examined. The section concludes with an examination of the various forms of retail premises and ownership structure that can be made available to a retailer, and explains why particular combinations of retail premises and ownership appeal to different types of retailer.

The final section draws together some of the previous findings, emphasising the role of property development and planning decisions in affecting retailer strategy. It examines some of the outcomes of the interaction between the requirements of property developers and land use planners. These include effects on size and location of stores as well as rental costs and land values. Other effects may include the decision on whether or not to internationalise, to introduce new merchandise and/or store formats, and to rationalise store portfolios through closures or sales of property.

The retail development process

This section presents a generalised picture of the ways in which retail premises come into existence. This includes a brief treatment of the various types of company involved, and the financial support and relationships that underlie retail development. Fuller accounts of commercial property development can be found in texts such as Cadman and Topping (1995), Ratcliffe and Stubbs (1996), and Millington (2000). A specialist text on retail development is Guy (1994a).

Any building used for retail display and sales must have at one time been constructed (although not always) for the purpose of retailing. Its construction would have taken place in order to provide some type of financial reward for the person or company responsible. If built by or for the retailer then the reward comes from profitable retailing. More usually, however, the premises are built by or for a property developer, in which case the financial reward takes place following construction, through sale to a retailer. Alternatively the sale may be deferred, in which case the developer remains the owner of the property and leases the property to a retailer, who becomes a tenant. In this case the owner forgoes a short-term reward, but the property becomes a long-term investment, and a capital asset that may be needed as collateral when further development is considered. In this case the original developer, or the company to which the property is sold, becomes a landlord who collects rent from the retailer concerned, in exchange for a legal right to occupy the premises for the sale of certain goods and/or services.

The developer has to find money in the first place in order to purchase the land required, carry out any site improvements and pay construction costs. In most cases this money is provided by a financial institution such as a bank, building society or (in the case of major developments) a company that has large amounts of money available for investment, such as an insurance company or a pension fund. The financial institution will expect a return on its own investment in the property development which is sufficient to justify that investment rather than some other property, or a non-property investment such as company shares. As property development will normally lead to an increase in land value the investor may wish to share in this increase, through acting as joint or sole developer, for example.

In some cases retailers act as developers on their own behalf. This is normally the case where the company has specialist requirements for store design and location, has a heavy programme of store openings and has the necessary funds or access to funds that can finance the development. In the United Kingdom, this behaviour is typical of the largest food retailers. Most other retailers do not build their own stores, but prefer to lease them from specialist retail developers and/or shopping centre landlords. Reasons for this are discussed later in this section.

Figure 7.1 sums up the position. Money flows from consumer to retailer, from retailer to developer and from developer to financier. At each stage the recipient aims to make a profit in either the short or long term. These financial flows are governed by institutional relationships between these parties.

The institutional relationship between retailer and landlord is particularly important. The rent paid is determined by negotiation between the two parties. The results of this negotiation usually mean that rents are similar to those already being paid for similar properties. The retailer leases the property, usually for a period of 15 or 25 years in the United Kingdom, but the rent may be altered – again by negotiation – every 5 years through a process of rent review. Landlords are legally entitled to insist that rents can only be reviewed upwards. If the retailer cannot accept this, or wishes to vacate the property for some other reason, it is his or her responsibility to find another tenant for the premises.

Many commentators have thus concluded that in the United Kingdom landlords (who, in the case of major town centres or out-of-centre schemes, are almost always large property companies and financial institutions) hold the upper hand. A retailer can be faced with increasing rent demands even if sales and margins are static or declining. For these and other reasons some retailers prefer to own their stores outright. The largest food retailers in the United Kingdom such as Tesco, Sainsbury and Asda have bought sites and built the majority of their stores themselves in the last 25 years or so. Table 7.1 summarises the factors that influence the choice of whether to own or rent stores.

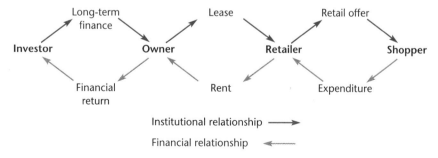

Figure 7.1   Financial flows within the development process

Table 7.1 Retail premises: own or rent

	Strategic reason	Economic reason
Own	Freedom to innovate (new locations, new layouts)	Avoid rent rises and service charges
	Add to capital assets	Use site value to lever finance
	Long-term potential to upgrade, redevelop	
Rent	Expand or reduce store portfolio more rapidly	Make explicit all costs associated with premises
	Opportunity to experiment without long-term commitment	Future costs more predictable, facilitates financial planning

It should be noted that in other parts of western Europe the terms of leases are generally more in favour of the retailer. For example, in Germany rents normally increase at the rate of national price inflation. Whilst this can improve the cost equation for the retailer it can also reduce the value of retail property for the investor. This means that there is less incentive to increase the value of retail areas through improvement or redevelopment. This may be one reason why there has been more development of shopping malls within town and city centres in the United Kingdom than elsewhere in Europe.

Self-assessment Question 1 *Imagine you are fund manager for a major investment company. What type(s) of retail property should you attempt to buy in order to obtain the best long-term return on your initial investment? In order to research this question you are advised to look at reports and newsletters published by property consultancies such as CB Hillier Parker, Cushman Wakefield, Healey and Baker, or Donaldsons (these can be accessed free of charge via the Internet).*

Land use planning

Before examining the main formats for retail development we need to be aware of one of the most important influences on the types and locations of modern retailing. In all developed countries there is to a greater or lesser extent control by the state (national, regional or local government) over new retail development. This control is exercised in what is assumed to be the public interest. This rather vague term may encompass the following:

- protection of adjoining land and properties from loss of privacy, excessive surface water run-off, polluting waste products, noise, traffic hazards, etc.;
- protection of attractive landscapes from urban development;
- reduction of traffic congestion and pollution caused by shoppers using private cars;
- control over the impact that modern large-scale retailing may have on older shopping areas, through taking away some of their trade;

- protection for 'small' retailers from 'unfair competition' by chain stores;
- attempts to guide new retail development into town centre locations, because of their cultural and social importance.

Not all of these aims are found in every country. In most parts of the United States, for example, land use planning is minimal in nature and serves mainly to protect the environmental quality of residential neighbourhoods. In some European countries protecting small retailers is an essential part of policy. In the United Kingdom enhancement of town centre retailing is probably the most important feature of policy at present. An increasing concern in most of western Europe is the control of the growth in private car journeys: governments are seeking to make retail destinations more suited to walking, cycling or public transport use by consumers.

Whilst broad policy is usually framed at central government level, day-to-day planning decisions on retail development are the responsibility of local government. In the United Kingdom a retail developer has to apply to the local authority concerned for planning permission and development should not begin until permission has been given. If permission is refused there is no compensation, but the developer may appeal to the central government department concerned. In many cases the original refusal is overturned and the development can then take place. Table 7.2 shows a simplified summary of those development activities that require permission. Some of these may seem very minor in importance: the emphasis tends to be on physical changes to the premises rather than changes in goods sold or methods of retailing.

The planning system in the United Kingdom is, in comparison with most other systems in the developed world, noted for its flexibility. Much discretion is given to local planning authorities over detailed matters, although they are expected to follow national policy guidelines. Deciding whether to approve a planning application usually involves simultaneous consideration of several factors.

Table 7.2 Retail development activities that require planning permission in the United Kingdom

Type of activity	Information typically required
Intent to develop at a particular location (outline planning consent)	Total floor area, means of access for goods and customers, car parking spaces
Erection of new building for retail purposes, and supporting activity on adjacent land (full planning consent)	As above, also: physical appearance of building, layout of entire site, numbers to be employed
Extension of existing retail building, alteration to access and car parking.	Floor area and purpose of extension, alterations to car parking and access.
Demolition or alteration (external or internal) of building listed for historic or architectural interest (listed building consent)	Full details
Change of use of a non-retail building and/or site to retail use	Existing use, layout, numbers employed, car parking, access; proposed changes
Display of advertisements off site (advertisement control).	Full details

These may include:

- policies for retail development in the statutory Development Plan prepared by the local authority;
- government policies, as set out in Planning Policy Guidance Note 6 (in England), and other documents in Wales, Scotland and Northern Ireland (these policies are summarised in Box 7.1);
- the appearance and layout of the proposed building(s) and their relationship with surrounding areas;
- traffic access and the need to maintain free flow of traffic on major roads;
- the type of development, including the types of goods to be sold;
- the employment opportunities likely to occur;
- environmental improvements that would occur as a result of the development, such as restoration of derelict or contaminated land.

Box 7.1
Retail planning policy in the United Kingdom: a recent government statement

1. General objectives

- to secure accessible, efficient, competitive and innovative retail provision for all the communities of Wales, in both urban and rural areas;
- to promote town, district, local and village centres as the most appropriate locations for retailing and for functions complementary to it;
- to enhance the vitality, attractiveness and viability of town, district, local and village centres;
- to promote access to these centres by public transport, walking and cycling.

2. Control over New Development
When determining a planning application for retail, leisure or other uses best located in a town centre, including extensions to existing developments, local planning authorities should take into account:

Official wording	Unofficial interpretation
Compatibility with the Unitary Development Plan strategy	Proposals should be consistent with the approved development plan for the local authority concerned
Consideration of the need for the development	The proposer should explain the need (both quantitative and qualitative) for the scheme
The sequential approach to site selection	Proposals should be located within town centres, or (if no town centre site is available) on the edge of town centres. Proposers of off-centre sites must show that no town centre or edge-of-centre sites are available
The impact on existing centres	Proposals should not significantly affect the vitality and viability of existing town, district, local or village centres
Accessibility by a variety of modes of travel	The scheme should be accessible by public transport, bicycle and on foot
The impact on overall travel patterns	The scheme should not lead to an increase in overall private car travel

Source: based on National Assembly for Wales (2002), Section 10

Of these matters, the Development Plan policies and central government policies are likely to outweigh other considerations, particularly for major proposals for new retailing. However, for minor changes or proposals that generally conform to existing policy the other considerations become more important. It is possible for an application that is acceptable on general policy grounds (for example, new retail development within an existing town centre) to be refused on grounds of buildings design or vehicle access. It is also possible for proposals that appear not to fit in with general policies to be approved, if other considerations such as employment provision or environmental improvement are seen as being particularly important by the local authority concerned. However, central government departments can 'call in' such cases for their own decision, sometimes against local authority wishes.

Planning policies and the ways in which they are operated vary considerably amongst other European countries and it is difficult to summarise them briefly (for a more detailed analysis, see Guy (1998a)). However two frequent characteristics should be noted. First, several countries such as France, Ireland, Germany, Denmark and Norway have size limits for individual stores, imposed through legislation or central government regulation of the planning system. In Ireland, for example, food stores of over 3,000 square metres of sales area are not permitted (the limit is raised to 3,500 square metres in the Greater Dublin area). Secondly, in most European countries there is less concern over detailed matters such as design and layout: if a proposal is in conformity with the zoning rules for a particular area then it can normally be built subject to 'building control' approval of minor details.

The general effects of planning control over retail development in western Europe can be summarised briefly. Retailers that usually prefer to locate in town or city centres and are prepared to rent shop units can expand rapidly subject only to availability of suitable premises, since their expansion should be in line with town planning policies. If planning policies also encourage the development of town centre shopping malls this will increase the availability of modern, well-serviced premises in the best locations.

However, retailers that wish to trade from large units readily accessible by car will find expansion much more difficult. Of necessity most such stores are located on cheaper land outside existing retail areas. Policies that restrict such development will obviously make it difficult for expanding retailers to find suitable sites. Furthermore, the growing shortage of suitable locations leads to inflation of retail rents and land prices. In the United Kingdom for example, rents for retail warehouse parks (see the next section) have consistently risen at rates well above the average for retail property (Guy 1998b), due partly to an increasing shortage of new schemes and the increasing desirability of existing schemes as longer-term property investments.

Planning control has also affected retailers' locational strategies. In the United Kingdom for example, large-scale regional shopping centres of the type that were built in the late 1980s (see below) are no longer permitted. Increasingly developers are seeking town centre sites for retail developments. Supermarkets are increasingly being built within or on the edge of town centres, whereas in the 1980s they were often built on the edge of urban areas, located some distance from existing retail facilities.

Types of retail development

This section describes the main physical forms of retail development found in modern western economies.

Planned and unplanned development

A fundamental distinction in describing retail facilities lies between planned and unplanned development. Planned development is the result of a deliberate decision to provide a specially built retail environment at a particular place; it is usually, although not always, carried out by a property developer rather than a retailer. The outcome is usually a planned centre. Planned retailing takes several physical forms that are described later in this section.

Unplanned retailing is the result of individual decisions, usually by retailers, to provide retail premises, often through conversion of residential or industrial buildings. Unplanned retailing can occur in isolated locations (for example 'corner shops' in older residential areas), or in clusters. The term unplanned centre can be used to describe a spatial cluster of unplanned retailing, for example in the central areas of towns and cities. In the following explanation the neutral term retail area is used to describe any occurrence in space of either unplanned or planned retailing.

In describing retail areas, two basic features should be recognised: location and the physical nature of the development. Location can be used in two senses:

- *absolute location*: the exact place where the retail area is located, identifiable for example by a post code;
- *relative location*: a relationship in space to other retailing and to the local catchment population.

Location, in the latter sense, can be categorised according to spatial relationships with both other retailing and consumers. Given that most retailing occurs within towns and cities a simple description of location with relation to consumers might be inner urban and outer urban. The relationship with other retailing can be described simply as in centre and out of centre, using 'centre' to describe both planned and unplanned retailing.

Figure 7.2 shows a simple classification of retail location within an urban area. The inner/outer and in/out-of-centre dimensions are used, together with an extra

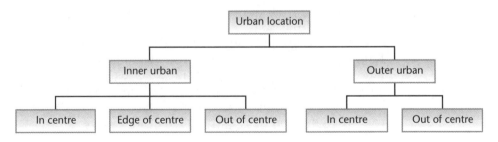

Figure 7.2 Locational classification

'edge-of-centre' category relating to inner urban. This describes the common situation where a central retail area can be expanded through new development on a site previously used for some other purpose.

The in/out-of-centre distinction is particularly important in western Europe as it interfaces with land use planning control. As explained earlier, planners generally prefer new development to take place within existing retail areas, especially town and city centres in which a mixture of unplanned and planned development normally exist. On the other hand, out-of-centre locations are preferred by many retailers and developers. This is because they are less constrained by existing buildings and the sites may also be simpler and cheaper to purchase than land within retail areas. This establishes areas of conflict and compromise between developers and planners, which are discussed later in this chapter.

Planned retail development

Retail development can be categorised in several ways (Guy 1998c). A simple categorisation employs physical characteristics. In rising order of complexity there are as follows:

- a single store with its own car park;
- a group of stores of similar size and appearance, on separate sites but with some shared features such as car parking;
- a linked group of stores, often linear or L-shaped, with common car parking;
- an 'open' mall with stores of various sizes facing each other across one or more pedestrian ways;
- an enclosed mall with stores of various sizes under one roof; such malls may be built on several levels and feature climate control.

The following discussion of planned retail developments is based upon this simple typology (Figure 7.3). Comments on typical location and ownership patterns are also made.

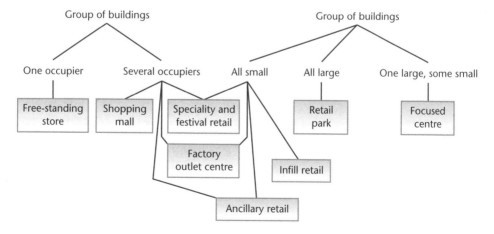

Figure 7.3   Planned retail developments

Single stores, often known as free-standing stores, are usually developed by the retailer occupying the store. Examples include Tesco, Sainsbury, Asda and Safeway (food stores in the United Kingdom), and Ikea (furniture and furnishings in several European countries). There are several reasons why retailers of this type prefer to develop their own stores including:

- adherence to proven design and layout principles, leading to standardised products that can be built without the need for specialist development expertise;
- the ability to finance new store development, often through cash flow rather than borrowings;
- realisation of greater profits from store development, or acceptance of a lower return on investment than would be necessary for a developer-led scheme;
- creation of a portfolio of 'fixed capital assets' which can be used to lever further funds for investment.

Table 7.3 illustrates how free-standing stores are typically classified in western Europe. The term 'hypermarket', for example, is usually defined as a store of at least 2,500 square metres of sales area, operating on one level and owned by a food retailer, although the goods sold will include non-foods. However, in the United Kingdom the term 'superstore' is typically used to describe such a store, and the term 'hypermarket', which is now rarely used in British practice, relates to stores with at least 5,000 square metres of sales area.

Such stores occupy substantial areas – for example a hypermarket may require some 3–4 hectares of land, to include the store itself, car parking, access areas for goods delivery and a petrol filling station. For this reason they are usually located in suburban areas where large undeveloped sites are more readily available.

Table 7.3 Classification of free-standing stores

Sales area (m^2)	Convenience shopping	Comparison shopping
Under 1,000	Convenience store	Fast food restaurant
1,000–2,500	Supermarket	Retail warehouse, Fachmarkt (Germany)
Over 2,500	Superstore (UK), Hypermarket (rest of Europe)	Retail warehouse, Non-food superstore

Planned shopping centres

Most new store development is however carried out by property companies. These typically build groups of stores, which are then rented to individual tenants. Table 7.4 provides a classification of such stores, based upon physical characteristics, which are described further in Box 7.2.

Table 7.4 A typology of planned shopping developments

Type of development	Anchor store	Size range (m²)	Trip purpose
Focused centre	Supermarket or hypermarket	5,000–20,000	Convenience shopping
Retail park	None	5,000–30,000	Household shopping
Shopping mall	Hypermarket or department store	10,000–100,000	Comparison shopping
Regional centre	Department stores	50,000–150,000	Comparison shopping, leisure
Factory outlet centre	None	5,000–30,000	Comparison shopping, leisure
Speciality centre	None	5,000–20,000	Leisure

Box 7.2
Characteristics of planned shopping centres

The focused centre: these have typically been built to serve surrounding residential areas with convenience shopping needs, and consist of a supermarket, hypermarket or (in North America) discount department store plus some small shop units. They are often known as local centres or neighbourhood centres in North America; as district centres in the United Kingdom and *centres intercommunaux* in France (Reynolds 1993).

The retail park: these schemes are usually built in off-centre locations. They consist of several large stores and were originally intended to sell bulky 'household goods' such as furniture, washing machines, DIY materials, etc. These were then supplemented with a wider range of household furnishings, electrical items, etc. More recently retail parks in the United Kingdom have begun to sell clothing, shoes and other personal/fashion goods (Guy 2000). The stores within a retail park may be physically separate, or joined together, or a mixture of the two styles. Some retail parks include leisure areas such as cinemas or indoor bowling arenas.

The shopping mall: is in effect contained in one very large building, although some of the internal spaces may not be roofed over. Its lower size limit is often taken to be 10,000 m² of gross retail area. It includes one or more large 'anchor stores' (department or variety stores), and several (often over 50) smaller retail units. Such centres attempt to replicate the amount and variety of shopping space in long-established central shopping areas. Small comparison goods shops selling clothing, footwear, leisure and luxury items are particularly important, and help distinguish the centre from retail parks and other types of centre. 'Leisure' uses such as a food court, cinema or ice rink may feature in larger centres.

The regional shopping centre: is a large shopping mall, built in a free-standing position rather than as part of an existing central area. The lower size limit to this type of centre is often stated as 500,000 ft² (as in Guy 1994b), but limits as low as 30,000 m² have been used (for example in Reynolds 1993). Very large centres of over about

800,000 ft^2 (known in North America as super-regional centres) are usually built on two levels, in order to reduce the total land take of the centre and to shorten the amount of walking for shoppers within the centre itself. In such a centre the major stores will probably trade from both floors.

The factory outlet centre: is similar physically to a relatively small shopping mall but has no anchor store. The outlets sell price discounted goods and are usually leased by manufacturing or wholesale suppliers rather than retailers. The purpose is to sell surplus goods such as ends of ranges, outdated fashions, slightly imperfect specimens, etc. (Fernie 1995; Fernie and Fernie 1997).

The speciality centre may resemble a modern shopping mall or may be converted from one or more old buildings. There is no anchor store, and the retail outlets (mainly owned by independents) tend to specialise either in one type of goods or in goods designed for a visitor/tourist market. The term 'festival marketplace' has been used for some examples, mainly in North America, which have particularly strong tourist appeal.

Source: Guy (1998c)

Locational selection for planned development

Each of the store/centre types shown in Tables 7.3 and 7.4 tend to operate most successfully in particular kinds of location. Some developments consume large areas of land and require good road access, for both suppliers and customers. These tend to locate outside existing retail areas, because large areas of land are thus made available and rents are cheaper. Others need to be located in areas where there are already retail attractions. This can work in various ways.

The retail park, for example, is an agglomeration of medium- to large-sized stores, each of which tends to specialise in a different retail offer. A typical retail park might consist of a 'do-it-yourself' (home improvements) store, a furniture store, a carpet store, a home furnishings and lighting store, an office stationery store and a drive-through pizza or burger restaurant. Although these stores all sell different things the agglomeration is favoured by retailers because the stores together will attract shoppers looking to purchase a variety of household and comparison items in one shopping trip. It is also more practicable for the property company concerned to develop a group of such stores in one place than separate stores in several different places.

In other cases, stores will cluster because they sell fashion or speciality items such that a group of several competing stores makes a strong attraction for the shopper. The precise combination of style, size and price that the shopper wants is more likely to be available in a larger cluster of stores. These stores choose to locate in existing town centres, or sometimes off-centre malls, and have to pay for this enhanced level of visibility and accessibility through higher rents. Therefore a retail development that consists mainly of fashion stores will require a town centre location, where it can add variety and interest to the existing retail area.

Figure 7.4 shows typical combinations of shopping centre type, and location within urban areas. These are discussed in more detail in Guy (1998c).

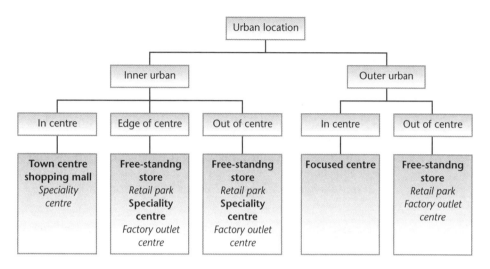

Figure 7.4 Locational classification of retail development

Planned redevelopment

Retail development does not always involve the use of new sites or even new buildings. It may take the form of a new use of existing buildings, or demolition of existing retailing and replacement by a new scheme. There are three common types of retail redevelopment:

- Conversion of older (non-retail) buildings that have architectural or historic significance, in order to add interest and a particular 'image' to the retail offer. Such developments are usually associated with 'speciality retailing', and are often mixed with bars, cafés and other leisure facilities to appeal to tourists and office workers. Locations are typically within a town centre, or in an area of tourist interest. There is some overlap here with the concept of the factory outlet centre, since many of these make use of historic buildings.
- A shopping centre will generally need renovation and upgrading during its period of life. This may be largely cosmetic and aimed at retaining the centre's appeal for existing tenants and customers or may involve substantial expansion or more efficient use of existing space.
- Outdated or 'tired' shopping centres can be completely demolished and replaced with more modern facilities. The 'life' of a conventional retail scheme such as a large food store or retail park is often held to be around 20–30 years. For accounting purposes it is usually assumed that a new development should generate enough revenue to pay back the initial investment over a period of 15 years (Guy 1995).

In a mixed market economy where planning controls over retail development are important, as in most of western Europe, the nature of the original planning consent given for a development can be important. In the United Kingdom a key factor that can affect redevelopment potential is whether the original scheme was given a restricted consent. The restriction could either affect the size of individual retail premises or the types of goods and services that can be provided. 'Open A1 consents', in which there are no restrictions on goods sold, are highly prized and lead to much higher rents and land values (Guy 1998b). A process known as 'active management' occurs when an open consent retail park is bought by a major property company or financial institution for investment purposes. Guy (2000) notes that this process can involve the following:

- more intensive use of existing buildings, for example by constructing mezzanine floors;
- improvement of customer facilities such as car parking and weather protection;
- replacement of low rent-paying retailers such as home improvements by higher rent payers such as sports goods and clothing.

Self-assessment Question 2 *Within any town centre you know summarise from your own observation the main differences in retail mix between 'planned' parts of the centre (covered malls or arcades) and 'unplanned' parts (groups of older buildings fronting the streets). Suggest reasons for these differences.*

The development process in relation to retailer requirements

This section relates the issues discussed above to some of the questions that a retail firm might pose when considering expansion, repositioning of outlets or even partial withdrawal from retailing. Are the types, sizes and locations of retail premises made available through the development process suited to my needs?

This reflects the type of retailing concerned. Individuals attempting to start a retail business generally seek premises that are cheap to buy or rent and small in size. This can make available a very wide choice of premises, although these tend to be in unplanned areas (such as inner city shopping ribbons) where there is little demand from more established retailers.

Retailers attempting to set up a network of stores (when, for example, expanding internationally or regionally) may find this much more difficult. Those who can use standardised premises that are already in existence are in the best position to expand rapidly. This includes comparison retailers seeking town and city centre premises, especially where they can profitably trade from the 100–400 square metre units typical of modern shopping malls. However, because of their location these are the most expensive premises to rent; furthermore, taking out a new lease may involve the retailer paying a substantial premium (that is, a one-off payment for the lease itself).

Box 7.3 provides an imaginary example. A sports shoe retailer ('Foot Fast') is looking to open new stores in the United Kingdom. Its opportunities to do so are limited by the unavailability of suitable premises, planning controls and the likelihood of high rent payments if suitable premises are found. In order to open a sufficient number of stores to gain adequate market share, the firm may have to compromise its original objectives – by trading from smaller stores than anticipated.

Box 7.3
Can Foot Fast set up a store portfolio in the United Kingdom?

Foot Fast is an imaginary company that both produces and sells a range of sports footwear and clothing. It is considering setting up some 30–50 stores within the United Kingdom over the next three years or so. Its ideal store configuration is:

- 2,000–3,000 m^2 sales area, on one level;
- around 100 free car parking spaces for customers;
- good access to the road network for goods delivery and customers;
- at least 100,000 catchment population within 10 minutes' car driving time;
- location close to other sports goods stores, and/or fashion stores, and/or outdoor leisure facilities.

The company does not want to build its own free-standing stores because of problems in finding sites and obtaining planning permission: this process is risky and will take too long. It is therefore seeking to rent existing premises. The stores available are:

Town centre location
Advantages:
- high profile location, accessible by public and private transport;
- proximity to fashion and sports goods stores;
- premises can easily be disposed of if location strategy changes.

Disadvantages:
- lack of availability of single-level large stores;
- high rents and business rates;
- no ground-level parking available.

Possible compromises:
- accept smaller premises and sell more limited range;
- trade from several floors in former department store;
- take secondary (lower-rent) location within town centre.

Off-centre retail park location
Advantages:
- availability of large, modern single-level premises;
- adequate free car parking space and road access;
- low rents compared with town centre (but rapidly rising).

Disadvantages:
- possible remoteness from sports goods, fashion stores or leisure facilities.

Possible compromise:
- only consider retail parks that include such stores or facilities.

Possible long-term strategy
Form alliance with property company to develop 'sports villages' that include the following:
- Foot Fast store;
- other sports and fashion-related stores;
- outdoor leisure and sports facilities.

Location:
- off-centre location preferred by developer because of land requirements and cost;
- edge-of-centre location preferred by planners because of accessibility by all transport modes.

Retailers that trade from large, single-level stores usually prefer out-of-centre locations. In the United Kingdom, there is a widespread system of existing retail parks, in which suitable space may be available to rent premises on a lease typically of 15 years. However, rents have risen sharply in recent years, reflecting the influence of retail planning policies in restricting new development. Cheaper premises, for example older free-standing retail warehouses, may be available in less accessible locations. Outside the United Kingdom, in western Europe, the market for such premises is less well organised and restrictive planning policies virtually rule out the new development of large, single-level stores in off-centre locations. For these and other reasons multinational retailers such as Wal-Mart, Ahold and Carrefour have been obliged to expand through takeovers and mergers rather than through developing new stores (Guy 2001). Increasingly such companies are recycling older large stores or shopping centres built on the edge of town in the 1960s and 1970s, when planning control was less strict.

Self-assessment Question 3 *Examine the options for expanding a store network for any major retailer operating at present in the United Kingdom, using a similar method to that in Box 7.3. You should select a retailer that makes its requirements clear through its website or through statements or advertisements in the trade press.*

How easily can a retailer develop new stores?

If the property development process – which tends to be conservative in nature – does not produce the premises an expanding retailer needs then the retailer may consider development itself. This requires availability of funds and some expertise in the property business. In western Europe the largest food retail companies have generally developed their own stores (see discussion above).

However, progress through the development of new stores is very much dependent on the type of stores required and the attitude of land use planning authorities. In several countries development of hypermarkets has been hampered in recent years by the imposition of controls (or even outright bans) by central government (Guy 1998a). This has resulted in changes in direction rather than a complete halt to new building. In the United Kingdom, for example, food retailers have tended to build smaller stores than previously, closer to town centres and in line with government policy (Wrigley 1998). They have also increasingly developed new space through enlarging existing stores, a process that attracts less hostility from planning authorities.

It has also been argued that a shortage in the supply of suitable premises can inhibit the early stages of growth in innovative retailing. In general terms it is noticeable that many innovations in store layout and merchandising methods originated in the United States, where retail premises can be developed easily and cheaply in the absence of strategic retail planning. In Europe the hypermarket took root in the 1960s, at a time when there was no legislation aimed at halting its growth. On the other hand countries such as Italy and Germany (where retail planning regulations are strict), have been widely criticised for their lack of innovation and preponderance of old-fashioned, small shops.

How easily can existing outlets be expanded or repositioned?

A physical expansion of an existing retail outlet counts legally as 'development' in the United Kingdom, and would require planning approval. In recent years government advice to local planning authorities has been that proposals for extensions, particularly to large food stores, should be assessed in the same way as would an application for a new store on that site. This means that extensions to stores that are outside existing town or district centres may be turned down by planners on grounds of policy. However, anecdotal evidence suggests that planning permission for store extensions is easier to obtain than is often the case for new stores.

Internal remerchandising or rearrangement of a store is not usually subject to planning approval in the United Kingdom. Exceptions occur where there are conditions attached to the original permission, such as control over the nature of the goods sold, or a limitation on the sales area within the building. These have been particularly common in the case of retail warehouses and have prevented many from changing their merchandise mix and selling 'high street' goods such as clothing and footwear (Guy 1998b).

How easily can existing outlets be closed?

There is no planning control over the closure of premises as such. However, closure programmes can involve serious implications for a company's property holdings and may be difficult to achieve in full over a short time period. Problems can include the following:

- difficulties in assigning rented properties, which involves finding new tenants who are willing to pay existing levels of rent and who meet the approval of the landlord;
- attempting to dispose of several large freehold or long leasehold properties all at the same time, in a sluggish property market;
- discrepancies between the valuation of properties being disposed of and the 'book values' of such properties as shown in company balance sheets;
- the need to obtain planning permission for a 'change of use', for example to business services or residential.

These problems have in some cases led to loss of share value or partial reversal of the original closure programme (Guy 1997; 1999).

Summary

This chapter has given an introduction to the complex topic of retail development. It has explained the ways in which new development is initiated, financed and given planning consent. It is clear that the requirements of both financial sources and government agencies have substantial impacts on rates of development as well as the location and other characteristics of new retailing. The discussion of types of planned retail development shows that a few of these types, such as hypermarkets and enclosed shopping malls, are common throughout most of the developed world; others, such as retail parks and regional shopping centres, are significant in only a few countries. The reasons for this tend to lie in variations in planning control systems rather than in developers' preferences.

These questions are important for retailers, particularly at crucial strategic junctures. Decisions on where and when to expand regionally or internationally, to reposition existing outlets or to downsize and operate through selective closures are partly dependent on the location and characteristics of retail premises and the institutional framework (both private and public) through which these properties are regulated. For example, cross-boundary expansion may take place either through building new outlets or through a takeover of another retail company. The decision will reflect (amongst other things) the amount of difficulty involved in developing new premises.

Property development and planning issues have been given relatively little attention in publications on retail strategy. It is hoped that this brief outline has indicated the importance of these topics.

Further readings

Fernie, J. (1995) 'The coming of the fourth wave: new forms of retail out-of-town development', *International Journal of Retail and Distribution Management*, 23(1): 4–11.

Guy, C.M. (1994a) *The Retail Development Process*, London: Routledge.

Guy, C.M. (2001) 'Internationalisation of large-format retailers and leisure providers in Western Europe: planning and property impacts', *International Journal of Retail and Distribution Management*, 29: 451–61.

Guy, C. and Lord, D. (1993) 'Transformation and the city centre' in R. Bromley and C. Thomas (eds), *Retail Change*, London: UCL Press.

Reynolds, J. (1993) 'The proliferation of the planned shopping centre', in: R. Bromley and C. Thomas (eds), *Retail Change: Contemporary issues*, London: UCL Press.

In addition you may find the following journals of interest:

- *Architects Journal;*
- *Estates Gazette;*
- *Planning;*
- *Retail Attraction;*
- *Retail Week.*

CHAPTER 8

The impact of retail planning on city centre development

Alan Hallsworth

Introduction

What does one have to fear from an out of town retail development? If a new development is large, relative to the existing nearby competition, and is seen by the shopping public as offering at least comparable (but inevitably newer) opportunities, then some effect on existing rivals can be anticipated. This in turn can increase customer choice, force down prices, promote innovation and prevent abuse by holders of monopolistic or oligopolistic power. What however if the type of retailer that appears is unfair or inappropriate and which, by its size and power, actually removes competitors from a marketplace?

The aim of this case study is to consider the impact that retail planning can have on city and town centre retailing. In the previous chapter we considered the *processes* behind retail development. In this chapter we consider the *implications* that stem from out-of-town and edge-of-town retail developments. The case first provides an overview of planning developments in the 1980s and early 1990s, as these times have been seen as one of the most significant periods for retail planning. Comparisons are provided with the United States and Canada and you will be asked to consider the implications for the consumer, the retailer and the town centre should approval be given for further edge and out-of-town retail developments in the future.

Background

Fears about the devastating effect that competition from major new shopping developments would have first surfaced in Britain in the early 1960s. A large, free-standing, car-based shopping mall or regional shopping centre (RSC) was proposed to be built near the Haydock Park racecourse on the main Manchester to Liverpool road and close by the M6 motorway. Academics in Town and Country Planning at Manchester University adapted some US market impact models and broadly predicted that the major centres of Manchester and Liverpool would be largely unaffected by such a development. However, mid-sized towns near to Haydock would lose trade.

These findings were enough to persuade British planning authorities not to proceed and many professionals and academics began to look more closely at the US experience. The timing was interesting, as the late 1960s were badly affected by urban riots in the United States and scenes of apparently derelict city centres were widely broadcast. Places such as Detroit were shown to have lost their flagship city centre department stores as spending power had decamped to largely untroubled and affluent suburbs. As the United States rapidly suburbanised (Canada did so more slowly) the wealthier populations commuted furthest and new shopping opportunities built up around these new suburban communities. With totally new communities set up, attractive shopping centres were provided. In many instances land for retail development was both inexpensive and freely available. These new forms of retail provision provided little incentive to commute back to the older city centre central business district (CBD) for shopping.

In the United Kingdom, large numbers of the working population looked to live outside of the city. This outflow of persons to small towns and villages placed pressure on the existing infrastructure and frequently engulfed the existing retail centres. This often led to an expansion of the pre-existing shopping provision rather than a totally new development being provided. As such, the competitive environment was slightly different from that of North America. Trends in retail competition are covered in depth elsewhere in this book so suffice it to say that, for the most part, UK high street retailing did not face the same scale of competition as that across the Atlantic. The UK high street (comparable, in reality, to an old-style North American CBD) had one further characteristic we need to note. Conformity, uniformity – some say boredom – born of a highly concentrated retail market dominated by powerful retail multiples. Boots the Chemist has long been regarded as the pinnacle of this – any centre worthy of note would have had a Boots. For many years the test of a major retail centre was: does it have a Marks & Spencer? Inevitably the planning researchers looking at Haydock (and this is nearly 40 years ago) counted the number and type of different retailers to find out how important a shopping centre could become.

In a parallel to what was happening out of town, UK planners were also undertaking a strategy of in-city retail development. Copying developments in the United States, these mall-style shopping centres were often placed at the heart of a city's retail offer. In a number of instances their creation led to the removal of existing retail provision and the construction of a wholly new, purpose-built offer within the city centre. Whilst there was some difficulty finding suitable sites the advantage of this form of development was that planning permission was easier to gain than for out-of-town centres. Despite these in-city malls being criticised for being ugly and incongruous their development was permitted as they reinforced rather than destabilised the familiar UK pattern of city centre retailing.

The new liberalism

After Haydock, out-of-town retail development was limited. The first major US-style RSC was at Brent Cross in North London. It took many years to develop and was not really out of town. (Incidentally, the staff filled up all the spaces on day one so a parking rethink was called for.) It was the election of Margaret Thatcher as prime minister in 1979 that signalled a change to existing planning legislation. Though elected as leader of the party of establishment and tradition she personally was a free market liberal and surrounded herself with like-minded followers. Developers sensed that new opportunities might emerge as old restrictions were torn up. Indeed there was a skyrocketing of applications for RSCs – prompted by liberalising statements from ministers. A classic example of the latter was the insistence of Nicholas Ridley (then the United Kingdom's most powerful planning figure as Secretary of State for the Environment) that it was beyond his power to control market forces. In a sense this statement was the undoing of the liberalisers as so many proposals came forward that it was clear they could not all be profitably developed. Major cities were soon surrounded by applications for mall after mall – akin to a medieval siege.

For example, Greater Manchester came to find itself with nine notable out-of-town proposals that were eventually considered together (Greater Manchester City Council and Roger Tym & Partners 1986). After a suitably long delay the one at Dumplington (now open as the Trafford Centre) was seen as the preferred proposal – subject to some traffic access requirements. The *Financial Times* summarised the issues well:

> Its supporters in one corner were the developers who claimed the £200m scheme would bolster Manchester's regeneration and its attempts to attract the Olympic Games, the retailers who argued it would be a magnet for shoppers throughout the Northwest and the politicians who believed it would generate 3,000 construction jobs and 6,000 permanent jobs thereafter. In the other corner were its critics; the property owners, retailers and local councillors who claimed that 1 million sq ft of new shops on the outskirts of Manchester would further damage business in the city (12 March 1993: 14).

Planning and development in the early 1980s evolved in two ways. The first and more predictable approach was that the planning system prepared to view proposals in batches. This delayed decisions and inevitably deterred some of the less feasible proposals. Others stuck with it, recognising the potential profits to be made. For most the wait was not worthwhile. The second way forward was, in effect, an unintended consequence of policies made elsewhere. The UK Budget of March 1980 – by the then Chancellor of the Exchequer, Sir Geoffrey Howe – created Enterprise Zones (EZ) 'free of planning red tape'. These were alleged to be a development of an idea from the United States.

The attractions of EZ status were considerable. The 1980 statement offered 100 per cent capital allowances, complete relief from development land tax, 100 per cent derating of industrial and commercial property and other incentives. In what some saw as an unfortunate compromise planning rules were cut. Possibly this was a reaction to the government's poor opinion poll ratings and a recession dominated by job losses in the industrial North. Inevitably, few sunrise industries wanted to locate on derelict factory land beyond the south-east of England – but there were those who could see a way to fill that space. They were encouraged in their activities by generous grants to reclaim land and put in an infrastructure. The plans that came to pass were for regional shopping centres and they succeeded largely because the planning battles that were holding up others did not apply to them.

The first and best known of those to push against the open door of Enterprise Zone profits was John Hall (later Sir John), a Newcastle-based developer. In 1984 he turned the site of the old Dunston power station in Gateshead into the Gateshead Metro Centre – at 2 million sq ft a truly out-of-town regional shopping centre. The Metro Centre proceeded in the absence of any evidence that the local area needed 2 million square feet or so of additional shopping space. This fact made little difference to retailers with interests in profit maximisation – the Metro Centre was the 'better retail mousetrap' that entrepreneurs always seek. Helpfully, a £3 million road interchange was constructed with 75 per cent funding from an urban development grant to make the Metro site accessible to potential customers. Tyne and Wear council was estimated to have invested £2 million in the road infrastructure in the area, ensuring that Metro Centre's private enterprise dream was well underpinned by public finance.

The issue of new national policy guidelines known in England and Wales as PPG6 in the mid/late 1980s formally sanctioned this more liberal approach to out-of-town retail development.

Post liberalism

The early 1990s saw a volte-face on the part of the incumbent government. First, new policy guidelines for England and Wales – a revised PPG6 published in July 1993 – noted the important contribution retail activity can make to securing the vitality and viability of town centres. It also stressed the importance of a 'suitable balance in providing for retail development between new town centre and out-of-centre retail facilities'.

Jones and Hillier (2000) note that this marked the beginning of a much more restrictive approach to out-of-town retail development. For example, in 1994 a planning policy guidance note, PPG13, was issued focusing upon the interrelationships between transport and land use (Department of the Environment 1993). It sought to encourage alternative means of transport that have less of an environmental impact. In so doing it was hoped to limit the number of motorised journeys and the reliance placed upon the private car as a mode of travel.

This mood was reflected in Parliament and from late 1993 onwards a number of ministerial speeches stressed the government's growing preference for new retail investment in town centre locations. A number of local authorities also held similar views, for example, in their examination of Cardiff, Guy and Lord (1993: 103) note:

> The City Council and County Council have consistently been opposed to the development of retailing outside the City centre. They have used their powers under . . . various . . . Acts to refuse permission for such development . . . there is no doubt that the Councils' attitudes have encouraged development in the City Centre.

The *Financial Times* added to the growing unease about large-scale out-of-town developments. They maintained that whilst earlier, successful RSC proposals such as the Metro Centre at Gateshead established themselves in the 1980s shopping boom, later proposals were coming at a time when: 'The harsher economic climate, and the

gradual expiry of leases in town centres may further encourage the retailer's deser-
tion of the High Street' (12 March 1993: 14).

In June 1996 a new version of PPG6 was published. The notion of achieving a
'suitable balance' between town centre and out-of-centre retailing was dropped in
favour of a new 'sequential approach' to site selection. This attempted to create a
process whereby local planning authorities and developers were encouraged to
look first for available sites or buildings in the town or city centre. Should suitable
sites be unavailable then edge-of-centre sites should be considered. Only as a final
option should out-of-town sites that are accessible by a choice of means of transport be considered (Jones and Hillier 2000). This tightening of the guidelines
reflected a number of governmental concerns. First, that the growth of out-of-town
developments was leading to a retail exodus from the high street, thus prompting
shop closures and the creation of retail deserts. Moreover the government was sensitive to the environmental lobby and the damaging effects that a growing volume
of motor car-based out-of-town shopping visits could have on the environment.

In May 1997 the Conservatives were defeated and a new Labour government
was elected. It reaffirmed the objectives of the 1996 policy guidance and stressed
its commitment to ensuring that city, town and district centres continued to act
as a focus for retail, office and leisure investment. Jones and Hillier (2000) note
that since this time government thinking on out-of-town development seems to
have hardened further. Commissioned research projects have pointed to the
adverse impact that large out-of-town food superstores have had on the quality of
the city centre environment. In November 1998 Richard Caborn, then minister for
the regions, was quoted as saying that the 'policy of putting town centres first is
here to stay' and insisted that the government was 'not trying to strike a balance
between town centres and out-of-town shopping'.

The popularity and impact of the larger centres

What the above chronological overview provides is an illustration of the popularity of a particular form of retailing. The obvious question that arises is why have
out-of-town and edge-of-town developments become so popular. A number of
explanations have been put forward. First, one could argue that such developments are a response to consumer change. Many persons find themselves cash rich
but time poor. With the increasing number of dual-income families and the
lengthening of the working day the concept of a one-stop shopping environment
has popular appeal. This is especially true if such developments are located on
travel to work routes. Secondly, the process of urban decentralisation has been a
feature of many towns and cities. As individuals have moved out of the centre and
into the suburbs out-of-town and edge-of-town retailing have become increasingly
popular. Moreover the massive increase in car ownership that has occurred has
improved the accessibility of consumers to this form of retailing.

Research from North America has also helped shed some light on the popularity of the out-of-town development. A nationwide US Gallup telephone survey of
1,000 adults indicated that almost one-third (31 per cent) of respondents viewed
shopping at a shopping centre as 'a recreational pastime'. A further 10 per cent

described it as 'partly a necessity' but also as 'partly leisure' (Jackson 1991). A regional or out-of-town mall would therefore seem to serve as a form of leisure activity. Individuals are therefore free to shop in safe, controlled and relatively pleasant surroundings.

Planners have also pointed to the economic benefits an out-of-town development such as an RSC can have. In addition to the number of people that it employs, a large-scale development can become a tourist attraction in its own right. Drawing on the example of the West Edmonton mall in Canada, researchers interviewed 2,500 visitors to the centre. They discovered that just under 50 per cent were from outside Alberta. At the same time, estimates were given that the mall was attracting between 35,000 and 39,000 visitors daily. This allowed the developers to suggest that approximately 3 million people were coming to Edmonton each year specifically because of the mall. It was later estimated that the mall attracted 9 million 'tourist' visits (from outside a 100-mile radius) per annum.

From a customer perspective out-of-town developments can have a positive influence. Shoppers are exposed to a brand new set of retail opportunities that are often superior to anything previously offered. In addition, the development may positively stimulate existing retailers and developers to spend money refurbishing their centres in order to remain competitive. For example, the Brent Cross shopping centre occupied an almost monopolistic position in London and as a consequence did not bother to refurbish until years after a comparable North American mall would have done. Consumers therefore benefit from the 'sharpening up' effect that competition brings.

It would of course be very misleading to view out-of-town developments as having only positive effects. Many different parties view such developments as having a series of negative impacts. Established retailers find their traditional markets undercut and are forced to close. Smaller, weaker centres are often unable to compete as the bigger retailers move out. As a consequence the area is often left with little or no retail provision. Those consumers who remain (typically the elderly or the immobile) find themselves more disadvantaged than before. Certainly new malls in remote locations dominantly appeal to the younger, more mobile and more affluent shopper.

We have already suggested that the issue is never straightforward and much depends on the robustness of rivals and on how change is measured. For example, both Newcastle and Birmingham are close to regional shopping centres. Both are large and robust centres in which a very great deal of retail investment has been made, as a consequence neither city could afford to see a collapse in its retail offer. In reality neither seems to have slipped much down the urban hierarchy as measured, for example, by the number of multiple retailers present. However, centres that were both smaller and closer to the new malls fared less well – Gateshead and Dudley are prime examples. The Gateshead situation was well covered in the 1980s by a series of reports from the Oxford Institute for Retail Management, which illustrated how much more robust Newcastle was than Gateshead and other smaller local centres. Newcastle, with its major Eldon Square mall, was well connected to the public transport system (and with refurbishment to assist a fightback) and had the location and the power to remain competitive. Smaller towns unfortunately did not.

A problem in assessing any change in retail trading patterns is the ability to isolate one influence from the range of factors that can impact upon competitiveness.

For example, in research undertaken by Roger Tym & Partners, many multiple stores near Merry Hill and Dudley reported that trade had fallen and that they believed this was due to the nearby RSC development. However, at this time there was an ongoing general shift of trade in the West Midlands away from smaller, weaker centres. Conversely, the huge revenues generated by such centres do not appear out of thin air – even in a prolonged economic upturn. Research on Merry Hill by Lowe (1991) outlined the way it had developed in phases – the first three dominated by retail shed developments. She noted that several multiple chains had deserted centres such as Dudley and taken space in the new mall. Indeed examples have arisen of retailers that do not favour out-of-town malls neverthe-less taking space in them – the argument being that if they do not they will lose trade to those who do. Whilst wisely accepting that ongoing store rationalisa-tions always mean that retailers regularly move into and out of centres, Lowe (1991) maintained that there were changes that 'exactly mirrored' a move into Merry Hill. For example, she noted that Marks & Spencer closed outlets in both Dudley and West Bromwich just weeks before a large Merry Hill store was opened.

The proposal

You work in the planning department of a large city council. Preliminary discus-sions have just begun with a major property development company specialising in the development of regional shopping centres. Details of the proposal are cur-rently quite vague as talks have been confidential and held between the most senior planning officials and the CEO of the property development company.

Inexplicably one local newspaper (citing an unattributable source) has managed to find details on a proposed development on the outskirts of the city. On its front page it notes that:

> The mall will be open by 2005 and is estimated to cost £900 million. It will have 4 department stores and 326 other stores and 27 entrances. It will have a 'Fantasyland' leisure element costing £120 million and will include an indoor roller coaster, fun fair and ice rink. The shopping concourse will be on two levels – a mile long . . . In addition, there will be a hotel, a bowling alley and a series of food courts and restaurants . . . Over 3.5 million tourists will be expected to visit the mall each year offering a welcome boost for the regional economy.

Within hours of hitting the news-stands the story has created considerable media attention. The press and public relations office at the council offices where you work has been inundated with calls asking whether the report is true or not. Some established retailers have phoned in asking about the accuracy of the report and the implications such a development would have for the central area of the city.

Of more immediate concern have been the phone calls from a number of elected council officials to your office asking about the report. Given that any such development would require their consent, they are naturally aggrieved they knew nothing about any such proposal. From your perspective it is unclear whether the news story is in any way related to the discussions that have taken place with the property company.

The director of planning comes into the office having been in discussions with the press and public relations office. He tells the department that a statement was due to be published by the council noting that no proposal for the development of a regional shopping centre had been received. Whilst this may temper the media interest it will not placate a number of council officials who feel they should be better informed of any such proposed developments.

The director comes across to your desk with the following task.

The task

Provide a briefing document for councillors that highlights the advantages and disadvantages of developing a regional shopping centre. In particular you should comment on the perceived attractiveness of such centres (from the consumers', suppliers' and retailers' perspective) and what are the potential dangers of having such a large-scale retail development on the outskirts of a city. You will be required to provide evidence from other such developments in order to substantiate your discussion. The views and experience of central government must naturally be taken into account when developing the brief.

CHAPTER 9

Revitalising the town centre: The example of Achmore

Andrew Paddison

Introduction

Town centres within the United Kingdom have undergone significant transition over the past three decades. The growth of edge-of-town and out-of-town retail parks has led to a change in shopping behaviour, with customers preferring the convenience and ease of access such locations provide. As a result many town centres have seen their volume of trade decline significantly. This case study examines how one town centre has sought to respond to the challenge of declining customer numbers and falling retail sales. Whilst the name of the town has been changed the activities and initiatives described are drawn from an actual case.

Background

Considerable debate still surrounds the best means of reacting to the issues that have arisen from the UK's town centres having undergone a significant (most often negative) transition. This is partly due to the wide and sometimes competing number of bodies involved with the town centre. For example, interested parties include retailers, property developers, investors and leisure operators; users include shoppers, visitors and residents; whilst intermediaries include local authority departments, community groups, local civic societies and town centre managers/management.

Bringing these multiple and disparate producer/user groups together is the challenge of various intermediaries within the town centre. These organisations are tasked with improving the functionality and aesthetic appeal of the town centre, so creating a greater incentive for the various target groups to use it. Accompanying this has been the recognition that many towns are in competition with one another (Page and Hardyman 1996); whilst, in addition, many locations have adopted marketing principles to sell themselves (Gold and Ward 1994). Consequently there is a greater rationale for different organisations to manage and develop the town centre 'product'. It is in this context that the role of town centre management (TCM), as a coordinated response, is of relevance.

Achmore: town and environment

Achmore is a medium-sized, free-standing market town. However it is only a relatively short travelling distance (approximately 40 minutes) from one of Scotland's largest cities. In addition transport links (by road and rail) are efficient and allow rapid movement to and from the town. This has had both positive and negative implications. It was advantageous to local traders, since the population in the hinterland of small villages and farms was able to access the town easily. However, the proximate location to the large city has also resulted in a loss of customer patronage. During the 1980s and early 1990s this city had capitalised and built on its existing strengths as a pre-eminent retail and service centre. Within its central business district a number of enclosed shopping centres had been constructed and the traditional shopping thoroughfares had been modernised. In addition the supporting infrastructure (such as car parks) had been enlarged and enhanced. In sum, it had become more attractive as a retailing destination and was able to attract visitors from adjoining districts such as Achmore.

Macro- and micro-level trends

By the early 1990s the local authority – Achmore Unitary Authority (AUA) – had recognised the negative repercussions of these customer shifts and correspondingly lower patronage levels. For Achmore's town centre the effects were particularly serious in that an increasing number of retailers were classified as having a destination rather than a proximity offer (higher value items bought infrequently, rather than low ticket convenience goods bought regularly). At the same time both survey and anecdotal evidence revealed that the bulk of customer leakage to larger centres was amongst destination shoppers. As a result Achmore was losing this valuable customer segment to competitor locations.

Whilst such macro-level changes, occurring at a regional scale, were undoubtedly important, a series of emergent threats and challenges were also arising at the micro-level. Since 1988 a number of retail parks had been built on the outskirts of Achmore. At first these locations contained only food retailers, but they had had an immediate impact upon the town centre. A number of the new tenants in the park had been drawn from the town centre and had vacated their smaller premises so as to capitalise on the new locations that afforded ample car parking space and greater flexibility. Those food retailers that vacated their premises created a gap in the town centre, which was filled by a number of independents and established multiples. Common to the vast majority of these new town centre tenants was their focus upon destination retailing. This was seen at the time as an opportunity to differentiate and distinguish the edge-of-town retail parks from the town centre. In essence both locations were positioned in different but complementary spheres of retailing. After this formative period, though, the retail mix of the retail parks started to diversify. Non-food retailers became more prevalent; in particular, electrical retailers and DIY stores began to establish themselves in these newly emerging parks. Some of these retailers had moved from the town centre, whilst others were totally new entrants. Regardless of their previous history the evolving tenant mix of retail parks presented a serious threat to the town centre.

In addition to these external pressures there were internal town centre issues to contend with. During the 1980s the level of investment in Achmore had failed to remain in line with that of other town centres. Consequently the overall level of environmental amenity had declined appreciably. This had manifested itself in numerous ways. Consumer surveys had revealed that the lack of car parking provision, relative to typical demand patterns, was a key constraint; in particular the town centre had a much smaller capacity than the retail parks. In addition only two minor side streets were pedestrianised, whilst the main shopping thoroughfare still had unrestricted vehicular access. Local shoppers cited this as a feature dissuading them from shopping due to the congestion and noise pollution. Compounding this were perceptual issues which needed to be addressed, in particular that Achmore was perceived to be an unsafe place at night. The town had also acquired a somewhat unfavourable image within the wider region. Issues that were frequently cited included the prevalence of litter, discarded chewing gum which marked the streets and an increasing number of vacant premises that were prone to vandalism. Some of these perceptions may have been unfounded. In the short term, though, these issues (whether they be perceived or real) necessitated action.

Achmore clearly had to contend with a number of external issues, the net result of which was to draw existing custom away. Exacerbating this was the realisation that, internally, the core 'product' (that is the retail offer) was now of a poorer quality, thus offering customers reduced utility and benefit. It was in such a context that TCM was recognised as a potential panacea which could provide a response and possible solution to these newly emergent threats. Traditionally Achmore had performed an important role as a market town and associated service centre for the surrounding area. Therefore a prosperous and vibrant town centre was of importance to the wider region, rather than simply the immediate environs. In essence there was a heightened appreciation of the economic development role that Achmore town centre played.

Leadership within the town centre

Immediately prior to the establishment of TCM there was no individual or entity entrusted with a remit to improve, develop and enhance the town centre 'product'. At this time there was a degree of scepticism from a number of key players in the public and private sectors. Individuals within the public sector viewed TCM as a threat that could usurp their position. Rather than exercising a degree of willingness to work with this new structural arrangement they viewed it as a threat, which could take responsibility for some of their existing functions. At the other end of the spectrum a small number of vocal and influential players amongst the local retail community were unsure as to its value. This uncertainty centred on the contention that TCM would be yet another mechanism of public sector intervention that would lack the resources, or clout, to effect real change. Proper and genuine consultation with this diverse range of stakeholders was, therefore, essential when selling the concept.

A board of directors was constituted with the responsibility of recruiting a town centre manager and the preparation of a three-year business plan for Achmore. This plan was divided into two sections: first, an overall mission statement that defined the key parameters and basic purpose and secondly, a more detailed action plan which articulated specific objectives into various categories – commercial performance and development, communication and marketing. These categories were then used as a framework when operationalising and implementing the various tactical measures.

Achmore TCM scheme: the first three years

As outlined in the original business plan, 'commercial performance and infra-structural development' was a key objective. There were a number of elements to this. In the first few years of TCM operation a key issue to resolve was whether the pedestrianised zone should be extended so as to incorporate the main shopping street. As indicated earlier, the relatively small number of pedestrianised streets in Achmore, together with the concentration on side streets, was perceived as a weakness. Consequently the newly appointed town centre manager identified this particular issue as a priority concern. At the outset, the decision to construct new pedestrianised zones or continue with the existing vehicular access had to be considered. Shoppers had to be able to access the town centre easily, although increased accessibility (in the form of continued vehicular access) could further undermine and erode the town's amenity and attractiveness.

Conflicting arguments that advocated a larger pedestrianised area or, alternatively, the status quo created a problematic situation for the town centre manager. In reaching a decision, though, he was able to harness and take advantage of the growing consensus amongst the stakeholders regarding vehicular numbers. This was that greater vehicle numbers would not be conducive to ensuring a safe and pleasant town centre. Adopting a polarised stance that could limit vehicular access, to the extent of damaging the commercial basis of the town centre, was also recognised as inappropriate. Consequently pedestrianised zones and associated car parking had to be designed as integral components of a traffic management strategy.

Sceptics contended that the new pedestrianised zones would create new 'no-go' areas in the evening, after the vast majority of shops and businesses had closed. This centred on the contention that there would be large areas of the town centre with neither traffic flow nor large numbers of pedestrians and this could create a forbidding and unwelcoming environment. When countering these assertions the town centre manager was able to point to preliminary evidence from close circuit television (CCTV) footage and accompanying police statistics. CCTV had been installed in the period immediately prior to the town centre manager being appointed. In terms of absolute numbers the occurrence of recorded incidents had declined appreciably – in both pedestrianised and non-pedestrianised zones. Anecdotal evidence, as well as data from research that had been conducted, pointed to the overall perception of security being more positive. In effect CCTV had largely neutralised and reversed the negative perceptions that the town centre had acquired. Using this evidence the town centre manager was able to argue conclusively that further pedestrianisation was both appropriate and warranted. At this stage he also utilised externally produced evidence (Dickins and Ford 1996) which noted that the proportion of main streets closed to traffic had increased from 5 per cent to 40 per cent since 1970.

Once the decision had been made to pedestrianise the high street and link it with the side streets, construction could commence. Inevitably, in the short term, the local traders suffered an element of disruption. In order to ameliorate the impact and any corresponding ill feeling, the town centre manager ensured that there was regular communication between himself and key traders so that any immediate issues could be raised and resolved quickly rather than becoming exacerbated. In the initial stage the question of deliveries to retail premises was cited as a problem. Since regular access was restricted, delivery drivers were constrained as to when they could discharge their loads. Through consultation with the relevant department in AUA the town centre manager was able to devise a solution: accompanying the extensive streetscape enhancements on the high street were a series of improvements to the access lanes to the rear of the retail premises.

Achieving a coordinated traffic management strategy necessitated that car parking was considered. In an earlier consultative stage, retailers had expressed legitimate concerns over the loss of car parking spaces adjacent to their premises. Representatives of the local traders' association surmised that many consumers could be dissuaded from patronising the high street retailers. Following discussions between the town centre manager and the traders association it emerged that ensuring a sufficient supply of car parking bays was paramount. During the period of conversion to a pedestrianised zone the existing car parking capacity was increased and reconfigured. Existing car parking capacity was modernised, whilst there was an increased orientation towards short-stay car parking spaces; in comparison, the previous system of vehicle charges had been slanted in favour of long-stay users. In order to ameliorate for any loss of on-street parking it was recognised that catering for the short-stay segment of the market was crucial. Essentially, the revised and more extensive car parking provision would help ensure a steadier flow of customers.

Accompanying the strategic efforts made to enhance accessibility were a number of measures aimed at improving the amenity of the town centre. Included within the plans for pedestrianisation were a number of physical features that were intended to give the town centre a greater aesthetic appeal. First, provision for clear signposting and information displays were incorporated into the pedestrianisation plans. Feedback indicated that a number of minor shopping streets were partially obscured and not immediately apparent to users. Signposting, therefore, had a clear rationale in allowing users to be routed through the town. At the same time there was felt to be a lack of general information on the town. In order to compensate for this, a number of information boards were designed. Reflecting the diverse range of producers, together with the differing needs of users, it was envisaged that these displays would include a comprehensive range of retail and non-retail information and would be sited prominently around the town.

TCM funding

Over the course of the first three years, the question of TCM funding and where this was sourced from became increasingly significant. At the outset the bulk of funding was derived from the public sector, in particular from AUA and the local economic development agency – Achmore Regional Development Agency. In total nearly 90 per cent of funding came from these two sources. Funding – which amounted to approximately £120,000 for three years – was spent on salaries for the town centre manager and his assistant, the town centre officer, and on office expenses. Initial funding allocations, however, proved inadequate in the longer term. Envisaged within the original business plan was the need for marketing campaigns directed to a variety of target markets, but to put these proposals into practice required finance on an ongoing basis.

Shortfalls in funding, together with the need to be proactive in marketing, necessitated that additional revenue streams were sought from local traders. In achieving this, though, the town centre manager encountered significant resistance. First, many traders objected to funding the town centre scheme, since they claimed – with some legitimacy – that they were already funding it through their business rates to AUA. Despite the strenuous efforts of the town centre manager only 65 out of 700 traders had contributed financially to TCM by the end of the third year; the exact amount being graduated according to the number of employees. Ironically the low level of contribution created some resentment amongst participative traders. Again with some element of justification, they pointed out that their fellow constituents were able to benefit from marketing campaigns without actually funding them. Continued funding could be jeopardised if the TCM could not demonstrate the additional benefits that were derived from making a financial contribution. Resolving this issue was identified as another key priority, since many activities (for example marketing the town centre and staging events such as the Christmas illuminations) had to be funded from additional revenue streams.

TCM marketing

Outlined within the original business plan was the recognition that a formalised marketing campaign, directed at different audiences through a range of mechanisms, was warranted. Prior to the institution of TCM many people and businesses had negative views of Achmore. Reversing these perceptions was an issue that needed to be addressed. Within the first few months of the town centre manager being appointed a generic campaign that extolled the merits of the town centre was launched, aimed at both internal and external audiences. Internally, the campaign intended to generate greater optimism and morale amongst local users and producers; externally, it was hoped that it might convert and bring new patronage or else reclaim custom that had defected to competing towns.

Morale-boosting campaigns that raised the town centre's profile and visibility were based on the rationale that they would lead, hopefully, to a more favourable perception of the town. In the long term, however, a more targeted series of seasonal and non-seasonal marketing activities needed to be developed. Information guides that detailed, both in a written format and pictorially, the facilities of the town were produced. These were distributed to all households within the town and placed in libraries, community centres and other public buildings. Rather than focus exclusively upon the immediate town, the campaign sought to draw in additional market segments. Public buildings in the surrounding town and villages were seen as appropriate locations to site brochures. Through such an approach Achmore TCM was attempting to stem some of the customer leakage to larger centres.

Seasonal events, such as the street illuminations at Christmas, required a requisite amount of marketing support. Publicity, in the form of favourable editorial coverage, was produced when the lights were switched on. In order to maintain the momentum of public interest, promotional flyers were inserted into the local newspaper, extolling the benefits of Christmas shopping in Achmore, relative to other locations, and highlighting a number of prominent retailers. Achmore's town centre manager was also aware of the need to ensure that there was no mismatch between expectations created during the marketing campaign and the reality experienced when visiting the town. Consequently the frequency of street cleaning patrols was increased in the period prior to Christmas. Justification for this was based on the premise that greater pedestrian flows would create a greater volume of waste, which in turn would undermine user perceptions of the town centre if not attended to. Appreciating the importance of this showed the primacy of integrating the broader strategic direction and vision for the town with the more specific operational tactics.

In addition to marketing campaigns targeted to users, innovative forms of marketing were directed at potential producers. Previous reviews of the town centre had indicated that the number of vacant premises, as a proportion of the total, had increased. Proactive measures that would reduce this figure were, therefore, warranted. Prior to TCM there had been no formal promotional mechanism to inform potential investors of the types of retail property available, so the town centre manager compiled a brochure outlining the complete range of property available. Operationally, this marketing strategy entailed the town centre manager updating the database and corresponding brochure at regular intervals. Strategically, this 'brokering' role encompassed all three of the key objectives – commercial performance, communication and marketing. Effective distribution was achieved through targeting the brochure to retail property companies and the location purchasing departments of retail/leisure chains.

Within a short period the validity of this marketing tactic became evident. Consolidation and contraction within the banking industry had led to several branch offices closing in the town centre. A number of these premises were of a sufficient size and scale to be suitable for conversion to public houses. Following a period of negotiation a large chain of public houses took the lease to one of these vacant premises. Synergy between the mission statement and twin objectives – namely 'commercial performance' and 'marketing' – was achieved, in that this tenant would help to revitalise the evening economy, reduce the level of retail vacancy and contribute to the physical resurgence of the town centre. In short, multiple objectives were fulfilled.

Summary

Towards the end of his initial three-year appointment the town centre manager reviewed the progress made during his tenure relative to the original business plan. When the progress was mapped against the plan he could legitimately claim to have achieved a number of important milestones. Armed with this evidence, the town centre manager and his colleagues were able to secure an additional three years of funding. Securing revenue from the existing public sector beneficiaries, however, was accompanied by a proviso that a number of emergent issues were tackled within the revised business plan. Auditing the progress of the first three years revealed a number of pertinent issues.

First, both internal members and external observers had questioned the current structural arrangements and composition of the board of directors. A consensus emerged that the number of members needed to be increased. Whilst the current members were deemed to have performed competently they were not sufficiently inclusive or encompassing in terms of the stakeholder groups represented.

Secondly, regardless of the structural arrangements in place, funding from the private sector needed to increase as a proportion of the total. Different solutions needed to be put forward.

Thirdly, the intensity and scope of marketing needed to increase. During the first three years it was felt that there had been insufficient dialogue with the local tourist board tasked to promote the town and the wider region. Liaising and engaging with this organisation, so as to synchronise any future marketing campaigns, was important. In addition the need for interaction and consultation with the community – both resident in the town centre and beyond – was acknowledged.

Finally, there was a need to formalise and regularise the system of TCM monitoring and performance evaluation. Evaluating the progress of Achmore's TCM had been rather sporadic and piecemeal in the first few years. After reviewing the experience of other TCM schemes it was recognised that a more systematic process was warranted.

Discussion questions

1. As a supporter and advocate of TCM what key argument(s) would you deploy when selling this concept to sceptics?

2. As a member of the board of directors, what key skills would you be looking for – and why – when preparing the future town centre manager's job specification?

3. What would you understand to be the key roles and responsibilities of a town centre manager?

4. What forms of marketing are most appropriate and for which target groups? Devise an action plan detailing the series of marketing campaigns that you deem appropriate.

5. When devising a formal mechanism of TCM performance evaluation and monitoring, what factors would you consider to be indicative of town centre 'success'?

PART 4

Retail marketing

CHAPTER 10

Retail marketing

Paul Freathy

Aim

The aim of this chapter is to develop your understanding of the marketing concept and its relevance to the retail sector.

Learning objectives

After completing this chapter you will be able to:

■ provide, in your own words, a general concept of marketing;

■ explain the relevance of the marketing concept to business organisations in general, and to retailers in particular;

■ recognise the dominant role of customer values in a marketing-oriented business;

■ describe the business activities that are derived from the implementation of a marketing approach;

■ state the relevance of marketing to retailing.

Introduction

One of the first questions asked on many undergraduate marketing programmes is: 'What is marketing?' At first this may appear to be a relatively easy question to answer (it is not selling!) and certainly there are no shortage of definitions. As you browse through the multitude of learned tomes you may come across authors who state that marketing is any of the following:

- having the right product, in the right place, at the right time;
- the delivery of a standard of living;
- the creation of time, place and possession utilities;

- the activities of buying, selling, transporting and storing goods;
- the establishment of contact;
- a set of human activities directed at facilitating and consummating exchanges;
- the act of selling goods which don't come back to people that do;
- distinguishing the unique function of the business;
- the total approach to running a company and building a business.

Two difficulties, at least, arise from this plethora of definitions: first, is any one the right one? Secondly, apart from the differences in the words and tone, are there any differences in meaning? Rather than becoming entangled in a discussion over which is the right or wrong definition it is perhaps more helpful to understand how and why marketing is important to a retailer. If we are able to understand the contribution that marketing makes to a business, its role and purpose should become clearer. In Chapter 4 we discussed the concept of strategic planning. One element of the retail planning process was the formulation of objectives. In particular, it was stated that such objectives should be quantifiable and allow the business to gauge a measure of its performance over a fixed period of time. If we build on this concept and begin with a very simple view of what leads to business success, we can hypothesise that: 'Business objectives are met through the achievement of customer objectives.'

What this means is quite straightforward. To ensure that a business achieves what it sets out to achieve, it must ensure that the wants, needs and desires of its customers are fulfilled. (After all, happy customers are most often loyal customers.) But many retailers find it extremely difficult continually to meet the needs of their customers. Whilst accepting that it is difficult in practice to consistently meet expectations, this chapter argues that for any retail business this approach is the only one that will lead to a sustained competitive advantage in the marketplace. Figure 10.1 highlights the relationship between customer values and objectives and the mission and business objectives.

For a retail business to survive and achieve the objectives it sets itself, it must generate sales revenue whilst at the same time minimising its costs. The primary means by which a retailer generates income is through the customer. As we know, customers will pay for goods and services that satisfy them and help them to achieve some of their objectives. How a customer perceives the value of a product or service will determine whether they will purchase it and how much they will be willing to pay. The greater the satisfaction with a product or service the more likely it is that sales revenue will be earned. As Drucker (1968: 52–3) pointed out:

> There is only one valid definition of business purpose: to *create a customer* . . . [Drucker's emphasis]. It is the customer who determines what a business is. For it is the customer, and he [*sic*] alone, who through being willing to pay for a good or for a service, converts economic resources into wealth, things into goods. What the business thinks it produces is not of first importance – especially not to the future of the business and to its success. What the customer thinks he is buying, what he considers 'value', is decisive – it determines what a business is, what it produces and whether it will prosper.

As the only source of sales revenue the customer must be a focal point for the design and implementation of business activity. Meeting customers' needs and

Mission
the guiding principles of the business are met through

Business objectives
are met through

Sales revenue
from the sale of the products that deliver

Customer perceived values
and therefore lead to the achievement of

Customer objectives

Figure 10.1   Achieving business goals by meeting customer objectives

satisfying their requirements represents a primary aim for the retailer. It is this emphasis on the role of the customer that is the distinguishing feature of marketing. Customers are central to the concept of marketing and the achievement of business objectives.

Customers, objectives and exchanges

A key element in the marketing literature is the concept of 'exchange'. Businesses generate sales revenue through an exchange process with customers. In simple terms, the retailer has a product or service that is offered in the marketplace; if the customer decides to take up the offer the transaction between the two parties is known as the exchange. Customers are willing to be involved in this exchange process because they have a use for the goods or services that the retailer has on offer. The customer will evaluate the product and on the basis of this evaluation will decide whether or not to purchase the good.

How we purchase, why we purchase and the way in which we purchase has been the focus of significant scientific investigation. One of the earliest approaches to understanding consumer behaviour saw customers as being wholly rational and concerned with maximising the satisfaction they will get from the product in use. 'Economic man' purchases products on the basis of objective, measurable criteria (Bentham 1907). For example, an individual who needed to purchase a number of grocery items would consider carefully the stores that stock the goods against a number of different criteria (such as price, quality and location). On the basis of this evaluation a choice would be made as to the preferred shopping destination.

Whilst we may recognise elements of 'economic man' in the way we shop, our behaviour is actually more complex. For example, take the following statement:

> I tend to frequent a couple of small grocery shops that are not far from where I live. I know I drive past a retail park on the way home from work and could easily stop to buy whatever I need. People tell me that these small shops are more expensive than the supermarkets – as if I didn't know! – but I am perfectly prepared to pay more for individual items. I enjoy discussing life, politics, religion and the world with the shop assistants. At these small shops I get a host of satisfactions that I do not get in a supermarket. I am not rich but I am certainly not economic man.

The above quote describes how many people live their lives today and does not fit with the notion of economic man. When individuals engage in an exchange they are also buying intangibles (perhaps detailed product knowledge, customer service, after-sales advice) as well as the actual product. The process of exchange therefore involves a transfer of psychological, social and other intangible entities. These are sometimes called the symbolic values of the product and represent the reason why we do not always purchase in a rationale, logical and consistent manner. It may be worth outlining briefly the two forms of value attached to each product:

- *Functional values*: this refers to what the product does, that is the function it performs, such as clothing bought to keep you warm and dry (and to stop people laughing at you in the street). The vast majority of goods have at least some element of functionality (for somebody). Whether we own a Skoda or a Porsche, a car has the function of transferring you from location A to location B. In a retail context, some companies base their whole offer on meeting the functional needs of the customer. The low price/no frills offer of companies such as Lidl, Aldi and Netto represent an emphasis on function – namely the availability of goods at low prices.
- *Symbolic values*: this refers to the additional values or meanings that may be attached to a product. These may be designed to reflect our lifestyle, our educational or social ideals or our membership of a group. For example, I could buy a perfectly acceptable work shirt for €25 (a function). However I might also want to represent myself as a discriminating and discerning individual and pay an extra €90 to get a shirt with a little polo player embroidered on it. Similarly, a football shirt can outwardly reflect your loyalty and signify your support for a particular team (e.g. Alloa Athletic). In a retail (as opposed to product) context the same principles apply. For example, the branding strategies employed by companies such as Harrods, Gap and The Body Shop are attempts to develop the retailer as a brand through the creation of strong, symbolic values.

Self-assessment Question 1 *Identify three retailers (one food, one fashion and one other) whose retail offer provides a high level of symbolic value. What are these values? Why do you think people subscribe to them?*

It is clear that we as consumers may chose to shop at a particular location or buy a particular product for reasons other than the utilitarian benefit it provides. If we accept that we are not always rational in our purchasing behaviour and that we sometimes chose products for their symbolic as well as their functional value we can understand Theodore Levy's famous (1959) quote that: *'People buy things not only for what they can do, but also for what they mean'* (Levy's emphasis).

To emphasise this point, Bagozzi (1975: 37) suggests the emergence of a 'marketing man', based on the following assumptions:

- Man [*sic*] is sometimes rational, sometimes irrational.
- He is motivated by tangible as well as intangible rewards, by internal (for example psychological) as well as external (for example economic) forces.
- He engages in utilitarian as well as symbolic exchanges involving psychological and social aspects.
- Although faced with incomplete information, he proceeds the best he can and makes at least rudimentary and sometimes unconscious calculations of the costs and benefits associated with social and economic exchanges.
- Although occasionally striving to maximise his profits, marketing man often settles for less than optimum gains in his exchanges.
- Finally, exchanges do not occur in isolation but are subject to a host of individual and social constraints: legal, ethical, normative (standards), coercive, and the like.

Given that our purchasing behaviour is far from logical and that we do not all follow in the footsteps of economic man, how do businesses better understand their consumers? How do you explain someone purchasing a car with high symbolic value (such as a Mercedes) and yet shopping in a discount supermarket? Why are some people highly sensitive about the price of one product (such as petrol) yet less so with others (such as the price of beer)? What are the factors that stimulate us to buy and do how these factors interact to determine buying decisions? As noted earlier, the study of consumer behaviour has become a broad and complex area of scientific study. At this stage in your study of marketing it is sufficient to recognise that no single factor influences the purchase decision, it is often a combination of the functional, utilitarian value of a good and the symbolic meaning that the individual attaches to the product.

So what is marketing?

So far we have established that marketing is part of the business process. It contributes to an organisation's attempt to achieve its stated objectives by understanding the values of the customer and meeting their needs. How this is done varies considerably, partly because different retail businesses have different views on the role, function and importance of marketing. (Ask a dozen managers how the marketing function operates in their business and expect 12 different replies.) Despite such a diversity of opinion it is generally possible to identify three different (although not mutually exclusive) approaches to marketing. Marketing may be seen as a:

- management process;
- business orientation;
- social philosophy.

The differences between these meanings are not only of academic interest but lead to important differences in the way that marketing is practised within the business. It is therefore helpful to examine these approaches in more detail.

Marketing as a management process: according to the Institute of Marketing, marketing is, 'responsible for identifying, anticipating and satisfying customer's requirements profitably'. The emphasis is on the management of activities commonly associated with marketing as a business function. For example, they include such activities as the following:

- researching customer and competitor characteristics;
- planning marketing strategies;
- developing products, price structures and sales and advertising campaigns.

This represents a good starting point to understand marketing as such a view is clearly concerned with the relationship between the firm's and the customers' objectives. It is somewhat limited however in describing the areas that this relationship should encompass. On the basis of this definition it would appear that only certain activities affect or influence customers. By focusing upon areas such as product development, pricing and promotion the values of the customer will be met. Whilst all these activities are important it can be argued that the firm/customer relationship is also determined by other factors, not just those which come under the responsibility of the marketing department.

Marketing as a business orientation: authors such as Kotler *et al.* (2001) have taken a broader approach to the concept of marketing. For example back in 1984 Kotler saw businesses having to have a: 'customers' needs and wants orientation backed by integrated marketing effort aimed at generating customer satisfaction as the key to satisfying organizational goals' (Kotler 1984: 22).

Kotler's view of marketing is different from the first definition in that it takes a wider perspective. There are of course similarities, for example 'customers' needs and wants' is basic to all marketing and stresses the central role of the customer in business decision making. However the 'integrated marketing effort' makes the point that it is the whole business that determines relationships with customers and not only the close-to-the-customer activities (these activities are discussed later).

The old quote that 'marketing is too important to be left to the marketing department' is appropriate here. There is little point in a retailer undertaking a consumer survey and developing an advertising strategy if the company's buyers have not been able to source the product or the logistics department is unable to deliver to the store on time. In order to ensure the values of the customer are met there is a need for an integrated approach between the different functions of the business.

This more integrated view of marketing broadens the perspective and requires the retailer to consider two questions:

- What is involved in marketing?
- Who is involved in company and customer relationships?

The generation of customer satisfaction still remains the key to satisfying organisational goals. It is achieved however through a total business approach rather than a particular set of 'marketing' activities.

Marketing as a social philosophy: this view of marketing is often a little difficult to comprehend at first. It is derived from the previous two views on marketing and makes explicit what is assumed in the above. In this sense it is not a different view from the previous approaches, rather it represents a further evolution of the marketing concept.

According to Baker (1985: 4) marketing is 'a process of exchange between individuals and/or organisations to the mutual benefit of the parties'. This view takes the process of exchange as its focus and makes the purpose of marketing the maximisation of value from the exchange. For example, the exchange of a product or service for money benefits the customer by satisfying a need and benefits the organisation by contributing to revenue.

This 'philosophical' view of marketing focuses on the concept of exchange and is concerned with an approach to thinking. The emphasis is on the customer and the need to bring the whole organisation round to sharing a customer focus and culture. Marketing is not merely a function of the marketing and related departments, rather it is *a way of thinking by all in the organisation*. It represents a basis for decision making and assumes that all the relationships we enter into are more productive if we recognise the values of those with whom we are dealing.

The three views of marketing described above are not mutually exclusive, rather they are developmental and represent an evolutionary approach to the satisfaction of customer values. As indicated in our discussion, a social philosophy view is the most comprehensive of the three and indicates that marketing is an approach to all exchange relationships that maximises the value from the exchange to all parties involved.

Self-assessment Question 2 *Look back at the definitions of marketing listed at the beginning of this chapter. What do you now understand by the term 'marketing'? How has your view of the marketing concept changed?*

Marketing: concept to practice

From our discussion so far it is evident that there is no one generally acceptable definition of marketing. What is clear, however, is that marketing combines both a philosophy of business and a practical approach. Much of effective marketing practice is pragmatically based and is determined by what Peters and Austin (1985) describe graphically as the 'smell of the customer'. Whilst smelling a customer may not be the most pleasant thought you have ever had (and may be illegal in many countries), in the context of marketing it is an essential element for turning theory into practice.

The smell metaphor demands that retailers obsessively seek advantage through enhanced closeness to the customer. It is only when we are very close to and intimate with something or someone that we can recognise their individual smell and any changes in it. If we, as a business, are to know and react to changing customer perceptions and characteristics we have to be so close we can 'smell' them.

Whilst they may use different terminology, many retailers now recognise the central importance of customers in their strategies and operations. The growing importance of the customer might be indicated by an increasingly extreme phraseology (Figure 10.2).

Amongst all the complexities and variables of the business environment there is at least one certainty – if not enough customers buy your product or service your business will fail. In an increasing number of markets the various competing products offered are functionally the same. This is particularly true in the consumer goods markets. For example, if we wish to purchase a pair of trainers, where do we go? To the local, independent sports shop? To a specialist sports goods retailer? To a supermarket or a hypermarket? To the Internet? Increasingly, advantage over competitors comes: 'not from the spectacular, or the technical, but from a persistent seeking of the mundane edge' (Peters and Austin 1985: 41).

The effectiveness of practical, pragmatic marketing comes from recognising that the mundane edge derives from customer needs, wants and perceived values.

Exchange and value

As the business world is complex, dynamic and uncertain, recognising the 'smell of the customer' is only the starting point in dealing with this world. We have maintained that the concept of exchange is fundamental to the delivery of customer values and ultimately business objectives. In this section we will examine the concept of exchange in more detail.

Exchange

Exchange occurs in all aspects of life, organisational and personal, and the process of exchange can be carried out in a variety of ways. For example, we can coerce

Figure 10.2 Approaches to customer understanding

people into exchanging things with us or in order to make a sale an assistant may mislead or lie to the customer. Such methods can be generalised under the 'I win, you lose' approach, or the less extreme 'I win, you might lose' (see Box 10.1). The difficulty with adopting such an approach to exchange relationships is that they only work in the short term, that is, until the lies are discovered or until the power to coerce is reduced.

In addition to being short term the 'I win, you lose' exchange is also seen as being regressive and inefficient. By definition this approach requires that any gain I make is offset by someone else's loss. No values are added to the total in the exchange. Only one set of values is used and one set of objectives is achieved.

The alternative to the 'I win, you lose' is the 'You win, I win' approach. From what we have already discussed in this chapter it should be clear that marketing is based on this latter approach and is an attempt to increase the total value of the exchange by ensuring that both parties gain. For example, in terms of business, the customer gains from the extra values the product or service provides and the business gains from the immediate and future revenues generated from a satisfied customer.

There is no doubt that the 'You win, I win' approach to exchange is the basis for long-term, mutually satisfying relationships. If you have doubts about this think about your own personal relationships and those that have been long and short term. For the business that requires not only to create but also to keep customers in order to survive and succeed 'You win, I win' is the most effective (and increasingly the only) way of doing this.

You win, I win: the process

The 'You win, I win' approach requires that we do several things that are difficult for many of us:

Box 10.1
'I win, you lose' or 'I lose, you win'?

During the 1990s many passengers complained about the high price of air travel between European cities. In order to qualify for cheaper fares passengers were required to stay a Saturday night at their destination. This led to a situation where it was cheaper to fly from Scotland to the United States via Amsterdam than it was to fly from Scotland to Amsterdam. Businesses in particular felt the pricing policies of the airlines discriminated against them. (People travelling on business do not/cannot spend a Saturday night away every time they travel.) Despite the criticisms and the negative publicity that these fares attracted, airlines continued to charge high prices for relatively short journeys. The power of the airlines was derived in many instances from a lack of competition in the market. However the deregulation of the air transport industry facilitated the development of the low cost carriers and led to a restructuring of the airlines pricing structure. Many passengers felt very little loyalty to the established carriers and therefore opted to use the discount airlines. As a result many airlines have been forced to undertake expensive marketing campaigns in order to entice customers back.

- recognise the importance of others;
- recognise that they might see the world differently from us;
- base our actions on their perceptions of the world.

None of these is easy and, in particular, basing our actions on others' perceptions requires a degree of belief and trust. That is sometimes difficult to achieve, however its achievement comes from a knowledge and understanding of the other party. The first stage in the process of exchange and the first activity of marketing is the development of an understanding of the customer – their characteristics, needs, wants, values and perceptions.

An understanding of the customer provides the retailer with an opportunity to create a set of products and services that the customer will want. If the customer values speed of delivery it should be provided; if the customer values individuality it should be provided; if the customer values personal attention it should be provided. Effective exchange relationships require that we share the values of the other party and that we take actions to create those values for the other party.

However, understanding and creating values is not enough. There seems little point in going to the trouble of understanding and creating customer value if we decide to keep this information to ourselves. For the exchange process to continue both parties must share meaning and that has to be communicated. For example, acting on market research information a retailer decides to stock a range of organic skin care products for men. Specifically aimed at the 22–35 age bracket, these products are designed to fill a current gap in the market. From a business perspective it is not enough to produce the values customers seek, it is also necessary to communicate the presence, availability, nature and desirability of what has been created.

All the effort that has gone into sharing values and meanings must result in an actual exchange – a delivery of values, that is, the physical exchange of products for money must take place (not necessarily at the same time or place). The product will be with the customer and, if the business's marketing is successful, the promised values to the customer will have been delivered.

It now becomes evident why, when we describe the exchange of value, we refer to it as a *process*. We can identify four distinct (but overlapping) stages in the value cycle. In order to deliver customer objectives and ultimately meet its own business objectives the retailer must achieve the following:

- understand its customer's values;
- create an offer that satisfies these values;
- communicate what has been created to the target audience;
- deliver the offer to the customer.

In the following section we will consider each of these stages in a little more depth.

Business–customer exchange process

The basic exchange process is illustrated in Figure 10.3. As you will note the cycle is continuous. This is because customer values are dynamic and in a state of continual change; they therefore need to be monitored, understood and reacted to.

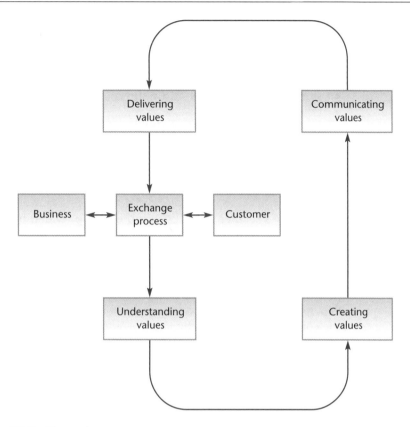

Figure 10.3   The exchange process

Understanding values

In order to create, communicate and deliver the right set of values the retailer must understand the customer. In activity terms this has traditionally been termed 'marketing research' but increasingly it is also linked to the development of 'direct' and 'database' marketing. Here are two typical questions that arise at this stage of the value cycle:

- What techniques can we employ to 'smell' our customers?
- What sources of information are available for understanding customer values?

The traditional starting point for the understanding of value in an organisation has been through its information systems. To get the best use of information many retail organisations establish company-wide systems that electronically integrate the various functional departments as well as their major suppliers. Davidson *et al.* (1988: 591–3) suggested that a retail management information system should comprise three main interconnecting elements:

- store elements, including ordering systems, space allocation, point of sale and energy management;
- corporate elements, including a general ledger system (payroll, cash management and personnel management), merchandise management and promotion;
- distribution centre elements, including order processing, purchase order management, inventory control and buying.

Ideally any user of such a system should be able to access all the available information on, for example, a particular product. It would therefore be possible to track that product by looking at:

- delivery patterns;
- stocks held centrally or at the stores;
- returns;
- orders by store, date or quantity;
- replenishment rates;
- sales against the pattern of promotion;
- sales against space allocated;
- efficient use of labour.

In addition a retailer may also use the data provided by sales and profit ledgers, electronic point of sales systems and personnel records. The idea will be to look at other types of raw data from within the organisation that may not normally be utilised for a particular form of analysis.

In Chapter 4, we discussed the concept of environmental scanning. This is the process that seeks information about events and relationships outside the business. Reports and publications may highlight trends in the industry, provide an overview of the competition or detail the latest technological and product developments. Often known as 'marketing intelligence' it represents a means by which the company's executives are kept informed about the changing conditions in the external environment.

On occasion it may be necessary for a retailer to focus upon a specific set of issues, such as what customers think of a new store layout, or whether a new customer service initiative is working. Market research is the process of generating data around given problems or areas of interest that can then be used in making marketing decisions. Lewison and DeLozier (1986) suggest that the areas where data will be collected:

- consumer attitudes towards the retailer and its merchandising efforts;
- consumer purchase motives and preferences;
- demographic and psychographic profiles of both customers and non-customers;
- buyer behaviour patterns and their relationship to the retailer's mode of operation;
- sales potential and consumer acceptance of product lines;
- advertising and personal selling effectiveness;
- locational attributes of the retailer's outlets;
- consumer service and price perceptions.

In practice the amount of market research undertaken will vary between organisations and according to the problem being addressed. In some cases it will provide the vast majority of the data, in others very little. Some companies may wish to undertake the research themselves, other retailers prefer to have outside bodies such as market research firms and universities conduct the research for them.

One further way in which a retailer may seek to understand the customer is through the use of marketing models. These are concerned essentially with the application of simulation and model-building techniques for marketing planning and control. Computer-based simulations are used to manipulate retailing factors, such as shelf-space allocations or alternative store locations, on paper (or screen) rather than in a real setting. A model of the controllable and uncontrollable factors (and their interactions) facing the retailer is constructed. These factors are then manipulated to determine their effects on the overall retail strategy. Simulations have become more popular for retailers as the level of mathematical and computer sophistication increases.

Creating values

Having attempted to understand the customer, the next stage in the cycle is the creation of value. As the quotation by Levy (1959) illustrated earlier, customer values are not always, or solely, related to the tangible and functional aspects of the product offered (see Box 10.2). Customers have values that relate not only to the product and its function but also to the intangible aspects and meanings of the product and with the services accompanying a product.

The implications of this are significant. Retailers should not think of a product purely as a physical, tangible object. When creating an offer for the consumer, retailers need to broaden the definition to include all the satisfactions and values that the customer gets from an exchange with the business. If we are therefore asked the relatively simple question, 'What is a product?' we may define it in the following terms:

- *Product*: this represents the object to be purchased. Retailers and manufacturers may seek to include a characteristic or component that may be used to distinguish it from competing products of similar quality (Stewart 1959). A product may be differentiated from the competition in a number of ways, for example in terms of quality (fashion), taste (food), speed (computers). Alternatively the product may seek to deliver symbolic values as discussed earlier.
- *System*: in this context refers to those factors that facilitate the exchange and often (but not exclusively) refers to the technological systems within the business. For example, if we take 10 minutes to choose the items we require in a supermarket but it takes us 40 minutes to pay for these items then the system is threatening to undermine the retailer's ability to deliver customer-related values.

Box 10.2
The added value challenge

Imagine for a moment that you intend to buy a brand new sports car. Although you have a couple of different models in mind you have not made a final decision. You have gathered sales literature on each model and read independent reports on the performance of each car. Both cars have received good reports in road tests and they are roughly comparable in price. As a consequence you may be happy to purchase either model. Your decision as to which car to purchase may therefore be based on other criteria. For example, you may have a number of technical questions about the car's performance and it is reasonable to expect that the sales staff are able to answer any questions you may have. You may also wish to purchase the car immediately and not want to wait whilst it is being manufactured. Given that you are making such an expensive purchase you may consider the level of after-sales service to be important. The key point to note here is that the decision to purchase the product is not based purely on the product itself but on other criteria that the consumer considers important.

Similarly, if we arrange to have a product delivered to our home but the retailer is unable to specify an arrival time we may be forced to wait in all day. Because of the inadequacies of this system it is unlikely that our values will be fully met.

Systems should therefore be designed to give customers maximum access to the service with minimum inconvenience. User-friendly systems can deliver customer values whilst non-friendly systems can destroy them.

- *People*: the issue of people will be discussed further when we consider customer service. In many cases the business, the product and the quality of delivery provided to the customer are embodied in the people they come into contact with. If customers expect high levels of product knowledge, good customer service skills and a level of common courtesy then it is at this stage in the value cycle that they are created. Typically training programmes, refresher courses and professional qualifications all contribute to the development of a skilled workforce and, ultimately, the delivery of customer-related values.

Self-assessment Question 3 *Consider the following statement from Levitt (1986: 77) and answer the questions below:*

A product is to the potential buyer, a complex cluster of value satisfactions. The generic 'thing' or 'essence' is not itself the product. It is merely, as in poker, the table stake, the minimum necessary at the outset to allow its producer into the game. But it's only a 'chance', only a right to enter play. Once entry is actually attained, the outcome depends on a great many other things.

What many other things might the business outcome depend on? If the availability of a range of goods at competitive prices is the retail product, what other factors may determine the outcome for the retailer?

Communicating values

Having understood their customers' values and then attempted to create a range of products and services to meet their needs, the next stage for the retailer is to develop a communications strategy that creates a common perception of the business and its products. (There is not much point having a better mousetrap if you keep it a secret.) Communications as a subject area is both wide and diverse. This is because what one communicates, how one communicates and the way in which one communicates is complex and will vary according to the type and needs of the business.

The general aim of marketing communications however is to share meaning with customers in order to facilitate the exchange. To achieve this, a business must first define its communications objectives. (It is a popular misconception that the only reason for communicating with the customer is in order to sell.) For example a retail business may wish to do any or all of the following:

- create awareness;
- stimulate interest;
- assist evaluation;
- trial;
- prompt action.

Such objectives will be stated in the common form of all business-related objectives, that is, they will be quantified and given time scales for achievement. For example, when a new store is being opened in a new location, communications objectives may include the following:

- creating awareness of the store and its shopping benefits amongst 75 per cent of the targeted customer groups within six months of opening;
- stimulating trial visits to the store amongst 55 per cent of the targeted customer groups within six months of opening;
- stimulating revisits amongst 50 per cent of targeted customers within six months of the store opening.

If a retailer meets its communications objectives this helps achieve both the customers' and the business's objectives. To do this however the retailer needs to provide a communications strategy that details the amount to be spent and the proposed methods of communication with the target audience.

One of the largest areas of spending in communications is payment for the means (medium) of transmission, that is deciding on how much you wish to spend on advertising, personal selling, publicity and sales promotion. Each represents an effective means of transmission in any particular situation. It is unlikely that any single one will perform all the communications tasks required, and most communications programmes require a 'mix' of the means. For example, in 2001 Tesco spent over £27 million (€42 million) on advertising in the press, on TV and radio. In addition it sent out 30 million letters to customers, gave away 160 million customer magazines and made 5 million telephone calls (*Retail Week*, 27th September 2002: 16).

Given the financial investment in marketing communications it is important to evaluate the success of any initiative. Fortunately today a range of techniques and systems are available to monitor and provide feedback on the effectiveness of a retailer's communications strategy. This is particularly important for advertising, where a common view is: 'I know that half my advertising money is wasted. The trouble is, I don't know which half.'

Delivering values

When we talk about the delivery of value we are generally referring to one of three things:

- *physical distribution*: getting the right goods in the right place at the right time;
- *channel management*: making sure that all players in the supply chain are working together to ensure the maximisation of customer value;
- *customer service*: when the actual physical exchange of products for money takes place and the promised values to the customer are delivered.

The first two topics are discussed later in the book (Sparks, Chapter 19 and Johansson, Chapter 21). In this section we will concentrate on the issue of customer service. Having gone through the process of understanding, creating and communicating it is often this final stage that fails to deliver customer value. How often have you gone into a store and been disappointed by the service? How often have you come away from a retail outlet feeling that the staff are not interested in helping you? Unfortunately such experiences are all too common in retailing. There is little point in getting the first three stages of the value cycle right if the fourth stage is ignored. When this occurs retailers end up 'over promising and under delivering' and their 'customer's expectations exceed their delivery performance'.

One way of conceptualising customer service is as a series of discrete yet inter-related set of stages operating within the exchange relationship. Sparks (1991) for example divided the delivery process into three phases: the pre-transaction, trans-action and post-transaction stages. As the name suggests, the pre-transaction stage occurs before the actual exchange takes place, and may even take place prior to the customer entering the store. For example, you may wish to phone the store to check if they stock a particular item or if they are open at a particular time. The service you receive will influence your views and perceptions of the company. Did you have to wait a long time before someone answered the phone? Were you then put on hold? Was your query answered satisfactorily? Even before you have entered the store you are developing a view about the company that may or may not reinforce the values you wish to gain from the exchange.

What you experience when doing this is a 'moment of truth'. This term was first used by Jan Carlzon (president of SAS airlines) to describe a customer's experience of the exchange relationship. He described how SAS had 50,000,000 contacts with its customers per year. Each one of these was a 'moment of truth', where the cus-tomer could add a tick or a cross to his or her mental report card. Each time the customer had contact with the business it would influence their future expectations of the product, service and business.

The next stage is the transaction stage and relates to the actual exchange itself. Theoretically, at least, if the value cycle has been adhered to the retailer will already have created an offer that meets the needs of the customer. Staff training programmes should have been conducted to ensure the necessary level of cus-tomer care. Services (that is, systems) such as laser scanning, rapid credit card approval, pre-wrap of best-selling gifts, speed registers, individual product keys on tills and packing at checkouts all speed up the transaction stage and contribute to a consumer's perception of the delivery process.

If a retailer seeks to develop an 'I win, you win' relationship with the customer then the post-transaction stage will remain an important part of the service offer. Typically this stage relates to issues such as product returns and complaint handling procedures. If a retailer is committed to developing a loyal customer base, issues such as customer complaints will be seen as an important feedback mech-anism designed to help improve the quality of the customer service offer. The philosophy to adopt is: if the customer takes the time and effort to complain then we should thank them for their effort and seek to investigate the issue as soon as possible. Unfortunately these views are not universally held. Box 10.3 details a real-life example from the financial services sector.

Box 10.3
Feedback? What feedback?

A few years ago I was teaching a group of financial managers about the importance of marketing. We began to discuss the need to develop customer loyalty and how customer complaints should be handled. There was general agreement that whilst no one liked to receive negative comments they did represent an important source of feedback. One individual who worked for a Chinese bank disagreed. In the sub-sequent discussion he remarked: 'At our bank we do not accept any complaints over the phone or face to face. If one of our customers has a grievance we ask them to put it in writing.' There was some obvious disquiet amongst other mangers to this approach. 'Furthermore,' he added, 'the vast majority of our clients are Chinese speaking; we therefore ask them to submit their complaints in English.' 'Do you get many complaints?' I asked. 'Not many,' he replied.

The delivery of value through the three transaction stages should theoretically become a seamless exercise. The difficulty lies in ensuring that this objective is actually met and consumer values are consistently delivered. Service and delivery breakdowns are unfortunately all too common in retailing. One approach to help-ing to reduce such failures is by conceptualising the delivery of value through Thomas's (1987) interfaces model. Thomas identified that delivery breakdowns occur through an interactive failure between management, staff, the retail system and consumers (Figure 10.4). Within retailing there are six primary interfaces; these are between the following:

- management and the customer;
- staff and the customer;
- management and the staff;
- customer and the system;
- management and the system;
- staff and the system.

Systems in this context are defined as the way in which the product or service is delivered. This represents a wide array of influential factors over which the provider needs to maintain control. The speed with which an order is taken, the queuing time, the provision of order status information and delivery times are all examples of how the system can influence the exchange process. There is a requirement there-fore for staff and management to be both fully conversant with the control systems and to reduce the complexity of the systems over which they have responsibility.

The relationship between staff and management also remains fundamentally important in the delivery of value and highlights the importance of good human resource management. Management needs to develop good working relations with staff as inadequately trained or poorly motivated individuals can undermine the exchange process and lead to poor delivery. Similarly the relationship between cus-tomers, staff and management is fundamental to a continued exchange process. As Figure 10.4 illustrates the model is iterative, not linear and the objective for any retailer is to maintain competitive advantage through the continual delivery of value.

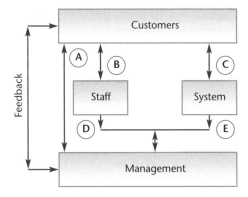

Figure 10.4   The interface model of customer care
Source: Thomas 1987

Summary

In this chapter we have provided a basic understanding of the marketing concept and have described what the adoption of a marketing approach implies for a business. Whilst it remains difficult to define what 'marketing' is, this chapter should have provided you with a framework for explaining the role of marketing in a retail context. Here is a summary of the main themes of the chapter:

- Marketing is concerned with the achievement of business objectives through the delivery of customer-related values and objectives.
- All retail organisations rely on an exchange of values to survive and grow.
- The 'smell of the customer' is the responsibility of everyone in the business and requires an obsession with seeking advantages through enhanced closeness to the customer.
- There is a logic of planned activity that derives from a focus on customer values which can be described in terms of a marketing cycle.
- Retailers, because of their closeness to customers, are directly and immediately affected by changes in the 'smell of the customer'. For retailers a marketing approach is not an alternative but an imperative.

Further reading

Gilbert, D. (2002) *Retail Marketing Management*, 2nd edn, London: FT/Prentice Hall.

McGoldrick, P. (2002) *Retail Marketing*, London: McGraw Hill.

Omar, O. (1999) *Retail Marketing*, London: FT/Prentice Hall.

Piercy, N. (2002) *Market-led Strategic Change*, London: Butterworth Heinemann.

Sullivan, M. and **Adcock, D.** (2002) *Retail Marketing*, London: Thompson Publishing.

You may also find the following journals useful:

- *European Journal of Marketing;*
- *International Journal of Retail and Distribution Management;*
- *Journal of Marketing Management;*
- *Journal of Retailing and Consumer Services;*
- *Marketing Intelligence and Planning;*
- *Service Industries Journal.*

CHAPTER 11

Using information to understand the customer

Eric Calderwood

Introduction

From Chapter 10 we can conclude that retail marketing covers a wide and diverse subject area, from market research to new product development, from advertising to customer service. One of the starting points for a successful retail venture, however, is an understanding of the customer base. Detailed information that informs the decision-making process is increasingly becoming a prerequisite of consistent managerial performance. In this case study we see how a detailed understanding of the consumer can help inform a business at a number of levels. Not only does it assist in evaluating the attractiveness of a potential acquisition (that is, identifying the right location) but it also helps in the development of the merchandise mix.

Background

Murray McGregor is the owner of a food store in a small rural community in Scotland, having taken over the family business some four years previously. By improving shop standards and introducing a wider range of products and services Murray has continually improved both the turnover and, more importantly, the net profit of the business. Whilst currently trading well, Murray is finding that additional turnover gains are becoming increasingly difficult to achieve. Recent improvements in sales have been dependent upon extending the variety of goods on offer as the existing product range has produced limited growth.

The town in which McGregor's Stores trades has a population of just over 3,000 people, most of whom work outside of the town. The provision of a by-pass some five years ago has improved the shopping environment of the high street but has eliminated most spending from so-called 'passing trade'. Nevertheless the town is popular with local residents, with a number of existing businesses apparently trading well (although some shop units are vacant).

Murray operates the most successful convenience shop in the town. Competition includes a small, more traditional grocer at the opposite end of the high street and a variety of local specialists including a baker, butcher, small fruit shop, a florist and a newsagent. Other neighbouring retail shops include the Post Office, chemist, small hardware shop and a coffee shop that also sell gifts. There are also three takeaway restaurants, a betting shop and two hairdressers.

The neighbouring large town, some 7 miles away, has a small shopping centre with a variety of food and non-food retailers and services. The largest and most influential food store is located on the edge of this town, closest to Murray's shop. This superstore, operated by Tesco, has a sales area of 25,000 square feet, trades from 08.00 until 22.00 and provides a full range of fresh foods plus a small range of non-food products. It also has a coffee shop and a petrol filling station. In addition, the grocery discounter Lidl trades just off the town centre.

In common with the rest of Europe, Scotland has been experiencing a decline in the number of small independent retailers as larger and more modern retail formats continue to increase their share of customer spend. Murray is well aware of this trend, as much of the local spending flows out of the village to the large town and particularly to the Tesco superstore. After talking to other local traders Murray believes that about half of his sales increases in the last four years have come at the expense of the other local shops. The remainder has come from increased prices and recapturing trade from the community that had previously been lost.

Murray knows that if he is to make any further gains in market share then he will either have to close (or acquire) some of his local competitors or take more trade from the superstore. Recently he has been considering expanding the business by acquiring a second shop in a neighbouring small town. This possible strategy had been encouraged by a series of articles appearing in *The Grocery Retailer* that featured the 'top 50' independent food retailers in the United Kingdom. A number of these had developed from family businesses and were not only surviving but were competing effectively. These ranged from Botterill's Convenience Stores, with over 30 shops and an annual turnover of £44 million, to a variety of medium-sized chains with an annual turnover of around £15 million (with between 14 and 18 shops). As the article had noted:

> The big supermarket chains may have increased their stranglehold over Britain's grocery sector in recent years, but that doesn't mean the day of the independent is over. There are plenty of privately run companies out there. And, somewhat against the odds, the best of them are thriving.

Current business

Murray's existing shop has a sales area of 2,000 square feet and provides a broad base of convenience goods, including food and household goods, alcoholic drinks, cigarettes and tobacco, newspapers and magazines as well as a selection of small non-food items. He operates a National Lottery terminal and has a video hire service. He does not have an automatic telling machine as he is located opposite the local branch of a national bank.

Average turnover (for the year to May 2002) was £23,665 per week, a 4 per cent increase over the previous year and over 50 per cent up on the first full year that he took responsibility for the store (year to May 1999) (Figure 11.1). The average transaction value had also risen to £4.25. Analysis of sales (based on scanning) has given Murray a good understanding of customer reaction to his existing offer and he uses this to continually review his range and introduce new products.

Murray also owns the small shop (*circa* 500 square feet) next door, which he lets to a small crafts shop for £3,500 per annum (the lease is due to expire in three years). The village newsagent (with home deliveries) trades on the other side of this shop.

A large proportion of Murray's trade is food and household goods (Figure 11.2), but he has always tried to differentiate his offer by providing a high level of customer service. This is becoming more difficult as other retailers are attempting to do the same by offering 'added-value' packages such as party planning with free glass hire, sale or return on wine for weddings, etc. Murray has considered a number of options, including the provision of freshly prepared party food and snacks. However, he does not think he has the expertise to expand into catering and he is not sure that the catchment population could sustain the investment in terms of equipment, training, etc.

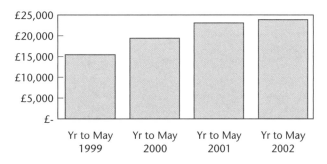

Figure 11.1 Average weekly turnover for McGregor's Stores

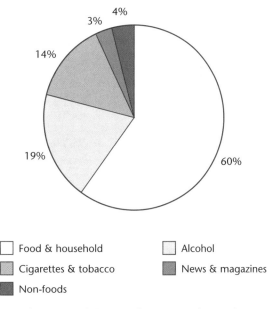

Figure 11.2 Breakdown of McGregor's Stores sales turnover by product group

Murray has developed a strong rapport with many of his customers and has encouraged his staff (who are all local) to maintain a friendly and helpful in-store atmosphere. Customers range from mums with small children to the elderly who use the shop as an extension of their pantry. There is also a strong local trade from people who drop into the shop on their way to or from work for cigarettes, beers or other convenience goods. The shop is kept busy throughout the day but the town centre is relatively quiet in the evenings and the shop closes at 21.00.

Profitability has steadily improved and in the last year the trading profit was £93,808 plus rent and commission payable of £16,176 to provide a net profit for the year of £109,984 (Table 11.1) (this does not include wages for Murray or his wife).

Table 11.1 Profit and loss account for McGregor's Stores for the year to 31 May 2002

	2002 £	2001 £
Sales	1,118,709	1,075,680
Opening stock	34,593	32,675
Purchases	912,154	891,766
	946,747	924,441
Closing stock	36,665	34,593
	910,082	889,848
Gross profit	**208,627**	**185,832**
Wages	46,425	43,422
Rates and insurance	9,491	9,322
Heat and light	6,565	5,263
Telephone	1,325	890
Stationery, wrapping and advertising	3,395	1,522
Repairs and renewals	1,121	1,488
Vehicle expenses	3,261	3,089
Accountancy fees	2,575	2,550
Bank interest and charges	18,286	17,558
Cleaning and sundries	2,487	2,049
Depreciation	19,888	14,252
	114,819	101,405
Trading profit	**93,808**	**84,427**
Rent receivable	3,500	3,250
National Lottery commission	7,496	7,382
Phone card commission	2,322	1,425
Power card commission	2,858	2,245
	16,176	14,302
Net profit for year	**109,984**	**98,729**

Source: after Dawson (2000a)

Potential business acquisition

Murray has learned that the owner of the grocer/newsagent store in the neighbouring village could be tempted to sell his business. The store is located in a slightly larger conurbation but the business does not trade as strongly as McGregor's Stores, suggesting that there may be potential for further growth (Table 11.2). Limited trading information on the 'target' business is available and Murray has decided to explore the potential acquisition in more detail before taking the idea further.

Table 11.2 Profit and loss account for the potential acquisition for the year to 28 February 2002

	2002 £	2001 £
Sales	670,819	691,566
Opening stock	26,100	24,598
Purchases	558,059	572,691
	584,159	597,289
Closing stock	28,311	26,100
	555,848	571,189
Gross profit	114,971	120,377
Wages	25,929	24,028
Rates and insurance	7,590	7,053
Heat and light	4,151	4,167
Telephone	1,195	487
Stationery, wrapping and advertising	1,167	1,276
Repairs and renewals	1,851	1,193
Vehicle expenses	1,606	1,325
Accountancy fees	2,125	2,025
Bank interest and charges	8,528	10,588
Cleaning and sundries	254	652
Depreciation	3,763	4,427
	58,159	57,221
Trading profit	56,812	63,156
Phone card commission	1,423	1,219
Power card commission	2,758	2,465
	4,181	3,684
Net profit for year	60,993	66,840

Source: after Dawson (2000a)

Turnover in the potential store acquisition is currently around £14,500 per week in a sales area of approximately 1,600 square feet. The store is noticeably busier in the mornings and evenings and a high proportion of the shop's trade is in tobacco products and newspapers (Figure 11.3). Although local residents visit for both forgotten as well as regularly purchased items, the average transaction value is only £3.15.

Local shopping provision is modest in the target town, with convenience retail being restricted to a butcher and newsagent in the town centre and a small grocer on the main housing estate. Other retail units include a chemist, a Ladbrookes betting shop and three takeway restaurants. Recently a national bank closed one of its branches in the high street.

Despite being located in the larger community and having relatively weak competitors the retail offer of the target shop has remained largely unchanged. Recently however it has been trying to add to its offer and now opens early and closes late. The shop falls under the influence of the same large superstore as Murray's existing shop, but the prospective acquisition is less than 2 miles from the superstore.

Comparison of characteristics/factors influencing the acquisition

Before committing himself Murray has recognised the need to improve his understanding of the local trading environment and the performance of the prospective business acquisition. He does not intend to buy a business with limited growth potential and believes that he should make a measured judgement based on sound analysis.

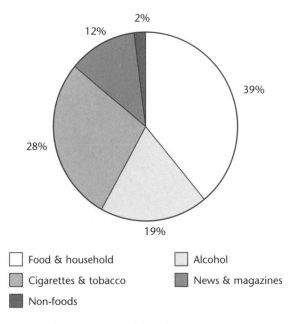

Figure 11.3 Sales turnover of proposed acquisition by product group

Initial analysis has shown Murray that he has three options of how to gather or acquire the essential data. He can gather data on the business and the local trading environment himself, he can draw on published information that is freely available or he can purchase specific information from a research company. Whilst continuing to work in his existing shop Murray has to balance the various costs of collecting the data (in terms of time and money) with the accuracy and speed with which such information can be accumulated. Murray began by comparing the two towns that the shops trade in and the neighbouring large town. His first objective was to identify what shopping and related services were available (Table 11.3). He then evaluated the relative attractiveness and the vitality of each town.

Despite having a smaller population, Murray's town offered a wider selection of shops, services and other local attractions. Whilst both small towns had important community anchors, such as a health centre, primary school and community centre, the home town had additional attractions such as a library and a petrol filling station. Both town centres had been more important in the past and vacant units suggest that external factors are influencing vitality. Car access was similar in both towns, with on-street parking in front of both shops. In addition there were local authority car parks off the main shopping streets.

Simple observation suggested to Murray that the target town centre was not as busy as the town in which he currently trades, so he counted pedestrians passing the two businesses at various times throughout the day to compare activity levels. The two towns were found to be quite different, with Murray's town being much busier during the day. In contrast, the target town was busier during the early morning (before 09.30) and in the evening (after 18.00). Overall he estimated that his town had approximately 50 per cent more pedestrians (Figure 11.4).

In attempting to better understand his customer base Murray also went to the local library. There he was able to draw on a number of published government surveys, including the Family Expenditure Survey (a random sample of private households in the United Kingdom), that provided information about household expenditure on key commodities and services. However, this data was not specific to local communities, and whilst the local authority planning department had been able to provide more localised data, this was a little outdated.

With more recent data, such as the 2001 Population Census, not yet published, and having recognised the weaknesses of using only the 1991 Census, Murray

Table 11.3 Comparison of retailers and services in home and target towns

	Home town centre		Target town centre	
	No.	%	No.	%
Convenience goods shops	6	30	4	33.3
Comparison goods shops	3	15	1	8.3
Services	9	45	5	41.7
Vacant	2	10	2	16.7
Total	**20**	**100**	**12**	**100**

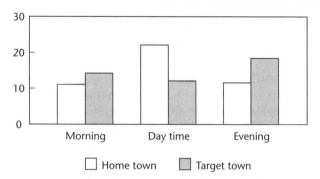

Figure 11.4 Comparison of pedestrian footfall in home and target towns

decided to purchase updated data from a specialist company – CACI. Its package of information products provided current data on the composition of the towns. For example, the Population and Household Profiles for the year 2000 is based on the 1991 Census data and updated by CACI's research on demographic and lifestyle information from millions of individual consumers. The information Murray purchased was presented in the form shown in Table 11.4.

Table 11.4 Extract from CACI population profile 2000

		Home town		Target town		National base
		Data	Data as %	Data	Data as %	Data as %
Total resident population		3,244		3,578		
Retired people		560	17.3	576	16.1	18.2
Lone parents		66	2.0	128	3.6	2.2
Aged	0–14	559	17.2	687	19.2	19.2
	15–24	390	12.0	406	11.3	12.1
	25–44	969	29.9	1,095	30.6	29.6
	45–64	863	26.6	913	25.6	23.4
	65+	463	14.3	477	13.3	15.6
Social grade	AB	350	13.2	193	6.8	21.9
	C1	625	23.6	861	30.4	28.7
	C2	902	34.1	668	23.6	21.9
	DE	769	29.1	1,114	39.3	27.5
Adults (17+) in private households		2,646		2,836		
	With no cars	541	20.4	727	25.6	25.4
	With 1 car	1,362	51.5	1,356	47.8	43.7
	With 2+ cars	743	28.1	753	26.6	30.9

Source: CACI (2000)

The resident population living within both towns has grown since the 1991 Census. CACI population projections of the home town indicate that it grew from 3,184 at the Census to 3,244 in 2000 (a modest increase of less than 2 per cent). During the same period the target town has grown from 3,420 to 3,578 (an increase of 4.6 per cent). Murray also noticed that whilst the research highlighted similarities between the demographic characteristics of the two catchments there were some noticeable differences in a number of economic measures (Table 11.5).

As consumers become more complex and fragmented the need for improved and more precise targeting grows. In most cases the traditional social classifications are no longer adequate or relevant to describe the current complex consumer characteristics. Geodemographic analysis combines the places where people live with their underlying lifestyle and demographic characteristics to provide a fuller understanding of the kind of people buying goods and services and their likely shopping behaviour.

To supplement this information Murray decided to purchase data from CACI's ACORN household classification. This is one of a number of geodemographic systems that categorise households in order to create a segmentation system (ACORN classifies people living in the United Kingdom into any one of 6 categories, 17 groups or 54 types) (Table 11.6).

Analysis of Murray's home town by ACORN categories highlights the predominance of one category (accounting for almost 60 per cent of the household categories present) – *Settling* households. These households are full of 'workers in the middle of the social spectrum who own their homes and lead a steady lifestyle'. Another important household category present is defined as *Striving*. This category contains people who 'find life toughest in the most difficult social conditions overall'.

Table 11.5 Extract from CACI household profile 2000

		Home town		Target town		National base
		Data	Data as %	Data	Data as %	Data as %
Total households		1,413		1,499		
	Single person households	369	26.1	388	25.9	29.5
Tenure	Owner occupied	981	69.4	701	46.8	64.0
	Rented	432	30.6	798	53.2	36.0
Dwelling types	Detached	172	12.2	215	14.3	20.9
	Semi-detached	314	22.2	488	32.6	28.5
	Terraced	456	32.3	459	30.6	28.9
	Flat	471	33.3	337	22.5	21.7
No. of rooms	1–2	58	4.1	51	3.4	5.5
	3–6	1,249	88.4	1,360	90.7	80.0
	7+	106	7.5	88	5.9	14.6

Source: CACI (2000)

Table 11.6 ACORN population categories (%)

	Home town	Target town	National base
Thriving	0.8	7.1	19.8
Expanding	6.6	15.8	11.5
Rising	3.5	0	8.9
Settling	59.3	3.0	25.6
Aspiring	7.5	17.2	12.1
Striving	22.2	56.9	21.9

Source: CACI (2000)

In contrast, the target town contains a different mix of ACORN household categories. In this area *Striving* households account for a much larger share of households. This category is supplemented by *Aspiring* (people who are running hard to better their lot – buying their council homes and pursuing their goals) and *Expanding* households (business people in better-off families – paying off mortgages and bringing up children).

From this Murray can begin to consider the likely shopping behaviour of potential customers. The research indicates that in his home town *Settling* households will give rise to two consumer types. First, Established Home-owning Areas, Skilled Workers (26.5 per cent of population) and secondly, Home Owners in Older Properties, Younger Workers (18.4 per cent) (Box 11.1).

Box 11.1
Shopping behaviour of customers in home town

Established Home-owning Areas, Skilled Workers (26.5 per cent of population)
These are very stable, traditional family neighbourhoods with a household structure biased towards married couples and families with older children. People in these neighbourhoods are more likely than average to think that known brands are better than own-label products. Grocery shopping is most likely to be done by car, and on a weekly or less frequent basis.

Home Owners in Older Properties, Younger Workers (18.4 per cent of population)
These neighbourhoods contain large numbers of young families and the proportions of women in couples who work are well above average. They are less likely than average to buy new brands and whilst consumption of fresh foods and frozen foods is low, the consumption of most packaged foods is average. More grocery shopping trips than average are made on foot.

In contrast, the target town displays a quite different profile, with a wider spread of household types present within the catchment area. *Striving* and *Aspiring* populations give rise to three likely types of consumer behaviour, as shown in Box 11.2.

Box 11.2
Shopping behaviour of customers in target town

Better-off Council Areas, New Home Owners (16.6 per cent of population)
These family neighbourhoods are relatively affluent areas where spending takes precedence over saving. The proportion of women in couples who work is high. They tend to be careful with money when shopping and to look for the lowest possible prices, although they are often tempted to buy new brands. Most grocery shopping trips are made by car although the proportion of people doing grocery shopping on a daily basis is above average. These people are very heavy consumers of a wide range of food products, partly because household sizes are large.

Council areas, Young Families, Some New Home Owners (11.0 per cent of population)
These neighbourhoods contain many young families. They are much less happy than average with their standard of living. They tend to look for the lowest prices when shopping and to budget very carefully. People in these neighbourhoods are much more likely than average to do grocery shopping daily and on foot. The diet here is not a healthy one as consumption of fresh foods, particularly fruit, is very low.

Council areas, Young Families, Many Lone Parents (11.0 per cent of population)
A key feature of the household structure in these areas is the very large proportion of single-parent families although there is also an above-average proportion of large families. These people are much less satisfied with their standard of living and spend time both budgeting carefully and searching for the lowest prices. The propensity to eat and drink out is well below average. Over a quarter of grocery shopping trips are made on foot and there is a higher than average level of daily food shopping.

Table 11.7 Average household expenditure: convenience goods extract from summary by COICOP group year 2002

	Average weekly spend in home town £	Average weekly spend in target town £	Average weekly spend in base £
Food	38.10	38.92	38.20
Non-alcoholic beverages	5.58	5.75	5.29
Alcoholic drink (excl. on-sales)	12.35	10.77	10.70
Tobacco	13.28	17.54	10.00
Goods & services for household maintenance	2.82	3.01	3.28
Pets	2.85	2.94	3.22
Newspapers, books & stationery	7.89	7.67	7.96
Personal care	6.42	6.60	7.33
Personal goods	0.47	0.56	0.80

Source: National Statistics (http://www.statistics.gov.uk)

Having considered the buying behaviour and shopping preferences of the catchment population CACI have calculated their spending on key product groupings. From this data Murray has extracted the current average family and total catchment expenditure for both his home town and the target town (Table 11.7).

Discussion questions

1. Murray uses three types of research to help understand his consumer base in the target town. Evaluate the strengths and weaknesses of each form of research.

2. What are the inherent dangers of Murray making his decision without undertaking such research?

3. Using the information contained within the case study, evaluate the attractiveness of the potential acquisition.

4. How might Murray use the information he has gathered to further improve the sales turnover, profitability and market share of his retail business?

CHAPTER 12

Fast Retailing:
We won't tell you what to wear

Keri Davies

Fast Retailing believes that when the clothes speak louder than the person, the person cannot be heard. (Company web site)

Introduction

This case study looks at the Japanese company Fast Retailing and its main brand, Uniqlo. In 2001, having grown to be one of the largest suppliers of casual clothing in the country, it was planning to extend its brand into other sectors at home and to spread the message of its clothing brand abroad, beginning with the United Kingdom and the People's Republic of China. This raised issues about just what were the factors that constituted its brand and could it be successful in transferring its brand and its operational model overseas?

Background

Fast Retailing began life in 1949 as a small private enterprise, Men's Shop Ogori Shoji, in Ube City, in western Japan's Yamaguchi Prefecture, a long way from the glitz of the main retail centres such as Tokyo, Osaka or Kyoto. By the early 1980s it had grown to be 'a backwater chain of 22 dowdy men's clothing emporiums', concentrating on jackets and formal shirts. The change came when the founder's son, Tadashi Yanai, took over as president in 1984. A graduate of Tokyo's prestigious Waseda University, he looked outside Japan and identified an increasing demand for more casual clothing. Most Japanese retailers at this time still focused on the high fashion/high price segment of the market.

The first Uniqlo (pronounced 'yuni-kuro') or 'Unique Clothing Warehouse' store opened on a back street in Hiroshima in 1984 and aimed to sell lower priced casual clothes for young people. The following year Uniqlo opened its first suburban or 'roadside' store. Yanai recalls:

'We were quick to note that it attracted customers of all ages and both sexes. Although up until that point we had been a store specialising in casual clothes for young people, we decided to change direction and market casual wear to all kinds of customers. Whereas in the past 'casual wear' had the image of cheap, rather flashy, trendy clothes just for the young, we saw no reason why they could not be marketed to customers of all ages and both sexes as basic clothing that people could wear comfortably on a daily basis. Our next challenge was to figure out how to manufacture such good, solid garments inexpensively.'

The early Uniqlo stores were seen as downmarket and the clothes they sold were cheap, maybe even frumpy. Or, as Jeremy Tonkin, an analyst with Commerz Securities Japan put it, 'Uniqlo used to be a suburban phenomenon. In the mid-1990s it basically served Japanese housewives in their silly aprons and fluffy slippers living out in Chiba.' The stores were perfect for stocking up on cheap items in quantity but not much beyond that.

But, as we will see, the company used the period to refine and hone its operations model, even changing its parent company's name to Fast Retailing in a move to express its business philosophy.

For the first years of its operation Uniqlo bought their stock from other manufacturers, but it was difficult for Yanai to get a competitive edge against established retailers. Designs were being set by the manufacturers, which took out one possibility, and price competition was difficult because manufacturers' prices didn't come down (despite the yen's appreciation against other Asian currencies and the dollar).

In 1985 and 1986 Yanai travelled to Hong Kong, where he found high quality casual wear made in China being sold at much lower prices than in Japan. On investigation he realised that this was often because he was looking at manufacturers who had gone into retailing.

> There is no boundary between manufacturing and retailing. There is no national border either. I realised that if we compete with them, we will lose. I thought this is what business should be, and that Hong Kong's way of doing business is more normal than ours. After starting business with major Hong Kong traders, I learned how to do business and the basic idea about business. This was a turning point for me.

Despite its initial drawbacks when incorrect sizes and colours were delivered to Japan, Fast Retailing's design and production model has become a key part of their business operation and of their competitive advantage. Without it their later success would probably not have been possible and certainly would not have been sustainable.

Supply chain management and customer responsiveness

The overall business model for Fast Retailing is shown in Figure 12.1. To create the right products the specifications for product planning, design, pattern making and tailoring are based on information gathered from market surveys, in-store customer feedback and its call centres. There are integrated programmes and systems to control

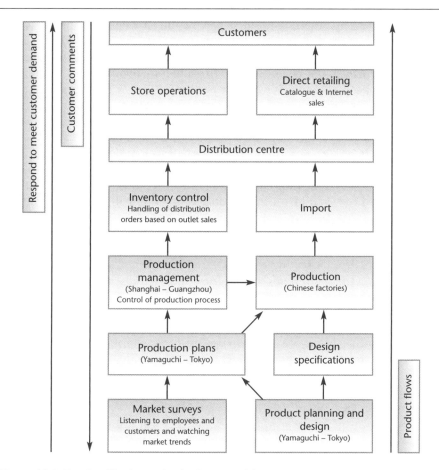

Figure 12.1 Fast Retailing's reactive business model
Source: after Fast Retailing web sites (www.uniqlo.co.jp)

all facets of product development from product design, fabric and materials development, procurement of raw materials, production, distribution and store selling.

By 2001 about 90 per cent of Uniqlo's products for Japan were being made in China, at 85 contracted factories, mostly around Shanghai and Guangzhou, run by roughly 60 companies. It has managed to maintain high standards in a region previously synonymous with cheap, poorly made items. Yet it does not own production facilities because Yanai sees them as having no added value. He prefers to cooperate with those who have production facilities (and the competencies to run them) and to help them to upgrade their production capabilities so that both sides can benefit. 'Once there are capital ties,' says Yanai, 'mutual dependence and excessive familiarity come into the picture. By limiting the relationship to commissioned production we can preserve a sense of tension and turn out high quality products.'

Fast Retailing was very careful over the joint venture partners selected in order to ensure that the quality of the output would be satisfactory. As the company's presence in China has grown so it has helped its partners to bring in both state-of-the-art machinery and outside expertise. In addition, it has implemented a set of practices borrowed from companies such as Toyota Motor Corp. under which product numbers and other clues allow the company to track down in which part of the production line any aberration originated and to solve the problem.

This, then, is the first part of the Fast Retailing business model. It is one that has shaken up both the Japanese clothing retail sector and the textile industry because of the sheer volume of Chinese imports handled by Fast Retailing and the impetus it has given to other firms to look overseas for cheaper products. Uniqlo has been able to achieve a 15 per cent after-tax margin whilst selling clothes at a 70 per cent discount to the rest of the market. In 2001 the Uniqlo stores in Tokyo were selling jean jackets for ¥2,900 (US$24), whilst the Japanese outlets of Gap were charging around ¥7,000 (US$60) and the Matsuya department store a whopping ¥20,000 (US$175). Nonetheless, Uniqlo still earned a gross profit of ¥1,400 (US$12) on each jacket.

But the Uniqlo managers are also at pains to point out that they are about much more than just using cheap production facilities. Yanai again:

> 'It is often said that Uniqlo has high profit margins because of China production or large volume sales. I do not agree . . . Uniqlo's genuine strength comes from assessing total risk and control and implementing low cost management that eliminates wastefulness to maximise added value.'

Uniqlo aims to offer lower priced fashionable and quality clothes in designer environments supported by a rapid response and sensitive supply chain. Uniqlo has stuck to its roots in casual clothing, concentrating on what it calls 'basic' products, that is, clothing for everyday use. Rather than just looking to this season's fashion, close attention is paid to colours, sizes, profiles and materials that can take the latest fashion features and translate them into wearable clothing at prices which match the underlying image of Uniqlo.

Customers in the stores are the focal points of all the organisation's activities. At the same time as sales budgets are established by week and by month, so are the production plans established for each product item in each factory (Figure 12.1). By having the right volume of products at the right time in the stores, whilst also keeping markdowns to a minimum, customers are encouraged to return to the stores to see what is new. All the in-store activities are geared to building lifetime bases of satisfied customers.

Within the sales organisation there is a high degree of performance motivation. Store managers can be promoted to *superstar* managers who assume responsibility for store performance as if it were their own business. Remuneration is closely linked to store sales performance and there is a strong company commitment to training and increasing the number of long-term contract employees. At the same time, poor performance at any level in the company receives its own reward.

Sales productivity is supported by concentrated marketing programmes. Uniqlo spends over 4 per cent of its annual sales on advertising and sales promotion. A key component of the marketing programme is the use of regular and dominant sales promotions in-store on core products where there is high confidence in the rate of sales. This drives customer foot traffic through the stores on a regular basis. Promotions are highlighted through in-store visual merchandising at the same time as placements in newspapers, magazines, events and television.

Brand building is also regarded as a key aspect of the marketing programme and involves every aspect of the company. The company strives to convey an integrated Uniqlo identity to its customers through stores, products, advertisements and all other media. It has also established a charitable arm that is involved in environmental projects and the donation or recycling of used Uniqlo clothing.

An enviable dilemma

For a decade or more, whilst Uniqlo put its business model into place, growth was slow but steady (Figures 12.2 and 12.3). Sticking primarily to suburban and

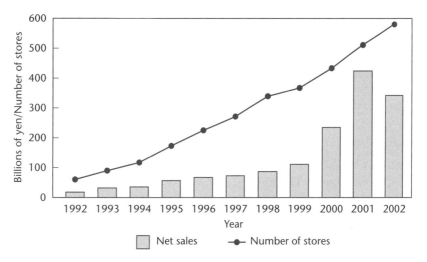

Figure 12.2 Fast Retailing Japan, number of stores and net sales, 1992–2002
Source: Annual reports

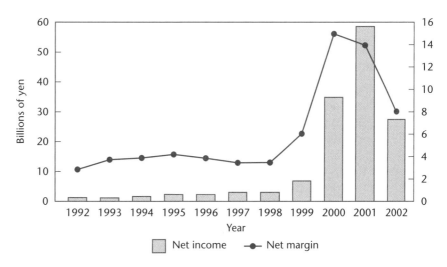

Figure 12.3 Fast Retailing Japan, net income and net margin, 1992–2002
Source: Annual reports

roadside locations it had reached over 300 stores by 1998; sales and net income grew slowly but steadily. In the late 1990s it began to move more into the mainstream of retailing when a decision was made that it would take outlets in shopping malls.

The company's big break came in late 1999. It was aided by the move amongst consumers away from higher priced 'status' brands towards cheaper items; defending himself from claims Uniqlo had actually worsened the economic situation in Japan, Yanai called his chain's prices 'good deflation'. Uniqlo pushed at an open door by hiring better designers (for its clothes and its stores) and began to create its brand image of clothing for all – basic (not overly fancy) clothing that could be mixed and matched with more expensive items to enhance the user's own personality. Suddenly the fortunes of the company changed, it became more exposed to the public and much more successful. Uniqlo itself traces the change to its decision to open its first stores in the ultra-fashionable districts of Tokyo such as Harajuku and Shibuya rather than stay in its traditional locations.

With opinion formers behind them the stores were immensely successful and sales and profit soared. Some Uniqlo stores were so crowded on weekends that employees had to limit numbers, leaving a long line of potential customers waiting outside. In 2000 Uniqlo sold more than 300 million individual items of clothing – the equivalent of 3 items per person in Japan. Its most famous item was a fleece jacket sold at a third of the price of competitors' and available in 30–40 colours. The items were so cheap that many families bought them, wore them for the winter and then threw them away on the first day of spring.

This rate of expansion gave Uniqlo problems, however. By 2002 there were nearly 600 stores and Fast Retailing was still planning to reach its target of 1,000 outlets. But as new stores opened so it became more difficult to sustain the growth rates of previous years. Analysts were also worried about Uniqlo becoming a fad. 'Consumers in Japan always seem to enthusiastically buy a particular brand for a few years and then desert that brand even faster when it's deemed to have fallen out of fashion, regardless of price', warns Jeremy Tonkin.

The fall in sales and net margin shown in Figures 12.2 and 12.3 seem to suggest that this point has been reached. It is also shown very clearly in Figure 12.4, which plots the percentage change in year-on-year sales for the company after allowing for changes in the number of stores in the chain. After sales increases of over 100 per cent in 2000 the declines reached over 40 per cent in some months in 2002.

The company needed to do something to win back favour. A number of the innovations to the supply chain noted above, such as reducing the initial production levels, were aimed at cutting costs from the existing operations and restoring Uniqlo's advantages. The company stressed that it had not expected the levels of growth experienced in 2000 and 2001 and had not planned for them to continue. Its Uniqlo operation in Japan will, therefore, continue to operate much as before and the emphasis has been on areas where it can look to expand outside its existing base.

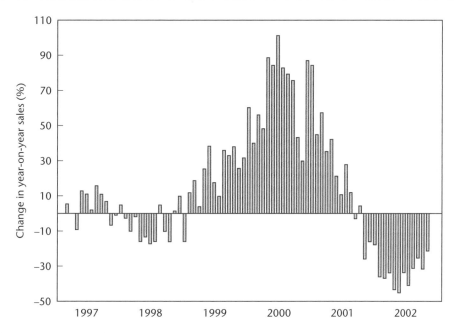

Figure 12.4 Fast Retailing year-on-year sales (comparable stores)
Source: Annual report

Uniqlo: areas for expansion

Faced with slower growth and even the possibility of saturation at home, Fast Retailing looked to use its clothing merchandising methods and networks to retail non-clothing items. Speaking to analysts in a briefing in Tokyo in 2001 Yanai outlined three long-term goals – diversification of the clothing business, launch of new businesses in areas such as food, and entry into major global markets. The firm would conduct feasibility studies and experiment with several marketing methods and outlets, including supermarkets. New businesses would be limited to those capable of generating annual revenue of over ¥100 billion (US$8.1 million) and realising a 10 per cent pre-tax profit-to-sales ratio in the short term. Fast Retailing would be willing to use mergers and acquisitions to enter new fields. As it does with clothing, Fast Retailing would manage the entire operation from product planning to retailing in order to maintain low prices.

Clothing diversification

In 1996/7 Uniqlo tried to diversify into separate stores for women's clothing, children's clothing and sportswear, but the stores were seen as too similar and confusing by consumers and were soon closed. In the following years Uniqlo started opening larger stores that allowed these different areas to be housed together and further areas such as baby clothes to be developed. Uniqlo has also established mail-order and Internet sales channels for their standard products.

In 2001 the company announced that it would diversify into uniforms and athletic outfits. The aim here was not produce a new line but to use its existing clothing lines, such as T-shirts and tops to tap into the market for casual clothing amongst staff in small businesses such as shops, restaurants, gyms, and so on. For a small fee company names and logos would be embroidered on to products bought off the shelf.

Launching new businesses: food retailing

Japan is the second biggest consumer market in the world – and the food industry is bigger than the clothing industry. By applying its established methods Yanai said that, 'We will be able to sell foods at one-tenth of supermarket prices by procuring food from large suppliers in the United States and China'. Typically ambitious, his plans called for the company to open several retail outlets for fresh food in 2004, with sales of ¥1–2 billion (US$8–16 million) expected in its initial year, rising to ¥10 billion (US$80 million) in the third year.

First, however, the company would establish a foothold in the food business through a mail-order and Internet membership operation. FR Foods Co. was established, selling products under the brand name 'SKIP'. In tie-ups with three Japanese agriculture-related companies FR Foods intended selling 100 food items via the Internet and mail order. Of these, 60 would be vegetables and 30 fruit, along with eggs, milk, juice and rice. The company planned to hire farmers to cultivate the produce under the supervision of external consultants in order to ensure the minimum possible use of agrochemicals and fertilizer. The farmers must follow guidelines in areas such as protein content and taste in order to maintain quality.

Unlike their clothes, the number of food products for sale would be limited and retail prices would be approximately 20 per cent higher than the same products sold in supermarkets. The number of member customers was initially expected to total around 15,000 and they would belong to a membership system called Skip Club. Products would be delivered by door-to-door parcel delivery truck – normally every other week.

FR Foods President Osamu Yunoki said, 'Prices are somewhat high because we stick to the safety of foods. We will continue cost-cutting efforts'. FR Foods planned to disclose to consumers the production histories of all of its fresh produce, company officials said. In 2001 and 2002 Japanese consumers had become very wary of food quality after a series of scandals involving Japanese companies, including accidental and deliberate mislabelling of the origin of meat products. Many food makers and leading supermarket chains had begun to introduce new systems and procedures to more effectively ensure the safety of their products. These steps covered the entire range of production processes, from sourcing ingredients to shipping, and this meant that their costs were rising also.

Nonetheless the analysts were not completely sure that consumers would be able to equate the success of Fast Retailing and Uniqlo with this new venture. 'The move doesn't appear immediately logical,' said Bryan Roberts, analyst with Planet Retail. 'It's an immensely competitive sector, and some of the established food retailers in Japan have been dropping like flies. The discount clothing retailer will not benefit from moving into the food area.'

Launching new businesses: electric cars

In September 2002 Fast shelved plans to begin selling electric cars in autumn 2002 through its Uniqlo causal clothing stores via a tie-up with toy maker Takara Co. The one-seat Q-Car was to be based on the Choro Q, Takara's miniature toy car. Fast Retailing had hoped the new car would help attract more customers to its stores, whilst Takara aimed to take advantage of Fast's extensive sales network. The two companies also intended to jointly develop toys aimed at adults, and interior goods. Takara was considering giving preferential treatment to Fast in supplying new products and producing goods that would be sold only through Uniqlo stores.

The plan was shelved because a special trial model was not completed on time. Despite the change in its plan, however, Yanai said the companies will continue seeking a business that will generate synergy effects, including the sale of a new product.

Retail internationalisation

Fast Retailing saw overseas expansion as a necessity rather than a preference because it expected the Japanese market to shrink overall. Even by 2000 it felt that it could not sustain year-on-year sales increases. Overseas sales accounted for under 1 per cent of revenues in 2002 but, Yanai said: 'By 2010, I want them to reach half of our total sales.'

When Fast Retailing announced its first plans to go overseas in 2000 analysts were not as optimistic, given the problems that other Japanese retailers had experienced when they had made a similar move. The company's response was to argue that it would stick to its core business model, replicating its Uniqlo operation overseas.

Management rationalised its choice of the United Kingdom for its first overseas foray as follows. For overseas expansion the primary destination should be the United States or Europe, given their large market sizes. The firm opted not to expand into the United States first because the creation of any meaningful impact and scale of operation would require a presence to be built up in a short space of time in several important cities, each of which might need around 50 stores. It was unlikely that the company had the resources or the power to carry out such an operation quickly.

It appeared to be much easier to create an impact in Europe. Fast Retailing chose London due to its offering a business environment friendly to foreign concerns, and consumers who seemed more likely to embrace the Uniqlo brand than would Parisians. 'We call the UK market the Olympics, and we want to be part of the Olympics,' said Yanai. 'Our concept, I believe, can translate to the global market anywhere. I did not look for a gap in the UK market. We are not a discounter. Our concept is really good casual clothing at a realistic price.'

After the United Kingdom Fast Retailing's first thoughts were to turn either to Germany or the United States. Instead they decided to take advantage of the further opening of the Chinese market to foreign retailers and foreign brands, along with the vastly increased consumer spending power in the coastal provinces around Shanghai and Guangzhou.

Retail internationalisation: United Kingdom

Fast Retailing opened its first four Uniqlo stores in the London area in September 2001, each testing a different store format and location, with a flagship store in the fashionable Knightsbridge district (almost next door to Harrods) to provide visibility and early publicity. The managing director of Uniqlo UK said:

> 'The UK is the most important project in the company. Unless we're successful in the UK, we cannot seek other markets. Our goal is to become a hybrid retailer combining the best of Uniqlo in Japan and the best practice of the UK market.'

After operating in the United Kingdom for several months the company disclosed that sizing, colours and the proportion of womenswear were all being adjusted for the British market, along with an increase in the proportion of UK-only lines. Compared to Japan, the UK operation faces hurdles such as higher shipping costs and tariffs and a range of import restrictions on its core made-in-China products. As the scale of the operation increases so it will allow the establishment of a new supply chain with contract manufacturers. Uniqlo UK aimed to sign contracts with manufacturers in low cost locations such as Turkey, Sri Lanka and eastern Europe rather than bringing the products in from China.

Even using its existing supply chain the company estimated that it could provide merchandise that would be 30–40 per cent cheaper than the equivalent offered by its likely competitors, including the discounters Matalan and Primark and speciality apparel retailers such as French Connection, Gap and Next. It was seen as sharing a price range with H&M but H&M was felt by analysts at the time to target a different customer group.

But Uniqlo has also tried to ally its pricing policies with an appeal to consumers' changing attitudes towards clothing brands and their prices. Much of its advertising and in-store merchandising is based around photographs and endorsements from members of the public – of all ages and income levels. A slogan painted on one London store carried Fast Retailing's unassuming attitude to its logical limits – 'You are not what you wear'.

The Uniqlo stores in the United Kingdom have tried to play down the parent company's overseas roots and shunned the 'Japaneseness' that was used by other companies such as Muji. The stores were designed by a British company, Conran & Partners, to emphasise the product, giving customers a 'clean, simple and accessible retail environment'. Genichi Tamatsuka, then chief executive of Uniqlo UK, said in January 2002:

> 'The reception to our existing London stores has exceeded our expectations and feedback from customers on our product quality, price and service has been very positive. The Christmas trading period has given us a clear indication that there is a place for Uniqlo product in the market.'

Uniqlo was already estimating that it was outselling its neighbourhood rivals in London by 2:1 or 3:1.

Mr Yanahira of ING Securities said that, compared with its competitors in the United Kingdom, 'They've got a good balance in both price and quality, and a nice variety of colours in their product line. So it's not impossible for them to succeed big overseas'.

The main problem identified was that they would have to expand quickly enough to get scale economies. Uniqlo had opened 20-odd stores by late 2002, sticking to the south east, Midlands and north west of England to capitalise on overhead and media costs. The company was aiming for 50 stores in total by the end of three years (and possibly 200 stores eventually). The aim was to break even fiscally in the United Kingdom by 2003 and to achieve a 10 per cent operating profit ratio by the third year (although that would still be a slimmer margin than Japan).

The initial costs of opening stores however meant that the UK operation posted a loss of some ¥3 billion (US$23 million) in the year to May 2002. And there was a high level of turnover amongst senior staff as the company looked to fine-tune its operations. In late 2002 there was further evidence of the desire to bring in local knowledge when Uniqlo recruited as UK managing director Bernie Foster, previously MD of The Body Shop and Miss Selfridge.

Summary

Fast Retailing allied a supply chain in which it controlled costs and output with a customer focus on 'basic' casual clothes, allowing it to provide good quality and design at relatively low prices, a proposition that Tadashi Yanai called 'good deflation'. It was helped by the environment in Japan as consumers moved away from a reliance on up-market brands to express themselves more through mixing and matching clothing and accessories from different sources. As it moved into new areas it tried to adapt the basic model to the new environment, rather than merely assuming that all consumers and consumer markets are the same.

Discussion questions

1. What were the key components of the Uniqlo brand as seen by Japanese consumers? What are the advantages and dangers of having such a clearly identifiable brand?

2. To what extent do you believe that the Uniqlo brand and its business model can be applied to other business areas?

3. FR Foods has chosen not to compete directly with the large supermarket retailers in the first instance. What are the likely opportunities and threats inherent in trying to grow their food business in line with Yanai's ambitions?

4. In trying to establish itself in the Chinese market higher costs meant that Fast Retailing had to shun the practice of setting prices lower than those of the competition in an effort to foster an upscale brand image. Whilst the company made most of its products in China it had no brand name recognition there compared to other Asian chains such as Giordano, Bossini and Crocodile. What were the dangers in this approach?

PART 5

Human resource management

CHAPTER 13

Human resource management issues in retailing

Adelina Broadbridge

Aim

The aim of this chapter is to provide you with an overview of employment in retailing and to analyse the changing structure of retail employment relationships in the United Kingdom. The central issues arise from the fact that changes in the structure of retailing have a substantial influence on the employment of people in the industry.

Learning objectives

By the end of this chapter you will be able to:

- describe the composition of employment in the retail industry;
- identify the employment characteristics of the retail industry;
- analyse the issues contributing to the changing structure and nature of retail employment;
- specify the HRM processes and techniques required by managers for the effective management of the workforce;
- appreciate some of the current HRM issues facing the UK retail industry.

Introduction

An understanding of the structure and nature of employment in the retail industry will set a context for the following two chapters, as well as providing a backdrop to any further study you may undertake on this topic area. The employment characteristics in retailing are influenced by both the micro environment (such as the structural changes ongoing in the industry) and the macro environment (such as the availability of labour).

Retailing has undergone much structural change since 1945, in response to changing consumer needs and the changing nature of the retail environment. The retail sector now has some of the most innovative and successful companies in the world. To survive, retailers must be professional in all areas of their business (which includes the management of people). Companies and managers need to understand modern HRM techniques to better manage their business. More companies are recognising that their employees are a major asset of their business. Strategic plans could not be made nor strategies executed without people. Where increasing importance is placed on service provision the customer – employee interface is all important. Employees can add value to the business and be a point of differentiation between one retailer and another. Therefore, the optimal use of employees, including the recruitment, retention, development and strategic planning of the workforce can provide additional competitive advantage in an industry that is paying closer attention to the importance of service levels and customer care programmes. The effective utilisation of staff can encourage customers' commitment to the business and contribute to the profitability of the company. In return, employees expect a safe and pleasant working environment, appropriate working conditions and remuneration.

Over the years figures on employment in retailing have been gathered by various government bodies and, because of differing methods of data collection, the statistics presented by different sources vary (although the trends are similar). Most data are based on the standard industrial classification of economic activities, which is the classification system used to provide a consistent industrial breakdown for UK official statistics. This classification was revised in 1968, 1980 and 1992. The 1992 Standard Industrial Classification (SIC 92) saw some major changes in the way retailing and wholesaling data are collected and presented. Therefore they are not strictly comparable to previous classifications.

Under SIC 92 the retail trade is included under section G, 'Wholesale and Retail Trade, and Repairs'. This section includes Code 50 (Sale, Maintenance and Repair of Motor Vehicles, Retail Sales of Automotive Fuel), Code 51 (Wholesale and Commission Trade, except Motor Vehicles and Motorcycles) and Code 52 (Retail Trade, except of Motor Vehicles and Motorcycles; Repair of Personal Goods). Unfortunately for scholars in retailing some of the figures now produced are aggregated data for the retail and wholesale industries and not for retailing alone. Furthermore, because of the way the data are collected, the SIC 92 no longer provides a meaningful sectoral analysis of employment in retailing, nor does it provide employment data according to the size of retail businesses. Other sources of retail data (such as the number of self-employment jobs) are aggregated with statistics on hotels and restaurants (section H of SIC 92) and transport, storage and communication (section I of SIC 92). Retail statistics are also published by the Census data (for example self employment, hours worked, age), but because of when they are collected (every 10 years) and published they can only be treated as approximations of the current picture.

The purpose of this chapter is not to provide you with a statistical examination of employment in the retail industry but to concentrate on some of the labour trends that have occurred. It is these trends that are important in understanding employment in retailing rather than any statistical analysis. When we do provide some statistical analyses they are, in the main, derived from the Labour Force

Survey. This is the largest regular household survey conducted in the United Kingdom and produces estimates each month that relate to the most recent quarterly period. It also meets international standards by producing data that are used to measure employment and unemployment according to the standard definition of the International Labour Organization.

Composition of retail employment

In June 2002 there were just over 2.7 million people employed in retailing (Office for National Statistics, 2002a). This represents 10 per cent of the total number of people employed in all industries and services in the United Kingdom. This figure excludes, however, those people in self-employment, unpaid family workers and those people who for whatever reason are not included within the official retail statistics. This will include those areas of work that are now subcontracted out by many retail companies, such as cleaning, catering and security jobs. It also includes those workers who are employed by concessions and so not included on the official payroll of the retail company. People working on perfumery and cosmetic counters of department stores and employed by the major perfumery houses are an example of this type of worker.

Over the last few decades there have been cyclical fluctuations in the absolute employment figures for retailing. This may be due to the state of the economy generally as trends for retail employment have been consistent with overall total employment trends in the United Kingdom. Although the absolute employment figures have been rising since 1994 those relating to full-time equivalent figures show a long-term decline. This suggests that much of the apparent rise in absolute employment figures is attributable to an increase in part-time working brought about by operational changes taking place within retail companies.

Self-employment and family members have traditionally been of great importance in the retail sector. Long-term trends, however, suggest an overall reduction in self-employment in retailing of approximately 50 per cent since 1961. At the beginning of the 1970s the independent sector accounted for almost half of all retail employees. However by the mid-1990s it accounted for less than a third. The growing market concentration in retailing, increased competition and reduction in retail outlets have combined to squeeze the independent sector and consequently to reduce the number of owners working in retailing.

The 1992 Standard Industrial Classification recategorised the kinds of businesses within the retail sector, which makes a sectoral analysis more difficult than in the past. However the food sector is the largest employer, with almost a third of all retail employees.

Gender distribution

In June 2002 there were approximately 1.8 million women and 978,200 men employed in retailing. Thus women workers outnumber men by a ratio of 2:1 and comprise 66.4 per cent of the retail workforce. Furthermore over one in seven of all women workers in the United Kingdom are employed in retailing. These trends have been consistent for many years. Closer examination of the sectors also reveals that women are additionally concentrated in certain retail areas, for example in clothing, footwear and leather goods; in mixed retail; confectionery and tobacco and food.

Furthermore, data collected from the Population Census and various company reports show that male and female workers are concentrated in different job categories. For example, in her analysis of the occupational structure of a multiple retail organisation Broadbridge (1996) found that gender segregation existed across the various job categories. The branch level statistics for the entire company showed that females comprise three-quarters of the workforce, confirming the general trend that retailing is an industry closely associated with the employment of women. Further analysis, however, showed that women predominated in non-managerial branch level posts. For example, 85 per cent of sales assistant staff were women (many of whom worked part time).

On first inspection the number of men and women employed in managerial branch positions was proportionately equal. However closer inspection showed that women outnumbered men at junior managerial positions (deputy depart-ment manager and department manager) by 2:1. The middle and senior managerial posts were found to be dominated by men: the higher the position in the occupational hierarchy the lower the percentage of women represented in these posts. Women occupied only 11 per cent of branch manager positions and 4 per cent of area management positions.

Similar trends were found for head office positions, where men were numer-ically dominant at managerial level (75 per cent). Moreover all the directors were male and only one senior management post (in personnel) was held by a woman. Broadbridge (1996) also noted that the company was a member of the Opportunity 2000 campaign (a government initiative whereby companies com-mitted themselves to increasing the quality and quantity of women's participation in the workforce by the year 2000).

Some comparative figures have been gathered for this same company for the year 2000. Similar trends as before are apparent. Of the total branch level staff, women comprised 73.8 per cent of the workforce. They continue to dominate the non-managerial positions and represent 82 per cent of all sales assistants. Three-quarters of supervisors (74.9 per cent) were female. At branch manager level some change was observed, with 24 per cent of females occupying these positions. However, on closer inspection (and in line with Broadbridge's (1996) findings), women are over-represented as managers in the smallest stores (stores are divided into six categories). Their representation in larger stores progressively decreases and less than 5 per cent are managers of the three largest store categories.

The gender segregation found by Broadbridge (1996) is similar elsewhere. Another major non-food UK retailer (and one also committed to the Opportunity 2000 campaign) had similar statistics in 1998. Women comprised 78.8 per cent of the store sales staff and 41 per cent of the total management. Again, fewer women were found to occupy the higher management positions. Women comprised 43 per cent of all junior managers, 33 per cent of middle managers, 17 per cent of senior managers and 8 per cent of the executive directors (just one woman).

Moreover the majority of women at senior and middle management levels were based at head office and mainly in the buying, merchandising and personnel functions. No senior managers outside head office were women, whilst the only woman on the executive board was in a personnel function.

In another article Broadbridge (1998) asked both male and female retail managers why they considered that women are under-represented in senior management positions in retailing. Both male and female respondents suggested that the reasons could be divided into two categories. The first category related to women's primary responsibilities for the household division of labour. Included here was the lack of child-care facilities together with the long anti-social hours of retailing and lack of flexitime provided. The second category related to organisational attitudes and included outdated attitudes to women's roles, company culture, a reluctance to change and the lack of female role models. These responses tend to support the outdated attitudes and cultural difficulties experienced by female managers and are symptomatic of how organisations have traditionally been defined by gendered custom and practice.

For women who seek a career in retail management the opportunities are apparently both fewer and qualitatively different from those available to men. So although retailing is an important employer of women it is only in certain sectors and certain job categories where women predominate in retailing.

Age distribution

Young people and school-leavers have always provided an important labour source for retailing companies. Retail work is also a source of income for young people still in receipt of formal education. Indeed some companies are heavily reliant on a student workforce. Whilst it has traditionally been common for students to work during vacation periods, since the 1990s there has been an increase in the number of students employed during term time (Broadbridge and Swanson, 2001). Most of this work is concentrated in the service industries, most notably in retailing, catering, hotels and bars (Income Data Services Report 1997; McKechnie et al. 1998; Barke et al. 2000). For example, Sainsbury's has been reported to employ 30,000 students, which represents a quarter (24.4 per cent) of their supermarket workforce (Labour Market Trends 1999). The importance of retailing work to students is likely to be even more paramount now that they are under increasing financial pressure. Ongoing work in this area by the author indicates that there are positive benefits for students working in retailing whilst still in higher education. These are not just financial, but additionally include the acquisition of general transferable skills and gaining employment experience to augment their CVs.

An interesting change occured during the late 1980s and early 1990s, mainly in response to demographic changes in the United Kingdom. Population projections realised that the birth rate was falling and so it was predicted that there would be a reduction in the number of young people available for employment in the future. This was accompanied by an increase in the number of older workers available for employment, due to early retirement and redundancy from other industries as well as people who were living longer. Proactive retail companies foresaw this trend and realised they needed to prepare for the shrinking pool of available youth labour. However, many employers had preconceived attitudes that older workers were not a reliable source of labour and had hitherto perhaps resisted their employment.

Work published at the beginning of the 1990s, however, started to challenge these assumptions. Hogarth and Barth (1991) identified a B&Q store in Macclesfield that (with the exception of the store manager) employed only workers over the age of 50. From this research they found several benefits of employing older workers, such as a greater knowledge about the product and being able to provide a better level of customer service. The older workers were also found to have more commitment to the job, which was additionally demonstrated by an improvement in retention patterns (absence and labour turnover). Hogarth and Barth's work demonstrated the fallacy of the perceived difficulties of employing older people and showed that they can cope with new technologies, are more reliable and can add value to the retail experience.

Retailing, however, remains a youthful industry, with relatively young managers at high levels and considerable numbers of young people working on the shop floor. Data collected in 2000 for a major multiple non-food UK retailer showed that over half its store staff (53.3 per cent) were under the age of 25, whilst just 20.4 per cent were over the age of 45. Such young and inexperienced staff are cheaper to employ but have particular induction and training needs that carry associated costs. Figures from this Labour Force Survey show that at the end of the 1990s over a quarter of the retail workforce was under the age of 25 whilst one in six was under the age of 20. The same survey also showed the level of reliance on an older workforce, with 29.5 per cent of retail employees being over the age of 45. Many retailers today claim to employ more older workers so that their workforce reflects their customer base.

Looking at age in more general terms, the Population Census data for 1991 shows that more men than women were represented in the age groups 21–34 (41 per cent and 23 per cent respectively), whilst more women than men were found in the 35–54 age groups (56 per cent and 29 per cent respectively). Taking into consideration occupational structure this may be attributed to young men embarking on a career in management and women returning to work, or combining working on a part-time basis with familial responsibilities.

Ethnic minority employment

Few official sources provide data on ethnic origins in retail distribution. Employment Department figures between 1987 and 1989 estimated that 95 per cent of the retail workforce is white and 5 per cent come from ethnic minorities. These percentages match the population of the United Kingsom generally. There are, however, some problems with these estimates. The first is the definition of ethnic minorities. The second is that these data do not include the self-employed and so the total figures exclude independent shopkeepers. Retailing is probably a far more important source of employment for ethnic minorities than official statistics suggest. Owen et al. (2000) report that the distribution industry (including restaurants and retail businesses) is the largest single source of service sector jobs for men from ethnic minority groups. They also report that women from ethnic minority groups are slightly more likely than white women to work in distribution. Twomey (2001) further claims that high proportions of Indian and Pakistani women work in the retail trade.

Figures derived from one major non-food UK retail company reported that in 1998 5.41 per cent of their total employees were of ethnic minority status. Of these 94 per cent were employed as store staff and 6 per cent employed in a management capacity (compared with 8 per cent of all employees). Furthermore it was at the lowest management grades that most ethnic minorities were employed. Another major non-food UK retail company reported in 2000 that a total of 5.2 per cent of store employees were from an ethnic minority group. As Twomey (2001) reported, the majority of these were Indian and Pakistani. The same company reported a total of 1.1 per cent of head office employees being from an ethnic minority group.

Characteristics related to the composition of the labour market

Part-time working

Part-time working is fundamentally important to retail organisations because of their hours of opening and the peaks in the trading day and week. Management's ability to match staffing levels to customer flow is a vital tool in improving retail efficiency and providing an enhanced service. Retailers offer part-time work to reduce costs, to extend operating hours or to meet variable demands. Therefore much of the rise in absolute employment figures we discussed earlier may be explained by the increase in part-time working.

Part-time working is also synonymous with the employment of female workers. The period 1961–71 saw increased employment in retailing. This allowed the addition of part-time labour throughout all the main sectors of retailing with an element of substitution of male and female full-time employees by female part-time employees. Since 1971 the pattern of employment has been more one of substitution of female full-time employees by female part-timers. Currently over one in five of all female part-time workers in the United Kingdom work in retailing.

Part-time employment tends to be concentrated in certain sectors of retailing, namely the food, confectionery and tobacco sectors, where part-time workers outnumber full-timers by 2:1. This can be explained, in part, by the trading hours of these sectors and the need to match staffing levels to customer flow patterns. Dispensing chemists also employ over half their staff on a part-time basis whilst the retail of clothing, textiles and household goods employs almost half their staff on a part-time basis.

The trends in part-time employment in retailing therefore have changed over time. In 1974 the split between female full-time and part-time retail jobs in the United Kingdom was almost equal at 48 per cent and 52 per cent respectively. Since 1974 the gap has been widening and by June 2002, 67.8 per cent of the female retail workforce in the United Kingdom worked part time (see Table 13.1). This trend has been steady, indicating a move towards employing more women on a part-time basis.

Table 13.1 Composition of the employee labour force in retailing, June 2002 (thousands)

Retail	Male		Female		Total	
Full-time	604.5	[51.4%]	571.4	[48.6%]	1175.9	[100%]
	(61.8%)		(32.2%)		(42.2%)	
Part-time	373.7	[23.7%]	1201.7	[76.3%]	1575.4	[100%]
	(38.2%)		(67.8%)		(57.8%)	
Total	978.2	[35.6%]	1773.1	[64.4%]	2751.2	[100%]
	(100%)		(100%)		(100%)	

Source: Office for National Statistics, Labour Market Trends (2002a)

A statistical breakdown of the number of male employees working on a full-time or part-time basis in retailing has only been available since 1985; this is because it was previously estimated that an insignificant proportion of men worked on a part-time basis. Since then the growth in males working part time has risen dramatically. As Table 13.1 shows, 61.8 per cent of the male retail workforce worked full time compared with 38.2 per cent who worked part time. So two-thirds of the female retail workforce, and one-third of the male retail workforce work on a part-time basis. These proportions increased during the 1990s (although they have levelled out over the last couple of years) and suggest that those jobs which are traditionally defined as less skilled are more susceptible to part-time employment arrangements. This was confirmed by Broadbridge's (1996) findings, which showed that less than 1 per cent of the managerial jobs across the organisation were of a part-time nature, the highest being junior assistant manager (a trial job share in one small branch).

Management in the past has achieved certain cost benefits in employing part-time rather than full-time employees, for example, National Insurance payments for two part-timers were often lower than for one full-time employee. However, recent legislative changes have had an impact on the use of part-timers and the hours they work; for example, the European Part-time Workers Regulations became fully operational in 2000. This gave part-time workers new rights in the workplace and ensured equal treatment in all areas of work and in terms and conditions of employment. The extent to which these regulations will be effective is open to question. As Stredwick and Ellis (1998) argued, little overall protection is implied and discrimination against part-time employees can still take place if it can be justified objectively, such as on the basis of length of service, time worked or earnings qualifications. Furthermore, casual part-time workers can be excluded altogether by member states.

However, some of the major multiples have indicated a trend towards employing more full-time staff in the future. MTI (1998) reported that Tesco intended to have more full-time jobs because of the link between full-time employment and customer loyalty/service. Others have considered moving towards employing more full-time staff in an effort to help reduce labour turnover rates amongst sales floor staff. It will be interesting, therefore, to see whether the proportion of full-time to part-time staff changes over the next few years. Whilst the increased sophistication and use of information from new technologies enables improved labour scheduling, and the extension of trading hours encourages the potential growth of part-time working, employers may choose to employ more full-time staff via flexible working arrangements in the future. As well as maintaining customer service levels this may be more cost effective depending on the outcomes of the Directive.

High labour turnover

Retailing is traditionally known as an industry with a high labour turnover. Official figures are not available owing to individual retail companies' sensitivity in making public such figures, however some figures for major UK retailers suggest that labour turnover is generally around 40 per cent. It is difficult to generalise though, as differences occur in the methods of calculation. For example, one major high street retailer reported a staff turnover of 45 per cent in 2000. The comparative turnover figure for management staff was 11 per cent. Other companies report a crude separation rate of over 50 per cent (Mockford 1996; Bridle 1998). With certain categories of staff, most notably those working part time and at non-managerial levels, the turnover can run in excess of 90 per cent (Ambrose 1996; Mockford 1996; Savage 1997). It may be claimed that labour turnover is lower in medium and small-sized retail businesses, although there are no data to support this. Clearly the economic climate impacts on labour turnover figures, so that during the 1990s most companies did not suffer the high labour turnover rates of the 1980s. For example, one major grocery retailer who suffered a 70 per cent turnover rate at the beginning of the 1990s reported it had fallen to 37 per cent by the mid-1990s.

Although labour turnover can provide some opportunities to reduce employment numbers by natural wastage, it can be a very real problem for retail companies. The costs of recruitment and training can be high. For example, one of the large supermarket multiples estimated the cost of recruiting a cashier in the late 1990s to be approximately £700. Other associated problems with staff turnover rates are the disruption and lack of continuity, and the loss of skills and knowledge that can result in reduced customer service and reduced sales and profits. High turnover would appear to be concentrated in certain jobs and with certain types of employee. For example, turnover is more prevalent with sales assistants and younger employees than it is with managers or older employees. Low pay and routine work contributes to labour turnover levels, as was found by Ambrose (1996) and Savage (1997).

Low unionisation

Several unions represent the retail sector, for example the Union of Shop, Distributive and Allied Workers (USDAW), the Transport and General Workers Union and the General and Municipal Boilermakers Union. In some parts of retailing such as transport there is a high level of union representation, but in general, retailing is considered to have low union activity with many major retailers not being unionised at all.

The main union is USDAW, which at 31 December 2001 had 310,337 members. Of these members 68 per cent work in retailing (48 per cent of their membership is with food retailers, 12 per cent with cooperatives and 8 per cent with non-food retailers). Of the remaining USDAW members, some work in wholesale distribution and wholesale grocery. Union density in the wholesale and retail industry in 2000 remains low at 11 per cent (Sneade 2001). Of all the industrial sectors only hotels and restaurants have a lower union density than the wholesale and retail trade.

USDAW membership figures have followed a cyclical pattern since 1961. Between 1961 and 1968 there was a general decline in membership, followed by a general upward trend until 1980. Since 1980 membership has fallen and this has been influenced by political (legislative), economic and cultural factors. For example, successive Conservative governments in the 1980s and early 1990s, introduced several bills curbing union power and effectiveness. The recession and high levels of unemployment weakened the industrial and collective bargaining power of the employee, whilst changes in employer/employee relations (particularly with the introduction of HRM techniques) have tended to move industrial relations on to an individual basis. This undermines the collective nature of union representation and relevance and alters the culture of industrial relations.

Sneade (2001) reported that 18 per cent of all employees in the wholesale and retail trade are covered by collective agreements. Employees situated in workplaces where there were 25 or more employees were more likely to have their pay affected by collective agreements than those in smaller workplaces. USDAW comments that it has major agreements in both the food and non-food sectors of retailing. It is mainly represented in the retail food sector, with the Co-operative Group having the highest number of USDAW members. It also has major agreements with Tesco, Sainsbury and Morrisons. The union also reports that it has individual agreements in the non-food sector with companies such as Woolworth's and is well represented in the clothing, footwear, electrical and department store sectors. It claims poor representation in the DIY sector. Whilst there is relatively high incidence of membership in some companies there are an extensive number of retail companies not recognising unions at all.

Of the 2001 USDAW figures, men comprised 40 per cent of the members whilst women comprised 60 per cent, a ratio that has been stable since the mid-1970s and reflects the overall proportions of men and women employed in retailing. Membership figures for part-time workers have gradually increased since the 1960s and in 2001 about a third of USDAW's members worked on a part-time basis (compared to 58 per cent of the retail workforce).

Some of the characteristics of the retail workforce go some way to explaining the low overall union membership density. For example, Cully and Woodland (1998) explain that those employees less likely to be unionised tend to be those working part time, temporary workers and those with short lengths of service (up to one year's service), youths (particularly those under the age of 20), women, those working in small workplaces (with less than 25 employees) and companies in the private sector. The fragmentation of employing units (see below) may also be a contributory reason for why retailing has a low union density.

USDAW report that in 2001 they recruited 69,615 members but lost 70,145 members. Rather than being a disenchantment with union activities this can be explained by the high labour turnover rates.

Low pay

Retailing has traditionally been considered a low paid industry. In 1972 the average weekly wage of shop salesmen and male sales assistants was ranked third from the bottom in the scale of average weekly full-time workers, whilst the corresponding position for shop saleswomen and female sales assistants was the bottom of the scale.

In 1974, Robinson and Wallace commented: 'The concentration of female employment, the high proportions of juvenile and part-time workers, the fragmentation of employing units, the limited incidence of collective bargaining . . . are features widely regarded as symptomatic of low pay sectors of employment' (38).

The work by Broadbridge (1995) also confirms that sales assistants and check-out operators were amongst the lowest paid workers in the United Kingdom in the 1990s. Analysis of the New Earnings Survey data for 2000 reveals that this position has not changed over the years. Indeed the average earnings index in retail distribution is lower than the average earnings index for the whole of the UK economy. Low pay can contribute to poor morale and high labour turnover. In practice there is a wide range of pay levels that vary according to the type of store, location and type of job performed. The range of earnings in the retail sector is significant, with senior retail management commanding very high salaries (look at some retail companies' annual reports to see the salary levels of directors and senior employees), whilst many sales assistants receive low wages. Large companies tend to have higher wage rates for hourly employees than small shops, often because of the collective agreements mentioned earlier.

Table 13.2 Composition of earnings of full-time sales assistants

	1990	1995	2000
Average gross weekly earnings (£)[1]			
Male	177.4	202.7	251.2
Female	126.2	165.4	198.8
Female earnings as a percentage of male earnings	71.1	81.6	79.1
Average gross hourly earnings (£)[2]			
Male	423.9	496.0	607.0
Female	326.9	424.0	513.0
Female earnings as a percentage of male earnings	77.1	85.5	84.5
% of earnings on commission			
Male	11.2	11.1	10.3
Female	2.6	2.6	3.1
Overtime pay %			
Male	4.5	4.3	5.4
Female	2.0	3.0	3.7
Average commission earned (£)			
Male	19.9	22.4	25.9
Female	3.3	4.3	6.1
Total weekly hours			
Male	40.6	40.6	40.3
Female	38.4	38.7	38.3

[1] Excluding those whose pay was affected by absence
[2] Excluding overtime pay and overtime hours
Source: Office for National Statistics (2002b), New Earnings Survey (1990, 1995, 2000)

The figures provided in Table 13.2 indicate that the average hourly earnings for sales assistants is about £5 to £6 per hour. Many companies however pay less than this. Whilst there was speculation that the introduction of a national minimum wage (NMW) would have disastrous effects on the retail sector many of the multiple retail companies have been unaffected as they pay rates above the minimum hourly rate (currently £4.20 per hour). Added to this is the fact that trainees or younger employees can be paid a lower rate or excluded from the NMW provisions altogether. It is likely that the introduction of the NMW has impacted more on small and medium-sized retail companies than upon major retail multiples.

Wilkinson (1998) shows there are large numbers of low paid employees in wholesale and retail industries and they account for 24 per cent of all the low paid in the United Kingdom. White (1999) notes that a third of low paid employees in the retail industries receive overtime payments. Overtime is more common among low paid employees in 'non-specialised stores' (such as supermarkets) than in other areas of retailing. By contrast, incentive pay (including commission) is most prevalent amongst employees selling household items, such as furniture and white goods. Men have more opportunities to earn commission payments than women (see Table 13.2 and Broadbridge 1991).

We have now examined the composition of the employment structure in retailing as well as some of the characteristics of the retail industry that are related to that structure; for example, the reliance upon part-time work means that it attracts particular types of workers, whilst its low pay status means it employs more women than men in lower level positions. However, what is interesting is that many of the trends have not changed significantly since Backman's (1957) research into the characteristics of retail trade employment. He concluded that the retail trade employed a significant proportion of women and youths, whilst it was characterised by a large amount of seasonal and part-time employment and low unionisation.

Self-assessment Question 1 *Thinking about the composition and characteristics of the retail labour market, what HRM strategies do retail companies need to consider to ensure they maintain an effective workforce?*

Issues affecting employment change in retailing

In Chapter 1, Burt and Sparks discussed some of the significant developments that have occurred in the retail sector. They placed this in the context of general environmental change and considered some of the main trends such as market consolidation and changes in location and operating scale. All these changes have an impact on the composition of employment and demand for labour in retailing. The aim here is to provide an outline of *some* of these issues:

- market concentration;
- technological change;
- centralisation;
- new approaches to working;
- retail location and operating scale;
- organisational restructuring.

Market concentration

There has been a steady decline in the number of retail businesses and outlets as businesses have consolidated and the market has become more concentrated. The market concentration in retailing generally has had implications on employment levels so that nowadays there is less employment in the independent sector. For example, employment in single outlet retailers was just 30 per cent in 1994 (Central Statistical Office 1996) compared to 47 per cent in 1971. This reinforces the overall decline of owners working in retailing. The proportion of employment in multiple chains has similarly been rising steadily as the influence of these retailers grows. In 1994 multiple retailers with at least 10 outlets employed 59 per cent of all persons engaged in retailing.

As retail market concentration has increased so it has become more noticeable that large companies are large employers of labour. However, it is clear that some polarities exist in retail employment. Independent shops might employ just one person, or perhaps other family members, whilst the largest retail employer, Tesco, employs almost 100,000 (Times Books 1998). Moreover 8 of the top 10 retail companies employ over 40,000 people whilst, many have over 10,000 employees (Times Books 1998). As they are national retailers this means that the employment pattern is dispersed, although some single units such as superstores, department stores and head offices can employ substantial numbers at any one site. As the retail market has become more concentrated and more professional in its approach, so large multiple retailers are able to offer a career in retail management. Thus there has been an increase in staff development activities as firms realise that direct and positive management is necessary in order to survive against growing competition. At the other end of the scale Liff and Turner (1999) consider how owners of small shops have responded to changing market conditions. They conclude that the unattractiveness of the wages and terms and conditions of employment (such as long hours) offered by small shops meant that they continued to experience labour shortages.

Technological change

The use of technology within retailing has always been seen as a labour-saving opportunity. It allows management to control, monitor and utilise labour more effectively. New technologies have rapidly penetrated most activities in retailing and allow control and decision making to be centralised at head office.

Self-assessment Question 2 *List the technological changes that have occurred in retailing which have impacted on people's jobs.*

Technological changes have affected jobs at every level in retailing. So, for example, in recent years there has been job rescheduling on the shop floor, back stockroom, warehouse and head office. This has resulted in greater labour productivity levels, but also resulted in less skilled, more monotonous and stressful jobs. The introduction of new technologies has also led to a loss of some types of jobs (such as clerical head office jobs because of the introduction of electronic data transmission) but an increase in other occupations (for example highly skilled specialists at head office to handle decision-making processes).

The jobs most affected by the introduction of new technologies are at the lower skilled, clerical and manual levels. Actual job losses do not always occur; changes in work rescheduling may result, but this depends on the store size, trading hours and desired customer service level. In addition, many companies claim they have few or no redundancies but when staff leave they are often not replaced, so there is natural wastage because of high labour turnover. Some of the technological changes have served to deskill some jobs, whilst others demand highly skilled employees. This results in a polarisation of the workforce into low skilled sales workers and highly skilled managers and technologists.

Centralisation

Market concentration and technological advances have meant that the major retailers have become increasingly centralised. More power has switched away from branches to head office buyers and product managers. Thompson (1993) argues that centralisation can bring major economies and efficiencies but it carries the risk that branch managers 'decentralise upwards' by referring difficult decisions to their area managers or head office. Branches become more standardised with consistent policies for stocking and display.

Front-line branch staff have been empowered in respect of certain aspects of customer service but little else. Thompson (1993) outlines the consequential impact on store managers:

- they now are fundamentally responsible for organising and dealing with staffing within the store;
- they have become cost controllers but with an ability to affect service effectiveness;
- they have little control/influence on product ranges, local prices and special promotions; instead they mainly implement the strategies and policies decided centrally;
- they are responsible for money and security and for compliance with the Health and Safety at Work Act;
- they are sometimes given discretion for local purchases and charitable donations.

Thompson (1993) concludes that centralisation has brought efficiency benefits and offers further opportunities through improved IT. But branch staff feel that their influence is quite limited. This is compounded when head office staff are perceived to make errors of judgement – often because of their isolation from the front line. There is a need for more effective listening and feedback mechanisms to provide for better two-way communications and to allow branches more influence and power of intervention. Centralisation at head offices also means that fewer opportunities are available for senior managerial positions at a regional level. However, individual managers may see this as an opportunity to get on the faster track to the top. It also requires a labour force specialist in many functions to cope with the technological and market concentration changes taking place.

New approaches to working

The length of the trading week for many retail companies, particularly those in the multiple food, DIY and electrical sectors, is often almost double the normal working week. Furthermore, many retailers now trade 7 days a week, with some outlets operating 24 hours a day, and many retail stores work on a 24-hour cycle with replenishment being carried out when the store is closed. In addition, Internet shopping has placed new demands on the retail workforce. All these permutations require careful staff scheduling.

Self-assessment Question 3 *What flexible working practices exist or may be adopted in the future by retail companies, and what are the principle benefits of flexible working arrangements for employers and employees?*

The different working arrangements available in retailing led Kirby (1993) to argue that one of the main attractions of employment in the sector has been the flexibility of working hours. However, this flexible workforce is comprised almost entirely of those in unskilled or semi-skilled, non-managerial positions. Managerial retail positions are traditionally full time (Broadbridge 1996; 1998). In practice the hours worked in retailing can vary between a few per week (as little as eight for some sales assistants) to very many (over 60 hours per week for some managers). So whilst companies have tailored their non-managerial employment to respond to changes in the macro and micro environment, managerial positions have not received similar attention. The reasons for this are less to do with the practicalities of offering flexible working arrangements for managerial staff (as demonstrated below) and more to do with the way organisational culture has been formed and allowed to develop. The implications of managers working long hours (which includes taking work home and being involved in work-related travel) have hitherto been overlooked, although recent research has indicated increasing concern about the number of hours worked and the feelings of job-related stress, and the resultant effects this has on life outside work (Broadbridge 1999; 2001a).

Working long hours regularly can carry serious health and safety implications (Hewitt 1993; Harrington 1994) and working beyond 40 hours a week may be counter productive (Cooper and Lewis 1993). This could result in deficient work performance, loss of productivity, reduced customer service standards and a decreased company image and profits. Yet in a survey conducted with 132 retail managers the author found that 86 per cent of managers worked over 40 hours per week. Moreover, 22 per cent worked between 51 and 60 hours per week and 11 per cent reported working beyond 61 hours per week. Furthermore 42.4 per cent stated that they took work home with them more than one evening a week, whilst the average number of days they spent travelling on company business (including an overnight stay away from home) was 20 days per annum.

Work overload, time pressures and deadlines and long working hours were the top three factors that put pressure on retail managers. The managers wanted more flexible working arrangements so as to allow them to achieve a better balance between their professional and family lives. However, most retail companies were found not to offer flexible working arrangements for their senior staff, despite the fact that three-quarters (75 per cent) of retail managers stated that some aspects of their job could be done via flexitime, two-thirds (66 per cent) said they could undertake some of their work at home, and half (56 per cent) could conduct their jobs over fewer days a week (such as three 12-hour days).

The findings showed that middle managers in particular seemed able to work via flexible working arrangements. Working at home was the most flexible working arrangement for senior managers whilst flexitime was the most flexible working arrangement for junior and middle managers. Head office locations were particularly suited to flexible working arrangements, such as home working and working several days per week. However, even two-thirds of branch level managerial staff (who are driven by customer demand and opening hours) reported being able to work via flexitime arrangements. All this signifies that introducing more flexible working arrangements for retail managerial staff may help to reduce the pressure they experience. Such a reconsideration of work schedules may better accommodate the changing nature of the role of retail managers, as well as the changing workforce (for example dual career households) and ensuring a better work–life balance.

Retail location and operating scale

The changing location of much retailing has also affected employment patterns. Again polarities exist, so that some areas will offer few or no retail employment opportunities (for example some rural areas of Scotland) whilst other areas may offer many thousands of retail jobs (for example city centres or shopping centres such as Bluewater or Braehead). The off-centre or suburban locations of stores are often more attractive to married women in suburban housing than, for example, to single young women. The modernisation of retailing, particularly through the development of new stores in new locations, has upgraded the retail environment. Job changes and environmental improvements coupled with attractive hours of work and flexibility have made retailing much more attractive to many female employees. Changes in operating scale have meant that large superstore and department store formats employ many people at any one site (perhaps 300–400) and have a senior management team to support their operations. Small satellite stores employ fewer people and may even be managed by a manager of a nearby store rather than having a dedicated store manager.

Organisational restructuring

During the 1990s considerable organisational restructuring occurred within the retail environment in response to many of the micro-environmental changes taking place in the industry. In many cases this has resulted in fewer levels of management in the hierarchy, and thus has restricted career development opportunities, leaving many shop floor staff 'empowered' and more multi-skilled.

Small retailers often do not provide training for their staff but there is likely to be more staff development in the large retail companies. In the search for competitive differentiation increased emphasis has been placed on customer service, product knowledge and customer care. This means a more thoroughly trained workforce, with training taking in skills additional to those currently taught. There has been a corresponding increase in the professionalism in the management of the industry.

Prospects for retail employment

When considering the prospects for retail employment we must take account of both the changes happening within the industry and those occurring outside.

Self-assessment Question 4 *What macro-level changes can impact on the retail employment structure and the demand for labour?*

Retail companies must consider changes that are happening in the external environment, how these changes are likely to affect the business, and subsequently the employment structure of the business. A change in consumer spending and disposable income levels may have consequential effects on retail employment levels. The cyclical fluctuations in absolute employment figures may be accounted for by the general state of the economy.

In preparation for the changing structure of the labour force, retailers must also reconsider their recruitment policies and training programmes so as to recruit and retain their future workforce during a period of fierce competition for workers in all industries. They have to use more creative approaches to recruitment because they need to compete with other employees for a shrinking pool of recruits.

Retailing has traditionally suffered from an image problem and failed to attract the best graduates (Schmidt and Corbett 1994; Retail Week 1996), but with the increasing professionalism of the industry a career in retailing may become more appealing. This was not the case, however, according to research with undergraduate management students at one UK university (Broadbridge 2001b). Just 2.6 per cent of the 369 students surveyed selected retailing as their preferred career option (although 30.7 per cent might be persuaded to consider it as a career). The top five attributes students associated with a career in retailing were 'consumer oriented', 'people oriented', 'poor salary', 'limited advancement' and 'poor working hours' – all attributes that may be derived from their experience as consumers or shop floor sales assistants. Many were unaware of what a career in retailing entailed or the opportunities it offered. Without such knowledge students cannot be expected to make informed decisions regarding retailing as a career choice. Retailers must concentrate their activities on demonstrating to graduates that the sector can provide an interesting, challenging and varied career. They could begin such a process by exposing students who have part-time jobs in retailing to the various parts of the business and explaining the variety of career advancement opportunities. They also need to collaborate more closely with careers officers and retail providers in higher education to ensure that students are exposed to and aware of the challenges that a career in retailing can provide.

The retail industry is a major employer of labour and human resource management is a vital task for company efficiency. This is true whether the company has tens of thousands of employees dispersed across the world or is in a single location with several hundred employees. The management of a wide variety of personnel categories and job tasks is complex and continuously evolving. Many elements of employee use in retailing have, therefore, changed over recent years.

Summary

This chapter examined the composition of the employment structure in the distributive trades and considered the trends in figures on absolute employment, self-employment and sector employment. It then looked at the characteristics of retail employees, concluding that the industry is an important employer of women, part-timers and youths. It identified some of the employment characteristics of the retail industry as being a high labour turnover, low unionisation and low pay. It then analysed the issues affecting employment change in retailing, such as market concentration, technological changes, new approaches to working and organisational restructuring.

Further reading

There are two textbooks that expand on the general principles contained in this chapter.

Armstrong, M. (2001) *A Handbook of Human Resource Management Practice*, London: Kogan Page.

Torrington, D., Hall, L. and **Taylor, S.** (2002) *Human Resource Management*, London: FT/Prentice Hall.

Journal articles that focus specifically on HRM issues in the retail sector include:

Broadbridge, A. (1996) 'Female and male managers: equal progression?' *The International Review of Retail, Distribution and Consumer Research*, 6(3): 259–79.

Broadbridge, A. (1998) 'Barriers in the career progression of retail managers', *The International Review of Retail, Distribution and Consumer Research*, 8(1): 53–78.

Liff, S. and **Turner, S.** (1999) 'Working in a corner shop: are employee relations changing in response to competitive pressures?' *Employee Relations*, 21(4): 418–29.

In addition the following journals may be of interest:

- *Employee Relations;*
- *Human Resource Management Journal;*
- *Industrial Relations Journal;*
- *International Journal of Human Resource Management;*
- *International Review of Retail, Distribution and Consumer Research;*
- *Journal of Retailing and Consumer Services.*

CHAPTER 14

Labour turnover in the retail industry

Jim Hendrie

Introduction

The previous chapter provided a detailed overview of the retail labour market. It noted in particular that many individuals who worked in the retail sector were young, female and employed on a part-time basis. It was also noted the retail labour market was characterised by a high level of staff turnover. Individuals tend to move from one job to another with a high degree of regularity. This level of transition can cause difficulties for the retailer who may be continually recruiting staff, constantly training and struggling to cover certain shifts.

In the following case study we examine the causes behind labour turnover and ask you to put forward ideas for dealing with the issues that emerge. The chapter is based on actual research for a multiple outlet retailer. Whilst the names of the companies have been changed the facts contained within the case and the survey details are accurate.

Background

Ashley's operates in a highly competitive market selling cosmetics, toiletries and related items at very competitive prices. The market in which the company trades had sales of some £3.28 billion in 2001 and is part of a growing retail sector. Indeed forecasts indicate that by 2004 the market will increase by over 30 per cent to reach £4.75 billion.

Whilst the market has traditionally been dominated by two major players, Brabsons and Chandlers, a large number of independent retailers also exist. The cosmetics and toiletries market has also become increasingly attractive to the major grocery chains. Information on the BBC News web site (2000) reflects this. Although it shows that Brabsons hold a 26 per cent share of the market it suggests that the grocery multiples have a larger combined share than the specialists.

Ashley's was founded in the late 1970s by an entrepreneurial family. They slowly but surely built a business that was based on low prices to the consumer and low operating costs to the owners. The strategy was to open news shops as funds became available. The family built the business to a chain of 25 stores before deciding to sell. Under the new owners, Ashley's business was expanded, slowly at first, then rapidly up to the present day. It now has stores located throughout the country. Approximately two years ago the business expanded overseas and it now has a total of over 100 stores, with plans to grow further both by new store openings and acquisition.

Ashley's has not been alone in developing discount formats, with many regional chains forming across the country. The company faces direct competition from other retailers such as Dubois, Esters and Franklins (a recent entrant to the market). These discounters, plus Brabsons, Chandlers, the independent stores and the grocery multiples create a highly competitive market sector. Table 14.1 shows the number of stores each 'specialist' competitor has nationally.

Table 14.1 Store Numbers

Group	Number of stores
Brabsons	1,400
Chandlers	800
Franklins	230
Ashley's	109
EstersΔ	50
Dubois	26

A major change that has taken place in recent months has been the sale of Chandlers, initially to a private European firm, then to a major player from the Far East. This has resulted in both Franklins and Chandlers being owned by the same group, which now has over 1,000 stores nationwide. It has the capacity for further growth and the potential to dominate both discount and standard retailing formats.

Meanwhile the grocers continue to exert pressure on the market, the latest report on the market confirms this when it notes: 'In 1990 the specialists were the dominant distribution channel with a share of 58%, followed by the grocers with 29%. By 2006, Verdict expects this to have been reversed' (www.verdictonline.co.uk).

Ashley's labour turnover

As the business has grown and the market has become more competitive there has been a need to recruit, train and develop staff at all levels. Inevitably as this expansion has taken place there has been an increase in labour turnover. Ashley's historical labour turnover is shown in Table 14.2.

Table 14.2 Ashley's labour turnover

Year	Staff in post	Starters	Leavers	Turnover (%)
1996	445	397	197	44.27
1997	566	586	461	81.45
1998	662	590	498	75.23
1999	847	617	468	55.25
2000	1,043	792	764	73.25
2001	1,098	809	758	69.03

Source: Company records (1996–2001)

There are a number of ways in which labour turnover can be calculated. Ashley's uses the separation rate, defined by ACAS (1994: 30), as 'The simplest and most usual way of measuring labour turnover'. It is calculated as follows:

$$\frac{\text{Number of leavers}}{\text{Average no employed}} \times 100.$$

Gaining comparable labour turnover figures is very difficult, as most businesses consider this to be sensitive information, the different types of competitors also makes it difficult to compare performance. However comparisons can be made with Ashley's parent company, which trades in a different market. Its labour turnover figures have ranged from 32 per cent in 1996 to 75 per cent the following year and are currently around the 60 per cent mark. Table 14.3 shows other businesses and their labour turnover figures.

Further comparisons are also possible. An Income Data Services (IDS) report in December 2000 detailed research undertaken by the Chartered Institute for Personnel Development. This research noted that labour turnover in the wholesale and retail trades was running at 56 per cent in the year to December 2000. It is

Table 14.3 Labour turnover comparisons

Company	Turnover (%)
Prêt a manger (sandwich shops)	90
Welcome Break (motorway services)	60
Parent company	60
CWS Retail Operations Scotland (food)	41
Sainsbury (food)	35
Retail food store average	33
Tesco (food)	30
Budgens (food)	30
Asda (food)	24

Source: Company reports (2000–2)

clear that Ashley's labour turnover is higher than average and for that reason alone it should be examined.

Labour turnover costs

For Ashley's the level of labour turnover has not only proved to be disruptive to the business but has also become costly. A simple formula supplied by the Institute of Personnel Management (IPM) suggests that the costs associated with replacing employees at store level is approximately 37.5 per cent of the jobholder's annual wage cost. This accounts for recruitment time, lost productivity, training and other costs (such as uniforms, etc.). Using this formula the cost of labour turnover to Ashley's in the year 2001 would have been close to £1.6 million.

A study by the IDS (2000) maintained that the typical cost of replacing an employee is actually higher than the IPM suggests. IDS estimates that the cost associated with replacing a member of staff is around 60 per cent of their salary. Given that the average salary at Ashley's is £6,000, this would mean that the average cost of replacing each member of staff was £3,600 and the total annual cost within the company was close to £2.7 million. Clearly, whatever figure is applied, labour turnover represents a major expense for the company.

Labour turnover statistics

Up until 2002 Ashley's had, like most other companies, recorded labour turnover figures as part of the human resources (HR) function. It produced reports for senior management showing the actual figures year by year. If required the HR department to disaggregate these reports further and provide details on turnover by age, length of service and the number of hours worked. However, apart from reporting these figures, little was done and the information was not used in a proactive manner.

Analysis of turnover figures for the company in 2001 revealed some key messages:

- 73 per cent of those leaving the business worked 16 hours or less;
- 58 per cent of those leaving had less than six months' service;
- 35 per cent of those who left were under 18 and 33 per cent between the ages of 18 and 25.

It was also interesting to note a higher level of turnover in city centre stores. There was also a high turnover level at the company's warehouse and distribution centre.

The only other source of information on labour turnover (and more importantly reasons for its happening) was from exit interviews with staff. However, due to poor return rates, exit interviews had been stopped in January 2000, and thus another source of information on why staff were leaving the business had been lost. The last available set of exit interviews (for the whole group, including Ashley's) is shown in Table 14.4.

Table 14.4 Exit interview results

Reason for leaving	Number reporting	% reporting
Other employment	231	31.82
Domestic/personal	113	15.56
Management attitude	102	14.05
Further education	53	7.30
Move to FT employment	48	6.61
Pay/benefits	38	5.23
Insufficient hours	29	3.99
Health	20	2.75
Travel problems	18	2.48
Working conditions	16	2.20
Retirement	14	1.93
Maternity	10	1.38
Lack of career prospects	10	1.38
Working patterns	8	1.10
Job content	7	0.96
Conflict with colleagues	5	0.69
Insufficient training	4	0.55
Total Return rate 39.89%	726	100.00

Source: Human Resources Department year-end statistics to January 2000

Current initiatives

Senior management in the parent company recognised at the beginning of 2002 that labour turnover was an issue in all parts of the business and set up a Labour Turnover and Staff Retention committee. Its remit was to investigate the causes of labour turnover throughout the business and to come up with recommendations for improvements. The committee comprised management from Ashley's, the parent company, and senior human resources executives. The initial meeting in January 2002 of this committee established the points shown in Box 14.1.

Box 14.1
Outcome of Labour Turnover and Staff Retention committee meeting

- Company-wide labour turnover including Ashley's was above industry norms.
- There were clearly difficulties in recruiting staff in city centres and areas of major conurbation.
- The cost of turnover was agreed to be at least £2.5 million to the whole business.
- Analysis of labour turnover statistics was required and independent research work would allow a deeper examination in this area.
- Comparison was required to investigate what other companies were doing and also to establish how remuneration packages compared.
- Some form of survey was required to seek the views of staff.

The committee commissioned outside consultants to carry out some focus groups with managers from both the parent company and Ashley's, their aim being to identify the reasons for the high labour turnover. The groups established what these managers thought were the key satisfiers and dissatisfiers in the business at the moment. Although this research was company wide the fact that Ashley's managers were involved meant that the findings were relevant (Tables 14.5 and 14.6).

At the same time as the focus groups were being conducted the committee arranged for a staff survey to be carried out. A randomly selected sample of staff from both the parent company and Ashley's were chosen. One element of the research focused upon

Table 14.5 Factors that satisfy staff at work

Ranking	Satisfier
1	Benefits
2	Salaries
3	Management attitudes
4	Working patterns
5	Management development opportunities
6	Staff seen as valuable resource

Source: Labour Turnover and Retention Committee (May 2002)

Table 14.6 Factors that dissatisfy staff at work

Ranking	Dissatisfiers
1	City centre pay rates
2	Junior pay rates
3	Staff facilities
4	Retention of mature staff
5	Low contracted hours
6	Ideas not listened to

Source: Labour Turnover and Retention Committee (May 2002)

Table 14.7 Reasons for working for the company (group wide)

Ranking	Top six	Ranking	Bottom six
1	Work location convenience	1	Staff facilities/uniform
2	Customer contact	2	Training/development opportunities
3	Management attitude	3	Career expectations not met
4	Suits domestic/study requirements	4	Rates of pay
5	Contract hours	5	Lack of communication
6	Social relationships	6	Other benefits (holidays/sick pay)

Source: Labour Turnover and Retention Committee (May 2002)

what was good and bad about working for the business. This led to the 'top 6 good points' and the 'bottom 6' (which effectively were the bad points) (Table 14.7).

On completion of its investigations the Labour Turnover Committee prepared a report and made a presentation to both senior management and other key managers of the parent company in June 2002. They made the following recommendations to senior management:

- the abolition of junior pay rates;
- the introduction of a 'city centre' weighting allowance;
- the improvement of staff facilities;
- the changing of staff contracts to minimum acceptable levels;
- the improvement of training and development in the business;
- the recruitment of mature staff;
- the need for more flexible employment contracts, such as 'term-time' contracts for students;
- the need to continue to develop company-wide communications;
- the need to work more on 'valuing people'.

The hard message to management was that doing nothing was not an option.

Research at Ashley's

In order to fully understand the issues surrounding labour turnover in Ashley's the company undertook additional research in the spring of 2002. Building upon the group results, this research was carried out in four stages (Table 14.8).

Secondary desk research

The results of the research work carried out by the Labour Turnover and Staff Retention Committee was the main source of secondary data. It had conducted its own small-scale survey of a random sample of all staff and had established that things such as management attitude and working patterns were seen to staff as satisfiers whilst pay, facilities and contract hours had been seen as dissatisfiers. The results highlighted areas around contracted hours, training, pay, management

Table 14.8 Research stages

Stage	Type of research	Activities involved
1	Secondary research	Researching the work of the Labour Turnover and Staff Retention Committee
2	Exploratory research	Reviewing historical data; discussions with key players
3	Primary research	Calculation of labour turnover costs
4	Empirical research	Questionnaire design, administration and analysis

Source: Labour Turnover and Retention Committee (May 2002)

style and staff facilities as being potential reasons for turnover. This gave a clear direction as to the areas to explore further.

Exploratory research

The initial exploratory research carried out was to review how labour turnover is measured in Ashley's. This involved a review of the available historical information and discussions with management seeking their views on the problem. The exploratory research phase also established that the company calculated total labour turnover by branch as follows:

- on a crude separation method of calculation;
- by hours worked;
- by length of service.

However the research also revealed that Ashley's were 'guilty' of the following:

- it had stopped carrying out exit interviews with its leavers;
- it did not routinely calculate a stability index (measuring the extent to which its experienced workforce is being retained);
- it did not clearly separate controlled 'organisational'-led turnover (redundancy, dismissal, early retirement) from uncontrolled turnover (when people leave of their own free will).

The data was analysed over a three-year period to identify trends and to better understand the key drivers of labour turnover in Ashley's.

Primary research

This stage of the research identified the cost of labour turnover to the business. This involved using the company computer database on turnover and agreeing costs with management. By using various recognised formulae the research was able to determine costs based on the turnover figures for the year ended January 2001.

It was also established that 80 per cent of recorded staff turnover within the company occurred amongst part-time staff working 24 hours a week or less. Clearly when this was established, a prime consideration was to seek the views of these staff. Payroll information suggested that there were around 600 employees within this category and, given their ease of identification, a full census was possible.

Empirical research

This part of the research saw the design and administration of an employee questionnaire. It sought to establish what were the satisfiers and dissatisfiers of working in the business and what staff considered to be the main causes of labour turnover.

The questionnaire was postal, and made use of the company's internal mail system. This had the advantage of allowing the research to reach the entire target audience simply, cheaply, quickly and efficiently. On completion of the questionnaire staff were asked to seal it in an envelope and return it. The process was specifically designed in this way to ensure that staff felt reassured about the privacy of their questionnaire replies.

Analysis of results

Ashley's received 325 replies from the original 598 questionnaires issued.

Personal details

The data shown in Table 14.9 confirmed that the spread of replies was representative of the main groups of staff that were actually driving the labour turnover at Ashley's and therefore any issues raised would be valid.

Further identification of respondents was sought by asking them to indicate what their job title was. The replies split very much along the lines of Table 14.9:

- 30.5 per cent were either school age or student assistants, working less than 9 hours;
- 50.2 per cent were part-timers, working between 10 and 16 hours;
- 19 per cent were in first-line management positions, working between 17 and 24 hours.

As company records had shown a significant proportion of overall turnover occurs amongst staff with less than six months service it was also important that the questionnaire sought to establish the length of service each of the respondents had with the company, as shown in Table 14.10.

Table 14.9 Contract hours worked by respondents

Contract hours	Number	%
Between 0 and 9 hours	96	29.5
Between 10 and 16 hours	163	50.2
Between 17 and 24 hours	65	20.0
No answer	1	0.3

Table 14.10 Length of service of respondents

Length of service	Number	%
0 to 3 months	26	8.0
4 to 6 months	28	8.6
7 to 12 months	66	20.3
13 to 24 months	72	22.2
25 to 36 months	50	15.4
Over 37 months	82	25.2
No response	1	0.3

In terms of age and sex of respondents the following also became clear from the analysis:

- 99 per cent of respondents were female, reflecting the lack of males employed;
- 30 per cent were below 18 years of age;
- 14 per cent were below 25 years of age;
- 43 per cent were between 26 and 50 years of age;
- 13 per cent were over 51 years of age.

Biographical

These questions were used to establish more background statistical information on the types of staff who were responding to the research questionnaire. The main details are summarised below:

- 45 per cent of respondents were single;
- 45 per cent were married or lived with a partner;
- 56 per cent had children;
- 36 per cent had three or fewer children living at home;
- 20 per cent had no formal qualifications, but 80 per cent had some qualification;
- 55 per cent were educated to post-16 level;
- 5 per cent had a first or higher degree.

Work environment

The questionnaire revealed that staff at Ashley's felt the company: (a) had a good reputation (75 per cent); and (b) was a good employer (70 per cent). On the negative side: less than 30 per cent felt that working at Ashley's had helped their career; less than 60% felt they knew the company's goals. With almost 50 per cent of staff currently under the age of 25, career development is often of central importance and it would appear from these findings that opportunities for improvement exist. Ashley's had also spent significant time communicating its business strategy, and to find a large number of staff unsure of the goals of the business was worrying.

Ashley's had also embarked on a 'change management' programme. The questionnaire seemed to indicate that this initiative was working:

- 86 per cent felt their manager treated them with respect;
- 73 per cent felt they were listened to;
- 78 per cent felt encouraged to achieve their targets.

As the relationship between management and staff is a key driver of labour turnover these figures were seen as encouraging. The research also questioned staff about the work they undertook and their relationship with their colleagues. Overall, staff were positive in their replies:

- 88 per cent liked working for Ashley's;
- 85 per cent liked working for their manager;
- 95 per cent liked their workmates;

- 88 per cent enjoyed their work;
- 92 per cent liked dealing with the public.

With such a positive assessment it appeared that this element of the work environment contributed little to labour turnover. Work pressure is often a cause of labour turnover and the research sought to try and understand how staff felt about this important area. The replies were that 58 per cent felt they did not work under pressure; whilst 51 per cent felt they did not often have to work extra hours.

This showed that over 40 per cent of staff either felt pressure or were not confident enough to reply in the positive. Those feeling under greatest work pressure and feeling the need to have to work additional hours were part-time staff. This may be expected, as it is this group of staff who have to cover any shortfall in shop hours due to staff shortages. The research also showed that amongst senior sales and deputies only 35 per cent felt under no pressure and 25 per cent felt they did not have to work many extra hours.

A large percentage of respondents either expressed a 'neutral' view or felt unhappy. This group of staff may feel under more pressure than most, as they are both part time and part of the management team of each shop. They therefore have to cope with the twin pressures of managing in a fast moving environment as well as having to work extra hours.

As the research itself was aimed at finding out what was driving labour turnover it was important to seek staff views on this subject. Staff were asked about the following:

- what they liked about working for Ashley's (Table 14.11);
- what they disliked about working for Ashley's (Table 14.12).

The data contained in Tables 14.11 and 14.12 suggest that the 'likes' revolve around the job itself, working with colleagues, meeting the general public, pay and hours of work. However the figures also show that staff have a series of 'dislikes'. It is very possible that these areas are a source of what is driving labour turnover. To try and confirm these as the causes the research asked respondents what the business should do to reduce labour turnover (Table 14.13).

Table 14.11 Staff likes

Ranking	Likes	% of total responses
1	Workmates	65.8
2	Meeting the public	49.5
3	The hours of work	45.5
4	The pay	27.1
5	The work experience	22.2
6	Their management	15.7
7	Company reputation	6.2
8	The training	3.4

Table 14.12 Staff dislikes

Ranking	Dislikes	% of total responses
1	Hours of work	31.7
2	Pay rates	27.4
3	Staffing levels	19.7
4	Lack of staff recognition	17.2
	Staff facilities	17.2
6	Staff uniform	15.7
7	The work itself	13.2
8	Working under pressure	11.1
9	Company communications	9.5
10	Lack of training	4.3
	The customers	4.3
12	In-store security	4.0

Table 14.13 How to improve staff retention

Ranking	How to stop staff leaving Ashley's	% of total responses
1	Improve pay	32.0
2	Improve hours of work	24.9
3	Improve staff recognition	11.1
4	Improve staffing levels	10.8
5	Improve communications	9.2
6	Change nothing	6.8
7	Improve staff facilities	5.2
8	Improve staff opportunities	2.2
9	Improve training	1.5
10	Lower expectations of staff	0.6

The last area of questioning in the area of work environment asked staff to rank in order of importance why individuals worked for Ashley's and why they left (Table 14.14).

Remuneration and hours of work were seen by many as basic needs and were therefore the main reasons why staff chose to work for Ashley's. Paradoxically they were also the reasons why staff left. Convenience is also a factor, as many of Ashley's stores are located in the heart of local communities, allowing staff to fit work around their own needs. There is also a lack of alternatives that, in turn, reduces employment choice. Although not perhaps the ringing endorsement the company would seek, it remains an important factor.

Table 14.14 Ranking of staff opinions for staying with/ leaving Ashley's

Rank	Reasons to work at Ashley's	Rank score	Rank	Reasons to leave Ashley's	Rank score
1	The money	2.43	1	Not enough hours	2.44
2	Suits childcare	2.07	2	Poor pay	2.23
3	Career	1.97	3	No career prospects	2.07
4	Good work conditions	1.81	4	Expected to work too many extra hours	1.99
5	No other jobs	1.79	5	Unsuitable hours	1.92
6	Work near home	1.78	6	Poor training	1.75
7	Reputation	1.70	7	Poor staff facilities	1.73
8	To meet people	1.67	8	Fear of redundancy	1.65
9	The hours of work	1.43	9	Staff views not listened to	1.62

Personality and attitudinal questions

A series of questions were aimed at assessing how satisfied or dissatisfied the respondents were about working for the company. Staff were asked about their levels of satisfaction in their current job role (Table 14.15).

The research also identified a high degree of satisfaction amongst staff:

- 93 per cent were satisfied with their work colleagues;
- 88 per cent were satisfied with the job they were doing;
- 88 per cent were satisfied with their manager;
- 82 per cent were satisfied with their hours of work;
- 78 per cent were satisfied with the level of job security;
- 76 per cent were satisfied with the training;
- 70 per cent were satisfied with the extra hours to be worked.

The areas of least satisfaction are noted below:

- 60 per cent were dissatisfied with the level of pay;
- 52 per cent were dissatisfied with the staff uniforms;
- 50 per cent were dissatisfied with the staff facilities;

Table 14.15 Level of staff satisfaction

Level of satisfaction	Number	% of total
Very satisfied	97	29.8
Quite satisfied	189	58.2
Not very satisfied	28	8.6
Dissatisfied	4	1.2
No response	7	2.2

- 50 per cent were dissatisfied with the branch staffing levels;
- 43 per cent were dissatisfied with their promotional opportunities;
- 41 per cent were dissatisfied with their future promotion prospects;
- 26 per cent were dissatisfied with branch staff shortages.

With regard to pay, two staff groups felt most aggrieved: part-timers of school age and senior sales assistants. The business does not pay 'adult rates' until the age of 18 (unlike a lot of other retailers) and the difference in pay between a junior and senior sales assistant is only 12p per hour. Neither group of staff is at all happy with this situation and this is probably leading to labour turnover.

In concluding the research, staff were asked simply to indicate what they would be doing in one year's time (Table 14.16).

Table 14.16 What staff will be doing in a year's time

What I will be doing in one year	Number	% of all respondents
The same job	181	55.7
Been promoted	24	7.4
Been made redundant	3	0.9
Working for another company	34	10.5
Not working	4	1.2
In further education	74	22.8
No response	5	1.5

Discussion questions

1. Provide a brief assessment of the causes of labour turnover within Ashley's.

2. Put forward a detailed strategy for reducing labour turnover within the company.

3. Is any further information required in order to put forward your recommendations?

4. What influence will the structure of the market and the level of competition have upon the strategies put forward?

CHAPTER 15

Superquinn: The specialists in fresh foods

Gordon O'Connor

Introduction

Superquinn represents one of the most innovative retail companies currently operating in the grocery sector. The basis of their success lies in their emphasis on providing the customer with fresh products delivered with high levels of customer service. It has managed to operate in an increasingly competitive retail environment by differentiating its offer and clearly positioning itself in the eyes of the consumer. It is this case, more than any in *The Retailing Book*, that demonstrates why successful retailing is predicated upon an interdependency between functions such as marketing and human resource management.

Market background

The Irish grocery sector has undergone significant change over the last decade and remains a highly competitive retail market. The size of the market is estimated to be €10 billion, with retailers serving over 3 million customers (Institute of Grocery Distribution (IGD) 2002). Traditionally established multiples such as Superquinn and Dunnes Stores have competed against independent retailers and voluntary chains such as Spar, Mace, SuperValu and Centra.

In 1997 the UK retailer Tesco entered the Irish market with its purchase of Power Supermarkets. The company now has 76 outlets and controls 16.5 per cent of the grocery market. In 1999 Lidl entered the Irish market, closely followed by Aldi. In just over two years these two discount operations have established a combined market share of around 5 per cent.

Large store development is likely to be limited in the future. Despite relatively good economic prospects there are few cities with sufficient populations able to sustain hypermarket development. Moreover, strict planning regulations limit the size of any new stores. Supermarkets and superstores are likely to remain the dominant format in the future (IGD 2002).

The company

Superquinn is a 100 per cent Irish-owned private retail company founded and managed by the Quinn family. It was started by an entrepreneur, Feargal Quinn, and his father Eammon in 1960. Initially they opened one shop in the border town of Dundalk. The original shop was 2,000 square feet in size and employed eight people. From those modest beginnings the Superquinn of today has 19 stores ranging in size from 20,000 square feet to 50,000 square feet, serving over 250,000 customers per week and employing over 5,500 colleagues (staff). For the first 34 years of its existence it concentrated its retailing efforts in the greater Dublin area, where over one-third of the population of Ireland reside.

In 1994 it modified this strategy by going nationwide and it now has stores in a number of major cities around Ireland. Since its foundation the company has grown organically. In the majority of cases when Superquinn opens a new store it also acts as the property developer and the landlord to adjoining units. Typically the company aims to attract an eclectic mix of retailers, including pharmacies, newsagents, restaurants, florist and dry cleaners. This strategy has both advantages and disadvantages. On the positive side it provides Superquinn with a regular and sustainable source of income. On the negative side, having such a wide array of tenants restricts the range of products and services that the supermarket can sell.

What has underpinned Superquinn's success from the very beginning has been its focus on fresh food and customer service. The company's mission statement is 'to be a world-class team renowned for excellence in fresh food and customer service'. Superquinn has adopted the view that good value is what attracts the customer and good service is what keeps them coming back. This was summed up in the company slogan, which was adopted in 1981: 'Come for the prices, and you'll stay for the service.'

Feargal Quinn, the executive chairman, believes that the biggest and most effective method of advertising is through word of mouth. He is constantly encouraging colleagues to create 'raving fans', that is, customers who speak so highly of the company that their friends and family also shop in Superquinn. As he notes: 'Existing customers can either bring back business themselves, or they can create new business for us by referral' (Quinn 1990: 32).

Fresh food strategy

The company made a decision very early on not to sell drapery, homewares or hardware, rather it focused on becoming the 'best at fresh foods'. Over the past 42 years it has consistently pursued this strategy and gained a worldwide reputation for fresh food shopping. As a means of differentiating itself from the competition the company has undertaken a series of initiatives, including the following.

In-store bakery: in 1973 Superquinn opened its first in-store bakery. After a short period the concept was expanded to all stores and the decision was taken that all bread and cakes not sold by the end of the trading day were to be given to local charities, thus ensuring the quality of the product. This manufacturing department is at the entrance to all stores and sets the tone for the shopping experience – fresh, fresh, fresh.

In-store sausage kitchen: in 1981 the first in-store sausage kitchens were introduced. This successful concept was rolled out to all stores and now represents a vital part of the fresh food offering. Superquinn currently sell over 30 million sausages per year in their 19 stores. This product is more expensive than the competition's but, despite this, it is the leader in all markets in which the company operates.

Salad kitchen: in 1983, in an effort to reduce waste in the fresh produce departments, a salad kitchen was trialled in one store. The idea was conceived after a number of managers returned from a field trip to the United States. All fruit and vegetables that were coming close to the sell-by date were removed from sale. They were then cleaned, processed and, where necessary, dressings were added. These products were an instant success with customers. Currently the salad kitchen accounts for over 1.5 per cent of total sales and provides the company with a gross margin of over 40 per cent.

Tender-cut beef: in 1990 as issues of food safety became more prevalent, Superquinn introduced its 'Beef Traceability' scheme. This initiative was designed to ensure that only beef from approved farms could be sold in Superquinn. This scheme has subsequently developed and now includes DNA tracing back to the animals' farm of origin. All cattle slaughtered must be under 30 months old, fed on a grass-based diet, with all feeds and medicines documented and fully traceable. These stringent regulations were in place prior to the BSE scare in the mid-1990s and Superquinn was the only retailer in Europe to see its beef sales rise during this period.

Select chickens: these were the next fresh food commodity that Superquinn focused on. Working closely with their poultry partner the company ensures that only Irish chickens are sold under the 'Superquinn Select' brand. The chickens can only come from approved farms, which have open-plan housing to provide the bird with ample space. The feed for the chickens is cereal based and does not contain any meat and bone meal or poultry offal meal and is free from any genetically modified ingredients. Every chicken produced has the name of the farmer printed on the label for the customers to see. It is not only in Ireland that Superquinn is recognised as the world leader in food safety and traceability. In 2000 the company was the winner of the Institute of Grocery Distribution UK supply chain excellence award.

Super Fresh: each head of lettuce that Superquinn sells has the day of the week it was picked printed on the pack. The company policy is that every head of lettuce picked on a Monday can be sold up to midday on Tuesday, thus ensuring the product the customer receives is 'Super Fresh'. This policy also applies to cabbages and mushrooms.

Customer service strategy

Since its foundation Superquinn has focused upon delivering value through customer care, and it is now recognised as one of the market leaders for service in Ireland. It employs more colleagues per store than any of its competitors. In 1991 Superquinn was the first supermarket to receive the Quality mark for service in Ireland, an award it retains to this day. In 2000 Superquinn was awarded the 'Excellence Through People' award, a state-sponsored award given to companies that excel in the training of their colleagues. Amongst the many and varied initiatives that the company has employed, are the following.

Bag packing: in Superquinn it takes two colleagues to operate a checkout. This is because the company offers all customers the option of having their bags packed. This major point of difference helps Superquinn attract a wide range of customers, most noticeably mothers with babies and the elderly.

Umbrella/Carry-out service: the company employs colleagues called service operators. As part of the service offer, their role is to assist customers with their groceries. They are equipped with rainwear for themselves and umbrellas for the customers to protect them when they carry their purchases to the car.

Trolley host: when a customer arrives at Superquinn they are handed their trolley by a trolley host or a greeter who welcomes them and gives them their trolley together with a copy of the latest special offers.

Playhouse: there is a playhouse in all stores for customers with small children. Until recently this was a free service, but a nominal fee is now charged. The playhouse is fully supervised and health board approved and it affords customers the opportunity to shop in comfort whilst their children are cared for. For first-time users of the playhouse the parent is given a 'bleeper' as reassurance – if the child does not settle the customer can be discretely contacted. The playhouse leader frequently organises colouring competitions and face painting and in one store a basic computer skills course is run for 5 and 6 year olds. The playhouse is one of the most popular features of a Superquinn store and even offers free nappies for babies in the changing area.

Pennies from heaven: Superquinn has always focused its customer service efforts at the checkout area, and one of the services that receives most attention is also one of the simplest. At each checkout there is a container with cents, and beside it is a sign reading: 'In need of a cent or have one to spare, take one or leave one, that's why we're there.' These cents are used for customers' bills that total, for example, €10.03 or €20.02. When this occurs the operators tell the customers to take the odd change from the container so that they won't have to change a large note. If the bill next time is, say, €9.98 then the customer can, if they choose, leave the loose coins in the container for the next customer. Customers appreciate this service, as do the cashiers, as it makes the job of cash management much easier.

Sweet-free checkouts: during one of the many meetings that Feargal Quinn held with customers it was noted that one of the biggest frustrations with shopping was 'pester power'. Every time customers got to the checkouts their children would pester them to buy sweets. In an attempt to please customers and resolve this issue, Superquinn removed all sweets from checkouts. Whilst this initiative led to a dramatic fall in sweet sales, the company soon noticed a large increase in the number of customers with children shopping in their stores.

Bunny bags: every fresh produce department has a display unit with a statue of a rabbit beside it. The unit is filled with leaves that have fallen off cabbage heads and the customer is encouraged to take the leaves home, free of charge, for their pet rabbits.

Broccoli saw: this was introduced to the fruit and vegetable departments after customers complained that they did not want to pay for stalks. To avoid paying they broke off the broccoli stems and left the broken stalks on the display. A Superquinn colleague decided to collect the stems and make broccoli salad with mayonnaise and nuts. This is now sold for up to five times the price of the broccoli. To help provide the raw materials for this new salad, and to give customers a service that is unique to Superquinn, a saw is provided and customers are encouraged to cut off the stalks if they do not want them.

Grape scissors: the grape scissors idea came from a colleague in the fruit and vegetable department. He noticed that in every box there was a large quantity of 'loose' grapes that fell off as customers tried to make the bunches smaller. In an effort to reduce this waste he placed a pair of scissors beside the grapes and put up a sign saying, 'For your added convenience we now have scissors to cut grapes'. Overnight this became a huge success and reduced the waste by over 90 per cent.

Two's a crowd: this idea came from the United States. During a trip abroad one manager noticed an egg timer at an airport check-in desk and enquired what it was for. It was explained that when a customer arrives at the desk the clerk starts the egg timer. If the passenger has not been checked through by the time all the sand reaches the bottom they get $10 off their next flight. When the manager applied this to Superquinn he decided to offer £1.00 to any customer who was third in a checkout queue and if the store failed to open another checkout within 60 seconds.

Superclub, Superscan and Goofs: in 1992 Superquinn was the first retailer in Europe to introduce a customer loyalty scheme. Entitled Superclub, it currently has over 200,000 members, with one-third of all households in Ireland being regular users. This scheme is similar to many in the United Kingdom and Ireland and has over 20 partners, including Texaco and Irish Ferries. The main difference between the Superclub loyalty scheme and others is that the scheme is gift based.

The Superclub card has many unique features, most noticeably the ability to display the customer's name on the EPOS screen. Superquinn colleagues are encouraged to call customers by their name so as to build up the personal relationship that is so important in retailing. As Feargal Quinn notes: 'In using their name, we are treating customers straight away as an individual, not a statistic, or a number or a member of an anonymous class like "passengers" or "customers"' (Quinn, 1990:110).

The Superclub card also gives Superquinn the opportunity to provide its customers with the Superscan facility. This is a self-scanning system that speeds up the customers' shopping and introduces efficiencies into the checking-out process for Superquinn. No other supermarket in the Republic of Ireland has self-scanning.

For retailers selling large volumes of goods throughout the week, quality control is a major issue. To ensure that customers receive products in the ideal condition Superquinn invented 'Goofs'. The company has drawn up an extensive list of products, and guarantees the quality of each item sold in store. This list is published and given to every customer. If the company 'goofs' and any of its products fall below the standard it sets itself, the customer identifying the Goof is rewarded with Superclub loyalty points.

Although the concept was originally designed to create a sense of fun and atmosphere within the store Superquinn now has over 250,000 quality controllers (customers) who inspect their products every week. Customers are rewarded for their diligence, whilst managers are provided with a valuable and instant source of feedback. Each Goof costs the company Superclub points and, although some retailers would feel that this is money not well spent, Superquinn maintains that it reinforces its commitment to customer service.

'Superquinn 4 Food': in 1999 Superquinn was the first supermarket in Ireland to launch Internet shopping. This business has grown steadily and is now being further developed as the company sees this channel contributing over 10 per cent of total sales by the year 2005.

The Boomerang Principle

Over the years Superquinn has welcomed thousands of foreign visitors to its stores. They come to see this small company from a small country on the periphery of Europe. They are amazed that Superquinn can have so many 'points of difference' and can have so many of their colleagues focused upon just one objective – getting the customer to enjoy the experience of shopping and returning week after week. A question that inevitably arises is 'What is the secret of the company's success?'

To enlighten their guests, and to partly answer the question, visitors are presented with a gold tie-pin in the shape of a boomerang. This gift symbolises the ethos and philosophy of the company. When new colleagues join Superquinn they are given a similar tie-pin during their induction training, which makes the job of explaining the 'boomerang principle' easier. Whether it is 'pennies from heaven', no sweets at the checkouts or two's a crowd, the aim is to get the customer to come back – just like a boomerang.

One of the key differentiating factors that separates the company from many of its competitors is the emphasis it places on empowering its colleagues; for example, individuals have always been encouraged to be innovative and look for ways of further improving the business. If they put forward a suggestion that is introduced into the company they get rewarded financially. The company has a formal suggestion scheme call 'Bright Ideas' that generates a significant number of new ideas.

The company also encourages both cooperation and competition between its stores; for example, there have been a number of 'twinning' competitions whereby colleagues from one store exchange ideas with a neighbouring Superquinn store. They compete with teams from other twinned stores, the objective being to copy more ideas than any other team. The winners of the competition (which is usually a 'working' holiday in the United States) are the two stores that implement the best ideas.

Another very productive source of ideas has been field trips to Europe and the United States. Generally a group of store managers will attend a conference and visit a number of stores. These visits are designed to identify best practice, innovation and alternative methods of retailing. When the group return it must present to the board of directors the findings of their field trip. The salad kitchen and the sausage kitchen are perhaps the two most noticeable 'finds' from such visits.

Another major way that Superquinn differentiates itself from its competitors is by having fun (perhaps this has something to do with the fact that the Quinn family were originally in the entertainment industry, or maybe Superquinn colleagues just like dressing up). Whatever the reason, it has become part of the established culture of the business and colleagues like to celebrate a wide variety of events in fancy dress. For example, on a number of occasions Superquinn has won first prize in the national St Patrick's Day parade. When one speaks to colleagues about why they enjoy marching in a banana costume through the streets of Dublin, the answer is that they don't enjoy the marching but they wouldn't miss the party afterwards 'for all the tea in China'!

Seasonal occasions afford plenty of opportunities for dressing up in Superquinn. At Christmas the checkout colleagues all wear Santa hats or flashing earrings. At Easter time you are likely to find a colleague dressed up as a giant chicken or a similar character. For colleagues who work in the fruit and vegetable department, Hallowe'en is without doubt the best time of the year. They not only dress up as Dracula and Frankenstein, they convert the whole department into a virtual haunted house or graveyard. This creates great fun in the store for both customers and colleagues.

When colleagues celebrate their birthday they are provided with a cake. Similarly, when a department has a very successful week a bottle of champagne is opened, and when the store receives a commendation in the food safety audit the colleagues receive a free breakfast. In short, no matter how trivial the occasion may seem, Superquinn colleagues are encouraged to celebrate it.

Summary

Superquinn is an example of how a small private company can compete successfully against the biggest retailers in Europe. The question is whether this formula can continue to be sustained in a market that is maturing and becoming intensely competitive.

As noted at the beginning of this case study, competition in the Irish market increased with the arrival of foreign competition. Superquinn, like all existing players, has been forced to examine all its operational efficiencies, whilst at the same time maintaining very high service levels. The company is seeking to strip out costs from the business without damaging its customer offering. Whilst this is necessary to maintain competitiveness it carries with it a degree of risk, as the points of difference that have underpinned the company's success are amongst the easiest to remove.

Superquinn has prospered over the last 42 years by employing a 'World-class team of Colleagues' who are both innovative and focused. The company is now entering a stage in its development where it must take a broader strategic view, as the customer of tomorrow will be more demanding, discerning and price driven. For Superquinn to continue to grow its market share, it must build upon the cultural foundations that have created its success. All parts of the organisation need to have a clear understanding of how and why the company has been successful. This can only be possible if the values of the Boomerang Principle are enshrined in the company – it is this challenge that lies ahead for the management team of the future.

Task

As a retail manager from overseas you have just visited Superquinn in Ireland on a study tour. Having returned home you have been asked to compile a management report for your CEO. You are required to provide a detailed analysis of the company and to summarise the factors behind Superquinn's success. (You should avoid merely listing all the different initiatives you have seen.)

The CEO of your company has a HRM background and is particularly interested in the contribution that people make to the business. You should consider the extent to which the company's success is predicated on the actions and activities of its colleagues and how Superquinn manages to continually motivate its staff. In answering these questions you may wish to consider the importance of culture and the role of empowerment.

Given your knowledge of the retail labour market (Chapter 13), what would be the difficulties of simply copying these ideas and importing them into your business?

PART 6

Buying and merchandising

CHAPTER 16

Retail buying and merchandising

Susan Fiorito and Paul Freathy

Aim

The aim of this chapter is to provide an understanding of the buying and merchandise process and how it contributes to the achievement of business objectives.

Learning objectives

After completing the chapter you will be able to:

- understand the relationship between corporate strategic planning and the buyers' tactical planning process;
- appreciate the complexity and importance of forecasting demand for products rather than forecasting sales;
- understand the role and function of buyers and merchandisers;
- have a basic understanding of the merchandise management process;
- understand the importance of supplier evaluations.

Introduction

The buying and merchandise process is complex and ever changing and there are considerable variations in how retailers purchase and manage stock. Factors such as the size of the company, the merchandise to be purchased, the resources available, the state of the economy and the culture of the organisation all influence the structure and operation of the buying and merchandise function. Even terminology differs between companies. For example, a 'merchandiser' may indicate a senior role in one firm and a relatively junior position in another. As a consequence it is difficult (but not impossible) to write a definitive account of what buying and merchandising actually comprises. What is provided in this chapter is a general introduction to the subject area. Should you decide to investigate the topic more closely you will almost certainly find variations to what is described below.

The challenge: managing product life cycles

The variety of products available on the market continues to increase significantly each year. In virtually all sectors, from the food industry to home building products, retailers have to make decisions over which products to stock. Imagine the problems faced by a typical department or grocery store. It must cater to a diverse clientele: men, women and children with varied tastes, disparate income levels and, for clothing stores, a wide range of physical measurements. Retailers must deal with seasonal changes that affect the number and types of products they carry. If the company has retail outlets in different geographic regions its product offerings must reflect any differences in style, weather, income and culture. In addition, consumer tastes vary and sometimes shift very quickly, even within a season. The combination of these factors means a retailer may have to carry an enormous range of different products. The more diverse the customer base the larger the number of individual products as measured in stock keeping units (SKU) that must be carried (Table 16.1).

All product categories share one common descriptor – the product life cycle (PLC). The PLC is the period of time over which a particular item, classification, fabric, colour, style, etc. will sell well enough to provide the retailer with a profitable return. During each phase of the PLC, three factors will usually change: the price, the number of manufacturers and the product itself. Knowing approximately which phase the product is situated in the PLC, will help the buying and merchandising team to predict how well the product will sell over time. Product categories typically follow a predictable sales pattern as the product moves from one phase to the next in the PLC. Sales typically start off low, increase, plateau and then ultimately decline. Yet the shape (or degree and speed of demand) of that pattern varies from product to product. Six phases of the PLC will be presented

Table 16.1 Number of SKUs held by retail type

Retail channel	Examples	Estimated number of distinct SKUs
Discount retailer	Aldi, Lidl, Netto	600–2,000
Grocery superstore	Safeway, Tesco	24–40,000
Category killer	Toys-Я-Us	80,000
Hypermarket	Wal-Mart	100-150,000
Department store		
Standard	Takashimaya	800,000
Flagship	Harrods	1–2 million

Source: after Harvard Center for Textile and Apparel Research (Abernathy et al. 1999)

here with a brief description of the buyer's actions in each phase and a listing of common characteristics. Following this will be a brief description of how the PLC phases vary in their shape.

Stage 1: introduction or trial phase. The buyers' aim is to help a new product through the initial phase, whilst not committing too many resources. The focus should be on maintaining low product inventory, seeking knowledgeable suppliers that can provide good technical services and paying careful attention to quality control. The characteristics of this phase include the following:

- low sales;
- uncertainty of how long the phase will last;
- losses or low profits, due to high initial advertising and promotion costs;
- inexperienced retail personnel;
- inexperienced customers;
- the vulnerability of the product;
- relatively few distributors (wholesale or retail);
- the product is often produced and marketed on a trial or pilot basis.

The arrival of the DVD player serves as an example here. Its introduction on to the market has been met with both enthusiasm and caution. Customers in particular have been unsure about the product, the different formats and the technical specifications attached to each SKU. When we are told that an individual player can offer DVD-R, DVD-RW (VM), DVD+RW and DVD–RW (VRM) capabilities the result can be customer confusion, resulting in low sales. It is therefore important for the retailer at this stage to ensure that customers are informed and sales personnel are adequately trained (again this highlights the need for cooperation between different functions within the organisation).

Stage 2: growth phase. The buyer now has to try to obtain the right level of product flow from suppliers. It will be necessary to look out for new sources of supply, ensure quality control is maintained and build bigger inventories or schedule more frequent deliveries of the product. The characteristics of this phase include the following:

- rapid rise of sales in a short time;
- much less vulnerability than at the former phase:
- possibility of substantial profits;
- many other suppliers becoming available;
- the product is now in full-scale production.

Again technology provides a recent example. The huge increase in the number of individuals owning and using mobile phones during the 1990s demonstrates how quickly a market can grow. In a relatively short period of time a variety of different retailers, including electrical specialists, grocers and dedicated phone shops were offering 'personal communications packages'.

Stage 3: maturity phase. The product enters this phase when the rate of growth of sales stabilises. The buyer is faced with optimising the return on existing stocks whilst also beginning to reduce the company's forward commitment. As demand is more predictable more favourable supply contracts should be obtained. The buyer now looks for lower cost prices without sacrificing quality, watches out for cut-price retail competitors and minimises all peripheral costs associated with the product. The characteristics of this phase are as follows:

- Sales continue to increase, but at a decreasing rate.
- Most retail competitors are stocking the product.
- Price competition begins.
- Profits begin to decline.

Many food products can be categorised as being in the mature phase. Fresh vegetables such as tomatoes, carrots, potatoes and cabbage all have relatively predictable demand patterns and are stocked by the main grocery retailers. Emphasis is placed upon working with suppliers to see if costs can be driven out of the supply chain and quality can be further improved.

Stage 4: saturation phase. This phase has many characteristics of the maturity phase but is now more extreme. The buyer should put more emphasis on cost cutting in all areas, balance inventory levels carefully, make the best of rampant price-cutting, expect gradual erosion of the quality in the goods and look for low cost substitutes. The characteristics of this phase include the following:

- It is no longer possible to increase sales with this item.
- Profits decline sharply.
- Competition is extremely severe.

Some would argue that the mobile phone market has already reached this phase in the product life cycle. Having saturated the high street with retail outlets offering similar product lines there has, in the last couple of years, been a shake out in the market. A number of specialist companies have reduced their store portfolio or withdrawn from the market completely.

Stage 5: decline phase. Eventually the saturation phase gives way to the decline phase, where sales are declining and profits are eliminated. Faced with this situation the buyer has to continue to reduce the company's commitment to the product and begin developing a withdrawal plan.

For example, in the early 1990s owning a handheld pager was the current equivalent of having a mobile phone. The adoption and use of the product was widespread and it was used by many as a form of personal communication. In a relatively short period of time sales of pagers have virtually ceased. Whilst some retailers continue to stock a small selection, their usage today is extremely limited.

Stage 6: abandonment phase. During this final stage in the PLC the buyer has to delete the product and eliminate all further company commitment to it. The buyer should dispose of surpluses and buy new or replacement items that can be recommended as suitable alternatives.

The examples often cited here are the replacement of the vinyl LP with the CD and the typewriter with the personal computer. It is worth noting that the CD itself may soon be surpassed by the DVD.

Every product eventually passes through the PLC. However the time it takes for products to move through each stage and the intensity of sales during the different phases varies according to many consumer and product dimensions. One argument of relevance here is that the life cycle of many products is shortening, that is, the period between introduction and abandonment has been reduced as the use of technology to communicate 'new' and 'better' products has increased. Today customers demand the latest model, the newest products and the most up-to-date fashions.

The speed that a product moves through the PLC will help determine what type of good it can be classed as. Generally four types of products can be recognised.

Fads: these products generate considerable sales over a short period of time, often less than a season. Fads are often illogical and unpredictable. The art of managing a fad is recognising it in its earliest stages and immediately locking up distribution rights before your competitor. Fads are a very risky business and require constant attention of the buyer.

For example, the sale of merchandise associated with children's films often has a very lucrative but ultimately short shelf-life. Well-known characters such as Pochahontas, Babe and Shrek have the potential to generate significant revenues over a relatively short time period.

Fashion: these products typically last several seasons. Sales are similar to a fad in that a specific style or SKU can vary dramatically over time. Examples of fashionable products may include red trouser braces, leg warmers and the ubiquitous shell suit.

Staple or basic: these products are in continuous demand over an extended period of time. Products such as milk, sugar, white paint, black socks and jeans are all considered to be staples. These items are thought to be essential by the retailer and it is the buying and merchandising team's responsibility to ensure that these products are always available.

Seasonal merchandise: these products generate sales that fluctuate dramatically according to the time of year. For example, turkey at Christmas, suntan lotion and swim wear during the summer and pumpkins at Hallowe'en. It is also worth noting that both fashion and staple merchandise usually have seasonal influences. Whilst it is possible to forecast accurately the timing of peaks and troughs associated with staple items, determining the demand for seasonal fashion items remains a significant challenge.

From our discussions so far we have determined two things. First, that in order to satisfy increased consumer demand there exists a greater proliferation of products in the market than ever before. Secondly, changes in consumer behaviour have meant that the average life expectancy of many products has been considerably reduced. For the retailer, these developments mediate against complacency and ensure that the products on offer must continue to satisfy customer need. In the next section we will consider the contribution that an ordered and systematic buying and merchandising function can make to ensuring optimum product availability.

Self-assessment Question 1 *Identify and describe one item (either clothing, electronics or food) that best depicts the six different phases of the product life cycle. Describe how the product moved through each of phase of the PLC and detail the marketing approach used within each phase.*

The buying and merchandising function

One theme in this book has been the need to satisfy customer goals in order to meet business objectives. The buying and merchandise process is no different. The strategic decisions made at the corporate level will set the framework in which the retail buyer plans and sets their goals for each buying term. Planning and goal setting is at the heart of long-term, successful retail buying. Corporate decisions should influence the overall strategic plans of the buyer as they choose the products to buy within each product domain.

Planning and goal setting is typically both top down and bottom up. Senior executives set overall financial plans for the retail organisation whilst buyers set financial goals for their own department or category. These plans are then negotiated and one company plan is agreed upon. It is a fallacy that small business owners/managers have less need for financial information because of their personal involvement in day-to-day operations. Such a belief is dangerously deceptive. Most buyers are not expert accountants, nor should they be expected to be. They should however be capable of calculating gross margins and inventory turnover and know enough about the accounting process to be able to analyse their business and understand the results.

To ensure that these financial and business parameters are met, the firm's target market must be clearly defined. Given that a company cannot be all things to all people it is imperative that the buying and merchandising teams have a clear understanding of their customer base (after all, buyers cannot be expected to purchase products if they are unclear about who they are attempting to satisfy). As noted in Chapter 10, the focus on the customer must be company wide so that all functional areas are working in unison to meet the demands of the customer. Because the primary objective of any retail organisation is the sale of merchandise at a profit it is best if the choice of merchandise presents a clear message to consumers. For instance, in clothing, is the store known for its basic selection, its classic styles, its high fashion trends, or its modern and contemporary designers? In the grocery sector, is the store known for its international selection, the quality of its fresh goods or its low prices?

In addition, the buying and merchandising process must identify points of differentiation that distinguish the retailer from the competition. Service levels, store layout and advertising and promotion are typically used to differentiate one retail offer from the other. Buyers and merchandisers will be required to take risks and experiment with new products, concepts and brands. Success is derived from constantly reassessing and satisfying customers' needs. The outcome from such strategies should be quantified and monitored using indicators such as increases in sales, profit, gross and net margin and merchandise turns.

Increasingly attention has been focused on developing relationships within the supply chain. It has been recognised that cooperation between channel members can contribute to business success. Whilst many different forms of relationships exist many retailers see the traditional 'I win, you lose' approach to negotiations as counter productive. By working together and establishing mutual goals and objectives the focus is placed on developing 'I win, you win' scenarios. Successful companies will see themselves less as retailers or suppliers and more as part of a chain of specialists focused on satisfying customer needs.

It would appear from the above discussion that considerable expectations are placed on the buying and merchandising team. Identifying customer needs, working with other functional areas within the business, ensuring the right products are always available and developing alliances with supply chain partners, all fall within their remit.

Whilst the allocation of tasks varies significantly between different sectors and even competing retailers, research has attempted to profile their activities. Swindley (1992) for example concluded that the main responsibilities of UK buyers were as follows:

- the selection and evaluation of products;
- the sourcing, selection and appraisal of suppliers;
- negotiation on issues such as margins, quantities and marketing support;
- monitoring product sales;
- pricing decisions, including an influence over markdowns.

Wills (1999) notes that the merchandiser is essentially the retailer's business manager and undertakes a role that is much more strategic today than in the past. The merchandiser or merchandise manager works closely with the retail buyer in setting goals and objectives for the department and in carrying out those goals. Again the activities will vary but can include the following:

- establishing and developing a merchandise plan for each season based on past and future trends;
- constantly monitoring the performance of suppliers.
- controlling the initial allocation of stock to branches;
- setting a timetable for the warehouse to ensure goods are distributed for initial allocations and replenishment;
- monitoring sales and stock throughout the season to see how they conform to the initial plan (the merchandiser may consider markdowns, promotions, or stock disposal);
- reforecasting plans during the season, if necessary;
- placing repeat orders if a line is selling very well.

The merchandise management process

We have highlighted the challenges that face the retail buying and merchandising team in terms of the large numbers of products and suppliers and the changing nature of consumer demand. In this section we will consider the merchandise management process. This is concerned with the planning and controlling of the retailer's inventories and the acquisition, handling and monitoring of merchandise. Here the retailer attempts to offer the right quantities of the right product, at the right place, at the right time to satisfy the customer and to meet the company's financial goals.

However, before the buyer visits the market to purchase merchandise a significant amount of planning must be undertaken. Merchandise managers in large organisations are typically responsible for estimating and forecasting sales and planning required stock levels. The buyer then translates these projections into actual purchases and may hold the responsibility for allocations between colours, styles and sizes. It is important to keep in mind that there is considerable difference between forecasting staple or basic goods and fashion or one-time-purchase goods. Minimising initial orders and negotiating rapid replenishment cycles with manufacturers can reduce risk. As noted above, buyers must make decisions about thousands or even tens of thousands of items from hundreds or even thousands of suppliers. If the buying process is not organised in a systematic and orderly way chaos will result or worse – a profit won't be realised!

Forecasting demand

At the heart of merchandise planning is information. Although buyers and merchandisers need to be well briefed in order to make sound decisions what frequently happens is that data comes from diverse and often incompatible sources. In order to balance out conflicting pieces of information it is necessary to keep data as up to date as possible.

The typical questions that face a buying and merchandise team are: What products are customers going to be looking for this year? What styles and colours are going to be in greatest demand? Which fads should we stock? In order to be able to answer these questions and cope with an increasingly complex range and variety of goods, buyers and merchandisers need to be able to make accurate decisions on their merchandise selection. In practice this process is extremely difficult to manage. For example, a retail buyer may be required to forecast the demand for a product 12 months before that item appears in the store. Trying to predict how many men will be prepared to pay full price for an XL size polo shirt with a pocket (in other words, one particular SKU out of thousands) is at the very least a challenge!

How is this problem solved? A starting point may be the historical data which provides weekly sales of that shirt. Even now, however, questions arise: Should that data be studied for only one store or all stores? Should predictions be made a year ahead rather than a season ahead? The complexity of the problem even for a basic shirt or a shampoo is staggering.

When forecasting demand based on historical data, buyers and merchandisers need to consider four components.

Trend: what has been the pattern of demand over the medium to long term? Has there been a steady increase, decrease or variation over time? If a product has shown consistent growth over a number of years then the buying and merchandising team may wish to factor this into the forecast.

Seasonality: does the demand for the product vary over a 12-month period? There are seasonal peaks associated with many products (perfume on Valentine's Day, men's ties on Fathers' Day)

Cyclicality: this describes longer-term, gradual rises and declines that are typically associated with aggregate business activity. Examples include demand for new cars during times of economic prosperity and a decline during periods of recession.

Random fluctuations: these are the most difficult demand structures to assess and incorporate into inventory planning as they cannot be explained by trend, seasonality, cyclicality or any other factors (Abernathy *et al.* 1999). Random fluctuations in demand decrease the accuracy of the historical data. Buyers and merchandisers therefore utilise other internal and external sources of information. Internal sources include the following:

- *customer information*: this may include details of returned items, written complaints about the merchandise or specially commissioned market research;
- *store personnel information*: sales associates, department managers, store and division managers all have information about the product and customers' reactions to it.
- *marketing information*: can include feedback from staff and customers on promotions, special events and special sales.
- *one's own knowledge and experience*: this should always be considered and never underestimated.

External sources include the following:

- *trade news, trade shows, other buyers, magazines;*
- *economic forecasts supplied by the government and other bodies;*
- *market intelligence reports on the sector and the competition;*
- *information supplied by the company's suppliers/manufacturers/distributors;*
- *specialist research output such as demographics of a specific residential area.*

It should also be noted that some retailers have chosen software packages to assist their company with inventory management and forecasting. For example, the 'Arthur Enterprise Suite' merchandising planning and forecasting software is regarded as a key tool around the world. The system has been a technological pioneer that has helped to bring the retail industry from merchandise planning based on intuition and experience to one based on statistically valid analysis of data. Marks & Spencer was the first company in the United Kingdom to utilise the Arthur planning and forecasting software (Reda 2001).

Taking forecasting to another level requires collaboration with one's suppliers. Collaborative forecasting is now being experimented with at several retail firms. For example, Chico's, a 300-unit, private-label women's speciality store in Fort Myers, FL reports that flexibility is essential to sound forecasting. A team of product developers and suppliers work together on forecasting using store-specific sales data and leveraging what they know about the preferences of its very targeted customers. Another example of collaborative forecasting is Superdrug, the 700-unit chain selling health and beauty aid products in the United Kingdom. The company has collaborated on planning and replenishment with Johnson & Johnson and wants eventually to expand their programme to include five suppliers.

The main goal of planning and forecasting is to maximise profitability by managing the inherent tension between stocking too much and stocking too little. This is not a new phenomenon – retailers of old grappled with this problem. But with increases in product variety and shortened product life cycles this tension has become increasingly acute, prompting inventory management practices to evolve to meet rapidly changing market demands.

Self-assessment Question 2 *Some retailers argue that forecasting has no place in modern supply chain management. Instead retailers and suppliers should collaborate together and work towards eliminating forecasting completely. Is such a strategy desirable? If so why? What are the practical difficulties involved in such an undertaking?*

Planning the range and assortment

Having gathered the relevant information from historical data and internal and external sources, the buying and merchandising teams will begin to plan the ranges they wish to purchase. This needs to be customer driven but also to include consideration of the financial budget and space availability. Range planning considers the width and depth of the merchandise carried by a store. Width (or breadth) relates to the number of different product categories stocked in a store; for example, department stores have a wider variety of products than shops just selling footwear. Depth (or assortment) relates to the number of SKUs within a particular product category. For example, if a grocery retailer decides to stock a particular brand of Scotch whisky a further series of decisions have to be made. Given that the whisky is sold in 20cl, 35cl, 37.5cl, 50cl, 75cl, 100cl, 114cl, 175cl, 200cl, 300cl sizes, the buyer has to decide which sizes are most likely to satisfy demand from customers. Similarly, when a clothing retailer decides to stock a range of men's suits the buying and merchandising specialists will have to consider which sizes, colours, fabrics, styles and price points to purchase.

When determining the variety and assortment of a product category, the buying and merchandising team must consider the profitability of the merchandise mix, the corporate philosophy towards the assortment, the physical characteristics of the store and the degree to which categories of merchandise complement each other (Levy and Weitz 2001). It is imperative that retailers constantly evaluate their merchandise for the most profitable mix of products. For example, a paint buyer for a DIY store will need to consider the overall gross margins that this product category makes for the company. If a paint manufacturer supplies a retailer, the buyer may wish to purchase white paint at almost the manufacturer's cost. This will allow the product to be sold cheaply and attract customers to the store. Other colours and associated items may then be sold at a higher price (and at a higher margin).

The corporate philosophy towards the assortment helps the buyer and merchandiser determine the number of styles and colours to purchase. For example, department store buyers and merchandisers are directed to limit the breadth of their assortments to fashion items that are in the growth and early maturity phases of the product life cycle. Department stores want to be known for carrying the most popular fashion items and thus must be able to move on to the next fashion trend as quickly as possible. Ordering in small quantities allows the buyers to constantly follow fashion trends by not purchasing items in great depth. Of course the more diversified the assortment, the less risk there is of not having what the customer wants to purchase. On the other hand too much diversity without depth of product can lead to stock-outs of certain sizes.

Whilst some retailers stock the same assortment in every store regardless of its location others have taken a more customer-focused approach. The availability of geographical information systems, consumer databases and sales data have allowed retailers to tailor their merchandise mix to the needs of the local market. Whilst a company may have two stores of a similar size, product assortments within each outlet may be very different depending on the location of each store. For the buyer and merchandiser the focus has shifted from cookie-cutter stores (that is, uniform customer assortments) to an understanding of the needs and wants of individuals at the local level.

When retailers add to their assortments they must determine which items to remove, since there is only a limited amount of floor space. In keeping with these decisions the retailer must also consider whether the merchandise under consideration complements other merchandise in the department. It is desirable for the retailer to know if one product stimulates the sale of other products. Similarly, if one product is out of stock, will it affect the sales of another product? For example, the customer may expect pasta and sauce to be always available, as the availability of one product will influence the demand for the other.

Product availability

Whilst it may be an objective to offer 100 per cent product availability, in practice all retailers experience stock-outs at some point. For those retailers who carry a large number of different SKUs, it is an everyday occurrence. Again, different retail sectors experience different challenges. For example, in the grocery sector, supply chain efficiencies combined with regular deliveries has meant that the retailer is required to hold only limited amounts of back-up stock. Product unavailability can usually be rectified quickly. In contrast, clothing and fashion retailers may be placing orders overseas, 12 months in advance. The ability to respond to changes in customer demand is therefore limited. Levy and Weitz (2001) indicate that choosing an appropriate amount of back-up stock is critical to successful assortment planning. If a retailer's back-up stock is too low sales may be lost, if it is too high resources will be tied up unnecessarily.

Levy and Weitz (2001) describe two kinds of back-up stock:

- *Cycle stock*: is used when the retailer is able to predict demand for a product and sets up a replenishment cycle. For example, a retailer orders 100 units of a particular SKU and over the next two weeks the majority of the inventory is sold. However before the store is out of stock the next order arrives. The cycle repeats itself and is reviewed periodically by the buyer and the supplier.
- *Base stock*: when a retailer can not predict demand for a product, they purchase back-up or buffer stock as a safety cushion. The aim here is avoid a stock-out before the buyer has been able to evaluate the selling history of the product and place another order or discontinue the line.

Sourcing and supplier relationships

Having identified their product requirements the buying and merchandising team needs to source the merchandise. The vast majority of retailers do not manufacture the goods they sell and therefore need to source products from a variety of different suppliers. The number of suppliers used, the location and nature of the trading relationship will, as with so many issues in retail buying and merchandising, vary considerably.

Essentially the choice of supplier and the type of methods by which products are sourced will revolve around the power relationships that exist within the supply chain. As we established in Chapter 1, the balance of power in the supply channel has tended to shift away from manufacturers towards retailers. This has partly been a result of the large product volumes being demanded by retailers and partly a result of own-brand developments.

One trend that has emerged amongst large food and non-food retailers has been the tendency to deal directly with producers rather than to have an intermediary. Buying direct from the supplier usually secures the best possible price (and the highest margin) as there is no one else in the chain to share the profit. However, there are disadvantages to this direct approach; for example, many manufacturers require large order quantities of any one item and lead times may be extended as goods are not supplied from stock but made to order. A further potential problem concerns the amount of control that a retailer can exert on a manufacturer of this type, particularly if they are located overseas. Retailers who source extensively from one overseas market frequently open a buying office to oversee local production and shipment.

Some large retailers still prefer to pay the premium to use a UK-based agent for at least some of their purchases in order to avoid risk and for ease of convenience – for example, poor quality goods may arrive from overseas that cannot be returned to the manufacturer. One alternative is to use an agent as an intermediary between the retailer and a manufacturer or primary producer. Agents charge a commission, sometimes to both the buyer and seller – this may be a transparent percentage but is frequently hidden in an overall cost price. Agents may be located either in the country of origin of the items they are supplying or in the country of importation. Sometimes they have offices in both locations.

Many retailers do not have the market power to deal directly with producers or do not require the services of an agent. Smaller retailers in particular rely upon wholesalers/distributors. The essential difference between wholesalers/distributors and agents is that the former carry stock. This enables retailers to purchase from them, either through pre-ordering merchandise or by the retailer calling on a distribution centre and physically taking goods away ('cash and carry'). There are a variety of different types of wholesaler/distributors. In the clothing business there are many companies that develop branded ranges which are supplied to small chains and independents. Examples include 'Peter Werth' in menswear or 'Copperknob' in womenswear. In the grocery trade, wholesale markets exist for fruit and vegetables – though the dominance of the supermarkets has meant a contraction of the number of middlemen in this and other agricultural products. There are also wholesalers such as C. J. Lang, Bookers and Makro who supply a range of food and non-food goods both nationally and internationally.

One supply source that has gained increasing prominence over the last few years is the 'grey market' (parallel importing). Here retailers attempt to import genuine products into the domestic market through 'alternative' distribution channels that rival the authorised channel. For example, Ang (2000) notes how a parallel importer in Singapore purchases Estée Lauder lipstick at $16 and sells it for

$22–$24. The retail price in authorised dealers is $34. A wide range of products have been sourced through the grey market including watches, fashion goods and even cars. Its legality has been challenged by Levi Strauss in the European Court, which upheld its view that Tesco was acting illegally in sourcing from an unauthorised distributor. Whilst parallel importing offers opportunities for some retailers to boost sales revenues, supply is often sporadic and cannot be guaranteed. For the majority of retailers who use it, the grey market represents a secondary rather than a primary supply channel.

Almost all retailers sell merchandise that has originated from outside the domestic market. For small-scale retailers that purchase from wholesalers the buying process is likely to be the same regardless of the product's origin. For larger retailers that are able to demand significant quantities there is often the motivation to source internationally (Liu and McGoldrick 1995). These motivations include:

- The opportunity to source merchandise at lower cost or at better value than can be obtained in the domestic market. The cost of labour, property and raw materials are often significantly cheaper overseas. Developing markets such as China and the Philippines have positioned themselves as centres for manufacturing.
- The availability of merchandise that can not be sourced in the home market. With food this may be because the climate is too cold or because seasonality limits the length of the growing season. In addition, branded goods, such as watches, videos and cameras are often manufactured overseas. This gives the retailer little alternative other than to source outside of the home country.

While there are obvious advantages to 'direct' international sourcing there are also a number of potential drawbacks including the following:

- *Lead times*: this is probably one of the most important issues for a retailer when considering direct international purchasing. This is particularly critical in fashion or seasonally driven lines, where a delay might markedly affect the opportunity to sell-through a range at the optimum time.
- *Communication*: this can also be a problem (though less so in the era of the Internet and video conferencing). For example, when negotiations are conducted through a translator misinterpretation can lead to a genuine misunderstanding of the buyer's requirements.
- *Culture*: although cultural barriers are less problematic than they once were, a failure to respect or adhere to cultural norms has the potential to undermine supply chain relationships. Many retailers and suppliers now have considerable experience in dealing with alternative cultures and have a greater understanding of the different approaches to business.
- *A loss of control*: this is perhaps the greatest fear for buyers and merchandisers. As the physical distance between retailer and supplier increases, the level of day-to-day control that can be exerted declines. Issues such as transportation, quality control and product sampling are just three examples of where control difficulties can arise in international buying.

Product selection and development

The actual interaction between retailer and supplier takes many forms. In some instances retail buyers and merchandisers will embark upon detailed face-to-face discussions with their suppliers. In other instances business may be conducted over the phone (or the Internet). Sometimes talks are conducted at the retailer's headquarters, on other occasions they may be held at the supplier's premises. Depending on the nature of the relationship many different issues can be discussed. For some it will merely be a discussion about price and volume, for others it will cover a range of tangible and intangible issues and may take place over a period of weeks, months or on a continuous basis. Issues that are often discussed include the following:

Physical properties: these are the tangible aspects of the product including its size, weight, components or ingredients. The buyers or merchandisers may provide the supplier with feedback from consumers and suggest modifications to the product. For example, the removal of genetically modified ingredients from a number of food products came about in part from the feedback retailers received from customers.

Packaging: this performs a number of functions including protection (the wrapper around a pat of butter), aesthetic appeal (the design on a CD cover) and a contribution to brand identity (Toblerone chocolate). Packaging is therefore relevant in attracting consumers to a product. As supply chain partnerships grow retailers work closely with manufacturers to minimise packaging waste, helping to both allay environmental concerns and reduce production costs. McDonald's, for example, reduced the weight of their hamburger box from 6g to 4.7g and saved 454 tonnes of plastic in one year. In other markets the company has gone even further, eliminating their familiar polystyrene 'clam shell' packaging in favour of recyclable cardboard containers (McDonald's 2001).

Style: product styling and design has historically been associated with fashion items such as clothing and footwear. Design however has been recognised as a way of differentiating the retail offer, with product categories such as home furnishings, electrical appliances and gardening equipment all incorporating a stylistic element into their product specification.

Utility: a product's utility is concerned with its performance. Issues such as maintenance, durability and health and safety concerns are relevant to consumers and should therefore also be relevant to buyers. For example, before deciding whether to stock a particular range of chocolates a confectionery buyer may wish the supplier to provide details of the ingredients used and the manufacturing process undertaken.

Product quality: quality control may be a task of the buyer but in many large retailers it is now a separate department. Often product inspections take place on a number of different occasions, such as, during the manufacturing process, at the warehouse after delivery and on-site at stores once the merchandise has been distributed.

Brand: the role of branding was discussed in Chapter 10. To the customer it is an *intangible* product feature, but one that has considerable relevance to a potential purchase decision. The extent to which consumers display brand loyalty for a product category has important implications for the buying process. For example, a retail category such as photographic equipment, which is dominated by brands, will require a different buying approach to most grocery categories, where own branding can now represent well over 50 per cent of all products sold. In the latter context the retail buyer is invariably more than just a product selector and the buying team will almost certainly contain designers and other specialists.

Supplier analysis

Continual analysis of supplier performance is necessary even when channel relationships have been stable. This analysis can pinpoint problems that may exist so that they can be solved quickly and without delay. One system suggested by Levy and Weitz (2001) is the multiple-attribute method, which uses weighted average scores for each supplier. This score is based on the importance of various issues and the supplier's performance on those issues. To illustrate the multiple-attribute method for evaluating suppliers, see Box 16.1.

Box 16.1
The evaluation process for a men's shirt supplier

Whilst there are many different ways in which a supplier's performance can be evaluated, the following method is relatively simple and transparent. For simplicity we have broken the process down into five stages:

Stage one: develop a list of issues to consider in evaluating the suppliers in your area. A balance should be made between having too few or too many criteria. If the list is too short relevant issues may be ignored; if it is too long the evaluation may be too cumbersome. Balance the list so that one dimension of supplier performance is not given too much or too little attention. For example, it would not be advisable to have three issues dealing with supplier promotional assistance and only one issue dealing with product characteristics. This would result in an unbalanced set of issues and a less reliable performance measure.

Stage two: the buyer and the merchandiser should determine importance weights for each issue in the first column. In the chart overleaf a 10-point scale has been used, where '1' equals very unimportant and '10' equals very important. Although all issues are important they must not all be rated with the highest score since this would be unrealistic for any supplier to achieve. List the importance of each issue according to customer priorities and the characteristics of the product being evaluated.

Stage three: make a judgement about each individual brand's performance on each issue (listed under column headings of Brand A, Brand B and Brand C). This procedure should be a group decision of the buyer, merchandiser and category manager.

Stage four: the overall performance of the suppliers is calculated by combining the importance and the performance scores. To do this, multiply the importance score for each issue by the performance for each brand or supplier. For example, under supplier reputation importance is '9' and we multiply that by '7', which is the performance of Brand A. The result is a score of '63'. Note that it does not pay if the supplier performs very well on an issue that is either unimportant to the buying group or unimportant to the customer.

Stage five: to determine the supplier's overall rating, sum the product for each brand for all issues. See the example below where Brand B with a score of '310' outperformed the other two brands.

Performance Evaluations of Individual Brands

Issues	Importance evaluation of issues	Brand A	Brand B	Brand C
(1)	(2)	(3)	(4)	(5)
Supplier reputation	9	7	5	6
Service	8	4	9	7
Product fashionability	7	8	5	6
Merchandise quality	6	5	7	6
Mark-up opportunity	6	6	4	5
Meets delivery dates	6	5	6	7
Country of origin	4	5	5	5
Selling history	4	7	6	3
Promotional assistance	3	3	4	3
Overall evaluation		304	310	301

Self-assessment Question 3 *If you are currently working in the retail industry or if you are able to interview a retail buyer or manager, develop your own Performance Evaluation Chart (see Box 16.1) for three brands within either the grocery or the clothing industry. Revise the issues column according to the manager's perspective of the product category. Keep in mind that each issue should not be rated as 'very important'. Be sure to change the importance evaluation for each issue. List the actual brands in the three columns and calculate an overall evaluation score for each. Write a brief description of your results.*

Summary

This chapter has provided a brief introduction to the buying and merchandising process. Changing consumer demands has meant that the life cycle of many products has become shorter whilst the range of goods on offer has increased. Although there is often no shortage of products to choose from, success will often depend upon selecting the right mix of products with the best margins attainable. The context in which buyers and merchandisers operate has therefore become increasingly competitive and dynamic.

The chapter has also stressed the wide variations to be found between different buying and merchandising functions. Whilst the basic managerial tasks have been explained and the main dimensions of merchandise planning have been discussed, it is important to note that we have not considered an 'ideal' or 'correct' approach. The aim has been to outline the primary tasks and responsibilities considered to be important when buying and merchandising products in the retail sector.

Further reading

Elliot, F. and **Morpeth, J.** (2000) *Retail Buying Techniques*, Chalford, Gloucestershire: Management Books 2000.

Diamond, J. and **Pintel, G.** (2001) *Retail Buying*, 6th edn, Englwood Cliffs, NJ: Prentice-Hall.

Varley, R. (2001) *Retail Product Management: Buying and merchandising*, London: Routledge.

The following journals also contain articles related to the buying and merchandising process:

- *International Journal of Retail and Distribution Management;*
- *International Review of Retail, Distribution and Consumer Research;*
- *Journal of Fashion Marketing and Management;*
- *Journal of Retailing and Consumer Services;*
- *Service Industries Journal.*

You may also wish to view the magazines published for particular retail trades.

- *Drapers Record;*
- *Retail Week.*
- *The Grocer.*

CHAPTER 17

Buying and merchandising in the retail fashion industry

Grete Birtwistle

Introduction

In Chapter 16 we highlighted the diversity of approaches that characterised the buying and merchandising process. The nature of the products being bought, the size of the company, the culture of the business and the sector in which the retailer operated were all influential factors. In the following case we examine in detail how a leading fashion retailer undertakes its buying and merchandising activities. The Next retail chain has a portfolio of stores in the United Kingdom and overseas. In addition, it operates a retail catalogue and e-tail web site. The company's buying and merchandising teams have been central to its success. This case details how Next designs its products, selects its suppliers, purchases the goods and displays the merchandise. It identifies the factors that have differentiated the company from its competitors and comments on the issues which have remained critical to its success.

Background

During the 1980s and 1990s fashion retailing experienced several major changes, the most important of which was the increased number of retailers promoting fashion merchandise on the high street. The competition in the middle market has come from a variety of sources. Specialist fashion retailers such as Next, Top Shop, Wallis, Dorothy Perkins, Miss Selfridge and River Island compete with established variety retailers, such as Marks & Spencer and Bhs. Department stores, such as Debenhams, House of Fraser and the John Lewis Partnership also operate in the market, as do grocery retailers such as Asda with its George clothing range. Discount retailers such as Matalan, New Look and Primark have made competitive inroads, as have the factory outlet centres and international chains such as Zara, Mango, Gap and H&M. This multitude of players has led the UK fashion scene to be described as one of the most competitive in Europe (Whitefield 2001).

The middle market of fashion retailing has never been more concentrated and competitive. Multiple clothing retailers have in excess of 70 per cent of all clothing sales in the United Kingdom (Hines and Bruce 2001). Marks & Spencer continues to have the largest market share (approximately 12 per cent), though this figure has come under pressure in recent years. Whilst many companies operating in this sector are finding business very difficult, Next Retail Ltd appears in recent years to have developed a buying and merchandising formula that has produced double-digit growth, increased turnover and improved profitability.

The history of Next

The Next brand was created in 1982 by the menswear fashion retailer Joseph Hepworth and Sons Ltd. Hepworth's was traditionally a gentleman's tailor selling made-to-measure suits and latterly, off-the-peg formal wear. This market however was declining. Consequently the company decided to diversify and create a format selling ladieswear spearheaded by George Davies, its merchandise director. Next initially traded from 70 outlets.

The company focused on selling quality merchandise and developed an air of exclusivity by presenting products in up-market surroundings using minimalist display techniques (Gardner and Sheppard 1989). The ladieswear trading format became so successful that the company expanded the concept to include menswear. In 1984 a number of Next for Men outlets were opened. The aim was to target a younger, fashion-conscious, male consumer with ranges of clothes that would satisfy the need for both formal work clothes and leisure wear. Although many retailers were already using market segmentation strategies to position their stores, Next became the most publicised retailer to clearly target specific lifestyle groups (Easey 1995). This led to the company extending the brand to include a range of home furnishings in 1985 and childrenswear in 1987. A year later the retailer launched a catalogue, the Next Directory, for which it won the Royal Mail Gold Award for the most outstanding consumer campaign of 1988. In 1993 the buying and merchandising departments of the Retail and Directory divisions were merged, leading to a brand strategy of common ranges across both formats (Next 1998).

The Next mission statement is 'To be the natural choice retailer in the UK for fashion-aware men and women who expect style, distinction and quality from their clothing' (Next 1998). In addition the company promotes the brand through its multiple channels with the strap line 'One brand – two methods of shopping'.

The Next brand is designed to appeal to the 20–35-year-old male or female customer with an ABC1 socio-economic profile. The average age is 26, but many customers are older. The merchandise in stores is varied frequently through phase changes and also by issuing individual styles throughout the year. Garments are designed to be purchased individually but can be coordinated to create an outfit. The number of styles offered in each store is closely matched to the space available, the local customer profile and the optimum display formula.

The economic recession of the 1980s hit Next particularly hard due to over-expansion, extended borrowing and a lack of financial controls. In 1988 George Davies and his wife, the then product director at Next, left the company following a boardroom coup. David Jones took over as chief executive and restructured the business, strengthened the Next brand to ensure good profit growth and increased market share (Cunningham 1998a). The recovery was based on outlets having a strong store design, developing core ranges and by clearly identifying the needs and wants of the customer base (Bubb 1992). By 1994 Next had over 300 outlets and the Next Directory was a trading success.

In 1998 a profit warning was issued by David Jones. The company admitted having selected a range of ladieswear clothing that was too fashionable for their regular customers. Moreover, they suffered an over-stock problem in 1997 and an under-stock problem of best sellers in 1998. Fortunately this appeared to have been a short-term problem particularly affecting ladieswear and not menswear (Corporate Intelligence 1998; Cunningham 1998b; Rankine 1998). Customers and shareholders continued to have faith in the strength of the brand (Anon 1998) and Next was voted 'Retailer of the Decade' by Retail Week in 1998.

In 2001 Simon Wolfson took over as chief executive. He had joined the company in 1990 as a sales assistant and was made an assistant to David Jones in 1991. He joined the board in 1997 and became managing director of the Next brand in 1999. Wolfson comes from a retailing family (Lord Wolfson retired as chairman of Great Universal Stores in 2000) and is said to be particularly adept at anticipating industry trends (Patten 2001).

Store profile

By 1993 Next traded from 267 outlets and had a market share of 2.3 per cent. The sales per square foot were approximately £350, and the average size of a Next store was 2,500 square foot (Verdict 1994). By July 2001 sales density in stores averaged £800 per square feet (Craven 2001). The company also increased the size of its stores and now has 9 outlets over 20,000 square feet (the largest store being Liverpool at 44,000 square feet). In addition, Next purchased 13 former C&A stores when the latter ceased operating in the United Kingdom in 2000. By 2001 the company traded from 333 stores in the United Kingdom and Eire and had approximately 1.85 million square feet of selling space. Currently its share of the clothing market is 4 per cent but the company aims to increase this to 8 per cent over the next six years.

The Next brand is aimed at the top end of the middle market and the company is committed to providing stylish, good quality products at affordable prices. Next clothing is mainly sold in outlets with ladieswear, menswear and childrenswear. However, larger stores also sell home furnishings (Next 1998). The majority of the stores are on prime high street sites (often near a Marks & Spencer's outlet) or in prestige, out-of-town shopping centres such as Brent Cross, Meadow Hall, Lakeside at Thurrock and Bluewater Park. There are 41 franchised stores in Europe and Asia (Next 2001).

Next Directory

The Next Directory promotes the same product ranges as the stores and has the same buying and merchandising team. Being mail order, the production of the

Directory demands that range selection is earlier than it would be for retail alone. This is to allow time for photo-shoots, artwork, printing and catalogue production. The aim is to co-ordinate the Directory's distribution to customers with the delivery of the season's new ranges to stores. A preview Directory is distributed to a small number of customers which enables the company to monitor reactions to the merchandise and make accurate forecasts on future range demands (more detail on the preview is provided later in the chapter).

In 1999 the Directory was also made available online. Customers could now purchase goods via the catalogue or order products directly from the web site. By 2001 the Directory had over a million active customers and sales had increased 18 per cent compared to the previous period. Of the Directory's total orders, 10 per cent are now placed over the Internet.

Buying and merchandising

Next was one of the first retailers to adopt a concept known as 'edited retailing'. Products are selected by designers, buyers and merchandisers to offer the customer a limited but coordinated look. It enables the retailer to have a low stock holding but the opportunity to link or cross sell (Easey 1995).

Next is acknowledged to have a strong design and buying team and stores only sell own-brand goods with the Next label. The quality and style of all the Next ranges were improved after an extensive marketing research exercise in 1992 (RI 1992; TMS 1992). The strengthening of product quality along with strong price points helped Next recover their position on the high street and Next's original mission of offering stylish quality clothes at affordable prices has remained evident (Retail Review 1996).

The product cycle

The Next collection has two seasons: Spring/Summer (launched in January/February) and Autumn/Winter (launched in August/September). Each collection of clothing, produced centrally from Next's head office, is the result of approximately 12 months' planning by the product teams. New phases within each season's range are designed to be delivered every six weeks to ensure stores always look fresh and different and hence maintain customers' interest. The phases also allow for climatic changes as well as providing the opportunity to introduce new colours (Next 1998).

The buying cycle remains the same be it for ladieswear, menswear, childrenswear or accessories (Figure 17.1). The buying and merchandising teams are split into individual product departments and sub-grouped into product categories, such as formal wear – suits or casual wear – knitwear. Each department is headed by a department director who leads a team of two buying managers and two merchandising managers, one each for formal wear and casual wear. Teams below the manager level consist of sub-groups of buyers and merchandisers (Figure 17.2).

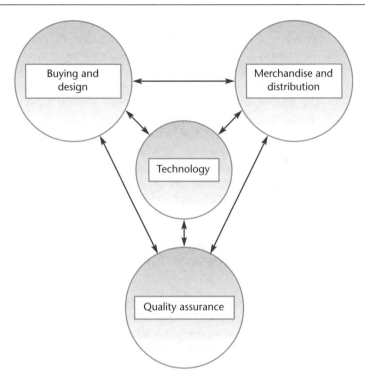

Figure 17.1 The buying cycle

For example, men's formal wear has three teams: tailoring, shoes/belts and accessories. Men's casualwear has five teams: shirts/ties, jeans/casual jackets, knitwear, jerseywear/resortwear, and sportswear. This centralised control has the advantages of providing economies of scale, consistency in quality, distinct style and design of garments and a standardised look that is the key success of Next.

Design presentations (sampling)

The product cycle follows a standard twice-yearly pattern (Figure 17.3). First, the designers travel to the main shows in Milan, Paris and New York to research trends and gain inspiration for the new ranges. The outcome of this is a series of 'mood boards' that enable selectors to gain a 'feel' for the ranges and individual themes which will be most in demand; one range recently introduced into Next was inspired by the film *Moulin Rouge*. Designers back up these mood boards with a 'bible' of colour swatches, print ideas and theme details – in essence a portfolio of current fashion trends. It is perused extensively at the forthcoming cloth fairs where the buyers ensure that Next is taking a direction in keeping with international prediction.

The design teams work on themes for the forthcoming season and liaise with the buying team in sampling garments. The introduction of computer-aided design allows designs to be produced in multiple colours thus providing significant time savings. Moreover, it allows designs (whether from an original sketch or a scanned image) to be manipulated. The outcome is a degree of flexibility that would be difficult to achieve from a manual process.

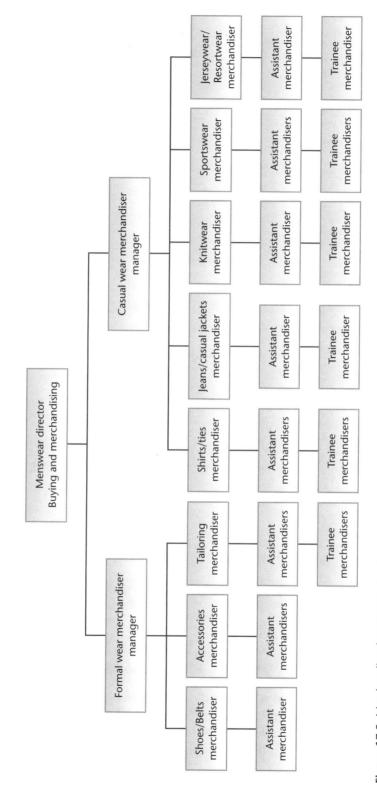

Figure 17.2 Merchandise department structure

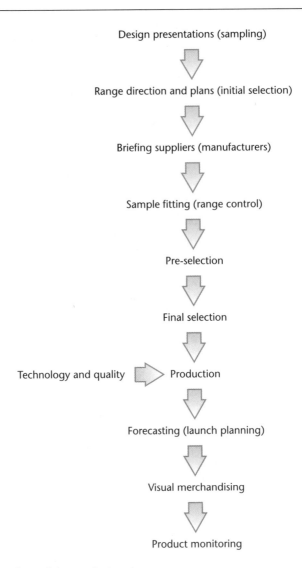

Figure 17.3 Flow chart of the product cycle

Range direction and plans (initial selection)

After the sampling stage, the cycle continues with a range review – a presentation by the merchandisers to the buyers and designers. The previous season's sales figures and sales trends are examined and the highs and lows of that season are assessed. Poor sellers are analysed in terms of what went wrong and why customers did not purchase specific lines. The aim is to consider what lessons can be learned when preparing for the forthcoming season. In particular, merchandisers identify best-selling items in terms of styles and colours and inform the buyers and designers of options that should be adapted or copied in readiness for the next season. The aim is to develop a strategy that optimises sales and maximises profitability. In addition, supplier performance is reviewed to judge whether new suppliers should be identified. The merchandisers utilise a PC-based forecasting and modelling tool to allow the improved planning and forecasting of trends and open-to-buy (Next 1998).

Briefing suppliers (manufacturers)

Whilst the initial selection is taking place buyers, merchandisers and the quality team select relevant suppliers, based on previous performance. Main manufacturers are based in Turkey, Portugal, Sri Lanka and Hong Kong and the company also intends to source from North Africa. At this stage designers add initial measurements, cloth and accessory details to the sketches. The suppliers then produce samples to be presented to the company's product teams. This is the first stage of the selection process.

Sample fitting (range control)

The samples will then be fitted on to a standard size 12 or 'medium' model and comments and amendments will be passed on to the supplier. Once the fitting, sizing and styling is approved by the retailer a 'sealed sample' is produced. This is the standard garment used to gauge any future production and will enable the supplier to quote Next an accurate price based on the exact fit, detail of work and quality of the fabric used.

Pre-selection

The buyers propose a range to be selected by the whole buying and merchandising team. Designers and buyers as well as merchandisers make sure both style and commercial criteria are met. The range is based on the previous product history, analysis of best and poor sellers, major new trends, price points and a few 'long shots' (products that may not fit the criteria but are considered to be worth taking a risk with). Designs are finalised and the exact details of each garment is specified (such as extra decorative elements and buttons). The addition of extra features or using a better quality cloth will increase the price point at which the garment can be purchased and thus the margin it can provide. All samples are reviewed, options considered and potential problems discussed and evaluated.

Final selection

A 'final-selection' meeting is held to show the complete ranges to directors, merchandisers and other key personnel, including staff from stores. The aim of this meeting is to gain overall approval for the merchandise. Samples are looked at by product group and options discussed. This in reality means looking at the ranges a store will be provided with and the coordination of garments within a specific range. Choice of manufacturer, pricing details and margin achievements are also agreed and each garment is allocated an item number by which it can be tracked. In addition, the grading of ranges and garments is undertaken to decide which products should be allocated to all stores and which should be delivered to specific stores. Top stores receive the full range whereas smaller stores receive a selection of the ranges. Details of labelling, such as care labels, seasons' codes, manufacturer number and logo labels are agreed as well as packaging presentation. Following final selection all relevant paperwork is circulated to members of the product teams and the suppliers.

Technology and quality

The company insists on implementing stringent quality procedures. Yarn, fabric, leather and accessories are submitted to a number of tests. These include the testing of physical strength – the tensile strength of fabric and seams; physical performance – pilling tests; dimensional stability – washing stability; and colour-fastness – for dry cleaning and washing. Once a fabric has passed all the various tests it is then confirmed for production.

Production

The range is now complete and production time is booked with suppliers. The buyers concentrate on the next season and hand over the monitoring of the range to the quality assurance team and merchandisers who will ensure it is produced at the right time, in the right quantity and of the right quality. Garments in all stages of production are regularly inspected for fit, style and quality. These checks ensure that the final product meets the quality criteria at the first attempt. If these criteria are not met, the product is returned to the supplier and the process will begin again. The quality department works very closely with the retail buyers and merchandisers who discuss supplier performance.

Forecasting (launch planning)

The Directory is used to sample customer reaction to certain lines. Photographic shots are arranged, a working layout of the Directory is planned and copy is checked. Key customers are issued with a preview Directory. This provides them with a discount on lines ordered but that cannot yet be delivered. The pattern of these orders informs the merchandisers of predicted best sellers for the forthcoming season and allows them to amend the quantity planned with the manufacturers. Continuous 'in-house' checks are made on the suppliers during production to ensure that schedules are being met and standards maintained. Orders are shipped to Next and are received at the central distribution depot. The final stage is the delivery of merchandise to the stores in time for a new season or a new phase.

Visual merchandising

Window displays and branch merchandising techniques are tested in a series of mock shops located at the company's head office. Once finalised, pictures and product details are sent to all stores. Publicity in the way of editorials is sought, the

Directory is printed and issued and web pages updated with the new ranges. Product training for all managers is planned and essential fashion shows are prepared. All of these components are considered crucial in the campaign to promote the Next brand and its image on the high street.

All store management receive product training at head office twice a year, which in turn is cascaded down to all staff on the shop floor. In addition shops are kept up to date with special promotions and advertorials through a promotions calendar document.

The window displays are the main promotional activity of the company. The purpose of the windows is to increase sales by displaying stock in the most positive and commercial manner. The product is the focus of the display since it sets the standard for the whole store. Graphics are produced to support and promote each phase. The aim is to create an innovative, imaginative, yet relaxing store environment, which strongly promotes the product and helps customers to shop efficiently.

When new ranges are launched instructions and new layouts are sent to all stores. Visual merchandising and the display of products is deemed very important by the company; for example, products on display are checked daily for creasing. Moreover, there is a dedicated and trained display team that visits all the stores on a three-week cycle to renew both window and internal displays.

Store designs are continually being reviewed and new space utilisation has improved the look of store layouts without making them too congested. Having experimented with various logos and facias in the past the company has become increasingly focused on developing core ranges for their customers.

Product monitoring

The product cycle is not quite complete. Even when the ranges are available in the stores the various teams are assessing individual garments for performance, best sellers and availability. The buyers do this by visiting stores and speaking with customers and store staff. Any information gained even at this late stage may be an essential 'tip' for the next season.

Summary

Next aims to sell 'affordable collectables'. This means that products are competitively priced, of lasting quality and embody 'contemporary styling' and 'classic good taste'. The objective for the designers and buyers is to produce ranges that look as good this year as they will the next year. The strength of the company lies in its ability to interpret fashion rather than to lead or follow it. The Next designers add fashion detail to classic designs.

The company has enjoyed continued success over the last 10 years based on the key strategy of offering customers a distinctive, stylish, quality product, providing good value for money in an efficient, friendly environment. The buying and merchandising team has a key role to ensure that this reputation is maintained.

Discussion questions

1. Identify the factors that affect stock levels and highlight how this may impinge on sales.

2. The company has a plan to increase average store size. How will this influence the way the company buys and merchandises stock?

3. What factors do you think buyers and merchandisers take into consideration when planning ranges for a new season?

4. What are the benefits to customers and the company of having central buying and merchandising departments?

5. How does a company cope with unusual weather conditions such as a cold, wet summer or a dry, warm winter?

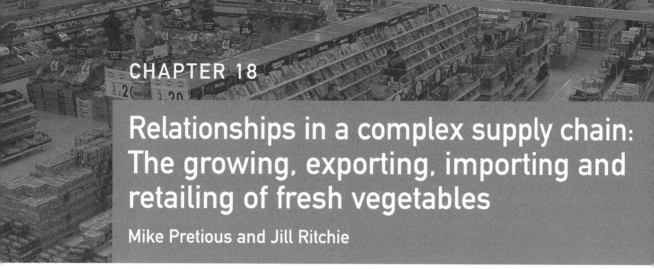

CHAPTER 18

Relationships in a complex supply chain: The growing, exporting, importing and retailing of fresh vegetables

Mike Pretious and Jill Ritchie

Introduction

Chapter 16 provided a detailed analysis of the buying and merchandising process and introduced the notion of collaborative relationships within the supply chain. It highlighted the importance of supplier selection and drew attention to the challenges that lie in sourcing overseas. Many of the issues that were identified manifest themselves in this case study. The channel for fresh vegetables is representative of many supply chains in that it provides examples of market concentration, consolidation and the exercise of market power.

The UK grocery retail market

The last two decades have witnessed arguably the most dramatic revolution that the UK food retailing industry has ever seen (Seth and Randall, 2001). Two closely linked changes have underpinned this transformation. First, mergers and acquisitions during the 1980s have altered the market structure of grocery retailing, leading to increased levels of concentration in the industry. The 'big four' chains of Tesco, Sainsbury, Asda and Safeway account for over 50 per cent of grocery sales (Harvey, 2000). Secondly, there has been a trend towards fewer, larger supermarkets, usually located away from the city centre and offering extended ranges of food (and increasingly non-food) products. Grocery retailing in the United Kingdom is now characterised by largely oligopolistic competition, with the major players vigorously competing for market share using a combination of price-driven promotions, own-brand developments and other customer service initiatives, such as loyalty cards.

The UK grocery consumer

Demographic factors and shifts in consumer demand for food products have meant that UK grocery retailers have had to adapt their core offer in recent years. Key social changes include the breakdown of the traditional family structure, the increase in the number of women in the workforce and the ageing population. The routine, daily cooking of meals from scratch is in decline, partly because of the above factors, though in contrast to this trend there has been an upsurge in the 'occasional' preparation of special meals using more esoteric ingredients. Generally, however, today's 'time-poor' consumers demand convenience foods that allow for fast preparation and consumption. 'Snacking', the eating of food on the move or at unconventional times, is also markedly increasing. These social changes have encouraged retailer innovations in packaging and choice and fuelled the growth of added-value 'meal solutions'.

Increasing health awareness is also a major factor in the changing climate of UK food retailing and the market is growing for low fat/low calorie foods and vegetarian options. Greater consumer understanding of food safety and environmental issues as a result of the BSE and 'foot and mouth' epidemics and the controversy over genetically modified foods, has also fuelled demand for food products that are perceived as safer and of better quality. All the major grocery retailers now label at least some of their products with healthy eating symbols, helping consumers make more informed purchases. There has also been significant growth in the availability and consumption of organic products. UK retail sales of organic food in 1999 reached over £390 million, up from £150 million in 1995 (Jones 2000).

Opportunities certainly appear to exist for suppliers and retailers to further develop innovative products, for example by making linkages between the concept of convenience and healthy or organic foods. However, the majority of UK consumers continue to be price sensitive for staple food products and the marketing focus of the major grocery chains reflects this emphasis on the need for value.

The fresh fruit and vegetables sector

Notwithstanding the potential opportunities for organic produce (see Wycherley 2002 for a full discussion of current marketing practices in this sector), the fresh fruit and vegetable trade in the United Kingdom is experiencing difficulties. These product categories overall are showing little growth and any new products that are introduced tend to displace sales of existing lines. Despite this, the major grocery retailers have seen fresh fruit and vegetables as a key attraction to customers due to their visual appeal and the fact that their limited storage life means frequent purchases. In addition, consumers with higher incomes buy proportionately more fresh fruit and vegetables. Margins too are higher than the average for other food items. Fearne and Hughes (1999: 121) sum up the position as follows:

> Fresh produce has become what retailers describe as a 'destination' category – fresh fruit and vegetables is one of the few categories (along with fresh meat and wine) for which shoppers will switch stores. It is also one of the two remaining categories (along with meat) which is virtually all own label and thus over which they can exert considerable influence and control.

One consequence of the interest shown by the supermarket chains in the fruit and vegetable category has been the decline in the number of specialist greengrocers. This reflects the common trend in other food retailing sectors away from independents towards large-scale operators. In turn this has led to the greengrocery wholesale industry experiencing significant decline (see, for example, White 2000). When greengrocery retailing was fragmented and most agricultural and horticultural producers were still quite small, wholesalers had power in the supply chain. Suppliers fed the wholesale markets that then sold on to local shops and traders. However, the relationships that retailers had with the growers were indirect and discontinuous and therefore the production side had no incentive to meet the exact specifications that the major chains demanded. Increasingly these larger retailers sought to purchase product direct from the farm, or from an intermediary who could better coordinate their requirements than a traditional wholesaler, such as one that would grade, pre-pack and process the product.

The main reason for importing fresh fruit and vegetables into the United Kingdom is because of the better outdoor growing climates overseas. However some items, including many pea and bean products, require intensive cultivation and are imported because labour costs in the United Kingdom make year-round production uneconomic. Historical links with the British Empire and subsequently the Commonwealth have meant that there exists a well-developed infrastructure of fruit and vegetable importers in the United Kingdom, which then sell the product on to retailers. However, in recent years the pressure exerted by retailers on wholesalers of UK-sourced fruit and vegetables has been extended to importers, and is now being felt further upstream in the supply chain by exporters and primary producers. Whilst the major multiples still prefer, in the majority of cases, to deal with an importer rather than direct with an overseas grower, there is an increasing expectation for one or more of these participants in the supply chain to involve themselves in 'added-value' activities such as processing. However, there are few specialist fruit and vegetable importers in the United Kingdom that can offer the facilities and expertise demanded by the larger chains. Moreover the tendency for the multiples to reduce the number of suppliers they purchase from is consolidating this part of the fresh produce supply chain still further.

The Sunveg[1] Group: company background

Sunveg operates in one of the larger East African countries. The issues that confront the business at national level are resonant throughout the continent of Africa. Though the country it trades from is stable, democracy is relatively new to the political environment and the government is striving with the twin aims of ensuring stability in the indigenous population whilst attempting to attract inward investment and trade through a programme of economic reforms. In addition, the local transport and communications infrastructure, whilst markedly improved over the last 20 years, is still relatively primitive.

Five major companies dominate vegetable exports from this country. These are Farm Supplies, Growfresh, Sunveg, Commonwealth Exporters and Kilimanjaro, which together account for 80 per cent of the business. Some years ago the industry was much more fragmented, but as customer demands have increased and

---

[1] All names and the exact location of the company discussed in the case have been changed to maintain commercial confidentiality. Any similarity of name to that of an existing business is not intended by the authors.

margins reduced there has been significant rationalisation due to the investment required to upgrade facilities.

The Sunveg Group is a major producer and exporter of chilled fresh vegetables. Incorporated in the late 1970s the group operates as a number of different companies, which together produce a wide range of high quality products and offer year-round supply to European supermarket chains. Initially Sunveg concentrated on the purchase of Asian vegetables from smallholders and the sale of these on a consignment basis to Asian wholesalers in the United Kingdom. From these small beginnings Sunveg developed new lines and moved into the mainstream European market, becoming one of the top five vegetable exporters from its country. The company's expansion was further assisted in the mid-1990s by the advancement of a loan facility of US$1 million towards a planned US$3.9 million expansion in their packing operation. The result was a dramatic shift in their customer base, away from the traditional bulk vegetable business and towards the value-added, pre-packaged sector. Export volumes stood in the year 2000 at nearly 4,500 tonnes, of which nearly 1,000 tonnes is prepared (washed and ready to eat). Sunveg has a particularly strong customer base in the United Kingdom, where it is a main supplier to several of the major supermarket chains.

The company itself owns four farms: Tanka River Farm Ltd, Valley Growers Ltd, Ridgeway Farm Ltd. and Sloma Ltd. Sunveg has a policy of producing at least 50 per cent of its export requirements from its own production units. The more technically complex crops, such as salad onions, are produced in-house, whilst crops that are more straightforward to grow, such as French beans, tend to be sourced from producers outside the company. Whilst these units are not owned by Sunveg they are heavily controlled by them, for example the planting/production programmes and the spray/fertiliser regimes are all set in-house. Sunveg has three main 'outgrowers', which are all large-scale commercial farming operations: Mbanga Ltd, Thantamont Farm and Vitality Holdings.

The supply chain from farm to retailer

Figure 18.1 illustrates the main stages the product goes through, from the farm on which the raw material is grown to the local supermarket in the United Kingdom. Due to the high perishability and short shelf-life of fresh produce the supply chain must be highly efficient and reliable. Each stage must be precisely coordinated to reduce handling time and costs.

Every farm affiliated to Sunveg is given their growing programme at the beginning of each season and seed is bought and delivered for the schedule. The crop plantations are closely monitored and the progress through their life cycle is recorded (traceability is a compulsory requirement for supplying the major UK retailers). Every single crop down to an individual bean must be accounted for, since if there is a problem further down the supply chain it is vital to be able to track the product back to its original source. Each crop plantation is therefore given a serial number, which remains with it until the end of its journey to the retailer. Every farm belonging to Sunveg has its own grading, packing and cold store facilities, although the standards vary slightly between the farms. As soon as

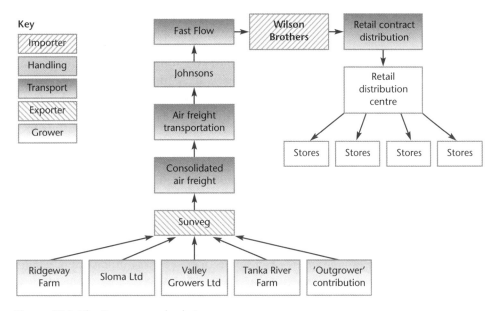

Figure 18.1 The Sunveg supply chain

crops are harvested it is paramount that they are taken care of appropriately. Once picked the raw material is cooled using a chill blaster and kept in a cold store for grading and packing into labelled pallets.

Each of the four farms belonging to Sunveg has its own trucks for transporting the raw materials to the group headquarters in the capital city. Some of the farms have arranged to pick up smallholder produce on the way. Once at the pack house the pallets will be offloaded into the relevant cold store. Some will go to the prepared cold store ready for processing under 'high care' conditions and the rest will go to the 'semi-prepared' building. Every day the pack house manager devises a packing programme to be completed during the two 10-hour shifts that make up a day. Each table is numbered and members of staff follow their own particular programme. During the day the quality control team will conduct a range of tests and set up experiments to determine the shelf-life and other properties of the crop. Everything is recorded meticulously and filed for future reference. It is also part of the quality control remit to check hygiene standards amongst the staff. In the 'prepared' section especially it is absolutely crucial to uphold the highest standards of cleanliness, and there is a strict procedure that everyone must adhere to when entering the pack house.

After any preparation is complete the processed vegetables are weighed, packed, labelled and boxed up, then blast chilled again and packed into airfreight pallets for transportation to the airport. Even though the headquarters are only a five-minute drive from the airport it is necessary to maintain temperature control. Consolidated Air Freight, Sunveg's own in-house cargo handler, deals with this part of the journey and arranges airfreight to the United Kingdom. Sunveg uses three main air transporters, subsidiaries of major airlines that have high flight frequencies to this part of Africa and refrigerated compartments available on their aircraft. Once in the United Kingdom, Johnsons, the handling agent, will offload the consignment and transport it to its cold store at the airport. From there FastFlow, a contract haulier, will collect the product and take charge of clearance and customs at the airport. The products will then be taken to Wilson Brothers, the importer and marketing agent. There the vegetables will be taken out of their outer boxes, labelled if required, and put into designated supermarket packaging. Third party logistics companies contracted by the retailers will pick up the product from Wilson Brothers and take it to their regional distribution centres. The retailers will sort the products in these depots and load them into trucks to be delivered to their network of stores.

Relationships in the supply chain

The key feature of the supply chain described above is the network of relationships it involves. This network is complex, and the interactions within it do not altogether correspond to the descriptions of emergent best practice in retailer/supplier relationships as discussed in the literature. Much recent commentary stresses the gradual shift towards supply chain management as an ethos and partnership as a paradigm (see, for example, Davies 1996; Kumar 1996; Fernie 1998). Authors such as Wilson (1996) and White (2000) attempt to unravel the specific nuances of the fresh produce supply chain, but it is Hogarth-Scott (1999), in a wide-ranging article examining supply chain relationships in the food industry, who perhaps best articulates the issues raised in the case. In it, she characterises interorganisational retailer–supplier relationships as having three key dimensions: power/dependency, trust/control and commitment. It is in this context that the relationships in the case will be examined.

The primary relationships from Sunveg's perspective are with the growers and with Wilson Brothers, their UK-based importer. Sunveg has the power to exercise choice over which growers supply it and the procedures of these suppliers in raising and processing the crops. However Sunveg are largely dependent on Wilson Brothers to effectively market their products. Wilson Brothers thus has some power over Sunveg (though Sunveg might be able to shift to another importer), but its most important relationships are with the retailers that source produce from them. Interestingly, it does not appear that the relationship with a particular buyer is especially relevant, though it is clear that the growers, Sunveg and Wilson Brothers must combine to offer the retailer a product which is viable:

> 'The crucial thing about a relationship is understanding the commercial success criteria for each party. In other words no matter how well you get on with individuals, it needs to be based on a good commercial understanding that what is expected of us as a marketing company we can deliver, and what we expect in terms of quality standards, continuity and promises can also be delivered. So relationships have to be based on clarity of what equals success.' (James Kirkpatrick, Managing Director, Wilson Brothers)

Given the structure of grocery retailing in the United Kingdom, it is the major multiples that have the real power in the supply chain. Each link in the chain has to be perceived by the retailer to be adding value, or else the possibility of disintermediation becomes real:

'The problem you get is that as the growers and retailers get bigger, the retailers start bypassing you and go direct to source. Also you're working on tiny margins so as the markets firm up or go soft and as competition comes in, you really struggle since you have no defensible barriers.' (John Ames, Finance Director, Wilson Brothers)

From the point of view of one retailer supplied by Wilson's there is clearly a desire to build a relationship with the grower and the exporter in addition to their day-to-day contacts with the importer. Such desire appears to be based more on developing an emotional bond than on any economic benefit, and in this regard the retailer is seeking commitment from the growers:

'The relationship is primarily with the importer, but I am very keen that we build relationships with the growers and get them passionate about supplying us.' (Ian Aitchison, buyer, major grocery retailer)

It is worth remembering at this stage our discussions from Chapter 10. The 'product' sold to the retailer is not just a consignment of vegetables but a set of services that add value to the exchange. So long as each member of the supply chain performs a useful function retailers prefer to utilise the specific skills and expertise of the exporter and importer. The trend towards category management suggests that there is at least some mutual respect in this relationship, despite the latent power of the retailer:

'I think that the whole spirit of category management is that the supermarkets' strategy will be built together with its supply base. We are actually helping develop their strategy. If we are really in control of our sector as category managers we should be going to them with ideas and telling them we want to work with them. So it's not done to us, it's done with us.' (James Kirkpatrick, Managing Director, Wilson Brothers)

This appreciation of the role of each member of the supply chain is mirrored in the attitude of Sunveg towards Wilson Brothers:

'What they bring, if you have the right importer, is knowledge . . . It's about how close you can get to the customer to understand their needs'. (Hugh Jameson, Managing Director, Sunveg)

One important way for supply chain members to add value for the retailer, and thus differentiate themselves from the competition, is through new product development (NPD). This is perhaps the best way in which the weaker supply chain members can generate commitment from the retailer:

'If you're a good agent then you'll take the initiative. You will work with your customer, who will also have an NPD stream. If the customer comes up with an idea, you as the agent will say "yeah that's a good idea, I'll go and talk to some growers and I'm sure we can put something together for you". Then we'll give them a range of innovations and the supermarket will choose.' (John Ames, Finance Director, Wilson Brothers)

However, such a proactive approach from the importer appears to occur less often than the retailers would like. This weakens their commitment to the importer and re-emphasises where the power in the supply chain truly lies:

> 'It should be a combination of ideas, and occasionally it is, but I have to say that importers generally aren't good at innovation. They're very good at marketing volume, but not very good at coming up with ideas for new added-value products. So it's usually down to the retailers. I would actually like to see the exporter getting involved in innovation from their end though.' (Ian Aitchison, buyer, major grocery retailer)

Summary

Sunveg's operation is at the fulcrum of a complex network of relationships. Looking back along the supply chain, the company is vertically integrated as it owns many of the farms that supply its core products (the vegetables that are ultimately imported and sold in UK retailers). Looking forwards, it controls through ownership, packing and transportation up to the point of export. These services, or secondary products, represent its key strengths and offer the opportunity for it to differentiate itself from other companies in the sector.

The relationship between Sunveg and Wilson Brothers can be characterised as a true partnership, in so far as each participant is mutually dependent and the power wielded by each is comparable. Sunveg requires Wilson Brothers to maintain strong communication channels with the retailers and to be efficient in terms of the services it provides in the Untied Kingdom. Should Sunveg perceive Wilson Brothers to be ineffective it can switch to an alternative importer. Wilson Brothers cannot operate its business at all without the core product of vegetables and is also heavily reliant on Sunveg's services. However, if there are problems with the quality of either of these products then the company might choose to purchase from alternative growers.

The relationships between the suppliers, Sunveg and Wilson Brothers and the major retailers are less balanced and appear to be based more on convenience than a true partnership ethos. The retailers seem to prefer dealing with an importer, though potentially they have the opportunity to either buy directly from an exporter or to negotiate supply terms with individual growers. They also have the choice of sourcing from a portfolio of importers, depending on market conditions and other factors. The commitment in these relationships is much greater from the supplier side and the power, albeit latent, clearly lies with the retailers.

Discussion questions

1. Perform a SWOT analysis on Sunveg. How in your view can this company capitalise on its strengths and minimise its weaknesses in its indirect dealings with the major grocery multiples?

2. What would be the advantages and disadvantages to the retailer in eliminating from the supply chain as described:

    i. the exporter, Sunveg;

    ii. the importer, Wilson Brothers;

    iii. both the exporter and the importer, leaving the buyer to deal direct with the growers?

3. Using evidence from the case plus your own knowledge, what further changes in the end-consumer market for fruit and vegetables can you envisage over the next 10 years?

PART 7

Retail logistics

CHAPTER 19

Retail logistics

Leigh Sparks

Aim

The aim of this chapter is to introduce students to retail logistics and the ways in which they support the retail offer.

Learning objectives

By the end of this chapter, students should be able to:

- understand the nature and components of retail logistics;
- comprehend the retail logistics transformation that has occurred in recent decades;
- document the importance of retail logistics;
- describe possible future constraints and issues for retail logistics.

Introduction

We take it for granted that products will be available to buy in the shops. The cornucopia of goods available in a supermarket or a department store sometimes masks the hard work that goes into getting the right products to the right place at the right time and in the right condition. We expect our lettuces to be fresh, the new Playstation to be available on launch day and our clothes to be in good condition and ready to wear. With the introduction of e-commerce we have come to expect 24-hour availability and home delivery at a time of our choosing.

As the earlier chapters in this book have shown, retailing has changed; our beliefs and needs as consumers have also altered. Our willingness to wait to be satisfied or served is reduced and we expect and demand instant product availability and gratification. If all this has changed then it should be obvious that the supply or logistics system which gets products from production through retailing to consumption has also had to be transformed. Physical distribution and materials management have been replaced by supply chain management, logistics management and a concern for the whole of the supply chain (Figure 19.1). McKinsey Global Institute (1998) declared the British grocery retailing industry world-class, based in part on its highly effective logistics system.

This transformation derives from cost and service requirements as well as consumer and retailer change. Elements of logistics are remarkably expensive if not controlled effectively. Holding stock or inventory in warehouses just in case it is needed is a costly activity. The stock itself is expensive and might not sell or it could become obsolete. Warehouses generally are expensive to build, operate and maintain. Vehicles to transport goods between warehouses and stores are major cost centres in terms of both capital and running costs. There is thus a cost imperative to making sure that logistics is carried out effectively and efficiently.

At the same time there can be service benefits. By appropriate integration of demand and supply, mainly through the widespread use of information technology and systems, retailers can provide a better service to consumers by, for example, having fresher, higher quality produce arriving to meet consumer demand. With the appropriate logistics, products should be of a better quality, could be cheaper, have a longer shelf-life, and there should be far fewer instances of stock-outs. If operating properly a good logistics system can both reduce costs and improve service, providing a competitive advantage for the retailer.

Self-assessment Question 1 *Product channels – Think about the last product you bought – this could be large or small, food or non-food. Where did it come from? How did it get from its point of production and into your hands? What issues do you think there are in ensuring the supply of this product?*

This chapter examines this logistics transformation (see also Sparks 1998). It looks at the changes in supply in recent years and the implications of these changes. New techniques and methods are introduced and considered. Constraints on

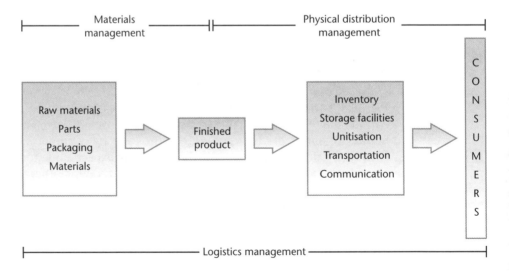

Figure 19.1 Logistic management

logistics change are also discussed, together with future issues that confront retail logistics systems.

The logistics task

Retailing and logistics are concerned with product availability. Many have described this as 'getting the right products to the right place at the right time'. Unfortunately that description does not do justice to the amount of effort that goes into a logistics supply system and the multitude of ways that it can go wrong. The very simplicity of the statement suggests logistics is an easy process. The real trick however lies in making logistics look easy, day in and day out, whilst reacting to volatile changes in consumer demand.

For example, if the temperature rises and the sun comes out in an untypical Scottish summer then demand for ice cream, soft drinks and even salad items rises dramatically. How does a retailer make sure they remain in stock and capture this transient demand? Or we might think about Valentine's Day, and how demand for certain products in the days before increases exponentially. If a retailer stocks Valentine's cards and demand does not materialise then the retailer has stock that will not sell. There is little demand for Valentine's cards on 15 February.

The examples above demonstrate that retailers must be concerned with the flows of product *and* information within the business and the supply chain. In order to make products available, retailers have to manage their logistics in terms of product movement and demand management. They need to know what is selling in the stores and both anticipate and react quickly to changes in this demand. At the same time they need to be able to move less demand-volatile products in an efficient and cost-effective manner.

The logistics management task is therefore concerned with managing the components of the 'logistics mix'. We can identify five components:

- *Storage facilities*: these might be warehouses or distribution centres or simply the stock rooms of retail stores. Retailers manage these facilities to enable them to keep stock in anticipation of, or to react to, demand for products.
- *Inventory*: all retailers hold stock to some extent. The question for retailers is the amount of stock or inventory (finished products and/or component parts) that has to be held for each product and the location of this stock to meet demand changes.
- *Transportation*: most products have to be transported in some way at some stage of their journey from production to consumption. Retailers therefore have to manage a transport operation that might involve different forms of transport, different sizes of vehicle and the scheduling and availability of drivers and vehicles.
- *Unitisation and packaging*: consumers generally buy products in small quantities. They sometimes make purchase decisions based on product presentation and packaging. Retailers are concerned to get products that are easy to handle in logistics terms, do not cost too much to package or handle, yet retain their selling ability on the shelves.

- *Communications*: to get products to where we want them it is necessary to have information, not only about demand and supply, but also about volumes, stock, prices and movements. Retailers have thus become increasingly concerned with being able to capture data at appropriate points in the system and to use that information to have a more efficient and effective logistics operation.

It should be clear that all of these elements are interlinked. If a retailer gets good sales data from the checkout system then the scheduling of transport and the level of stock holding become more straightforward. If the level of inventory can be reduced then perhaps fewer warehouses are needed. If communications and transport can be effectively linked then a retailer can move from keeping stock in a warehouse to running a distribution centre that sorts products for immediate store delivery, that is, approaching a 'just-in-time' system.

It should also be clear that retailers could not do all of this on their own. They are involved in the selling of goods and services to the consumer. Retailers take products from manufacturers and suppliers and therefore have a direct interest in their logistics systems. If a retailer is effective, but its suppliers are not, then errors and delays in supply from the manufacturer will impact on the retailer and its consumers, either in terms of higher prices or stock-outs (no products available on the shelves). If a retailer can integrate its logistics system with that of its suppliers such problems can be minimised. Much more importantly however the entire supply chain can then be optimised and managed as a single entity. This brings potential advantages of cost reductions *and* service enhancement, not only for the retailer but also for the supplier. It should also mean that products reach the stores more rapidly, thus better meeting transient customer demand.

For example, Benetton can obtain data on what is selling from its entire chain of stores on a daily or even real-time basis. This knowledge can be transmitted to production facilities to ensure supply is increased or decreased accordingly. For single-colour garments, products can be held in an un-dyed state, with dyeing occurring only when demand is known (a process we can term 'postponement' as the final decision on product colour is postponed until the demand is known). The distribution operation delivers tailored amounts of products to individual stores by a fast response system, for example flying products to national locations. Reacting to demand in this way maximises selling opportunities whilst minimising 'obsolete' product risks.

In the grocery sector, Tesco works with its fresh food producers to ensure that products are picked in reaction to demand levels and distributed rapidly to stores through the distribution centres. By being in the shop more quickly the freshness is maximised and shelf-life is extended. The consumer gets a better quality product but at the same time wastage costs are reduced. The system is cheaper but also provides a better service.

We could also think about the reverse proposition. If demand is not coordinated with supply then there is a danger of over or under production. For example, if sales increase one week production will rise to meet this demand. If sales go down the next week production may not be switched off quickly enough. Variations in orders, storage needs and production multiply and become exaggerated as the system and the component companies seek to react to situations that have already changed. This is known as the Forrester Effect (small disturbances at the sales point can become magnified as the effects spread through the supply chain). The effect may be brought on by poor retail buying strategies, poor transmission of demand data, storage requirements and availability, competitor pricing, promotion and advertising, etc. In each situation costs rise considerably for logistics and thus eventually for the consumer.

The description above of the logistics task leaves open one aspect. These are highly advanced and complex operations: suppliers might be spread across the world, a retailer may have thousands of stores with tens of thousands of individual product lines and may make millions of individual sales per day. Utilising data to ensure effective operations amongst retailers and suppliers, head office, stores and distribution centres, vehicles and drivers, is not straightforward. There is thus always a tension between overall complexity and the desire for the simplest possible process. One way in which retailers, particularly in the United Kingdom, have reacted to this tension is by contracting out (or outsourcing) aspects of these operations to specialist logistics service providers.

Many of the vehicles you see on the motorway bearing retailers' logos are not owned by the retailers but are provided by logistics specialists. Many of the distribution centres at motorway interchanges may bear retailers' names, but they are run by logistics services providers. Companies such as Hays, Wincanton, Exel or Christian Salvesen operate numerous facilities and activities on behalf of major retailers, not only in the United Kingdom, but in Continental Europe and beyond. By specialising in the operation of certain tasks the overall logistics supply system becomes more efficient. This is not to say that retailers have no interest in what is done in their name. On the contrary, contracting out requires retailers to manage through knowledge and information. Data on all aspects of performance are collected and compared, sometimes with operations run by the retailers themselves just for this purpose. Tesco, for example, operates a couple of distribution centres itself to enable it to benchmark the performance of the other subcontracted centres.

If we think about Amazon.co.uk we can see this subcontracting process in operation. Amazon does not distribute products itself, but subcontracts the delivery of products to specialist firms such as Federal Express, UPS or the Royal Mail. The company saves itself the problems and cost of setting up a specialist system by using networks already in place.

Summarising the discussion above, the logistics task can be described as follows:

> The process of strategically managing the procurement, movement and storage of materials, parts and finished inventory (and the related information flows) through the organisation and its marketing channels in such a way that current and future profitability are maximised through the cost effective fulfilment of orders. (Christopher 1998: 4)

Managing the logistics mix in an integrated supply chain whilst aiming to balance cost and service requirements are the essential elements of logistics management (Figure 19.2). Figure 19.2 and the above discussion might suggest that getting the 'right products to the right place at the right time' is straight-forward. There have been many disasters in retail logistics, however, and it is an area where, when things go wrong, the costs of the problem accelerate quickly.

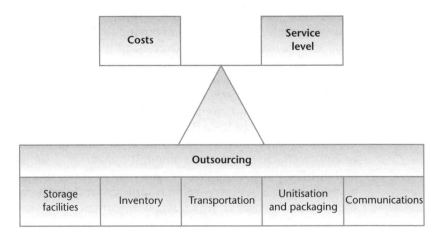

Figure 19.2 The management task in logistics

Box 19.1 provides a recent example. The company had stock, but it was in the wrong place. With no stock on the store shelves, consumers went elsewhere. This means lost sales and profits in the short term and possibly in the long term. Retail buyers for the company will have had their predictions and purchase estimates upset, and so supply and demand will not match easily. Getting this back in balance will take more than just getting the goods to the stores.

As retailers have begun to embrace this logistics approach and examine their supply chains many have realised that, to carry out logistics properly, there has to be a transformation of approach and operations. It is to this we now turn.

Box 19.1
Carelessness at Mothercare leaves cupboard bare

Helen Slingsby
Guardian

Tuesday 9 October 2001
Sales at Mothercare have dived by 6% in the last three weeks after its move to a new hi-tech distribution centre caused problems.

The childrenswear retailer admitted yesterday that staff shortcomings meant its heralded autumn/winter clothing range had languished at the new Northamptonshire warehouse, causing huge stock shortages in its stores.

Chief Executive Chris Martin, who was recruited to turn around the chain, admitted the setback was 'exceptionally frustrating' given that like-for-like sales until this period had been up about 10%, and that the new range had been well received.

It was doubly frustrating, he said, as management of the Daventry warehouse is subcontracted to a third party, Tibbett & Britten. 'Some of their staff just weren't doing their job,' said a source.

Tibbett has responded by placing a senior director at the building to sort out the problems and establish a proper flow of stock to the stores. Asked if he was considering legal action, Mr Martin said: 'This is a five-year relationship. We are working it through together.'

He added that a fifth less stock than usual had been in the shops but stressed that it was 'now coming through'. In a trading statement Mr Martin revealed that sales rose by 9.6% for the 26 weeks to September 28 with like-for-like sales up by 7.6%. Brokers at Charterhouse Securities cut their recommendation from hold to sell after the news. But Seymour Pierce retail analyst Richard Ratner said: 'If they sort the warehouse problems out in the next few weeks I won't be unduly concerned, particularly as the 2.1 percentage point improvement in margin was better than expected.' Mothercare will forge ahead with the roll-out of its larger Mothercare World format after Christmas.

Retail logistics transformation

When Tesco opened its new 16,000 square feet store in Leicester in 1961 it claimed it was the largest grocery store in Europe. Today Tesco's *average* store size in the United Kingdom is almost twice this and in eastern Europe the company is opening hypermarkets 10 times as large as this pioneering store. As the scale, location and product range of Tesco have changed, the systems for supplying new stores have undergone a fundamental shift in operations and approach. New store formats demand new logistics. The logistics required for a new hypermarket are vastly different to those required for the smaller stores it replaces. Such differences are one component of the logistics transformation.

Retailers were once effectively the passive recipients of products, which were allocated to stores by manufacturers in anticipation of demand. Today retailers are the active controllers of product supply in response to known customer demand. They control, organise and manage the supply chain from production to consumption. This is the essence of the retail logistics transformation that has taken place.

Times have changed and retail logistics has also changed. Retailers are the channel captains and set the pace in logistics. Having extended their channel control and focused on efficiency and effectiveness, retailers are now attempting to engender a more cooperative and collaborative stance in many aspects of logistics. They are recognising that there are still gains to be made on standards and efficiency, but that these are probably only obtained as channel gains (that is, in association with manufacturers and logistics services providers) rather than at the single firm level.

Table 19.1 charts this history of innovation in logistics by major grocery retailers. The stages are characterised by a movement from a manufacturer-controlled, transport-oriented system to a retail led and replenishment focused technology-rich supply chain. This transformation began in the food retail sector, but has spread to other retail sectors such as DIY and clothing. Figure 19.3 shows the effect this assertion of leadership and maintenance of control has had on the stockholding levels of Tesco. The figure illustrates clearly the shift from disorderly systems through the enhancement of efficiency to the current low-stock position.

Table 19.1 Major logistics innovations by multiple grocery retailers

Period	Problem	Innovation	Consequences
1960s and 1970s	Disorderly delivery by suppliers to supermarkets; queues of vehicles led to both inefficiency and disruption	Introduction of regional distribution centres (RDCs) to channel goods from suppliers to supermarkets operated by retailers	(1) Strict timing of supplier delivery to RDC imposed by retailers (2) Retailers build and operate RDC (3) Retailer operates own delivery fleet between RDC and supermarkets within its catchment area
1980s	Retailers becoming too committed to operating logistics services in support of retail activity	Operations of retailer-owned RDCs and vehicle fleets outsourced to specialist freight companies	(1) Retailers can concentrate on 'core business' of retailing (2) Retailer achieves better financial return from capital investment in supermarkets than in RDCs and vehicles
1980s and 1990s	Available floorspace at retail outlets being under used; too much floorspace used for storage	Conversion of storage floorspace at supermarkets to sales floorspace; corporate strategy and brand development	(1) Better sales revenue potential at retail outlets (2) RDCs absorb products formerly kept in store at supermarkets (3) Just-in-time (JIT) delivery used from RDC to replenish supermarket shelves
1990s to date	Requirement for better customer service and cost control over a range of formats and channels; range of products expands	Reorganisation of DCs; some development of stockless centres; store-based Internet delivery systems	(1) Better in-store quality and stock position (2) Technological expansion through operations (3) Rapid rollout of Internet operations

Source: after Cooper *et al.* (1991)

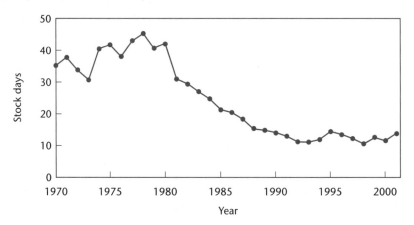

Figure 19.3 Stock days in Tesco 1970–2001

McKinnon (1996) has reviewed and summarised the key components of this logistics transformation. He identified six trends, all of which are closely related and mutually reinforcing.

Increased control over secondary distribution: retailers have increased their control over secondary distribution (that is, warehouse to shop) by channelling an increasing proportion of their supplies through distribution centres (DCs). In some sectors such as grocery, this process is now virtually complete. British retailers exert much tighter control over the supply chain than their counterparts in most other countries. Their logistical operations are heavily dependent on information technology, particularly the large integrated stock replenishment systems that control the movement and storage of an enormous number of separate products.

Restructured logistical systems: retailers have reduced inventory and generally improved efficiency through the development of 'composite distribution' (the distribution of mixed temperature items through the same distribution centre and on the same vehicle) and centralisation in specialist warehouses of slower moving stock. In the case of mixed retail businesses the establishment of 'common stock rooms' (where stock is shared across a number of stores, with demand deciding to which store stock is allocated) is developed.

Adoption of 'quick response' (QR): the aim has been to cut inventory levels and improve the speed of product flow. This has involved reducing order lead time and moving to a more frequent delivery of smaller consignments both internally (between DC and shop) and externally (between supplier and DC). This has greatly increased both the rate of stock turn and the amount of product being 'cross-docked' rather than stored at DCs. QR was made possible by the development of electronic data interchange and electronic point of sale, the latter driving the 'sales-based ordering' systems that most of the larger retailers have installed. In other words as an item is sold and scanned in a shop this data is used to inform replenishment and reordering systems and thus react quickly to demand. Sharing such data with key suppliers further integrates production with the supply function. Major UK retailers have been faster to adopt these technologies than their counterparts in other European countries, though they still have to diffuse to many medium-sized and small retail businesses.

Rationalisation of primary distribution (that is, factory to warehouse): partly as a result of QR pressures and partly as a result of intensifying competition, retailers have extended their control upstream of the DC (from the DC to the manufacturer). In an effort to improve the utilisation of their logistical assets many have integrated their secondary and primary distribution operations and run them as a single 'network system'. This reduces waste and improves efficiency.

Introduction of supply chain management (SCM) and efficient consumer response (ECR): having improved the efficiency of their logistics operations many retailers have closely collaborated with suppliers to maximise the efficiency of the retail supply chain as a whole. SCM and ECR (see later) provide a management framework within which retailers and suppliers can more effectively coordinate their activities. The underpinning technologies for ECR have been well established in the United Kingdom, so conditions have been ripe for the application of this principle.

Increased return flow of packaged material and handling equipment for recycling/reuse: retailers have become much more heavily involved in this 'reverse logistics' operation. This trend has been reinforced by the introduction of the EU packaging directive (see later). Although the United Kingdom currently lags behind other European countries, particularly Germany, in this field, there remain opportunities to develop new forms of reusable container and new reverse logistics systems to manage their circulation.

These components of the logistics transformation emphasise a number of themes. More detail on these themes in the retail context can be found in Fernie and Sparks (1998), which contains a number of case examples and illustrations, as well as a discussion of the broader points.

The retail logistics transformation has placed considerable emphasis on doing the 'right' things in logistics. Central to achieving this aim has been the use of information technology to aid data capture and on new approaches to managing the supply chain. As Box 19.2 suggests, competitive advantage can be gained by looking

---

Box 19.2
ZARA – Time-based competition in a fashion market

Zara is one of Spain's most successful and dynamic apparel companies, producing fashionable clothing to appeal to an international target market of 18–35 year olds. Zara's rapid growth and ongoing success in such a fiercely competitive environment is based on the dual objectives of working without stocks and responding quickly to market needs. It does this as well as, or even more effectively than, its internationally acclaimed rivals such as Benetton or The Gap. Zara has developed one of the most effective quick-response systems in its industry.

The process of supplying goods to the stores begins with cross-functional teams working within Zara's design department at the company headquarters in La Coruna. The designs reflect the latest in international fashion trends, with inspiration gleaned through visits to fashion shows, competitors' stores, university campuses, pubs, cafés and clubs plus any other venues or events deemed to be relevant to the lifestyles of the target customers. The team's understanding of directional fashion trends is further guided by regular inflows of EPOS data and other information from all of the company's stores and sites around the world.

If a proposed design is accepted commercial specialists proceed to negotiate with suppliers, agree purchase prices, analyse costs and margins and fix a standard cross-currency price position for the garments. The size of the production run and launch dates are also determined at this point. A global sourcing policy, organised through the company's buying offices in the United Kingdom, China and the Netherlands, and using a broad supplier base, provides the widest possible selection of fashion fabrics whilst reducing the risk of dependence on any source or supplier. Approximately 40 per cent of garments – those with the broadest and least transient appeal – are imported as finished goods from low cost manufacturing centres in the Far East. The rest are produced by quick response in Spain, using Zara's own highly automated factories and a network of smaller contractors.

Only those operations that enhance cost efficiency through economies of scale are conducted in-house (such as dyeing, cutting, labelling and packaging). All other manufacturing activities, including the labour-intensive finishing stages, are completed by networks of more than 300 small, exclusive subcontractors, each specialising in one particular part of the production process or garment type. The system is flexible enough to cope with sudden changes in demand, though production is always kept at a level slightly below expected sales, to keep stock moving. Zara has opted for under supply, viewing it as a lesser evil than holding slow-moving or obsolete stock.

Finished goods are labelled, price tagged and packed at the company's distribution centre in La Coruna. From there they travel by third-party contractors by road and/or air to their penultimate destinations. The shops themselves receive deliveries of new stock on a twice-weekly basis, according to shop-by-shop stock allocations calculated by the design department. The whole production cycle takes only two weeks. In an industry where lead times of many months are still the norm Zara has reduced its lead time to a level unmatched by any of its European or North American competitors.

Source: adapted from Christopher (1998: 155–7)

at ways of driving stock out of the system and speeding up the process. Time in the system is enormously important, as the Zara example illustrates: reductions in the time it takes to get products to market and the time it takes to react to demand can produce major benefits. Some of these approaches and techniques have been mentioned above and we now turn to look at some of them more closely.

New approaches in retail logistics

The integrative logistics approach described thus far aims to produce a supply chain that is seamless from production to consumption. The aim is to move product appropriately and rapidly, both in terms of base flow ('a lean system') and in terms of rapid reaction to demand ('an agile system'). Aiding this are a variety of tools and approaches. In this section we examine quick response (QR) and Efficient Consumer Response before moving on to consider new integrating approaches that hold potential for the future, namely Collaborative Planning Forecasting and Replenishment and Internet exchanges.

QR and ECR

Both the concepts of QR and ECR originated in the United States and came about as a result of intense competition in the retail marketplace and a need to respond to changes in the external environment. New competitors were seen to be more efficient. Low cost manufacturing, allied to rapid delivery, was demonstrating the inefficiencies in existing retail channels. International comparisons on simple performance measures identified the United States as often over-stocked, over-supplied and slow to react to market changes or demand.

Quick response tends to be associated with the textile and apparel sector and was a reaction by US textile manufacturers to a loss in domestic market share to Far East suppliers in the 1980s. The council representing these US manufacturers commissioned Kurt Salmon Associates to study US apparel industry supply chains. The results were alarming, showing that the length of supply chain from raw material to consumer purchase was 66 weeks: 11 weeks was in plant time, 40 weeks in warehouses and 15 weeks in store. The consultants estimated the cost to finance such a chain was $25 billion per annum and prompted a number of industry-wide initiatives to speed up responsiveness.

The QR initiatives can be considered in a number of ways, but essentially they comprise a search for a reduction in the lead times of fabric supply, a reduction in the production throughput times and the establishment of relationships in the distribution chain. As such, product and information flows are made both more 'lean' and 'agile'. Zara (Box 19.2) provides a good example of this.

Efficient Consumer Response arrived later than QR. It was initiated by traditional US supermarket operators and their suppliers amid concerns of eroding profit margins. Once again Kurt Salmon Associates was commissioned to conduct the research. The results were equally revealing; in the US grocery supply chain it identified excessive inventories, a 104-day lead time from plant to customer with potential savings estimated to be $30 billion (10.8 per cent of sales turnover).

The main reason for such a large volume of stock being held was the fragmentation of the chain and the pushing of inventory through the warehouse network because of trade promotions and forward buying. Forward buying began in the 1970s when heavy discounting by manufacturers was used to circumvent price controls. Instead of being phased out, forward buying continued to be important. Grocery manufacturers also focused more on trade promotions at the expense of other elements of the promotional mix. Kurt Salmon also maintained that some retailers have 7,000 to 8,000 deals on file at any one time, with buyers and sales representatives spending 10–15 per cent of their time resolving price discrepancies, that is, an essentially unproductive activity. This is a classic example of how a lack of coordination ends up increasing volatility and costs, to which companies react by storing ever more product and acting ever more slowly. Competitors who re-engineer the supply chain can gain significant benefits.

ECR (http://www.ecrnet.org/ECR/ecr.home) is a global movement (mainly in the grocery industry) focusing on the total supply chain. Suppliers, manufacturers, wholesalers and retailers work closely together to fulfil the changing demands of the grocery consumer.

ECR can be categorised into category management, product replenishment and enabling technologies (Figure 19.4). Most companies have tended to focus on supply side initiatives at first (product replenishment improvements), tackling the demand side issue later (category management). It is probably in the category management area that greatest savings can be achieved because of the doubts raised about the success of new product introductions and the costs associated with promotions. Better coordination of such activities may improve efficiencies and cost effectiveness. The thinking behind this should be clear to you. New products and price promotions essentially disrupt 'normal' demand patterns. Whilst new demand may be created or new patterns of behaviour formed these are often at the expense of existing product demand. If this is the case then this activity is basically adding complication to the logistics and distribution functions. By adding complication and variation over product range (new product introductions) and time (promotional activity) costs and risks are increased. A stable or at least a better coordinated approach to such activities provides a better chance of success and less disruption and stability in distribution.

For either category management or product replenishment initiatives to work the enabling technologies have to be in place. For category management, loyalty card and EPOS data give indications of what is being bought, when, where and by whom. Once this is known appropriate category plans can be drawn up. As information flows back through the supply chain it is essential that it is standardised and comprehensible to all partners. Protocol in relation to EDI networks, item coding and database management are necessary to ensure that a breakdown in communications does not occur. Similarly, it is important that standardisation occurs with materials handling technologies to improve efficiencies in product handling and maximising unit loads (for example standardisation of pallet size and returnable trays to an agreed industry norm).

It is clear that ECR will not be a panacea for all companies (Kotzab 1999). Figure 19.4 provides a number of initiatives from which companies may choose, according to their own particular objectives. Each company will have a different starting point and a different agenda depending upon the current nature of supplier–retailer relationships. For example, whilst a large grocery retailer may deal with thousands of suppliers, it may have only a limited number of formal partnerships.

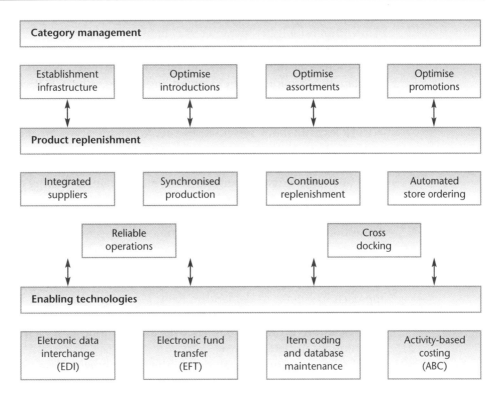

Figure 19.4 ECR improvement areas

Source: Coopers & Lybrand (1996)

Collaborative Planning Forecasting and Replenishment (CPFR) and Internet exchanges

The initial outline of ECR (Figure 19.4) has now been adapted by the introduction of 'integrators', which allow supply chain management (and ECR) to be fully exploited. Essentially these integrators are enhancements in the technological and data sharing areas. The two integrators most often mentioned are CPFR and retail exchanges.

CPFR is a business practice that aims to reduce inventory costs whilst improving product availability across the supply chain. Trading partners share forecast and results data over the Internet. CPFR technology analyses this data and alerts planners at each company to exceptional situations that could effect delivery or sales performance. Trading partners then collaborate to resolve these exceptions – adjusting plans, expediting orders, correcting data entry errors – to achieve better business outcomes. Full details of CPFR and its approach can be found at the CPFR web site (http://www.cpfr.org).

CPFR begins with an agreement between trading partners to develop a jointly owned, market-specific plan based on sound category management principles. The plan fundamentally describes what is going to be sold, how it will be merchandised and promoted, in what marketplace and during what time frame. It is accessible via agreed communication standards by either party who can adjust the plan within established parameters. Changes outside of the set parameters require the approval of the other party (which in turn may require negotiation). With CPFR a forecast can be agreed in advance and converted automatically into a delivery plan, thus avoiding the customary order processing. CPFR systems also capture mission-critical information such as promotion timing and supply constraints and can eliminate days of inventory from the entire supply chain.

CPFR expands and systematises the communication of critical data between trading partners, thereby increasing the visibility of planned and unplanned changes and uncovering problems in data integrity or planning assumptions. CPFR also allows trading partners to improve their forecasting and replenishment cycles by shedding light on which plans yield the best results. At the retail store, CPFR practices can increase sales by preventing out-of-stocks, especially during promotions. At head office, CPFR can empower category management strategies, thereby optimising product mix, promotion timing and margins across the chain. Retail distribution networks can carry less safety stock because of better partnerships with suppliers. Meanwhile, manufacturers can move from a make-to-stock approach to a make-to-demand strategy, resulting in reduced inventory, less product obsolescence and production cost savings. Throughout the supply chain CPFR efficiencies drive higher volumes over a lower total cost, resulting in improved return-on-assets performance.

CPFR has been running alongside the development of so-called retail Internet exchanges. The advent of the Internet has opened up the possibility to closer align suppliers with specific business practices. The most extensive retail example would be Wal-Mart's Retail Link. Wal-Mart defines this as:

> Information and an array of products that allow a supplier to impact all aspects of their business. By using the information available in Retail Link suppliers can plan, execute and analyse their businesses – thus providing better service to our common customers. Retail Link is a website that is accessible to any area within your company. Wal-Mart requires all suppliers to participate in Retail Link because of the benefits it provides (Wal-Mart Stores, Supplier Proposal Guide: 14).

As all parties use common systems the benefits would appear to be faster and more reliable communications and an enhancement of planning, forecasting and replenishment. In the United Kingdom we can see a number of retailers moving the same way, most publicly Tesco with its Information Exchange. These closed communities offer the advantages of simplification, automation and elimination of problem areas. In essence they are the operationalisation of the integrative principles of logistics set out earlier.

Secondly, there has been a development of wider exchanges, utilising the massive business investment in Internet technology and capability. The basic principle behind such exchanges is to allow a marketspace where competitors, suppliers, etc. can collaborate to set standards and approaches. By utilising common tools and other standards opportunities for efficiency, wider sourcing and new markets may emerge (Figure 19.5).

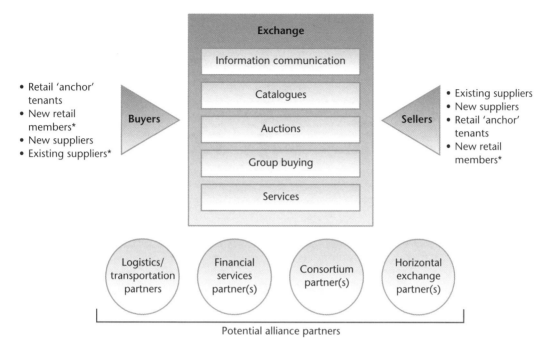

* Suppliers may buy excess products from the retailers and retailers may sell excess goods, fixtures, etc.

Figure 19.5 The composition of retail exchanges
Source: World Wide Retail Exchange information pack 2000

Two major retail exchanges have been developed, both with substantial membership from leading retailers worldwide: Global NetXchange (GNX, see http://www.gnx.com/) and WorldWide Retail Exchange (WWRE, see http://www.worldwideretailexchange.org).

GNX claims to be a globally integrated retail supply chain network, leveraging the Internet to seamlessly connect trading partners across extended retail supply chains. This open network could drastically change the way retailers collaborate with their global supply chain partners. WWRE sees exchanges as revolutionising trading relations. This occurs through the creation of open systems in which firms can form short or long-term relationships with one or many partners. Buyers and suppliers that have previously had trouble reaching each other can now connect. Suppliers can gain access to more buyers. Buyers can participate easily and view items from multiple suppliers. The electronic interface will lower transaction costs for both buyer and seller and this transparency will possibly drive down prices. Exchanges also allow the possibility of the development and implementation of new e-commerce business models (for example online auctions).

The overall aim is to provide efficiencies on current operations and benefit from new business methods. Figure 19.6 sums up the potential benefits in the supply chain. Whilst exchanges are currently unproven, online auctions have taken place and buying through the exchanges is under way. The potential to reduce cost and to streamline supply is clear. Such exchanges may seem a little abstract at this

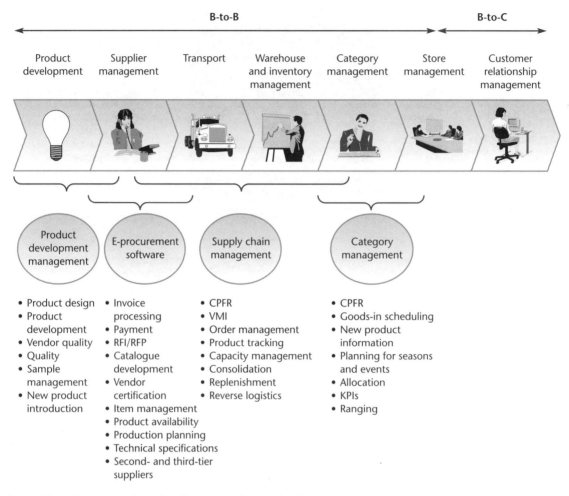

Figure 19.6 The impact of retail exchanges on the supply chain
Source: World Wide Retail Exchange information pack 2000

time, however integrative approaches such as these are fundamental to modern retail logistics. This consideration of such ideas allows us to summarise the key current issues in retail logistics generally.

First, it should be clear by now that the modern logistics system is heavily dependent on the use of information technology. Logistics now is as much about information movement as it is about product movement. Anyone who believed that retail logistics is all about boxes and lorries should have had to rethink. Of course it remains true that products have to be distributed. Vehicles and boxes are still involved. But increasingly it is the control of data and information that remains the key to a successful logistics system.

Secondly, the discussion above should have indicated that modern retail logistics is no longer a separate or functionally based activity. Within a company, warehousing and transport can not exist as separate operations. Instead logistics is all about integration, not only within a company but also increasingly outside the business with suppliers, logistics services providers and customers. Partnership is a strong component of modern retail logistics and an ability to work with other individuals and other companies is fundamental to success.

Thirdly, it should have become apparent that the 'reach' of retail logistics has expanded enormously. Companies used to manage local suppliers and products to and from local warehouses. Nowadays retailers are much more global in their outlook. Products are sourced from around the world and so the interactions and movements involved in logistics are now equally international.

Finally however we must not forget that logistics is about the movement of product, and much work is undertaken on improving the mechanics of this task. For example, a modern supermarket contains good examples of packaging and standardisation, the best of which make handling easier. Vehicle fleets may be equipped with GPS (global positioning satellite) systems and advanced tachograph and communications equipment, allowing real-time driver and vehicle performance monitoring. Such detailed analysis remains a key element of supply chain integration.

Self-assessment Question 2 *Supermarket handling systems – Go to your local large supermarket. Have a look at the fixtures and fittings from which products are sold. Identify those that are essentially handling systems that allow the product to be moved directly from the back-room of the store or the distribution centre direct to the shop floor. Why are these systems used for these products?*

The new approaches that have been outlined in this chapter provide a picture of retail logistics far removed from many people's preconceptions. To make supply chains work effectively requires this modern outlook. All the evidence is that this approach based on technology, partnerships and international activity will continue to develop.

Future issues for retail logistics

The picture we have built up thus far for logistics has emphasised cost and service improvements and a search for greater efficiency and effectiveness. We will now consider two influences on the future of retail logistics. These are: (a) environmental issues and (b) e-commerce.

Environmental issues

It could be argued that many of the logistics efficiencies described above have been generated by operating systems that are insufficiently environmentally aware. Logistics can have a major adverse impact upon the environment. Whilst improvements in vehicle design, engine efficiency, reusable handling systems and building standards have reduced the impacts, the distances products now have to travel has accentuated the problems. Environmental issues are thus one issue of future concern.

Reverse logistics: it has to be recognised that terminology in this area has been the subject of some confusion. A good starting point however is:

Reverse logistics is a process whereby companies can become more environmentally efficient through the recycling, re-use and reducing the amount of materials used. Viewed narrowly, it can be thought of as the reverse distribution of materials among channel members. A more holistic view of reverse logistics includes the reduction of materials in the forward system in such a way that fewer materials flow back, reuse of materials is possible, and recycling is facilitated. (Carter and Ellram 1998: 82)

Figure 19.7 puts these components together. It suggests that disposal is increasingly unacceptable and that companies should look to move up the pyramid, with resource reduction as the best option.

In a retail context it is relatively straightforward to think of elements that fit these definitions. Many retailers operate a recycling policy for consumers to use and for aspects of their stores' waste. In some countries there may be legal or fiscal encouragement, for example, no soft drink cans are allowed in Denmark and all glass bottles have deposits for return. Some recycling may be internalised in the company. Other material is sold on for external recycling purposes.

In the grocery industry the use of plastic trays and boxes to carry and distribute fresh product has become standard. Many DCs contain specialist centres for cleaning and reusing such equipment. This is an example of a reverse logistics system in that a channel has had to be created in order to move the containers back down the chain. In reality, the vehicles delivering to store often back-haul containers to distribution centres or to manufacturers.

One of the key drivers for change is government. In March 1997 the Packaging Waste regulations came into force. These are the requirements to meet the EU Directive on Packaging and Packaging Waste. The aim is to recover at least 50 per cent of the annual packaging waste created in the United Kingdom. All retailers with an annual turnover of £2 million or more are affected. A succinct guide to the Packaging Producer Responsibility Regulations can be found at *http://www.incpen.org/html/legislate.htm*. The main obligations on retailers are to do the following:

Figure 19.7 The reverse logistics hierarchy

Source: Carter and Ellram (1998)

- register with the authorities or join a registered collective scheme;
- provide data on packaging handled, recovered and recycled;
- recover and recycle certain percentages of packaging waste;
- provide a Certificate of Compliance.

The amount a business has to recover and recycle depends on its position in the channel, but retailers (selling to consumers or final users) have a current target of 48 per cent overall. Retailers can meet their obligations by either individually complying (primarily large companies) or by joining a collective scheme (14 approved compliance programmes are registered nationally). Members of a collective scheme do not have to meet individual obligations, as the scheme assumes this responsibility on behalf of its members. The cost of membership is set to reflect what your individual obligations would have been – in essence you buy a licence (a Packaging Recovery Note) not to recycle! Such regulations are not likely to disappear and are probably going to become more stringent in the future.

Self-assessment Question 3 *Waste – After your next shopping trip (preferably for food), when you have taken products home, sort out the packaging that you have 'purchased'. What type is it? What functions is it serving? Is it all needed? How much of it can you recycle? Do you recycle it or are you not bothered? What should be done to change behaviours (retailers', manufacturers' and consumers') and attitudes?*

Sustainable distribution: As a further plank in its policies, the government is committed to introducing legislation in the transport area. Following its transport White Paper, the government produced a consultation document that put forward a strategy for sustainable distribution. A full version of the strategy is available at http://www.detr.gov.uk/itwp/susdist/index.htm.

The aim of the strategy is to ensure that the future development of the distribution industry does not compromise the future needs of society, economy and environment. In short, pressure will be placed on business to become more efficient in its operations in terms of distribution (where efficiency is defined in terms of sustainability). Some of these pressures may be fiscal (that is, tax based) but others may well be more subtle. What is clear is that retail supply chains have an incentive to continue to improve performance in the environmental area and to avoid some of the worst excesses.

The model of logistics that has been illustrated in this chapter is not necessarily a sustainable one. Centralisation does have implications for transport and the environment, as well as for costs. Perhaps a resource reduction approach in this area would see a move back to more local sourcing, production and distribution systems – a response that is harder to manage but is perhaps more sustainable.

E-commerce

Numerous commentators have considered the future of Internet shopping and the predictions of its success have varied widely (see http://www.marketspace.org). Companies have come – and companies have gone. Yet all companies now are expected to have an Internet presence and to exploit the potential for consumer contact. But what will be the successful approaches?

When we think of Internet retailing (e-tailing) the name that often comes to mind is Amazon. In terms of brand recognition Amazon is an Internet colossus. The book market is a straightforward one in many ways. Amazon offers a web site that utilises some of the features of the Internet (online reviews, recommendations, order tracking, 1-click ordering) that make it different to the physical bookstore. The technology is used to provide a massive range of products, some of which are held by Amazon. Distribution is by third-party carrier to the home, whether it is by the Post Office or Federal Express. The Amazon model is essentially simple.

In non-food retailing of course, home shopping is nothing new and catalogues and specalogues have been around for centuries in various forms. Rapid delivery systems via specialist handlers ensure that the product reaches the customer in the shortest possible time. In this market the returns system has also had to be developed to take care of high levels of customer dissatisfaction with the purchases.

Box 19.3
Tesco.com: delivering home shopping

Tesco.com has become the world's largest Internet grocery system in a very short time. Unlike many of its competitors, it has opted for an in-store picking and home delivery operation, rather than starting with a dedicated distribution centre system. This choice came about for three reasons:

- Warehouse-based picking and delivery was not believed to be economic due to low penetration levels and drive times for vehicles being high.
- Customers confirmed that they did not want a reduced offer online as this destroyed the point of shopping at Tesco for them.
- Outside of London the possible penetration rates did not make a warehouse a valid option, even if other costs (such as picking were solved).

Since introduction there has been a very rapid rollout to effectively cover the United Kingdom through the network of stores. Each store involved has dedicated local delivery vehicles. There have been a few surprises:

- Fresh food has been a big seller online, whereas people had initially expected big, bulky replenishment items to be the most popular.
- People plan their online order better than their in-store trip (aided by the Clubcard and Internet item recall availability), so a higher proportion of spend is made with Tesco.
- The non-food item offer can be more extensive online than instore so sales in this area can be expanded.
- Knowledge is gained from the online shopping process of what items customers wanted to buy that were not in stock. This helps enhance the supply system.

Source: adapted from Jones (2001)

In the grocery market we can go from the product specialist site (for example Danish Kringle) to the full-blown standard food shop replacement. The mechanics of the latter are much more complex. Should delivery always be to the home? Does the recipient always have to be there? What is the replacement/out-of-stock policy? Will the picking be done at store or in a new centre? What is the service provision (human and otherwise)? Do we charge? Box 19.3 provides the example of Tesco.com, one of the most extensive home delivery Internet grocery systems. It illustrates how the company reached its decision to have store-based picking and delivery and what surprises it has found thus far.

In short, the Internet revolution at the consumer end of the market is exploding in experimentation. Some of this is profitable; most is not. Much of the effort is confusing. Some sites are portals to retailer operations so standard delivery solutions are used. Others are last-minute, time-dependent purchases so need expedited systems. Time-pressured fulfilment, for example at Christmas, has also proven to be problematic. Global purchasing by consumers may be taking place with all its attendant distribution (and regulatory) issues. The logistics choices are complex, though outsourcing to those with expertise is a popular solution at a cost (to the consumer?). Whatever the issues, the requirement for effective logistics exists in this market as in others (Foresight Retail Logistics Task Force 2000).

Summary

This chapter set out to introduce the subject of retail logistics and to demonstrate how retail logistics can support the retail offer. As retailing has been transformed in recent years, so too retail logistics has undergone a major transformation. Components of this include:

- enhanced retail control of the supply chain;
- introduction of management of the supply chain as an entity;
- vastly greater use of data and information technology;
- development of collaborative and partnership-based supply arrangements;
- the reconstruction and efficiency enhancement of the elements that make up the logistics mix.

This transformation has generated a renewed interest in the increasingly professional field of logistics. Many companies are looking for keen graduates to fill vacancies and the UK professional institute goes from strength to strength (http://www.iolt.org.uk). Without an effective and efficient supply chain retailers will be unable to compete in today's global marketplace.

Further reading

As an introduction to both logistics and retail logistics, the following would make a good starting point.

Christopher, M. (1998) *Logistics and Supply Chain Management*, London: FT/Prentice Hall.

Fernie, L. and **Sparks, L.** (eds) (1998) *Logistics and Retail Management*, London: Kogan Page.

Lowson, B., King, R. and **Hunter, A.** (1999) *Quick Response: Managing the supply chain to meet consumer demand*, Chichester: Wiley.

In addition, there are a number of journals in the area:

- *ECR Journal;*
- *International Journal of Logistics Management;*
- *International Journal of Physical Distribution and Logistics Management;*
- *International Journal of Retail and Distribution Management;*
- *International Review of Retail, Distribution and Consumer Research;*
- *Journal of Business Logistics;*
- *Logistics and Transport Focus;*
- *Logistics Information Management;*
- *Supply Chain Management: An International Journal.*

University logistics web sites

A number of universities have specialisms in logistics and supply chain management and have developed their web sites for the benefit of students. Examples include (correct at November 2002):

University	Web address
Cardiff	http://www.cf.ac.uk/carbs/lom/lerc/index.html
Cranfield	http://www.som.cranfield.ac.uk/som/cclt/
Heriot-Watt	http://www.sml.hw.ac.uk/logistics/
Huddersfield	http://www.hud.ac.uk/sas/trans/
Westminster	http://www.wmin.ac.uk/transport/

CHAPTER 20

Online shopping: The logistics issues

John Fernie and Alan McKinnon

Introduction

Much has happened since Amazon.com launched its book proposition on the market in July 1995. Consumers can now browse through millions of book titles, receive reviews of likely purchases and interact online with the retailer. As Internet access mushroomed globally, predictions of an exciting e-commerce age were promulgated by consultancies in the United States and Europe. The 'hype' exceeded reality and after a dotcom boom in the late 1990s stocks of pure players collapsed in 2000 with a wave of liquidations occurring. This chapter will focus on the role of logistics in e-tailing with particular reference to the grocery sector. E-fulfilment, especially the 'last mile' problem of delivering goods to the final customer, is often seen as the key to success in e-tailing. Before discussing these issues in detail it is important to review the nature and growth of online shopping and assess its future prospects.

The market

Non-store shopping is not new. Traditional mail order and its more up market 'specialogues' have accounted for around 4–5 per cent of retail sales in the United States and United Kingdom for many years (Morganosky and Fernie 1999). There is also a sense of déjà vu about the prospects of electronic commerce. In the late 1980s teleshopping was forecast to make major inroads into the retail market. It did not. The difference with the advent of the Internet by the mid to late 1990s was that the technology was more sophisticated and reliable and the growth of PC usage exponential. In the United States, 50 million people went onto the Net within five years (Freedman 2001). The trouble with this uptake of Internet technology was that forecasts of online retail sales were strongly *technological* rather than behavioural based. A report by the *Financial Times* in 1995 produced a conservative estimate that by 2000 in Europe, 10 to 15 per cent of food sales and 20 to 25 per cent of non-food sales would be made by home shopping (Mandeville 1995). In reality, online grocery sales throughout Europe were around 0.24 per cent in 2000 with non-food sales only making an impact in computer software, CDs, books and videos.

The position is much the same in the United States. Online retail sales accounted for around 1 per cent of all retail sales in 2000 and 2001 (Reynolds 2001). Perhaps the clue to this slow uptake of the new technology is that consumers are using e-commerce for purchasing other services. For example, Forrester Research shows that of the $20–$30 billion online consumer market in the United States in 1999 only 60 per cent accounted for the physical distribution of goods (Laseter *et al.* 2000). The other 40 per cent accounted for digitally delivered goods such as airline and event tickets, banking services, auctions and automobiles, which have a separate delivery network.

Research carried out in the late 1990s on retailers' Internet offerings would suggest that both US and UK 'bricks and mortar' retailers played a fairly passive role in adopting the technology (Morganosky 1997; Doherty *et al.* 1999). Their web sites were more informational than transactional and it was only the direct threat of pure players in the late 1990s that moved them to a more proactive approach to e-commerce. However, the pure e-tailers lacked the brand awareness of their traditional counterparts and needed capital to promote their brand image in addition to building an infrastructure to serve the online customer. Even Amazon.com with its recognisable brand could not record a profit until the last quarter of 2001, and so it was no surprise to witness the demise of pure players in 2000 and 2001. The shake-out of the sector has led to alliances (Amazon.com/Borders/Toys 'Я' Us; Safeway in the United States/Tesco) and takeover of financially weak pure players (Ahold/Peapod, Safeway/groceryworks.com). The name of the game in the decade 2000–10 is 'clicks and bricks'.

Although the rise and fall of Internet retailers has brought a touch of realism to the evolving market for online shopping, forecasts are still being made of it capturing up to 12.5 per cent of retail sales in both the United States and United Kingdom by 2005. This seems unduly optimistic in view of fulfilment and other problems, which still have to be overcome and will be discussed later in the chapter. Table 20.1 provides a forecast by Verdict Research of UK online sales by category in 2004/5. This confirms that sectors such as computer software, music and videos and books will continue to increase their penetration of these retail markets. In these product categories many consumers know what they want and online retailers are more competitive than their high street counterparts. It is interesting to note that Internet sales of electrical goods are forecast to rise from £18 million to £993 million between 1999 and 2005. Price is a key store choice variable in this sector and shopping online can yield significant savings to consumers.

The grocery sector

Despite the fact that online grocery sales account for less than 1 per cent of retail sales in most national markets this sector has attracted most attention from researchers and government bodies. Grocery shopping impacts upon all consumers – we all have to eat! However, our populations are getting older so shopping is more of a chore. Many younger, time-poor, affluent consumers also may hate to waste time buying groceries. Home delivery of groceries is reinventing

Table 20.1 Online shopping forecasts by product category 1999–2005

	1999		2004		2005	
	Online shopping £ (m)	Online as % of all retail sales	Online shopping £ (m)	Online as % of all retail sales	Online shopping £ (m)	Online as % of all retail sales
Grocery	165	0.20	3,665	3.7	4,960	4.9
Clothing & footwear	5	0.01	1,210	2.7	1,843	4.0
Computer software	122	9.97	934	35.6	1,502	51.9
Electricals	18	0.17	668	5.3	993	7.6
Music & video	85	2.87	592	16.0	782	20.4
Books	106	5.15	430	17.2	473	18.3
Health & beauty	1	0.01	213	1.6	355	2.5
Other	79	0.17	1,125	1.8	1,625	2.4
Total	**581**	**0.29**	**8,837**	**3.6**	**12,533**	**5.0**

Source: Verdict (2000: 126)

the wheel. One of the authors of this chapter was a message boy for Wm Low (now Tesco). In the 1960s and 1970s home delivery was a service to the customer from the store. In the early 1980s the UK government tried to encourage non-car-owning customers to shop via their local library to gain the benefits of cheaper prices from superstores. Tesco, at Gateshead and other trials in the Midlands experimented with this form of home delivery but pulled out when government subsidies were withdrawn. Ironically, the global market leader today is Tesco, which began experimenting with Internet-based shopping in 1996.

Because of the relatively recent nature of online grocery shopping, empirical evidence of the behaviour of online shoppers is limited. Morganosky and Cude (2000) were fortunate to receive permission from Schnucks Markets of St. Louis to survey their online shoppers. The results show that customers were generally positive about the experience. The majority of respondents (70 per cent) cited convenience and saving time as key factors for shopping online. Specific groups of online shoppers emerged, for example, mothers with young children and people with disabilities, including minor temporary disabilities that inhibited their access to a store. The two main e-grocers in the United Kingdom, Tesco and Sainsbury, claim that their online customers spend more than their conventional customers. Tesco also explodes the myth that online customers would not buy fresh products because of the so-called 'touch and feel' factor. Indeed the opposite is true – of the top 10 selling lines, 7 are fresh, with skinless chicken breasts at number one (Jones 2001).

Tesco, however, is one of the few success stories in e-grocery. In Europe, grocery retailers are powerful 'bricks and mortar' companies and the approach to Internet retailing has been reactive rather than proactive. Most Internet operations have been small and few pure players have entered the market to challenge the conventional supermarket chains.

The situation is different in the United States where a more fragmented, regionally oriented grocery retail structure has encouraged new entrants into the market. In the late 1980s this came in the form of Warehouse Clubs and Wal-Mart Supercenters; by the 1990s dotcom players began to challenge the traditional supermarket operators (Table 20.2 identifies the key players, with Tesco for comparison). Unfortunately these pure players have either gone into liquidation, scaled down their operations or been taken over by conventional grocery businesses.

Why have pure players failed? Laseter *et al.* (2000) identify four key challenges:

● limited online potential;
● high cost of delivery;
● selection–variety trade-offs;
● existing entrenched competition.

Ring and Tigert (2001) came to similar conclusions when comparing the Internet offering with the conventional 'bricks and mortar' experience. They looked at what consumers would lose out on in terms of the place, product, service and value for money by shopping online compared with store-based shopping. They also detailed the 'killer costs' of the pure play Internet grocers, notably the picking and delivery costs.

Table 20.2 The major existing and former e-grocers

	Tesco UK	Webvan USA	Streamline USA	Peapod USA
Background	The biggest supermarket chain in the UK	Started as a pure e-grocer in 1999	Started as a pure e-grocer in 1992	Started home delivery service before the Internet in 1989
Investments in e-grocer development	US$ 58 million	Approx. US$ 1,200 million	Approx. US$ 80 million	Approx. US$ 150 million
Main operational mode	Industrialised picking from the supermarket	Highly automated picking in distribution centre (DC)	Picking from the DC, reception boxes, value-adding services	Picking from both DC and from stores
Current status	The biggest e-grocer in the world. Expanding its operations outside the UK. Partnering with Safeway and Groceryworks	Operations ceased July 2001	Part of operations were sold to Peapod in September 2000. Remaining operations ceased in November 2000	Bought by global grocery retailer Royal Ahold. Second biggest e-grocer in the world

Source: Yrjola *et al.* (2002)

The gist of the argument presented by these critics is that the basic Internet model is flawed. Laseter *et al.* (2000) suggest that the Forrester Research forecast for 2004 is highly optimistic. Nevertheless, the researchers took Forrester's sales forecasts, assessed Internet penetration in the key US cities identified by pure players for their expansion plans, and built a forecast model on the drivers of local delivery economics – sales concentration and population density. They conclude that only New York City offers an attractive market in terms of online sales potential.

Even if the potential is there, the consumer has to be lured away from existing commitment to conventional retailing. Convenience is invariably ranked as the key choice variable in both store patronage and Internet usage surveys. For store shoppers convenience is about location, interaction with staff and the retail experience. Internet users tend to be more interested in the time saved by not having to visit shops. However, as Wilson-Jeanselme (2001) has shown, the 58 per cent net gain in convenience benefit is often eroded away by 'leakages' in the process of ordering to ultimate delivery. Furthermore, the next two key store choice variables in the United States tend to be price and assortment. With the exception of Webvan, pure players offered a limited number of stock keeping units compared with conventional supermarkets.

Price may have been competitive with stores but delivery charges pushed up the final price to the customer. In the highly competitive US grocery market customers will switch stores for only a 3–4 per cent differential in prices across leading competitors. Ring and Tigert (2001: 270) therefore pose the question: 'What percentage of households will pay substantially more for an inferior assortment (and perhaps quality) of groceries just for the convenience of having them delivered to their home?'

Yrjola *et al.* (2002) argue that e-grocery companies failed because an electronic copy of a supermarket does not work. They claim that e-grocery should be a complementary channel rather than a substitute and that companies should be investing in service innovations to give value to the customer. Building upon their research in Finland, Yrjola *et al.* (2002) maintain that the 'clicks and bricks' model will lead to success for e-grocery. Most of the difficulties for pure players relate to building a business and creating an order fulfilment system. Conventional retailers have established trust with their suppliers and customers. The customer needs a credible alternative to self-service and the Finnish researchers suggest that this has to be achieved at a local level where routine purchases can be shifted effectively to e-grocery.

To facilitate product selection web-based information technology can tailor the retail offer to the customer's needs. The virtual store can be more creative than the restrictions placed on the physical stocking of goods on shelves. However, manufacturers will need to provide 'pre-packaged' electronic product information for ordering on the Web.

E-fulfilment in the grocery sector

Regardless of the nature of the 'accepted' e-grocery model of the future, the 'last mile' problem continues to pose difficulties for e-grocers. In designing a home delivery system they must make two critical choices, between: (a) supplying customers from existing shops or dedicated fulfilment (or 'pick') centres and (b) providing attended or unattended delivery. These choices have a major impact on fulfilment costs, the standard of customer service, capital investment requirements and the rate of market penetration (Punakivi and Saranen 2001).

Shops versus fulfilment centres

Companies entering the e-grocery market have adopted markedly different fulfilment strategies (Figure 20.1). Webvan raised $360 million of share capital in October 1999 mainly to fund the construction of 26 dedicated fulfilment centres, each with over 300,000 square feet of floorspace. It remained committed to the fulfilment centre option until its bankruptcy in mid-2001. Tesco, on the other hand, has built the world's largest online grocery business in the United Kingdom entirely on shop-based fulfilment and appears to have no plans to develop pick-centres. By early 2002 it could supply 95 per cent of the UK population from 273 stores and was attracting 80,000 orders a week. Other companies have experimented with both strategies. The US company Peapod, for example, initially supplied orders from the shops of partner retailers. It then invested in dedicated fulfilment centres, but since its acquisition by Ahold in 2000 has increased its dependence on store-based picking. Sainsbury, in contrast, was originally wedded to the fulfilment centre concept but, as its online business has expanded, the proportion of orders delivered from shops has steadily increased. Asda, whose initial strategy was very similar, has closed its pick-centres and moved entirely to a shop-based model. Evidence has, therefore, been accumulating to suggest that it is more cost effective and competitive to serve home-based shoppers from existing retail outlets.

The use of existing shops offers a number of advantages. It minimises the amount of new investment required and increases the utilisation of retail assets. It also permits the pooling of retail inventory between conventional and online markets, improving the ratio of inventory to sales. This also gives online shoppers access to the full range of products available in the supermarket to which most of them will be accustomed. One of the main benefits of shop-based fulfilment is

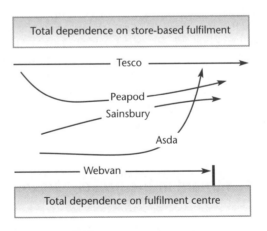

Figure 20.1 Evolution of e-grocery fulfilment strategies

that it enables the retailer to 'roll out' the service rapidly across a wide geographical market.

By fulfilling orders from existing shops retailers can achieve a fast rate of market penetration, but doubts have been expressed about the long-term sustainability of this strategy. Tulip (2002: 30) argues that:

> If Internet grocery shopping really took off it is hard to see how the in-store picking model could be sustained – aisles clogged with personal shoppers and car parks monopolised by delivery vehicles are unlikely to enhance the retail experience for traditional shoppers visiting the retail outlet.

Combining conventional and online retailing operations in existing shops can also adversely affect customer service in other ways. As the online shopper does not have access to a dedicated inventory it is not possible at the time of ordering to guarantee the availability of particular products. There may be sufficient product on the shelf when the order is placed, but by the time the picking operation gets under way, conventional shoppers may have purchased all the available stock. Where these in-store shoppers encounter a 'stock-out' they can decide themselves what alternative products to buy, if any. Most online shoppers must rely on the retailer to make suitable 'substitutions'. It is estimated that in the United Kingdom substitution rates of between 5 and 15 per cent are typical in online grocery operations. Often these substitutions are a poor second best, and impair the overall quality of customer service.

Conflicts between conventional and online retailing are likely to intensify at the back of the store as well as at the 'front end'. Back store-room areas, where much of the assembly and packing of home orders is undertaken, will become increasingly congested. Over the past 20 years the trend has been for retailers to reduce the amount of back storage space in shops as in-store inventory levels have dropped and quick-response replenishment become the norm. This now limits the capacity of these retail outlets to assume the additional role of online fulfilment centre. Where sufficient land is available shops can be enlarged to accommodate a higher volume of home shopping business. New shops can also be purpose built to integrate conventional retailing and online fulfilment. The Dutch retailer Ahold has coined the term 'wareroom' to describe a dedicated pick facility co-located with a conventional supermarket (Mees 2000).

Most of the purpose-built fulfilment centres so far constructed are on separate sites and overcome most of the problems of fulfilling orders from existing shops. They can be designed specifically for the multiple picking of online orders, incorporate mechanised picking systems and provide much more efficient reception facilities for inbound and outbound vehicles. As their inventory is assigned solely to the online market, home shoppers can have greater confidence in the availability of products at the time of ordering. All of this comes at a high price however, both in terms of capital investment and operating costs. It is estimated, for instance, that Webvan's fulfilment centres cost an average of $36 million. Dedicated pick-centres must generate a high throughput to earn the e-tailers an adequate rate of return. They also require a high throughput to support a diverse product range. It is very costly to offer a broad range in the early stages of an e-tailing operation when sales volumes are low. Offering a limited range, however, can significantly reduce the appeal of online shopping and retard market growth. The collapse of Webvan, which tried, from an early stage, to offer a range of 55,000 items through purpose-built centres provides a salutary warning to other new entrants to the e-grocery market.

Another inventory-related problem that retailers using pick-centres have encountered is the difficulty of disposing of excess stocks of short-shelf-life product. E-tailing operations are just as susceptible to forecasting errors as conventional retailing. Where overstocking occurs in a shop, however, it is much easier and quicker to sell off the excess stock using price reductions or in-store merchandising techniques.

In summary, the shop-based fulfilment model has low start-up cost but is likely to prove more expensive in the longer term as retail outlets become more congested and service quality for both conventional and online shoppers deteriorates. The fulfilment centre model, on the other hand, has high initial capital and operating costs, but is likely to prove more cost effective in the longer term. In theory, therefore, one should be able to conduct a break-even analysis to determine at what level of online grocery sales it would become more efficient to supply homes from pick-centres rather than shops (Figure 20.2).

In reality, the cost functions are much more complex than suggested by the graph and are influenced by a range of factors specific to individual retailers, including the size and layout of shops, the nature of the upstream distribution system, the product range and the customer base. The configuration of the store-based fulfilment curve will also be highly sensitive to the allocation of retail overheads between the conventional and online shopping operations. 'Brick and click' retailers can make their e-grocery businesses appear more efficient, and even profitable, by loading a disproportionately high share of these overheads on to the conventional operation.

The relative efficiency of the two fulfilment models is likely to vary geographically. Companies might find it more cost effective to serve home shoppers in some

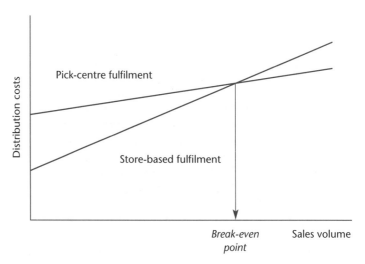

Figure 20.2   Break-even analysis of e-fulfilment systems

areas from shops and in other areas from pick-centres, depending on sales' densities and local competition.

Other complicating factors are the size and service area of the fulfilment centre. There has been much debate about the optimum size of pick-centres and, by implication, the number of centres required to serve the national market. One large UK supermarket estimated that it would require 18 such centres to provide national coverage, whilst another e-grocery business has indicated that 5–6 strategically located centres might suffice. Similar principles of warehousing planning apply to pick-centres as to distribution centres at a higher level in the supply chain. The more centralised the system the lower will be the capital investment and inventory levels. Fewer pick-centres, however, means longer average distances to customers' homes and higher delivery costs. The cost of transporting orders over longer distances can be reduced by inserting an extra tier of satellite depots between the pick-centre and the home (Figure 20.3). Orders bound for the same district can be trunked in a consolidated load to a local 'satellite' depot (or 'van centre') where they are broken down for onward delivery in small vans (Foresight Retail Logistics Task Force 2001). Webvan operated a hub–satellite system of this type, with each pick-centre supplying orders through a network of 10–12 satellites.

Solutions to the last mile problem

The US critics mentioned earlier in the chapter claimed that it was the order fulfilment and delivery costs which were the 'killer costs' undermining e-grocery

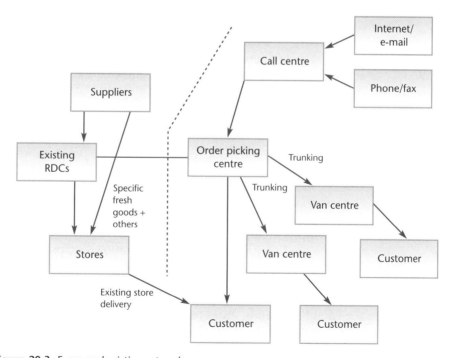

Figure 20.3 E-grocer logistics network
Source: Foresight Retail Logistics Task Force 2000

businesses. In the United Kingdom, it has been estimated that the average cost of order processing, picking and delivery for groceries is around £13 per order. As the charge to the customer is normally £5 per order it is clear that unless the order value is high, retailers will make a loss on every delivery.

The cost of the delivery operation is strongly influenced by time constraints, in particular the width of the 'time windows' within which orders are dropped at customers' homes. In deciding how wide a time window to offer online shoppers e-tailers must strike a competitive balance between customer convenience and delivery efficiency. From the customer's standpoint the ideal would be a guaranteed delivery within a very narrow time interval, minimising the encroachment on their lifestyle. It is very costly, however, to provide such 'time-definite' deliveries. Nockold (2001) modelled the effect of varying the width of time windows on home delivery costs in the London area. The window was initially set at three hours. He then reduced it by 25 per cent, then 50 per cent, and finally eliminated this time constraint. These options had the effect of cutting transport costs by, respectively, 6–12 per cent, 17–24 per cent and 27–37 per cent. His conclusion was that by having completely open delivery times, cost savings of up to a third were attainable.

Normally to achieve this degree of flexibility it must be possible to deliver orders when no one is at home to receive them. Unattended delivery can take various forms. According to market research the preferred option for around two-thirds of British households is to leave the goods with a neighbour (Verdict 2000). This applies mainly to non-food items, however. Because of their bulk and the need for refrigeration, few online grocery orders are left with neighbours. Instead home-based reception (or 'drop') boxes are being promoted as a technical solution to the problem of unattended delivery. These boxes can be divided into three broad categories:

- *integral boxes*: generally built into the home at the time of construction;
- *external fixed boxes*: attached to an outside wall;
- *external mobile (or 'delivery') boxes*: moved to and from the home and secured there temporarily by, for example, a steel cable linked to an electronic terminal.

These boxes come in various sizes and offer different types of electronic access. Most are well-enough insulated to maintain the temperature of frozen and chilled produce for 6–12 hours. In a comparison of fixed and mobile boxes, Punakivi *et al.* (2001) conclude that their operating costs are similar, assuming that the latter are only collected at the time of the next delivery. Mobile boxes, however, have a capital cost advantage because they are shared between many customers and can achieve much higher utilisation rates.

In the United States, unattended reception was pioneered, unsuccessfully, by Streamline. Its Stream Boxes were generally located in customers' garages that were equipped with keypad entry systems. Home access systems do not require the use of a reception box. One system, which is currently being trialled in 50 homes in the English Midlands, uses a telephone-linked electronic key pad to provide delivery staff with controlled access to garages and out-buildings (Rowlands, 2001). The key pads communicate with a central server allowing the 'home access' agency to alter the pin codes after each delivery. It is claimed that this system cuts average drop times from 10 minutes to 4 minutes and, if coupled with a 5-hour time window, would improve delivery productivity (measured in drops per vehicle per week) by 84 per cent. Home access systems offer greater flexibility than drop boxes and are much cheaper to install than an integral reception unit. Their main disadvantage is that they pose a significant security risk both to the goods being delivered and the home itself (McKinnon and Tallam, 2002).

A more radical means of cutting transport costs is by delivering to local collection points rather than to the home. These collection points can be existing outlets, such as corner shops, post offices or petrol stations, purpose-built centres or communal reception boxes. Few existing outlets have the capacity or refrigeration facilities to accommodate online grocery orders. This has led one property developer to propose the development of a network of specially designed collection centres (or 'e-stops') to handle a range of both food and non-food products. A much cheaper option is to install banks of reception boxes at central locations within neighbourhoods where orders can be deposited for collection. One company has adapted left luggage lockers into pick-up points for home-ordered products, but their size, shape and lack of refrigeration limits their suitability for the collection of online grocery orders. As e-grocery sales expand, however, there will be an increasing demand for communal reception facilities at apartment blocks.

The use of collection points economises on transport by sharply reducing the number of delivery locations and increasing the degree of load consolidation. It achieves this, however, at the expense of customer convenience, by requiring the online shopper to travel to the collection point to pick up the order. If the collection can be made in the course of an existing trip, say from work or to a petrol station, the loss of convenience may be acceptable. For most online grocery shoppers, however, this is unlikely to prove an attractive option.

Punakivi and Tanskanen (2002) have made a comparative study of the delivery costs for several 'last mile' options, using point of sales (POS) data from one of the largest supermarket chains in Finland. The dataset contained 1,639 shopping baskets of 1,450 anonymous household customers. In their analysis, five home delivery concepts were modelled (see Table 20.3). These ranged from the standard Tesco model of attended reception within two-hour delivery slots to unattended delivery to shared reception boxes in 'central locations'. Not surprisingly, the more the customer controlled the delivery time windows the higher were the delivery costs. The results of the modelling exercise show that transport costs for unattended delivery to shared reception boxes were 55–66 per cent lower than attended delivery within two-hour windows.

Outsourcing of home delivery operations

Most deliveries of online grocery orders are currently made on a dedicated basis either by the e-tailers themselves or third-party distributors working on their behalf. Most of the larger e-grocers have been keen to retain direct control of the 'last mile' to ensure a high level of service and maintain customer contact. This carries a transport cost penalty, however. By outsourcing home deliveries on a shared-user basis e-grocers could collectively reduce their transport costs by increasing drop densities and consolidating loads. A 'common distribution system'

Table 20.3 Comparison of home delivery concepts

Case	Home delivery concept and description	Example
1	Attended reception with two-hour delivery time windows Delivery hours 08:00–22:00 Customer locations based on POS data Number of orders per day varies from 20 to 720	Peapod.com, USA Tesco. com, UK
2	Home-based reception box concept Delivery time window 08:00–16:00 Customer locations based on POS data Number of orders per day varies from 20 to 720	SOK, Finland Streamline, USA
3A	Delivery box concept, with pick up of the box on the next delivery Delivery time window 08:00–16:00, pick up on next delivery Customer locations based on POS data Number of orders per day varies from 20 to 720	Homeport, UK
3B	Delivery box concept with pick up of the box on next day Delivery time window 08:00–16:00, pick up next day Customer locations based on POS data Number of orders per day varies from 20 to 720	Homeport, UK Sainsbury, UK Food Ferry, UK
4	Shared reception box concept Time window 08:00–16.00, 'by end of working hours' 5, 10, 20, 30 selected central locations of the shared reception box units Capacity of the shared reception box units varies: 8, 16, 24 and 32 customer-specific lockers per unit Utilisation rate of shared reception box units in the analysis: 50% and 75% Number of orders (20–720) per day varies according to the combination of the above elements	Hollming, Finland Boxcar Systems, USA ByBox holdings, UK

Source: Punakivi and Tanskanen (2002)

for grocery home deliveries would have to interface with different company IT systems and would probably require the insertion of an additional consolidation point in the home delivery channel (Foresight Retail Logistics Task Force 2001). Adding another node and link would offset some of the consolidation benefits. It is worth noting, though, that the Swiss online grocer LeShop manages to provide a low cost, next-day delivery across Switzerland by channelling home orders through the national postal service (Taylor 2002).

Summary

This chapter has identified a growing potential market for grocery online shopping. However, the main success stories to date tend to be in the traditional sectors of books, CDs, videos and computers. The grocery sector has attracted much attention, mainly because of the innovations of pure players in the United States. Unfortunately many of these companies have either gone into liquidation or have been taken over by powerful traditional grocery retailers.

Critics of the e-grocery models claim that profitability is an unattainable goal because of the 'killer costs' of order fulfilment and delivery. This is too negative a view. As the online grocery market expands the unit costs of these operations are likely to decline. In the medium to long term this may entail a transfer of order picking from existing retail outlets to purpose-built fulfilment centres. The development of these centres appears to have been premature. Once a mass market for online grocery shopping has been created and their early teething problems rectified, dedicated fulfilment centres are likely to become major hubs in the e-grocery logistics networks. The growth in volumes will improve the economics of last mile delivery operations by raising drop densities and vehicle load factors. This trend will be greatly reinforced if online shoppers can be persuaded to switch from attended delivery within narrow time windows to various forms of unattended delivery that have emerged over the past few years. The theoretical modelling work discussed in this chapter shows that the costs of e-fulfilment can be substantially reduced by the relaxation of time constraints and the use of reception boxes. Online retailers may have to incentivise consumers to invest in new home reception facilities by passing on some of the transport cost savings in lower delivery charges. Some may also have to consider joining shared-user delivery networks to ensure the longer-term viability of their home delivery operation. This would also reduce the amount of van traffic in residential areas, yielding environmental as well as economic benefits.

Discussion questions

1. Outline the reasons behind the growth of e-tailing and discuss why over-optimistic forecasts were not realised.

2. Review the advantages and disadvantages of the two main fulfilment models for grocery e-commerce.

3. Evaluate the proposed solution to overcoming the 'last mile' problem.

4. Discuss the likely nature of e-tailing in 2010 and the logistical infrastructure to support developments in the market.

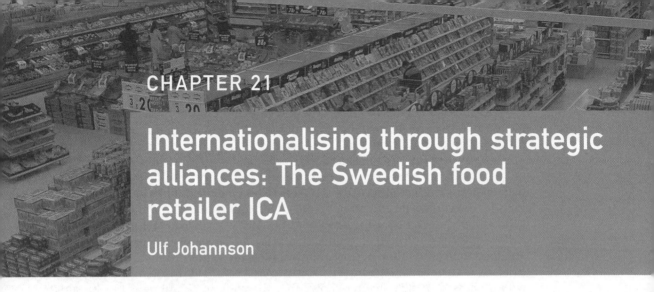

CHAPTER 21

Internationalising through strategic alliances: The Swedish food retailer ICA

Ulf Johannson

Introduction

One of the recurring themes in this book is that successful retailing is dependent on satisfying customer needs. Chapter 10 discussed the value cycle and the need to satisfy customer demand as a way of achieving business objectives. Similarly, Chapter 19 identified the role that logistics plays in ensuring product availability and customer satisfaction. This case focuses upon a further (related) method of delivering value to the customer. It considers how competitive advantage can be achieved through cooperation between supply channel members (vertical co-operation) and also between retailers (horizontal cooperation).

Background

For most companies the trading environment in which they operate is becoming increasingly borderless – markets are no longer confined to national boundaries and global competition has become a feature of the retail sector. From a Swedish perspective the European Union is a good illustration of this. It is no longer poss-ible to build 'fences' or barriers around particular parts of the Swedish market to protect them from what is happening in other (European) countries. As companies expand internationally the market continues to be reconfigured. The greatest threat may not come from a national or even a European-based retailer but may emerge from the other side of the world.

Some Swedish companies such as Electrolux, Volvo, SKF, IKEA and Ericsson are already global players and the notion of a borderless world is not a new phenom-enon. In other cases, for example the food sector, the Swedish entry into the European Union in 1995 meant companies have had to operate under a dramati-cally different set of trading conditions. Barriers that used to protect Swedish companies have disappeared or been significantly lowered. As Sweden was an important market for these indigenous retail companies this distinct new envi-ronment has provided them with a number of important challenges.

In order to develop a competitive edge in this liberalised market a number of retailers looked to build strategic alliances with both non-competitive retailers and to cooperate more fully with supply chain partners. The rationale for this was straightforward: if a network could be developed through intensified relationship building it would be one way of developing and growing in this new environment. However, such relationships do not just happen. In order to make them work, significant time and energy needs to be invested by all parties. A series of commitments may have to be made, and it may be necessary to have an explicit strategy that defines the company's approach to alliances. It therefore remains important for all involved to understand the expectations and demands that will occur through any form of cooperation.

The Swedish food industry

At the beginning of the 1990s a number of significant changes occurred within the Swedish food sector. The background was one of growing consumer discontent as the sector had been protected for many years by a wide number of rules and regulations. With fresh goods, for example, there existed a price guarantee (provided by the government) and also a guaranteed market. During the 1970s and 1980s the consumption of food decreased and for the government the cost of supporting the system increased significantly. In 1990 the Swedish parliament decided to change these conditions, meaning (amongst other things), that a gradual deregulation should take place. The goal was to transform a highly regulated sector into one that was market based. In other words the production of Swedish farmers should be limited such that supply equalled demand (at a reasonable price). This meant that the same economic conditions which applied to other businesses in Sweden would now apply to Swedish farmers. The rules and regulations that supported the export and storage of over-capacity was removed. Such action meant that the regulation of prices on imported food products (through the price and market guarantees) also disappeared. (Customs and tariffs provided protection at the borders for a limited period.)

The regulations described above – and the consequent deregulation – had an impact on the entire supply chain. For example, Swedish food retailers were dependent on Swedish food manufacturers (few retailers had non-domestic alternatives). The deregulation of the Swedish food sector therefore brought about a radical reconfiguration of relationships for all parties within the supply chain.

Swedish law through the so-called PBL (Planning and Building Law) had also, indirectly, protected the food retail sector in Sweden. This law gave the local authorities the right to decide who could open food stores in a particular region. This led to three established companies – ICA, KF and Dagab – developing a large portfolio of stores and having outlets in most of the regions in Sweden. Whilst the structure and operation of these organisations are beyond the scope of this case study it is necessary to note that they were insulated from competitive forces through a variety of different means. For example, an ICA outlet was 91 per cent independently owned, with the remaining 9 per cent being owned by a federation that supplied the store. Should an independent operator no longer wish to continue trading, the store had to be offered to the federation which, in turn, could offer the site to another independent operator. Stores were therefore not placed on the 'open market' unless the federation decided to dispose of them.

The Swedish competition authorities had long complained to the Swedish government that these arrangements and the PBL meant that competition was lower than would otherwise have been the case. Other investigations found that local authorities favoured the established firms when a new store was to be opened and new companies were consequently discriminated against.

Finally, in 1992 a paragraph to the PBL was added stating that increasing competition should also be a factor when deciding who could develop food stores. This made it easier for other retailers to establish food outlets in the Swedish market. The local authorities were no longer allowed to treat food stores in a special way and limit the establishment of new stores, instead they were supposed to pave the way for increased competition by allowing new retailers to enter the market.

Removing protectionism

The protection afforded to the Swedish food sector was not unique, indeed it was mirrored in many other European countries. The issues that the European food sector faced were highlighted in the so-called Ceccini Report (1988). In addition to concluding that the food sector (when compared to all industry sectors) made the greatest contribution in terms of jobs and added value, it also concluded that the market was fragmented and hampered by a number of obstacles to free trade.

The report noted that Swedish food companies selling products classified as farming products (such as meat and dairy goods) were protected from international competition. Also, the export opportunities for these companies were non-existent as other European countries operated protective systems similar to that in operation in Sweden. The costs of these restrictions were estimated at between 500 and 1,000 billion ECU per year and big efficiency gains could be expected if these obstacles were removed. The Ceccini Report (1988) also concluded that this situation had made European food companies nationally rather than internationally focused. Given the increasingly global nature of the retail marketplace and the growth of global competition, Europe risked being left behind.

In 1993 the Swedish parliament decided to align the Swedish farming and food industry to the conditions in the European Union (although some limited support for export activities was extended until 1 January 1995). As Sweden entered the European Union the manufacturing sector got access to an international market (which in turn got access to the Swedish market). As a result Swedish exports increased dramatically between 1994–1997, with the subsequent increase in imports being more modest. However imports from other EU countries have continued to increase since 1995 and now make up 65 per cent of the total imports into Sweden (the largest food exporters to Sweden are Denmark, Holland, Norway and Germany).

The structural developments that have taken place in Sweden's food sector are the same as in many other European countries. The process of consolidation is very much in evidence, with fewer and larger companies. With food manufacturing, the 1990s meant a number of mergers and acquisitions, involving companies in most product sectors of the industry. Some of these deals were pan-Nordic, for instance in 1995 the Norwegian conglomerate Orkla acquired Procordia Foods (formerly a part of the Volvo group) and the Dutch company CSM acquired the Swedish confectionery producer Malaco. More recently (during 2000), Sweden's biggest dairy company Arla merged with one of Europe's largest dairies, MD Food, to create the largest dairy company in Europe. Whilst farmer-owned cooperatives (through the farmer's federation LRF) still dominate Swedish food manufacturing, the market share of foreign-owned companies increased from 12 per cent in 1985 to 35 per cent in 1995 (and has continued to grow).

Reflecting another global trend, the number of retail food stores in Sweden has also decreased. For example, in 1991 there were 8,100 outlets; by 1996 this had fallen to 7,000 and by 2000 there were 6,400 food stores trading. At the same time the size of the average food store is becoming larger. Today approximately 55 per cent of all grocery sales in Sweden are derived from 10 per cent of stores. Unlike in the United Kingdom, food retailing in Sweden has traditionally been dominated (and still is) by two different types of federative organisations.

The first is where the store is owned and managed by an entrepreneur but is also attached to a central group. Typically a store is financed by the central office of the retail federation but the entrepreneur is allowed to gradually buy shares in the store – until he or she owns the whole store (the central office however retains the right to purchase the store if the owner wants to sell). This also means that (at least in theory) the owner/manager of the store decides how it is merchandised, managed, etc. Companies such as ICA and Dagab are examples of how this type of organisation has grown and prospered over the years. In 1996/7 they had around 45 per cent and 22 per cent of the Swedish food market respectively.

The second federation is consumer based. In many ways Swedish federations parallel UK cooperatives. Individual consumers can choose to join a federation on payment of a fee. This provides them with the right to become involved in influencing the policies and direction of the federation. Currently consumer federations have around 25 per cent of the Swedish food market. Whilst a process of consolidation has occurred a number of separate federations continue to exist. This means that consumer federations do not act as one body (for example towards suppliers) but more as a set of separate entities.

Building relationships in the new environment

The internationalisation of the food sector in Europe at the beginning of 1990s was limited. Few food products seemed to travel across borders and consumers were inclined to have a preference for their own country's retail offer. This made it difficult to pursue a standardised and non-differentiated retail strategy in relation to store concepts, suppliers and product assortment at the European level. This difficulty was compounded by the fact that markets in western Europe (and the United States) are mature and are characterised by intense competition involving established retailers. Entry would therefore require major investment to have any chance of being successful. Moreover market entry cannot be undertaken in a gradual, piecemeal fashion, as stores, distribution and the basic retail infrastructure has to be there from the outset.

Given that many retailers were confined to their own national boundaries, the 1980s saw the development of international alliances. The objective of these alliances was to cooperate on issues such as purchasing and product development. By 1992 there were eight alliances of significant scale involving major food retailers. Together the companies involved accounted for around 60 per cent of the total sales of grocery products in Europe. Most alliances involved companies from different European countries and were administrated by an office that coordinated activities. All three major food retailers in Sweden are either currently, or have been, involved in different strategic alliances with other European retailers. For example KF has a long tradition of international cooperation (mainly joint buying) with other consumer federations across Europe. Cooperation has been under the name NAF and has involved retailers from eight different countries. The nucleus of this cooperation were the consumer federations in the Nordic countries. Suppliers are identified by alliance members who then coordinate buying, create volume discounts and signal to each other where to find alternative suppliers. Buying for NAF is done through an office in Copenhagen, complemented by representatives in each country specialising in different product areas.

Another example of a strategic alliance is the Dagab group, which is a member of BIGS and Spar International. This alliance includes retailers and wholesalers from 20 different countries. Here, amongst other things, joint buying takes place and new store concepts are developed. There is also a joint ownership of an import company – United Nordic – (in association with three other Nordic food retailers). The third Swedish retailer involved in an international strategic alliance has been ICA. The remainder of this case study will examine the nature of this alliance.

ICA involvement in AMS

The number of members in AMS (Associated Marketing Services) has varied through the years, with as many as 13 retailers being involved. Initially the intention was that the alliance should comprise companies that held a dominant position in their home market (something that in practice was not possible).

Several trends in European retailing were seen as triggering the creation of AMS. One of the most significant was the formation of the European Union, which gave rise to the easier circulation of goods (something that could benefit retailers if they were able to coordinate their efforts). Also, from a retail perspective, European food manufacturers were seen as becoming increasingly powerful. Pan-European alliances provided the opportunity to match this growth. In addition, cooperation could provide better access to markets and give a more international outlook. The AMS therefore provided the opportunity for members to exchange information and communicate on best practices in order to increase productivity and improve supply chain management efficiencies.

ICA joined AMS in 1988, when it was a small organisation with a head office in Zug, Switzerland. ICA did not want to join a 'super organisation' with lots of overheads and costs to distribute amongst its members. Instead AMS was built on the premise that the actual work done in the alliance should take place within the member's own company and by persons employed by each organisation. In this way the costs of participating in the alliance could be kept to a minimum.

AMS had a board made up of the managing directors of each of the different member companies, a full-time managing director and an advisory board (comprising experts from the member companies). Work undertaken by AMS took place in the form of projects. The nature of each project was decided upon by member companies and participation was entirely voluntary (as a rule not all member companies participated in all projects). There was also a special steering group to ensure that the right types of project were given priority.

The purpose of AMS is, to quote the organisation's own material:

> co-operation with producers and suppliers of branded, own-branded or unbranded goods and services in order to identify opportunities for improving the entire delivery chain, reduce the cost of goods and services and take part in the yields from this co-operation. (AMS 1997)

The AMS has therefore also sought to improve and increase the efficiency of the supply chain by, amongst other things, cooperation with suppliers and several areas of cooperation between AMS members can be distinguished (see Figure 21.1).

As AMS partners joined forces, buying could be undertaken more efficiently and trading terms became more favourable for those involved. One major area of cooperation has been private-label development. The brand developed through AMS was known as 'Euroshopper'. However ICA also cooperated with the Nordic members of AMS and developed a second private label, 'Diva'. In the case of the Euroshopper brand some joint marketing efforts also took place. Although limited, attempts have also been made to source and market jointly the Eurobrand (Euro-cream cheese, Euro-nappy, Euro-kitchen paper, etc.). From ICA's point of view this

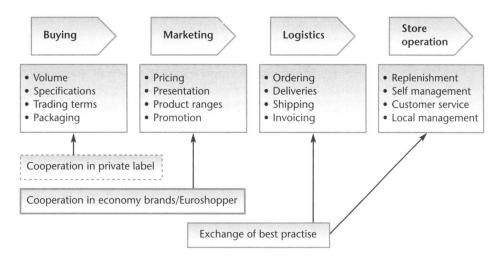

Figure 21.1 Different levels of cooperation in the AMS alliance

Source: AMS (1997)

was an issue of high priority and an area where it deemed it needed partnerships with other leading food retailers in order to succeed.

This was because the Swedish food retail market was a 'late developer' when it came to private brands. Most Swedish suppliers have resisted the pressure from retailers to deliver private-label products, instead they have attempted to market products under their own brand name (maintaining a brand identity reinforces the power of the manufacturer). Whilst there had been some attempt to develop private brands on the Swedish market in the 1970s, this initiative had been confined to one retailer, KF, and at that time had focused on commodity products (potatoes, rice, milk, sugar, etc.). By comparison, ICA had based its competitive advantage on delivering well-known manufacturer brands to consumers (in direct contrast to KF's preference for private brands). However, towards the end of the 1980s the position of KF gradually changed and they also started to stock recognised manufacturer brands on their shelves.

For ICA this represented a direct competitive threat and influenced strongly its decision to develop private-label products. Paradoxically both KF and ICA began to shift towards each other's market position. A second reason for ICA's change of strategy was the realisation that private brands could be used to increase profit levels in a low margin business. Net profit margins of 1–2 per cent in Swedish food retailing could be compared to the 5–6 per cent of Tesco, Sainsbury and other UK food retailers. Private-brand penetration in the United Kingdom was high (between 40 and 50 per cent) and was seen as making a significant contribution to overall profitability. Thus AMS could help ICA gain knowledge in this area by exchanging best practice, gaining access to new suppliers (which were more willing than Swedish suppliers to provide private-label products) and also take part in the creation of joint private-brand development.

There also existed a potential for ICA to communicate on logistics and store operations. From the outset it was quite clear that some of the members of AMS, such as Ahold (Netherlands), Safeway (UK) and Casino (France), were advanced in certain aspects of supply chain operation and that other partners could benefit greatly from their experience. From ICA's perspective getting access to supply chain solutions as well as information on how to create different types of store formats was valued very highly. For example, ICA had long operated a system of logistics based on distribution centres throughout Sweden. Most manufacturers delivered their products to the distribution centres, from where ICA distributed to its stores. Direct store delivery was the exception to the rule and applied mainly to bread, meat and dairy products. During the years leading up to ICA joining AMS there had been many structural changes in the set-up of distribution centres and also experiments concerning new supply chain solutions.

With fewer and bigger stores taking more and more market share it became increasingly difficult to defend a rigid distribution structure, based on delivery to the distribution system. For larger stores direct delivery was in many cases the most efficient solution. This, however, meant that the volume in distribution centres went down and the cost of supplying the remaining stores increased. Through AMS, ICA hoped that a solution to this issue could be developed.

During the 1980s and the beginning of the 1990s ICA (in common with other Swedish food retailers) identified the need for a new store concept, a move triggered by the arrival of the discount format. A number of questions however remained unanswered: What should this concept look like? How should it be implemented and run? What effects would a new format have on the existing store structure, customers and overall profitability? It was hoped that by being part of AMS, ICA would be able to draw on the experiences of other alliance members. Food retailers such as Ahold, Casino and Safeway were all experienced in the development of new store formats and it was hoped they could provide both the necessary information and expertise.

During 1999 there were well-developed plans to introduce ICA on to the Swedish stock exchange as had happened to another major food retailer, Axfood (formerly Dagab). However, in late autumn 1999 the Dutch food retailing group Ahold made a bid for ICA and the Norwegian Hakon group (also owned by ICA). The bid was accepted and, as of 2000, Ahold owned 50 per cent of the newly created Swedish food retailer ICA Ahold AB.

This change of structure had considerable implications for operations within ICA. In particular it led to a re-evaluation of the relationship with AMS. Ahold was also a member of the alliance and it soon became evident that the two companies needed a new strategy to fully benefit from the potential that AMS offered.

ICA's cooperation and operations within AMS are today operated through AES (Ahold European Sourcing). This is a separate department within Ahold, based in Zaandam in the Netherlands. One of its goals is to create buying synergies between OPCOs (operating companies). AES makes considerable effort to coordinate the OPCOs and develop private-label goods across the group. AMS is still regarded, by both ICA and Ahold, as having a useful function. The alliance continues to offer a number of benefits, including new product development and the opportunity to foster closer relationships with suppliers. AMS is still dedicated to developing own-label goods, especially economy brands (mainly Euroshopper). For AES (and ICA) AMS is still thus a critical body as own brands are becoming increasingly important in the Nordic countries.

Discussion questions

1. What are the positive and negative aspects of retail alliances in a deregulated market?

2. What areas of cooperation should ICA consider a priority when in the AMS alliance?

3. What are the implications for Swedish suppliers of Ahold's acquisition of ICA? How might suppliers react?

4. If ICA begins to use more foreign suppliers, what consequences could this have for the management of its supply chain?

PART 8

Retail futures

Retailing and the millennium

Nicholas Alexander and Paul Freathy

Introduction

The focus of this book has to this point been on understanding many of the contemporary issues that affect the retail sector. In these final three chapters we move the debate forward by speculating on how retailing and the retail sector may develop in the future. As you study further the subject of retailing you will undoubtedly come across many books, articles and management reports claiming to provide authoritative accounts on its future. Many are convincingly argued and some are brave enough to support their assertions with figures extrapolated from current trends. One word of warning: often such 'predictions' are often widely inaccurate, overly prescriptive and in many cases simply wrong.

Given the impossibility of predicting future events some sceptics would see such 'crystal ball' gazing as a meaningless and counter-productive activity. This is not necessarily a view to which we would subscribe. We hope this book has been able to demonstrate why planning for the future is of central importance for a retail business. Changing consumer tastes, increased competition and greater product availability make it all the more important that organisations consider how retailing will develop. In this chapter we will consider alternative retail scenarios, examine factors that can mediate future retail outcomes and consider the potential difficulties and pitfalls involved in this form of hypothesis. What the chapter will *not* provide is a definitive view of the future of retailing.

Problems of prediction

One of the problems with prediction is that it is often far too embedded in the present and the fears and expectations of the present. For example, a couple of years ago the warehouse club Costco announced its intention to enter the British market. Speculation and prediction at this time was focused on how this retail format would reconfigure the face of UK retailing. As it transpired, warehouse clubs were not wholeheartedly embraced by the UK public and their impact here has been negligible. Similarly, the beginning of the millennium heralded the dotcom boom. Many reports at this time commented on how retailing would be transformed in the space of a decade. Bricks would give way to clicks and retailing would never be the same again. If you have not already done so, you are encouraged to read Chapter 20 by Fernie and McKinnon. They highlight how the amount consumers spend on online grocery purchases has fallen significantly below the estimates of earlier reports.

This chapter is not about predicting a definitive vision of the future. Its aim is to provide a view on how we should seek to build scenarios about the future retail environment. It is therefore concerned with asking the question 'What could happen?' rather than answering the question 'What will happen?'

A further warning on the pitfalls of building future scenarios is probably appropriate, in particular the way in which commentators on retailing futures, treat the external environment. Two issues typically arise: first, it is often not recognised that in the majority of instances social, economic; political and cultural factors remain stable over time. Thus the *Nineteen Eighty-Four* (Orwell 1949) or *Brave New World* (Huxley 1932) logic of rapid and dramatic change too often creeps in. Thus within a few years the fundamentals of human interaction are revised as a result of political, social and economic change irrespective of cultural conventions that act as a brake on change. In essence retail change is more often evolutionary than revolutionary.

Conversely, future scenarios are by their nature poorly equipped to accommodate fundamental and rapid changes brought about by external events, for example, the events of 11 September 2001 may have altered the structure and operation of the air transport industry overnight. Despite such events having an immediate and dramatic effect upon the future of the industry they remain impossible to factor in. Scenarios cannot account for the unexpected or the unpredictable. Views of the future made in the present cannot account for factors such as strikes, wars and terrorist threats.

In a retail context, the changes that have occurred in the Czech Republic highlight the difficulties in predicting the future. The 1930s saw the development of early international retail activity through the Beta footwear operation (Hollander 1970). However, major political change and conflict altered the economic structure in the country from 1938, whilst the distribution and retailing systems became centrally planned from the late 1940s until the early 1990s. By the late 1990s the market had seen the arrival of large international operations from elsewhere in Europe and from the United States. From being an early innovator in the area of international retail activity the market had become the recipient of retail innovation. Who could have charted such events? In essence fact is stranger than fiction. The changes that took place lay beyond the predictive powers of the most insightful politicians, academics and social commentators and reinforces the view of some: that developing a view of the future of retailing is an interesting but ultimately fruitless exercise.

Self-assessment Question 1 *Given the difficulties highlighted in the above sections, why would anyone wish to develop future scenarios for the retail sector?*

The influence of the external environment

Despite the above reservations we would argue that developing alternative retail scenarios represents a worthwhile exercise. Both Chapter 1 and Chapter 4 highlighted the wide variety of external factors that influence the structure and operation of the market. These are often factors over which the retailer has no control and must yet react to. Their importance in this context lies in their ability to shape future retail forms. It is therefore worth considering briefly the ways in which external factors can influence the future. What is provided here is not an exhaustive list, but examples for illustration.

In most scenarios (whether retail or otherwise) that consider the future, technology plays a significant, if not a central role. But is technology assigned a more important position than it merits? Future scenarios often become submerged in new 'tools' for bringing about change and these tools end up taking on a central role in the new environment. In this context we immediately hear how technology will revolutionise our future, for example all our needs will very soon be available from the comfort of our own armchair. Not only will we be able to shop for food, clothes and leisure goods, we can avoid the trouble of going on holiday by putting on our virtual reality headset and being transported to the destination of our choice. No more queues, no more delays, no more bad service encounters. What could be simpler!

As human beings we are preternaturally inclined to accept this vision of a brave new world. The new environment transports us beyond the confines of the present and the drudgery of our existence to something that is different. It is a world in which our own inestimable talents and virtues will be truly recognised. Thus it is in pleasant contrast to the present.

The problem with this approach is that it places the technology at the heart of the change process. There is something of the alchemist's world view in it. It implies that life is some sort of experiment confined within a test tube, where the addition of a substance, in this case technology, will change base metals into gold. At its worst this interpretation of cause and effect ignores the context in which innovation occurs. The technology-based view of change appears to suggest that so called 'inventors' and 'scientists' spend their time locked away in darkened rooms inventing for the sake of inventing. The technology-based interpretation of events works well only if we factor out the realities of human existence – that is, the inventor needs to eat and has a mortgage.

A further factor mediating the technology-driven view of change is the notion of a 'social brake'. Just because there is a technological capability in existence does not mean consumers will automatically want to use it. For example, WAP (wireless application protocol) phones represented the next stage in personal communications and were set to dominate the market. In addition to the standard range of services this new form of mobile phone offered access to the Internet. Perhaps surprisingly (or not) consumer uptake on this next generation of phones has been slow.

Whilst it remains impossible to understand the structure of retailing today without reference to technology it would be inaccurate to suggest that current advancements will dictate the shape of retailing in the future. Availability does not always equate with adoption. Whilst we may be able to identify what technology is capable of delivering we cannot extrapolate from this a conclusive view on how it will influence the retail sector in the future.

In addition to the role of technology, earlier chapters highlighted other external factors that could influence the structure of retailing. For example, Chapter 4 discussed how retailers had to be aware of a range of economic factors such as interest rates, exchange rates and tax levels. What is sometimes ignored in such a discussion is the interaction between these different factors and how one may counteract the other. One of the best examples of this is in the discussion over e-commerce. We have already established that many forecasts concerning the growth of electronic commerce were wildly inaccurate. We should not overlook the vested economic interests that conspire to constrain and contain such change. For example, clicks may sound more advanced and exciting than bricks, but the real estate industry is a very large and heavily capitalised one (Winger 2001). The property value of some retailers may be far more significant than their trading value. Are those parties with significant financial interests in bricks and mortar retailing really going to embrace the potential changes that e-tailing has to offer? One reason why some commentators were wildly inaccurate in their predictions of e-commerce was their failure to understand the complexities of such market relationships. Even if electronic ordering becomes a substantial part of retail activity, existing economic interests will continue to play a substantial role in its development and future structural form.

The final external factor that we will use as an illustration is legislation. Numerous strategy and marketing textbooks require you to be aware of the legal parameters placed on firms. Legislation may prevent, contribute or reconfigure the structure of retailing. It will often be a contributory factor when explaining constant and consistent change within a retail sector. For example, the legislative provisions that restrict superstore growth in Ireland have prevented large-scale retail development. Providing the law remains unchanged the future structure of retailing in that country will be constrained by the prescribed legal framework. In contrast, the removal of the Large Stores Laws in Japan has provided US and European retailers with greater access to the market and contributed to retail structural change (Larke 1994; Alexander 1997). As a consequence predicting the future structure of the Japanese market remains more difficult. Finally, we can illustrate how the removal of a set of legislative provisions can completely reconfigure a retail sector and undermine all attempts at predicting future retail forms. The decision by the European Union in July 1999 to remove a passenger's entitlement to purchase duty free goods on intra-EU travel led to chaos in the travel retail industry. Revenues dropped by up to 40 per cent for some companies as customers became confused as to what they could and could not purchase. This highlights how political pressure and ultimately the removal of a legal entitlement can have a major impact on trading systems and distort expected changes in the market.

Self-assessment Question 2 *Choose a retail sector and identify the major external influences that have shaped its growth and development over the last decade. To what extent would it have been possible to predict these factors in advance?*

A vision of the future

Despite the difficulties identified above there is no shortage of pundits willing to give their vision of the future. These were Nicholas Negroponte's thoughts in July 1998:

> Already today, going to a bookstore may be the worst method of buying a particular book. All the elements are against you: weather, time, energy, price, not to mention availability. Instead, by logging on to, say, Amazon.com (my favorite), you can order the book in less time than it would take to call and see if your local bookseller has it in stock.

This description is part of the 'technology can shop for you' interpretation of future retailing and is in danger of putting technology at the centre of future developments. In Negroponte's opinion technology is going to be everywhere: in operations, customer service and especially in the supply chain. This view is reinforced by Welling (2000: 25), who maintains that: 'What is emerging, however, is not the demise of brick-and-mortar apparel retailing, but a new value supply chain model with amazingly sophisticated technologies that promises to concentrate the benefit of each step in the streamlined production-to-market process.'

Whilst not denying the importance of technology in understanding the future of retailing, Negroponte (1998) and Welling (2000) both go on to say there is a human dimension that can not be ignored. Although it may be easier for a consumer to get the book they want over the Internet, the social dimension to shopping means that individuals may value the experience of being in a store:

> Bookstores, of course, are no longer just for buying books. They are for browsing, meeting people, having coffee, and engaging in the serendipity of life – bumping into the unexpected. The real 'product' is not mere paper and ink, but a place to conduct educational and social entertainment. (Negroponte, 1998)

Here the dichotomy is highlighted. Whilst technology may offer the customer a rational, efficient means of purchasing the product, the importance of the social interaction can outweigh any such benefits. For some individuals the true pleasures are derived from the actual act of shopping. This willingness to value social contact over pure efficiency gains highlights the limitations of viewing retail change purely from a technological perspective. If you have not already done so you may wish to read the discussion in Chapter 10 on the differences between 'economic man' and 'marketing man'. A fundamental aspect of our behaviour as consumers is that we do not always buy a product purely for its functional properties. Rather we will shop at a particular store or purchase a particular product for the intangible values associated with it. Hence Levy's (1959) quote, which is mentioned on a number of occasions throughout this book: 'People buy things not only for what they can do, but also for what they mean.'

We must also ensure that our view of the future is not based purely on a specific form of contemporary retailing. For example, when Negroponte says 'Bookstores . . . are no longer just for buying books' he chooses to interpret the future by virtue of a debatable interpretation of the past. What is being implied is that in their present form bookstores only have one purpose: to sell books. This, however, is to view bookstores as an undifferentiated mass without acknowledging the range of different formats and market sectors they occupy. Whilst one may identify book-stores that equate to this definition and offer few added-value services, others do not. For example, in the film *Notting Hill*, the bookshop does not just sell books, it provides a range of services from fresh coffee to a considered opinion on the merchandise. In that, it is the 'traditional' bookshop. So will the bookshop of the future represent a radical departure from what we are currently used to? The answer is both yes and no. Retailers will continue to innovate and offer new 'added-value' services to the customer, whilst at the same time building on many of the existing benefits associated with book buying.

So what have we established thus far? It would seem from the above debate that retailing is not technology led, that an interplay of factors may work against the most widely predicted set of outcomes and that retail change is best viewed as an evolutionary rather than a revolutionary process. Furthermore the physical aspects of the store environment continue to remain important as individuals still value the opportunity to visit a retail outlet and personally conduct transactions. From this reading, we could conclude that the retail sector is inherently conservative in nature and that change is neither welcomed nor wanted. That is not the intention, indeed we would maintain that the sector is dynamic, adaptive and embraces innovation. What is being argued is that retail change is the outcome of a multi-tude of factors continually interacting with each other, one consequence of which is that there is no prescribed future. If we return to the development of e-com-merce, for example, Welling (2000: 27) notes:

> The e-tailing revolution is giving consumers the ability to refuse to participate in retail arenas they find too time-consuming, inconvenient and – in the case of car-buying or even holiday shopping at crowded, stocked-out malls – just plain distasteful. For apparel brick-and-mortar retailers, the shield of protection against e-tailing that argues that consumers still want to touch and try on gar-ments before purchasing is wearing thin.

Are consumers time sensitive and eager for convenience above all else? Will they continue to value the physical shopping experience? Will an alternative form of retailing develop whereby:

> Stores will become giant display areas where shoppers can see, touch, feel and try out merchandise, but won't actually leave the store with the things they buy. Instead, purchases will be customized and delivered to shoppers' homes directly from the manufacturer (Mahler, 2000: 45)?

That sounds very advanced, and very beneficial to the retailer who now carries low inventory levels; however from a consumer's perspective it takes away the pleasure of immediate acquisition and the simple experience of shopping in the store. It does however engage the consumer in the purchase of an item as well as allowing social intercourse to take place. Which of the above scenarios remain accurate? Which is the true vision of the future? The answer is all of them yet none of them.

Visions of the future often contain mutually exclusive, even contradictory predictions. As such the notion that retailing will follow a singular, predetermined path is a view to which few subscribe. Similarly, it would be misleading to suggest that all those commentators who venture in speculation predict a retail world unrecognisable from our own. Some tell us that businesses are going to do it differently in the future because they will manage it better. For example, *The McKinsey Quarterly* carried an article in 2000 indicating that 'Ecosystems that cater to interrelated customer requirements may be the next thing in retailing' (Eagle *et al.* 2000).

In this scenario retailers build on customers' needs from the perspective of their existing core business or relationship. Future success will involve the ability to 'master multi-channel dynamics, partnering, and brand leverage'. This book should have demonstrated that many retailers have already embraced such challenges. Diversification, strategic alliances, supply chain partnerships, e-tailing and brand development are all characteristics of the retail sector.

Understanding the past through theories of retail change

To this point it appears that we have been quite elusive in putting forward our own vision or view of the future. We have instead highlighted the multitude of difficulties that arise when attempts are made to define how retailing is likely to develop. Perhaps the main point to be made thus far is that there is nothing inevitable about what retailing should look like in the future. As a student of retailing you may find this situation frustrating – what, how or who can help you gain a better appreciation of the future of retailing? Perhaps one answer to these questions lies in the theories that surround retail change.

When predicting the future it is useful to have a clear appreciation of the past. One of the problems encountered when attempting to understand the future is that the process of change may be too easily seen as something contemporary rather than a constant. New retail forms will often be the re-establishment of old patterns of activity, a limited knowledge of our retail past therefore limits our understanding of the future (Alexander and Akehurst 1999). For example, the Royal Exchange in London, which dates from the 1570s, had two floors of shops and is generally acknowledged to be the first ever shopping mall. Similarly Émile Zola published his novel *The Ladies Paradise* in 1883. It is concerned with the commercial development of the department store and is based in particular on the development of the Bon Marché in Paris from the 1850s. The growth of large stores, the demise of the small family enterprise, the extension of product ranges, the introduction of new technology and the development of competitive management systems are themes explored within the book. They are themes that would sit comfortably within a description of the development of retailing in the second half of the twentieth century. Indeed to read the book is to be made aware of the dangers of expecting anything entirely new within the retail environment. This revisiting of past formats and experiences is evident in some of the more popular theories of retail development.

The wheel of retailing (McNair 1958) has attracted considerable attention over the years (Brown 1987). The original hypothesis maintains that the majority of new retailers enter the market as low status, low margin and low price operators.

As they continue to trade they eventually develop more elaborate establishments and facilities, extending their product offer, level of service and their cost structure. Finally they move into a mature phase, becoming high cost, top heavy organisations that experience a declining return on investment and become vulnerable to new market entrants.

The theory is predicated on the 'upward movement' of the retail offering. (The development of more elaborate establishments is seen as trading up.) The 'wheel' provides the opportunity to reflect on the structure of retailing at a given point in time, therefore allowing some prediction of the future. The low cost, low frills origin of some high value, high service retailers such as Tesco is acknowledged and lends credibility to the 'wheel' theory.

In the United Kingdom one could argue that retailers such as Matalan are the modern equivalent of Marks & Spencer. The latter took advantage of the second industrial revolution. The business was in an ideal position to place products on the market at a time when the ability to mass produce consumer items coincided with an increased demand for such products. The company provided consumer groups with access to products from which they were previously excluded because of cost. Their success at this time was based on providing an offer at the low cost, low frills end of the market. Over time the company has traded up, improved its facilities, its level of service and its product offer. Does this place it in a vulnerable position, susceptible to competition from the likes of low cost operators such as Matalan?

Critics of the wheel have essentially been concerned with its failure to provide a robust interpretation of events. For example how have companies such as Tesco and Sainsbury survived in the face of increased competition from Continental discounters such as Aldi, Lidl and Netto? They have perhaps missed two essential points. First, 'laws' of retail development will not provide the certainty accepted in scientific endeavour. Secondly, the model alludes more to a trend than a certainty. In essence we talk about tendencies rather than absolutes. It is always possible to find exceptions to the rule, but this does not necessarily mean that the rules themselves are incorrect. Consequently, if viewed in this light, the wheel has a role to play in anticipating future trends in retail development.

A second theoretical approach that may help in understanding retail futures is the 'accordion theory' (Hollander 1966). Like the wheel of retailing, this theory has suffered from the expectations invested in it. However, those less critical of its application maintain that it has the capacity to indicate fundamental trends in the development of retailing.

The emergence of superstores and hypermarkets has been cited as examples that illustrate the applicability of the accordion theory. It is noted that many retailers have a tendency to add to product ranges and services to their existing merchandise mix. The accordion theory buys into the common human experience of increased complication and over extension, modified by a period of simplification and reductionism. As retail enterprises grow they acquire unnecessary baggage. The number of people at head office may grow and they may add new departments and product categories in store. Ultimately the organisation becomes overly complicated and unworkable. Then along come more efficient enterprises focused on consumers' real product needs rather than their lack of alternatives. Suddenly the unfashionable tie display in the 'gentlemen's clothing department' of the local department store is challenged by a retailer selling only ties that are selected for their consumer appeal by buyers who are able to focus on recognised consumer needs in that product area. This is not to argue that niche operations such as the Tie Rack and the Sock Shop are immune. These retailers, which emerged so strongly in the 1980s as a challenge to the established wide assortment retailer have a tendency to stock product groups not indicated by their name.

The accordion theory may also help in understanding the strategic activity of retailers. For example, in the United Kingdom the phenomenal growth of Next, the clothing retailer, saw new product areas being added to the core product range. In addition, the Next facia proliferated in a variety of store types on the high street. Next for Men, Next for Women, Next Originals, Next the Jewellers, Department X, Next 24 Hours and Next to Nothing were all added to the Next Group in the late 1980s and early 1990s. This over extension was followed by a period of consolidation in the face of increased competition and changing market conditions.

Advocates of the accordion theory maintain that it has applicability even at the corporate level. For example, in the 1990s the Kingfisher Group developed a portfolio of businesses that included Woolworth (variety), Superdrug (toiletries), Comet (electrical) and B&Q (DIY). Since then we have seen the removal of a number of these businesses from the portfolio. Superdrug has been sold off, Woolworth demerged and it is highly likely that Comet will be divested in the near future. Even at this most strategic level we see the characteristics inherent within the accordion theory, that is, extension followed by simplification and reductionism.

Whilst there is a danger in providing too many theoretical approaches to understanding the future of retailing, Gist's (1968) theory of retail conflict and resolution remains a useful framework to think about the future. In this interpretation of events, different types of retailing representing thesis and antithesis eventually bring about a new retail form (the synthesis of the two originals). The classic example is the lumberyard (thesis) catering for tradesmen and the hardware store (antithesis) selling directly to the consumer. The outcome was of course the DIY store (synthesis).

However it would be wrong to see this process as inevitable. A gap had to emerge and the benefits had to be recognised before the new concept could come into being. The success of DIY reflected changing consumption habits, with home ownership becoming the norm not the exception. As DIY stores grew greater volumes were demanded from suppliers and the purchasing power of the retailer increased. Eventually tradesmen could get their materials cheaper at the DIY store than the lumberyard and this form of retailing underwent significant decline.

Social change and hence altered purchasing behaviour are at the heart of retail change theories even if this is not always explicitly stated. Retail change will not occur unless consumer change occurs. Similarly, social change will introduce new forms of retailing but will not necessarily eradicate the old forms overnight. This is important as it helps explain why, for example, we find discount retailers operating successfully in a service-oriented marketplace. Consumer groups are diverse, they have different values and different needs, and the structure of retailing at any point in time represents a response to these demands.

Self-assessment Question 3 *For a sector of your choice evaluate whether any of the models identified above fit the pattern of change as you see it.*

The future

Building on the previous sections, the future of retailing therefore lies with the consumer rather than the retailer or any technology that the retailer may seek to employ. It is the changing requirements of the consumer that brings about change and future retailing practices. The structure of retailing is a response to consumers' behavioural changes in the context of their social, economic and political environments. These changes are confined within cultural norms. Thus there is no single future of retailing; there are competing versions of the future.

To accept this proposition is to abandon the notion that retailing follows some preordained path from simple retailing to modern retailing to advanced retailing. Determinism is a notion that underlies many of the assumptions about retail development and should be challenged. It is an inheritance from the social science origins of much retail thought embodied in and typified by studies such as Arndt's (1972).

The UK retail commentator is susceptible to the notion that innovation comes from the United States. The fear created by the incoming warehouse clubs of the early 1990s and of Wal-Mart in the late 1990s is evidence of this. Innovation, so the story goes, is a product of the advanced economy, advanced society and hence the consumption systems of the United States. However this fear or appreciation of the supposed driving forces of change ignores the wider cultural environment and probably says more about the dominant cultural forces in the United Kingdom than provide an objective appraisal of retail development.

Box 22.1 is an illustration of a situation where there are different sources of retail innovation competing for the future in one market space. The discount store did not replace the superstore (which itself is a UK version of the continental hypermarket) – rather it supplemented the retail structure. Thus within the global environment there is an ebb and flow of retail competition and development. What we are witnessing is a level of eclecticism where different retail forms are adopted and adapted to suit the cultural demands of the market.

A country's retail system will therefore be influenced by both emerging and existing trends. For example, in Brazil, consumers are said to have European tastes and shop like Americans. While US-style shopping malls have become a central feature of retail development in the country, the stores anchoring these malls are often European in origin. In the Brazilian marketplace, retailers such as Carrefour compete head on with US operations such as Wal-Mart.

Hong Kong is an Asian market that has been exposed to western forms of retailing for some time and, despite the pressure to conform to a global standard, traditional retail forms continue to flourish. For example, 'wet markets' (a feature of south and east Asia) continue to thrive. They do this because they meet customer needs within the existing culture of consumption (Goldman *et al.* 1999). No doubt a very, very long time ago someone said they would not survive.

The structure of retailing within any one market is therefore the outcome of an evolutionary process of innovation, adaptation and accommodation. A question that arises is whether we are ever likely to see a revolution in retailing. Can we

Box 22.1
Competition within the marketspace

The warehouse clubs engaged the attention of the large dominant superstore retailers in the United Kingdom in the early 1990s. Those superstore retailers launched legal appeals against the US incomer because they argued that the international operation by calling itself a club could operate from low cost sites designated as non-retail and thereby gain unfair competitive advantage. At the same time discount operations from Europe, such operations as Aldi and Netto, were also entering the market. Warehouse clubs appealed to the consumer who had the desire to and could buy in bulk because they had the space to store goods at home. The discount store offered non-brand cheap food. The latter has made more of an impression than the former. The warehouse club, a product of west coast US society, demanded a consumer infrastructure that was suited to the United States but not immediately accessible to UK consumers. The discount store was a product of prosperous European societies where cheap staple food items filled socio-economic requirements. The European option was more culturally relevant than the US option.

identify a scenario whereby processes and activities lead to a radically reconfigured retail system? If we take the e-commerce 'revolution', many commentators confidently predicted a fundamental change in our shopping behaviour and a redevelopment of our retail systems. (We have already commented on the accuracy of this prediction!)

Whilst revolutionary change in retailing is not unknown the examples are often confined to less developed retail markets. For example, what happens when you take a superstore format and place it in an agrarian market that is technologically backward, without a supporting infrastructure and a consumer base not used to self-service? Is this a revolution that will fundamentally alter the way in which people shop or is it a course of development that ignores the complexities of retail change enshrined in the retail theories above? Do such initiatives work? Do these markets need to be brought kicking and screaming into the twenty-first century? Or are they doomed to failure as they ignore the cultural differences that exist between societies and the social peculiarities that modify or reject imported innovation? Again, there is no right or wrong answer as there is no single outcome that can be assumed from such change. Put simply the revolution may work, or it may not. The important point in this context is not to automatically assume one outcome or the other.

Future scenarios

In 2000 the Department of Trade and Industry in the United Kingdom commissioned, through its Foresight programme, a series of Retail Scenarios for the year 2010 (Alexander *et al.* 2000). The scenarios addressed different retail environments and provided suggestions as to what could happen over the next decade. Whilst it is not essential that you read these scenarios, it is important to understand the general points that they attempted to make. The scenarios considered the role of electronic retailing, not only from a technological point of view but also from the setting in which such technologies would be employed (the point made earlier in this chapter). For example, they considered the future of the travel sector and its associated retail opportunities. In the other scenarios alternative retail experiences such as the department store and the convenience store are considered.

Despite taking significantly different viewpoints the scenarios are not mutually exclusive visions of the future, rather they represent a range of outcomes that could occur concurrently within the same society. Thus the department store scenario considers an environment where membership is based on the concept of exclusivity. In contrast the urban convenience store scenario is defined by social breakdown. It is a response not to a poor market but the lack of an infrastructure that holds a market together. The critical point here is that both scenarios could operate simultaneously within a retail marketplace. The existence of one does not preclude the other.

What the scenarios sought to do was challenge perceptions of the cohesion of retail forms and structures. There remains no predetermined set of outcomes that may be logically derived or extrapolated from the current retail system and the scenarios highlighted this fundamental issue. In the future retail environment where there is a widening gap between the rich and poor, the franchised and the disenfranchised, how will retailing evolve? The one conclusion about future retail forms and structures is that there can be no definitive conclusion.

One inference that we can draw however is that an understanding of the consumer is at the heart of any future scenario. The future of retailing will be derived from the consumer's desire for self-realisation and the constraints placed on achieving this aim. Whilst an understanding of consumer change is unlikely to help us predict the future it may help us to prepare for what may or may not occur. It allows the retailer to remain relevant to the consumer. An essential truth is that retailers often become more excited than their customers about their offering and, as a consequence, fail to respond to changing consumer values. For example, consumers do not go to supermarkets, superstores or hypermarkets because they like walking down 'industrialised' aisles under harsh lighting. They go because it is cheaper or more convenient than going elsewhere. Customers do not visit a store because they feel loyalty to the bricks and mortar, they go because of the benefits offered. If those benefits no longer flow then the future scenario for that retailer is clear – there is no future.

Summary

In considering the future of retailing, therefore, there is one golden rule: look at the consumer first. Despite the temptation, the first consideration should not be the available technology. Technology only makes new systems possible within the cultural and social parameters of the retail marketplace. Retailing is consumer driven, not technology led. If you want to know how retailing will change, look at yourself. What will be your future wants, needs and desires?

To understand the future one must also consider both the past and the present. Retail change has been a constant feature throughout history and is not located simply in the present. The present is important in that the competitive environment, economic and legislative controls and social drivers all have a mediating effect on future retail forms. Whilst it remains possible to speculate about a radical reconfiguration of retail form, the likelihood is that such factors ensure that future change will tend to be evolutionary rather than revolutionary in nature.

So, what of the future? Perhaps the simplest message is that there is no pre-ordained path that retailing will follow. Whilst it is possible to identify trends and likely developments it is impossible to say what will definitely occur. Indeed a number of different outcomes can concurrently occur within the same market-place. How can we therefore predict what will happen in our own country, let alone Europe or the rest of the world? The dynamic nature of the retail sector ensures that the future remains uncertain. Perhaps this is a strength in itself. Certainly retailing remains an exciting area to study – the process of continual change, adaptation and innovation characterises the sector and provides a challenge for all those who compete in the market. As a student of retailing you should seek to examine, to monitor and to understand these processes. You should allow yourselves the luxury of hypothesis and the indulgence of speculation whilst at all times acknowledging the dangers of prescription.

Further reading

If you wish to understand a little more about the theories of retail change then look at the following:

McGoldrick, P. (2002) *Retail Marketing*, London: McGraw Hill.

Chapter 1 provides more detail together with some additional readings on the subject.

The following two chapters focus on e-commerce and the future of payment systems. Below are listed additional readings to support these case studies.

E-commerce

Agrawal, V., Arjona, L. D. and **Lemmons, R.** (2001) 'E-performance: the path to rational exuberance', *The McKinsey Quarterly*, February, 31–43.

Bakos, Y. (2001) 'The emerging landscape for retail e-commerce', *Journal of Economic Perspectives*, 15(1) 69–80.

International Journal of Retail and Distribution Management (2002) Special issue on Aspects of electronic retailing, 30(10).

Reynolds, J. (2002) 'E-tail marketing', in P. McGoldrick (ed.), *Retail Marketing*, London: McGraw Hill.

Payment systems

Worthington, S. (1988) 'Credit cards in the United Kingdom: where the power lies in the battle between the banks and the retailers', *Journal of Marketing Management*, 4(1): 61–70.

Worthington, S. (2001) 'Affinity credit cards: a critical review', *International Journal of Retail and Distribution Management* 29(11): 485–508.

Worthington, S. and Edwards, V. (2000) 'Changes in payments markets, past, present and future: a comparison between Australia and the UK', *International Journal of Bank Marketing*, 18(5): 212–21.

CHAPTER 23

E-commerce and the future of retail delivery

Jonathan Reynolds

Introduction

One of the main conclusions stemming from the previous chapter is that retailing has no predetermined future. There is no chosen path, no single way forward for a retailer to follow. The future of retailing is defined by the decisions that individuals have made in the past and are making today. The main difficulty for a retailer is determining whether the decisions made will be the right ones for the business. Often the correct choice of strategy is far from obvious. Conflicting reports, erroneous forecasts and contradictory advice can all serve to make the process of decision making more difficult. Nevertheless businesses are regularly faced with the dilemma of whether or not to invest in a particular project or undertake a particular course of action. If they make the right choice it can mean growth, profitability and a competitive advantage for the organisation. If they get it wrong it can mean lost sales, low profits or ultimately the company failing altogether.

The following case study highlights the issues associated with making strategic decisions. It takes as its example a grocery retailer and illustrates the multitude of factors that can influence the decision of whether or not to invest in e-commerce.

The challenge

Frustrated, Jo Weller threw the remains of her morning Espresso into the bin and closed down the e-mail session. What had irritated her was the casual message from her boss, Hamilton's Marketing Director Simon Chambers.

```
-------
To:              Jo.Weller@Hamilton.com
From:            Simon.Chambers@Hamilton.com
Subj:            What are we going to do about e-commerce?

Jo:

Eleanor has been putting more pressure on marketing to come up with a defen-
sible view on e-commerce. She's sick of Tesco getting all the headlines and fed
up with city analysts asking smart-alec questions. I said you were our resident
expert on the marketing side. She's asked Jeff to put together the financial
pieces. Can you come up with a solid marketing brief for Friday so I can keep
her happy?

Si

-------
```

As if she didn't have enough to do, with the new organic range roll out and cov-
ering their backs on the salmonella scare. This had the makings of a major project.
Anyway, from what she'd been reading at the weekend, e-commerce was another
busted flush, wasn't it? And Hamilton's hadn't even got a web site of its own. Since
the high-tech stock market collapse a couple of years ago the pendulum in Europe,
much like that in the United States, had swung pretty firmly against home shopping. She'd been to an industry research meeting last month that, as she recalled,
put it in lowly bottom place out of 12 issues on the retail CEO's agenda (Table
23.1). Faced with this clear evidence of a 'busted flush', many established retailers
had breathed a sigh of relief and moved on to what they regarded as more immediate sources of profitability (like her organics roll out, she reminded herself).

On the other hand, Jo knew that Hamilton's CEO Eleanor Goodley's irritation
sprang from the fact that established businesses such as Tesco in the United

Table 23.1 'Top of mind' issues for retail grocery CEOs 1997–2002

Rank 2002	Issue	2001	2000	1999	1998	1997
1	Retail internationalisation	1	3	1	4	3
2	Food safety	4	5	11	–	–
3	Customer loyalty and retention	2	1	2	2	2
4	Global recession	4	–	–	–	–
5	The store offer	9	7	4	10	–
6	Retailer as a brand	8	6	5	–	–
7	Efficient consumer response	5	4	3	1	1
8	Recruitment and retention	8	11	8	11	11
9	Environment/sustainable development	12	11	10	12	12
10	B2B exchanges	3	–	–	–	–
11	Euro	6	9	6	6	–
12	Home shopping	7	2	9	7	6

Source: CIES (2002)

Kingdom were already generating around 3 per cent of turnover (which this year would be around £500 million) from online grocery sales. In addition, they were using the channel as a means to internationalise the business – something else she knew Eleanor had been getting a lot of criticism about. But Tesco was a very different business from Hamilton's – more mass market, more stores – with much more money to throw at the problem. Hamilton's had a market share of around 3 per cent compared to Tesco's 20 per cent and focused on being a niche fresh food retailer.

So, Jo mused, what price e-commerce for Hamilton's? The messages were in fact pretty mixed across the board on this. She'd seen pendulums swinging before and knew that extreme positions were unlikely to be sustained – perhaps the truth lay somewhere in between. But Hamilton's was not a rich organisation – was this a channel only for those companies with deep pockets? She knew that she would need to consider the largely conflicting evidence on the present and likely future scale and nature of e-commerce. What for example did other retail practitioners feel about its attractiveness as a means of growing market share and profitability, and what place should e-commerce have in Hamilton's 'retail mission'? Along the way Jo knew that she would also have to come to grips with one of the most enduring obstacles to effective business-to-consumer (B2C) e-commerce – retail home delivery.

The scale and nature of e-commerce

Jo pulled out some recent statistics on the penetration of e-commerce in the United States and across Europe from the Oxford marketspace web site.[1] What she found appeared to bear out the gloomiest interpretation of the facts. B2C e-commerce in the United States amounted to only just over 0.8 per cent of retail sales in the third quarter of 2001, according to the United States Department of Commerce, growing only to 1.2 per cent in the second quarter of 2002[2] (although this excluded ticket, travel and financial services sales). The NRF/Forrester Retail Index[3] also showed 2001 online sales little changed from 2000 levels. UK National Statistics put the value of e-commerce in retail, travel and catering at £7.6 billion (0.27 per cent of sales) in 2000.[4] Similar levels of penetration appeared to prevail in, for example, France.[5] Detailed evidence from US tracking surveys suggested, indeed, that domestic Internet users did not regard 'shopping' as anywhere near the most popular activity online (Figure 23.1). Use of the Internet for e-mail and browsing were far more popular pursuits, even amongst very experienced Internet users. (Jo smiled, recalling her three hours online the previous night looking for a web site specialising in the care of her beloved Maine Coon pet cats.) Internet adoption itself had slowed down in the United Kingdom to peak at around a 45 per cent penetration (Figure 23.2) and there was still a distinct bias towards younger, more educated and southern households (Figure 23.3).

[1] http://www.marketspace.org.uk
[2] http://www.census.gov/mrts/www/current.html
[3] http://www.inetstart.com/nrf_forrester_online_retail_inde.htm
[4] http://www.statistics.gov.uk/pdfdir/ecom0501.pdf
[5] Brousseau, E. (2000) 'Commerce électronique: ce que disent les chiffres et ce qu'il faudrait savoir', Economie et Statistique, 2001 Mai., http://www.insee.fr/fr/ffc/docs_ffc/ES339F.pdf

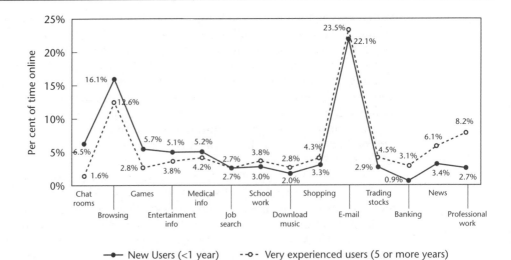

Figure 23.1 Shopping is not the 'killer application' online.
Source: UCLA (2001)

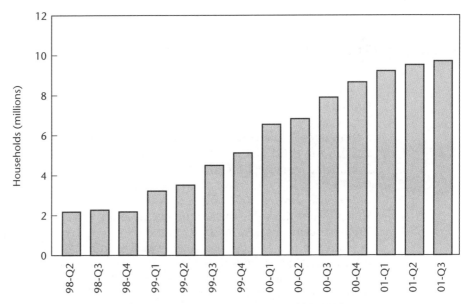

Figure 23.2 Penetration of UK household Internet access, 1998–2001
Source: OFTEL (2002)

She read on: 'Electronic commerce', declared one rather pompous academic,

is a misleading and ambiguous term. Statisticians have developed relatively clear definitions of what such activity entails, but, in so doing, have arrived at an excessively narrow focus which serves to ignore the many indirect effects of the Internet on retail sales through such effects as pre-sale marketing, brand-building and after-sales customer service, all of which might potentially lead to increased customer satisfaction and patronage, particularly for 'clicks and mortar' businesses.

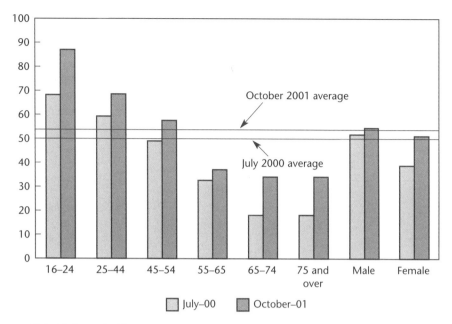

Figure 23.3 UK household access to the Internet by age and gender 2000–01
Source: National Statistics (2001)

She knew from her own marketing experience of seeking to measure advertising effectiveness that these so-called 'halo effects' were of course exceptionally difficult to measure for an individual business, let alone for the economy as whole. But the forecasters could not even give her a consistent estimate of likely future direct sales online. They all talked about 'the interplay between a series of driving forces' – technological, social, economic and regulatory – that would determine the pace of change in the eventual nature and scale of e-commerce.

Also, they suggested, European e-commerce appeared to be taking a very different technical course from that in the United States. Broadband, interactive TV and mobile platforms are much more evident in consumers' adoption patterns, with some European consumers (notably from the United Kingdom) having a higher likelihood of buying online than the usual simplistic innovation–adoption curve would suggest. But this again conflicted with recent evidence from the sector, with both Argos and Woolworth withdrawing from digital TV shopping trials in early 2002. Jo sighed. Her own experience of *Digital4U* interactive TV, demonstrated last weekend in her local electrical store, had been less than impressive. No wonder UK consumers were resisting buying wide-screen digital TVs; it looked as if the government was going to have to further delay the date for switching off the analogue signal.

Evidence from practitioners

But Jo knew that a wholesale retreat from the promise of e-commerce was by no means in evidence from all established retailers. Some retailers had proved considerably more

proficient than other sectors at exploiting the opportunities of new electronic channels to market. She dug out some recent research undertaken by KPMG (2001). This
showed that e-business in the United Kingdom was not having a uniform impact on
companies. The researchers had distinguished between e-pioneers, e-followers and e-
laggards (Table 23.2) and had remarked that, whilst e-pioneers were to be found in all
industry sectors, it was retailing which was characterised by an 'all-or-nothing'
approach to e-business (Figure 23.4). So, was Hamilton's 'all' or 'nothing' or, as ever,
stuck in the middle?

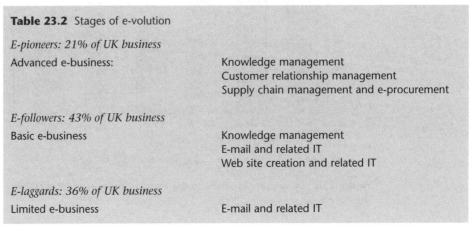

Table 23.2 Stages of e-volution

E-pioneers: 21% of UK business
Advanced e-business:

Knowledge management
Customer relationship management
Supply chain management and e-procurement

E-followers: 43% of UK business
Basic e-business

Knowledge management
E-mail and related IT
Web site creation and related IT

E-laggards: 36% of UK business
Limited e-business

E-mail and related IT

Source: KPMG Consulting (2001)

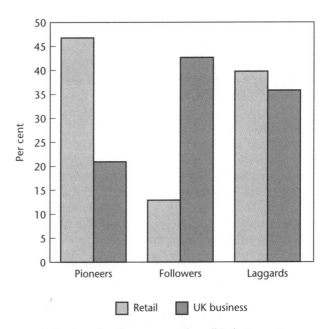

Figure 23.4 Degree of e-business involvement: retail vs all industry sectors
Source: KPMG Consulting (2001)

Further, work commissioned by telecommunications provider Energis (2001: 2) had commented, in a survey of the attitudes of over 250 European retailers to e-commerce in mid-2001:

While the financial markets are showing volatility in relation to technology and internet stocks, it is clear that e-tailers remain confident of future growth and are focused on their business goals. For the vast majority, their main concern is getting the people and technology in place to enable them to compete effectively.

Jo also reviewed the most recent evidence from the Internet audit firm Netvalue. Their reporting of 'e-Christmas' 2001 had been especially buoyant (Table 23.3). Jo was struck by a number of features of the December 2001 figures:

- the number of established retailers in the 'top 20' in terms of penetration as well as of conversion;
- the continued dominance of Amazon.com – attracting nearly one-fifth of all those online at some point during the month;
- despite this, the greater success of some traditional retailers in achieving high conversion rates, despite relatively low penetration.

Table 23.3 Top UK retail sites December 2001

Rank	Domain name	% reach	conversion rate
1	amazon.co.uk	19.77	21.03
2	amazon.com	12.50	6.04
3	tesco.com	8.96	14.26
4	argos.co.uk	8.87	13.51
5	comet.co.uk	5.74	5.55
6	bol.com	4.62	5.72
7	Jungle.com	4.41	14.52
8	dixons.co.uk	4.26	3.04
9	littlewoods.co.uk	4.18	10.57
10	pcworld.co.uk	4.15	8.24
11	whsmith.co.uk	4.05	4.12
12	Lastminute.com	3.63	4.98
13	cd-wow.com	3.32	ns
14	britannia-music.co.uk	3.20	34.55
15	wellbeing.com	3.04	15.01
16	johnlewis.com	3.00	3.18
17	adobe.com	2.90	3.53
18	littlewoods-index.com	2.87	6.10
19	ea.com	2.60	5.92
20	warnerbros.com	2.52	ns

Source: www.netvalue.com (2002)

The Tesco experience

One company directly relevant to Jo's research, which also figured prominently in the December figures, was Tesco (not least because of Eleanor's irritation with the company being held up against Hamilton's as a prime example of success online). Jo knew that she had to get a better handle on what Tesco had achieved, especially given all the disasters in the online market – particularly in grocery retailing. She turned to an Investext broker's report on the company.

Tesco, it appeared, had first trialled home shopping on the Internet in 1996, although it had dabbled in the area as early as 1980, when it had gained some experience operating a service using videotext at its Gateshead store. From these early beginnings Tesco now generated £500 million in turnover per annum from nearly 1,000,000 registered customers. Over 75,000 orders were processed each week, with an average order size of £85. Jo gasped – that was around three times the average basket size in Hamilton's and about twice Tesco's in-store basket size. The 300 outlets from which the Tesco.com service was available were able to reach some 94 per cent of the country's population. The Tesco.com web site already boasted an online market share of over 50 per cent – twice the company's conventional market share. Although the operation was notionally profitable, Jo noted that Tesco had reinvested much of this potential margin to extend the online business into non-foods – electricals, toys and books.

Tesco's operation was unconventional in that it used in-store picking and packing, rather than employing a dedicated warehouse. Jo frowned. She would need to check on the implications of that later. A dedicated fleet of vans delivered to homes during two-hour windows, using a variable delivery charge, which, at its maximum, was £5.

The broker estimated that in-store picking would give Tesco the potential of online sales of up to £1.6 billion before both the number of new stores that could be brought online and the picking capacity within those stores were exhausted. This was pretty impressive – up to 10 per cent of overall turnover could be generated that way and that was not insignificant. There would then probably need to be a move to warehouse-based distribution. It was also, the broker noted, a potentially interesting way to internationalise the business. Tesco had announced its intention to operate the home shopping business of the US Safeway stores on the west coast towards the end of 2001, using the experience and skills it had gained in the United Kingdom.

Prospects for retail delivery

The fulfilment aspect of e-commerce was something that had worried Jo for some time, particularly from the marketing point of view. Individual home delivery was something few traditional retail companies had any experience of and no other aspect of electronic commerce had been subject to more complaint by consumers than that of fulfilment. Over 35 per cent of UK consumers claimed that this was their most significant concern about e-commerce, according to recent survey evidence.

The so-called 'pure plays' had made an even bigger mess of it when they had tried (Figure 23.5) Contemporary debate appeared to centre around the identification of an appropriate operational design to deliver sustainable competitive advantage.

Whilst there was now a much better understanding of the implications of different business models for distribution costs, a paradox remained: as customer demand for home delivery increased the likelihood of consumers being at home to accept delivery was decreasing. A recent Department of Trade and Industry report – Foresight Retail Logistics Task Force (2001) – forecast that for grocery goods alone, annual home deliveries would increase tenfold between 2000 and 2005 from 6.6 million to 62.5 million. Should we have a share of that market, mused Jo – because if we don't it may be at the expense of our own store revenues, but if so, how do we achieve it?

Jo read further. It became clear that online grocers were presently using one of two models of distribution: store-based order picking or e-fulfilment centres. Whilst there were a number of other 'caching' strategies available (using intermediate locations as 'drop-off' points, for example, or collection boxes at the home – Figure 23.6) these were the two most popular routes to growth. Early work showed that e-fulfilment centres were cheaper to operate than store-based picking and packing operations, but companies such as Tesco had clearly found the latter more attractive, for a number of reasons. Jo wondered why.

She could see that the major challenge for store-based picking was the potential conflict that could arise between store-based customers and employees picking on behalf of remote customers; as a result, the store-based picking route has scaling limitations. She could also see that an e-fulfilment centre would carry with it particular benefits of its own.

Study: Internet Flower Sites Fail Mother's Day Test

By Lori Enos
E-Commerce Times
May 15, 2001

⊠ Send this Article   ⬚ Talkback
⬚ Print this Article   ⬚ Related Stories

With Mother's Day approaching, traffic to the major online flower retailers doubled in the first week of May – but the sites' delivery performance was shaky.   ● COMPLETE STORY ⤵

It was a disappointing Mother's Day for those who went online to send flowers, according to data released Tuesday by Nielsen//NetRatings and Keynote Systems.

The Internet performance firms reported that 25 percent of Mother's Day orders placed at three popular flower sites -- 1-800Flowers.com, Flowersdirect.com and Proflowers.com -- were not delivered on time.

In contrast, all four candy sites evaluated -- Chocoholic.com, Ethel M., Godiva, and See's Candies -- delivered 100 percent of Mother's Day orders on time, the firms said.

"Online users only care that they can get to the site, get there quickly and be confident that their orders will arrive on time," said Daniel Todd, chief technologist of public services at Keynote. "Therefore, sites need to be prepared."

Figure 23.5 Fulfilment failures in the United States
Source: www.Ecommercetimes.com (2001)

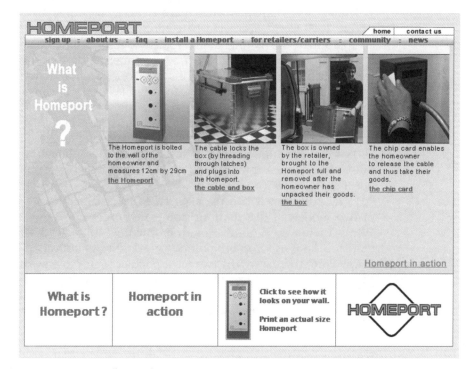

Figure 23.6 Home collection boxes
Source: Homeport (2001) (http://www.homeport.info/index.asp)

One company to try out warehouse-based fulfilment operations in the grocery sector had been Webvan, founded in the United States by a former managing partner of Andersen Consulting. Jo shuddered as she remembered the story:

> The company, along with HomeGrocer, which it bought last year, raised $1.2 billion – more than any other online retailer besides Amazon.com. With that war chest, it set out to build a futuristic nationwide network of distribution centers, expecting the service would become a phenomenon. Many signed up and loved the service. But the company has failed to attract the huge numbers of customers it needed – despite subsidizing the cost of delivery. Now Webvan hopes retrenchment will help them survive. (news clipping)

It had not survived. Having planned 26 automated warehouses across the United States, its most popular warehouse, in Oakland, Ca., only managed to achieve 25 per cent of its capacity in probably the world's most wired territory. Nevertheless, Jo noted that in the United Kingdom, both Asda and Sainsbury were exploring e-fulfilment centre options, although Sainsbury had started to consider a hybrid route to growth.

Hamilton's positioning

The final key component of Jo's assessment was to put all this information in the context of Hamilton's marketing strategy and positioning. Hamilton's was a niche retailer, appealing to an up-market, professional clientele, with relatively few stores in northern locations (Table 23.4). This contrasted with Asda, but particularly with Tesco, which commanded a much broader market appeal, but with concentrations amongst 25–34-year-olds. Hamilton's was especially noted for its strong presence in fresh foods and pioneering work in organic ranges. Its efforts in wines and spirits had also been rewarded through the 'Which? Wine Guides' for several years' running. The company's customers scored highly in terms of their loyalty and allegiance to the Hamilton's brand but, Jo wondered, were they the right kinds of people to embrace e-commerce?

Hamilton's market share had been increasing slowly, but was by no means growing at the speed of many of the company's competitors. For this reason the business had acquired a small number of a failing competitor's sites, which the business had spent a great deal of money reformatting (and which had eaten into

Table 23.4 Use of four facias for main grocery shopping 2001, main demographic components

	Tesco %	Asda %	Sainsbury %	Hamilton %
Total shoppers	20	20	19	7
Male	19	21	17	6
Female	21	19	21	7
16–24	16	24	11	3
25–34	18	26	18	6
35–44	22	24	19	7
45–54	19	22	20	12
55–64	29	13	21	10
65+	20	10	24	6
AB	29	12	24	15
C1	20	21	24	12
C2	20	24	14	3
D	15	26	14	1
E	11	15	17	4
London	22	11	37	17
South and south east	32	16	28	15
Midlands	16	19	22	7
South west	29	23	8	5
North	10	19	10	2
North west	16	29	12	2
Scotland and Wales	14	41	5	1

Note: Percentages refer to the demographic composition of shoppers and does not reflect the relative market share of each company.

Source: Market research

profits during 2001) (Table 23.5). Whilst sales had therefore grown respectably over the previous five years trading profit had not proved so consistent. Sales per square foot had also stagnated as many stores were over trading; likewise margins had come under significant pressure. In terms of priorities for investment, did e-commerce represent the correct internal use of resources?

Jo contemplated the brief she would have to write for the board; perhaps this would not be so straightforward after all.

Table 23.5 Hamilton's key performance indicators 1997–2001

Year ending February	1997	1998	1999	2000	2001
Turnover (incl. VAT) £m	1,545	1,693	1,784	1,899	2,095
Trading profit £m	71	74	54	59	47
Trading margin %	4.6	4.4	3.1	3.1	2.2
Sales per sq ft per year £	1,000	950	960	980	910

Discussion questions

1. Does e-commerce provide Hamilton's with a clear opportunity or would it prove an expensive diversion for the business? What would you advise Eleanor Goodley?

2. How do you think Hamilton's core customers would react to an online offer?

3. Would e-commerce provide Hamilton's with a viable route to expanding market share?

4. What are the pros and cons of the two main models of e-commerce fulfilment?

5. It has been suggested that there is only room for one or two key online players per category in B2C e-commerce. Why? Do you agree?

CHAPTER 24

The future of transaction systems

Steve Worthington

Introduction

It is appropriate that this chapter should be the concluding one of this book, as payment is usually the final action in the process of retailing goods and services. By the end of this chapter you should be able to appreciate:

- the evolution of different methods of payment, primarily in the United Kingdom, but also elsewhere around the world;
- the projected trends for these different methods over the next 10 years;
- retailer responses to these changes and their interests in entering the value chain of the payment system;
- the reasons behind the issuance of the so-called 'smart cards', based on integrated chips embedded into plastic cards and their use both as payment and loyalty mechanisms.

Towards a cashless society

In the United Kingdom the Credit Card Research Group (CCRG) is regarded as the authoritative voice on card payments. Its figures are based on information provided by all banks and building societies that issue credit cards (carrying the MasterCard and Visa acceptance marques) and debit cards (carrying the Switch/Solo or Visa/Electron acceptance marques).

The CCRG's review of card holder attitudes published in 2001 provides some evidence of the distance already travelled towards a cashless society and of the distance still to go:

- 94 per cent of card holders think that the credit card market is more competitive in 2001 than it was in 1999;
- 90 per cent of card holders are satisfied with their main card, with just 2 per cent dissatisfied;

- 83 per cent of card holders believe that credit cards have at least one advantage over other forms of borrowing;
- 43 per cent of card holders are unaware of having limited or zero liability for card fraud;
- 42 per cent of card holders can envisage a cashless society in which they make all their purchases – large and small – by card.

Thus whilst many card holders can see a cashless society on the horizon a more realistic appraisal of the current situation would be that we are moving to a less cash society, that is, one where the use of plastic payment cards continues to diminish the need for and the use of cash.

Cash

For the moment, however, cash remains the king of the payments market. The Association for Payment Clearing Services (APACS) offers an annual briefing, which provides an overview of the United Kingdom payments market. The APACS briefing for 2001 shows how cash has remained the majority payment method in volume terms over the past decade. APACS estimated that there were 28 billion cash payments in the United Kingdom in 1990 and, whilst this figure had dipped to 25 billion by 1998, in the year 2000 it rose again to 28 billion. In 2000 this represented nearly three-quarters of all payments in the United Kingdom and an estimated £260 billion in cash was acquired and used by individuals.

There are many reasons for the resilience of cash, such as that it is easier to access: in 1990 there were 17,300 automatic teller machines (ATMs) in the United Kingdom, by 2000 this number had doubled to 34,300. Over one-third of these were sited at locations such as supermarkets, railway stations and convenience stores. Higher daily allowances from these cash machines and the wider availability of 'cashback' at the point of sale (POS) are inducing consumers to move away from using paper cheques. Today two-thirds of adults (that is, those over 18 years of age) are regular users of ATMs.

The 34,300 ATMs in the United Kingdom dispensed £113 billion in 2 billion transactions in the year 2000 and APACS forecasts that the total volume of ATM withdrawals will rise to 2.9 billion by the year 2010. The greater preference amongst younger consumers to use cash machines and the ever increasing availability of ATMs are major factors behind these projections. The other substantial influence will be the introduction of automated benefit payments, which will result in many cash benefit recipients drawing cash from ATMs rather than over Post Office counters. In the year 2000 the Post Office dispensed £59 billion to around 14 million benefit recipients.

Nevertheless, APACS forecasts a decline in cash payment volumes over the next 10 years, from 28 billion in 2000 to 24 billion in 2010. One of the biggest influences on this will be the introduction of the electronic purse which, using smart card technology, will replace some low value cash payments, especially those made by coins. Cash, however, will remain the king of payment methods for the foreseeable future. Its familiarity, portability and ubiquity make it a formidable competitor to the other existing methods of payment.

Paper cheques

APACS reported that personal cheque volumes declined again in the year 2000, for the tenth year running. Table 24.1 charts payment trends from 1990 to 2000. The popularity of direct debits and plastic cards continues to erode the use of personal cheques for payment in areas such as regular bills and retail transactions. APACS forecasts that by 2010 only 4 million adults will use guaranteed cheques (as opposed to 10 million in 2000) and only 6 per cent of household bills will be paid by cheque.

One of the most notable changes in the payments markets since 1997 has been the fall in the volume of business-to-business cheques. Growth in electronic commerce and the use of electronic banking by businesses will continue to drive down the use of cheques. APACS forecasts that business-to-business cheque payments will fall from 846 million in 2000 to around 547 million in 2010. Cheque use for business-to-individual payments, such as payroll and pensions, is already low and volumes will continue to shrink as a result of substitution by direct debits.

The APACS 2001 briefing concludes that whilst there will remain some personal customers who prefer to use cheques and some retailers who will continue to refuse to accept credit or debit cards, cheques will become a minority payment method. In addition, personal cheque payment volume will decline from 1.4 billion in 2000 to around 890 million in 2010.

Debit cards

These plastic payment cards were introduced into the United Kingdom in 1987 and were positioned as a direct substitute for the paper cheque. Worthington (1988) details the introduction of the debit card and the successful resistance by retailers to the merchant service charges (MSCs) that the banks tried to impose.

The debit card has been a huge success in the United Kingdom, with four out of five adults holding one. Currently there are around 50 million in circulation under the acceptance marques of Switch/Solo and Visa/Electron. Over half of all debit card holders are regular users and in 2000 made an average 108 debit card payments. Total debit card spending grew by 23 per cent in 2000 to £79 billion, with 25p of every £1 spent on the high street being with a debit card. The average value of a debit card purchase is £32.50p with the average annual spend being £1,610. APACS reports that the volume of debit card purchases in 2000 was 2.3 billion, a 13.1 per cent increase on 1999. Table 24.1 illustrates this trend since 1990. APACS also forecasts that the number of debit card payments is likely to double over the next 10 years to 4.5 billion per annum.

Debit cards are not only used in locations such as supermarkets and petrol stations, but increasingly in other areas such as the service and utility sectors, for instance to pay dentist or electricity bills. Debit cards are multi-functional as they are also used to access cash through the ATM network and for cashback at the POS. The number of places and opportunities where a card holder can use a debit card will continue to grow and hence according to APACS there is still considerable

Table 24.1 Payment trends 1990–2000

Total transaction volumes in the UK (millions)	1990	1991	1992	1993	1994	1995	1996	1997	1998	1999	2000
All plastic card purchases	930	1,104	1,316	1,488	1,723	2,023	2,413	2,759	3,094	3,537	3,914
Debit card	192	359	522	659	808	1,004	1,270	1,503	1,736	2,062	2,337
Credit and charge card	690	699	724	748	815	908	1,025	1,128	1,224	1,344	1,452
Store card (estimate)	48	46	70	82	100	109	118	128	134	131	125
Plastic card withdrawals at ATMs and counters	1,045	1,112	1,199	1,277	1,372	1,512	1,656	1,809	1,917	2,025	2,092
Direct debit, standing orders, direct credits	1,741	1,848	1,962	2,047	2,196	2,042	2,613	2,826	3,056	3,255	3,470
Cheques	3,975	3,882	3,728	3,559	3,430	3,283	3,203	3,083	2,986	2,854	2,700
For payment	3,537	3,450	3,332	3,163	3,074	2,938	2,901	2,838	2,757	2,641	2,515
For cash acquisition	438	432	396	396	356	345	302	245	229	213	185
Total non-cash (plastic card, automated and paper)	7,691	7,946	8,205	8,371	8,721	9,220	9,885	10,477	11,053	11,672	12,176
Cash payments (estimate)	28,023	28,022	27,845	27,273	26,179	26,270	26,318	25,540	25,309	25,596	27,910
Post Office order book payments and passbook withdrawals	1,061	1,056	1,108	1,144	1,127	1,163	1,114	1,066	1,017	962	880
Total transaction volumes	36,775	37,025	37,158	36,788	36,026	36,654	37,318	37,083	37,379	38,230	40,966
The UK ATM network (banks and building societies)											
Number of ATMs (at year end)	17,300	18,100	18,700	19,100	20,000	20,900	22,100	23,200	24,600	28,300	34,300
ATM withdrawals (millions)	1,012	1,085	1,169	1,242	1,335	1,471	1,599	1,745	1,850	1,968	2,027
ATM cards (millions)	45	48	49	51	52	55	57	60	65	69	71

Source: APACS (2001)

potential for more people to catch the debit card habit. Most debit cards issued under the Switch or Visa acceptance marques are linked to current or savings accounts held with the card issuer and most transactions on these cards are offline (that is they are batched and then transmitted overnight to the bank). Solo and Electron were developed to allow online (real-time) transactions. Thus all transactions with these acceptance marques can be immediately checked and debited from the funds held in the card holder's account. Despite its success, however, the total value of debit card spending is still less than that for credit cards, reflecting the longer pedigree of the credit card and the fact that it is often used for higher value transactions.

Credit cards

Introduced into the United Kingdom in 1966, there are now over 50 million of these cards in issue, branded with either the MasterCard or Visa acceptance marques. The CCRG reports that in 2000 total credit card spending was £84 billion, an increase of 19 per cent on 1999, that the average value of a credit card purchase was £56.40p and the average credit card spend was £1,677. Furthermore, 20p of every £1 spent at high street retailers is with a credit card, and if this is combined with the debit card figure then 45p of every £1 spent in the high street is with a plastic payment card.

The credit card business is one of the most competitive sectors in the UK economy and the market has been transformed since the mid-1990s by the arrival of new card issuers who have grown to become major players. These newcomers include credit card issuers from the United States such as Capital One and MBNA and UK retailers such as Sainsbury and Tesco. By product innovation (balance transfers, teaser rates) and aggressive marketing (direct mail, in-store promotions) the newcomers and the already established players have succeeded in making the credit card an increasingly popular source of consumer credit. Such cards had 45 per cent of the £12 billion growth in outstanding unsecured (that is, non-mortgage) personal borrowing in 2000 and the total of outstanding balances on MasterCard and Visa credit cards was £34,341 million by the end of the year 2000.

A considerable proportion of credit card holders (between one-third and one-half) pay off their outstanding balance in full every month. Their reasons for using a credit card are twofold: first, to take advantage of the interest-free period and secondly, to participate in the incentive schemes run by a number of card issuers. The remaining credit card holders who do take the opportunity to 'revolve' their debt, pay interest at the prevailing annual percentage rate, as determined by their card issuer.

Credit cards are also the most popular way for adults to purchase items over the Internet. APACS estimates are that 60 million card payments were made online in 2000, three-quarters by credit card and one-quarter by debit card. The numbers of women making online purchases was thought to be equal to the number of men and although Internet buyers are concentrated in the lower age bands one in six of online buyers is aged 55 or over.

APACS concludes that although there are some signs of consolidation in the credit card market, particularly between card issuers, robust growth in credit card use by individuals is expected to continue. Use over the Internet is projected to grow strongly and the demographic base of card holders could widen to include more adults in the socio-economic groups C2 and D (the so-called under-served or sub-prime market). Thus APACS forecasts that personal credit card volumes are expected to rise from 1.3 billion in 2000 to 2.3 billion in 2010. There would also be a related rise in the value of credit card payments.

Besides personal credit card payments there has also been rapid growth in the use of credit cards for business-related purchases. Key factors underpinning this are the provision of management information and other value-added services to the business organisation, for example the control of employee expenditure on travel and entertainment (T & E). APACS recorded around 100 million business card transactions in 2000 and forecast that this will grow to around 300 million in 2010.

Charge cards

The original plastic payment cards were the T & E cards of Diners Club and American Express, and both of these still feature in today's payment market. Worthington (2001) gives a history of the development of the plastic payment card. The charge card is different from the credit card, in that all of the purchases made on a charge card are paid off in full at the end of the account period, that is each month. With a credit card, the card holder can choose not to pay the full amount and hence revolve some of the debt and pay interest on it. 'Revolving' credit cards are then different from charge cards, the latter sometimes being referred to as 'deferred debit' cards.

In order to fund their activities and make a profit the charge card issuers ask retailers to pay higher merchant service charges than for credit card transactions. This is because the charge cards do not have an income stream from interest payments and purchases made on charge cards are often of a higher value than those made with credit cards. The MSC is an *ad valorem* (that is a percentage of the total value of the transaction) payment paid by the retailer to the financial institution. For charge card payments it averages around 4 per cent; for credit card payments it averages around 1.5 per cent. Some retailers refuse to pay the MSC associated with charge cards and hence do not accept these cards as payment methods. As a consequence of this and other changes in the market, the volume and value of charge card transactions have stagnated in the United Kingdom. This has resulted in American Express moving into the credit card market and targeting younger card holders with its 'Blue' credit card. Retailer resistance to MSCs has also produced another variant of the credit card, the store card.

Store cards

Also known as private-label credit cards, these are cards issued by retailers to their customers. They enable purchases to be made in stores(s) and paid for later, either in full or by using the revolving credit facility. There are currently no authoritative statistics for store cards in the United Kingdom, but estimates place the number of cards on issue at around 18 million and APACS estimates that the volumes of transactions in 2000 was 125 million (Table 24.1). Some major retailers such as Marks & Spencer, the John Lewis Partnership and IKEA run their own store card operations, whilst others use third party providers such as GE Capital and Creation, to both finance and operate their store cards. Marks & Spencer has around 5 million of its own Chargecards in issue and it has used its store card customer database to cross-sell a variety of other financial services. The Marks & Spencer Chargecard was also originally the only credit card accepted in the company's stores, as it tried to minimise its MSCs (Worthington 1994). This situation changed in March 2000, when the company finally decided to accept MasterCard and Visa branded credit cards.

The sections above have described both the evolution of and the future prospects for the different methods of payment in the United Kingdom. The United States credit and debit card markets form the largest payment card market in the world, but the United Kingdom is the second largest and arguably the more sophisticated since it has equal numbers of credit and debit cards, whilst the United States is very credit card oriented. Other countries are exhibiting trends similar to that in the United Kingdom, for example, Worthington and Edwards (2000) report on the changes in the payments market in Australia, whilst Worthington (1998) reported on developments in Japan. There are a number of different players involved in each country, all of whom have a role to play in the evolution of the payments markets and in the movement towards a cashless society. The primary players are the card associations of MasterCard and Visa; the card issuing financial institutions that are members of the card associations; the banks who receive the transactions from the retailers; the consumers and card holders who choose which cards to hold and use. Finally there are the retailers, which choose which cards to accept as payment from their customers. Retailers, both individually and collectively, have increasingly strong views on payment methods and particularly so for plastic payment cards, as these become increasingly dominant at the POS.

Retailers' responses

All payment methods involve retailers incurring some form of cost and naturally they will endeavour to reduce these, whilst at the same time taking account of how best to serve the customer at the POS. Taking the existing payment methods in turn: cash is still the most popular as measured by volume of transactions. The retailer's costs include handling, counting, transportation, security and paying cash into the financial institution where they have their account. Retailers attempt to reduce these costs by offering other means of payment, particularly by plastic card and facilitated by the development of electronic funds transfer at the point of sale (EFTPOS) terminals. Some retailers both reduce costs and add services by offering cashback (where consumers use the POS as an ATM and draw cash directly from the retailer's till). This decreases their cash holding and is charged as a debit card transaction value (that is, the MSC is a fixed sum (pence) per transaction). Cashback has proved extremely popular, both for cash-rich retailers and cash-poor consumers, offering benefits to both at no extra cost.

Cheques also incur a charge when retailers pay them into their financial institution for clearing. The clearing process takes a number of days before value is realised and there are also handling, security and transportation costs. Hence with the introduction of the debit card retailers were keen to ensure that the costs to them were the same as for cheques – a fixed fee per transaction. Also given that the transaction via the EFTPOS terminal was quicker and more secure they could receive the value earlier than with cheques. As debit cards were also used as cheque guarantee cards retailers had the perfect opportunity when a customer was writing a cheque to suggest that the debit card be used as the payment method.

The debit card itself was warmly received by retailers and the number of outlets where debit cards are accepted still exceeds those for credit cards. This is because, pro rata, more consumers hold and use debit cards than credit cards and because the bank charges a fixed fee. When introducing a new payment method there is always the conundrum of the chicken and the egg: which comes first? Is it the number of acceptance points where the payment method can be used or the number of people holding and willing to use the new payments method? In the case of the debit card retailers could see the advantages of accepting this method of payment and hence the acceptance network grew rapidly and the conundrum was resolved.

The credit card too was welcomed, for besides offering a more convenient and portable way of payment it offered card holders a line of credit to facilitate their spending at the POS. This was not lost on retailers, many of whom then introduced their own private-label credit cards (store cards). Besides offering credit to their customers it also meant that they did not have to pay the MSC associated with the MasterCard and Visa credit cards or the American Express and Diners Club charge cards. These MSCs are again based on an *ad valorem* system. The origins of this lie in the history of charge and credit cards (Worthington 2001).

The smart card

Retailers are working together to fight the costs associated with the introduction of so-called 'smart cards'. These cards, with a chip embedded into the plastic card, are rapidly replacing the magnetic stripe technology associated with plastic payment cards over the past three decades. There are two fundamental reasons behind this, one short term, the other more medium term. The immediate reason is that the magnetic stripe technology is very prone to fraud and in particular to the creation of counterfeit cards. According to APACS fraud losses on UK-issued cards in 2000 rose to £292.6 million, up by 55 per cent on 1999. The majority of this increase was attributed to the use of counterfeit cards (+104 per cent) and to fraudulent remote transactions (mail order, telesales and Internet purchases). Counterfeiting represents the biggest proportion of card fraud, accounting for 35 per cent of total fraud losses and, to combat this, the United Kingdom is introducing smart cards.

All ATMs and EFTPOS terminals will have to be upgraded to read the chip on the new cards. It is also highly likely that card holder verification will be by personal identification number (PIN), rather than signature. PIN pads will therefore have to be attached to all terminals. UK retailers are reluctant to upgrade their own terminals as they see most of the benefits of fraud reduction going to the card issuers. If fraud is to be reduced then retailers will expect an even lower MSC.

The more medium-term attraction of smart cards is that the chip enables a number of functions to be carried out by the same piece of plastic. Whereas at the moment consumers need to carry separate credit, debit and loyalty cards, with a smart card all these functions could in theory be held on the chip of one card. Such potential multi-functionality raises the issue of who will be the issuer of the chip card. UK retailers are in a good position to be issuers of such cards – Sainsbury and Tesco already issue plastic payment cards and have loyalty schemes, whilst Boots is already using chip cards in both payment and loyalty functions.

The Boots Advantage card is the company's loyalty card and there are currently over 14 million in issue. All carry the customers' loyalty points earned on the chip. Boots, in partnership with the financial service provider Egg, also issued an Advantage credit card, where again the loyalty points earned are held on the chip. Such cards offer card holders portability and instant redemption of their loyalty points. They also provide the issuer with information, both from the application form and the ongoing use of the card. Worthington (2000) describes how loyalty cards are used by retailers to provide information for better customer segmentation, merchandising in store and for selling information to suppliers.

Smart cards will also provide the technology for the development of the electronic purse, which will enable consumers to pay for low value transactions by plastic cards. There is a large potential market for a coin substitute in the United Kingdom, with APACS estimating that there were over 9 billion coin payments below £1 in value in 2000. When such a product becomes available we would finally see plastic cards used in all three time-based payment situations: credit cards – pay later, debit card – pay now and electronic purse – pay before. When this occurs we will finally see the onset of the cashless society!

Discussion questions

1. Using the APACS website, www.apacs.org.uk, find out the latest figures on payment trends and discuss the reasons behind these.

2. Identify which multiple retailers offer their own plastic payment cards and describe the advantages to both customers and retailers of such payment cards.

3. Discuss the advantages and disadvantages to retailers of upgrading their EFTPOS terminals to accept smart cards and compare these to the costs and benefits faced by the card-issuing financial institutions.

4. Describe, using examples wherever possible, how you would introduce the electronic purse product, bearing in mind the conundrum of what comes first: acceptance locations or cards held and used?

Answers to self-assessment questions

Chapter 4

Question 3

Performance measures tend to be both financial and non-financial. In addition they are usually quantifiable and can be measured across a defined time period. Examples of financial performance measures include:

- gross/net profit;
- gross/net margin;
- ROI;
- ROCE;
- sales turnover;
- like for like sales.

Examples of non-financial performance indicators could include:

- staff turnover;
- staff absenteeism;
- the number of customer complaints;
- the number of delivery errors;
- the length of the order cycle time.

Chapter 7

Question 1

At the time of writing the following are most in favour: (a) 'high street' shop units in the prime areas of large town and city centres; (b) regional shopping centres and large shopping malls within city centres; and (c) retail warehouses. In the case of regional shopping centres and retail warehouses, their value reflects the increasing scarcity of good quality new schemes, due in part to planning restrictions.

Question 2

You should expect to find that the planned parts of the town centre are occupied mainly by international or national multiples, especially in clothing, footwear and personal or fashion goods. This reflects the importance of good location and purpose-built premises in secure, climate-controlled surroundings. In the unplanned part of the centre a much wider mix of retail types should be expected: fashion multiples in the best 'high street' sites, local companies and independents selling a wide range of goods in the lower-rent 'secondary' parts of the town centre.

Chapter 10

Question 1

There are no 'correct' answers to this question. The values that individuals may identify include quality, status, professionalism, discernment and sophistication. There are many reasons why a person may subscribe to these values, for example a sense of belonging, a statement of individuality or an indication of lifestyle.

Question 2

Many people who have not studied the concept of marketing usually equate marketing with sales. Some individuals are familiar with the four Ps. That is Product, Place, Price and Promotion. As long as a business ensures it gets these four variables right then it is a successful marketing business. In this chapter you should have learned that marketing is much more than this. Whilst sales are obviously an important part of the delivery of value, marketing embodies a much broader, more encompassing approach that starts and ends with the satisfaction of customer values.

Question 3

The core of an answer to this question should be the realisation that the physical product is only the starting point for business and marketing success. Whilst a range of goods at competitive prices may be the retailer's 'stake', the level of competition in retailing means that others have the same stake.

Potential customers will become actual customers if the retailer or wholesaler is able to add customer-related values to the basic product or service. Amongst the factors you listed you should have included the following:

- location;
- level of personal service;
- facilities for specific customers, for example the disabled or aged; customer bonuses for either regular or large sales or both.

Chapter 13

Question 1

More and more retail companies are recognising the need for strategic planning of their workforce, that is, how many people retail companies need now and in the future given the internal and external demand and supply of people. Once a strategic plan is in place a workforce plan is developed that examines how people will be recruited, utilised, developed and retained by the company. The HRM strategies retail companies need to consider to ensure they maintain an effective workforce are listed below, together with some of the issues surrounding these strategies in retailing.

Recruitment and retention
- availability of labour (types of employees);
- graduate recruitment (retailing has an image problem with graduates – Broadbridge 2001b; 2001c);
- regional variations – part-time workers are more difficult to recruit in the south-east of England;
- controlling absence management;
- controlling labour turnover.

Motivation and performance
- employ motivational strategies in order to retain employees: job design techniques (such as job rotation, job enlargement, job enrichment and team-working), reward systems and goal setting (such as financial rewards, store competitions, praise, recognition and feedback, involvement, autonomy and responsibility), management style and organisation climate (such as relationship between management and staff, empowerment, ideas held about the business and the people who work for it);
- labour management;
- labour scheduling and flexibility to enhance productivity levels;
- welfare management;
- work–life balance.

Developing effective people
- training for the job (the level of training is not always high);
- performance management and appraisal systems;
- career development issues (including mobility issues, enhancement of individual status of employees and progression opportunities, achieving a work–life balance, family-friendly policies);
- development of client-oriented skills and multi-skilling.

Communication and influence
- changes in work organisation have led to increased pressure to establish more teamwork and internal communication between workers;
- difficulties of the fragmentation of units;
- difficulties of head office and store communications;
- influencing others through power and communication;
- managing conflict.

Question 2

The introduction of new technology has impacted on people's jobs in various ways, and has resulted in various changes such as:

- the introduction of EPoS, EFTPoS and laser scanning systems at checkouts;
- the automation or computerisation of reordering systems;
- improved goods handling into stores and on to shelves;
- automatic calculation of replenishment cycles and order placements with suppliers;
- the pre-processing of many products (such as butchery and bakery);
- the use of computer models to administer labour productivity;
- the use of planograms and merchandising systems; these are visual plans showing the physical allocation of products within a grouping to provide a standardised in-store merchandising presentation (but room can be left for initiative or a default option);
- the automatic calculation of sales data and use of computers to indicate profitability (for example direct product profitability systems), but this can also lead to advanced decision making.

It is worth pointing out here that IT is neutral. It is how it is applied that enskills or deskills.

Question 3

Economic pressures (such as the need to increase competitiveness and reduce costs) are the most important reasons for introducing flexible working practices. Some of the flexible working practices that either exist or may be adopted in the future by retail companies include the working:

- *annual hours*: the replacement of a weekly-hours contract with one that covers the whole year. This provides the company with savings in labour costs, as well as helping to reduce absenteeism and improve teamworking and health and safety. For the employee it can result in stress through insecurity, and having to work unsociable hours because of a fear of losing the job.
- *term-time working*: which enables employees to remain on a permanent contract (either full time or part time) but gives them the right to take (unpaid) leave during school holidays. This helps to retain female staff, on whom many retailers rely.
- *zero hours*: in which employees are not guaranteed any work but are required to be available as and when the employer needs them. This provides cost savings but there are few benefits to the employees.
- *teleworking*: where employees work from home either totally or for part of their working week. With increasingly sophisticated technologies some retail companies have explored the feasibility of introducing such forms of work for some of their payroll staff.
- *call centres*: these have grown substantially over the last few years within some service areas. The growth of home and Internet shopping has meant the introduction of call centres to handle orders. Call centres could also be used to deal with general customer queries and complaints as part of the retail companies' commitment to maintain high customer service levels. Alternatively, these functions could be diverted to the employee's home to enable teleworking.

- *Subcontracting and outsourcing*: with the increasing range of specialist activities associated with retailing, some forms of work may be subcontracted or out-sourced to specialist service companies. Outsourcing is where the provision of a service or a specific retail function is handed over by the retail company to a third party to perform on its behalf. It differs from subcontracting in that the service/function was previously performed by the retail company; in sub-contracting, work has not customarily been carried out in-house. Amongst its benefits include an improved business focus, accessibility to world-class capa-bilities and accelerated re-engineering. An example of outsourcing in retailing is Sears, which outsourced its financial department. Outsourcing reduces the numbers employed by the main retail company and may cause changes in employment figures as indicated at the beginning of this chapter.

As more functions become increasingly specialised so it is expected the trend towards subcontracting traditional retail employment to specialised services will increase, which may further cause definitional problems for statistical purposes. This has already been witnessed by the types of retailing that may not appear on official statistics, such as the retailing of services.

Some of the benefits to employers include: reduced costs; increased pro-ductivity; increased competitiveness; improved customer service; improved ability to recruit and retain staff; increased staff motivation and commitment; better communication; improved ability to manage and respond to change; reduced absenteeism; improved teamworking; better organised training; a more open style of management.

The benefits to some employees include: improved ability to create a healthier balance between work and home commitments; increased job satisfaction; better security of employment; a stable income; the opportunity to develop new skills.

Question 4

Macro-level changes that can impact on the retail employment structure and the demand for labour can be considered by undertaking a PEST analysis.

Political
- government legislation;
- minimum wage;
- sunday trading;
- opening hours;
- political stability;
- European Union;
- the City;
- PPGG – planning regulations out of town.

Economic
- recession/boom;
- increased cost of employment;
- competitive environment;
- market concentration;

- UK move to post-industrial economy;
- inflation/consumer expenditure/interest rates;
- unemployment.

Social Environment
- demographics – age;
- working women;
- change in lifestyle;
- increased mobility;
- early retirement;
- job sharing;
- new approaches to working;
- standard of living/distribution of income;
- education and health;
- increased leisure time;.
- individualism.

Technological
- polarisation of skills;
- communications;
- teleshopping/Internet;
- quality and service;
- new products;
- speed of change, adoption of new technology.

Chapter 16

Question 2

Despite significant improvements in forecasting there will always remain a certain degree of uncertainty. Whilst it is acknowledged that removing forecasting altogether may be an impossible task, emphasis has been upon reducing the length of the forecasting period. As collaboration within the supply chain has become a more widely accepted management practice, detailed discussions with suppliers have looked at ways of flexibly responding to customer demand. Close communications (sometimes on a day-to-day basis) is one element to this approach. Reducing the forecasting period benefits the retailer in that orders can be more closely aligned to customer needs and stock-outs are less likely to occur. From the supplier's perspective, production can be kept 'lean' and the investment in 'work in progress' minimised. The difficulties in achieving this level of cooperation however should not underestimated. It requires both parties to be open and honest and be prepared to collaborate and share information. This may be contrary to the standard practice within the industry or against the current culture of the company.

Chapter 22

Question 1

There are a number of different reasons why it is important to understand the future. Perhaps one of the most important from a retail context is the need to remain competitive in the long term. For a retailer it is important to have an idea of what the future may or may not bring. Whilst it is obviously impossible to consider all events and all scenarios it is often useful to have a contingency plan should a series of events occur. Without an attempt to look to the future and build a series of scenarios this task becomes almost impossible.

Question 2

There is no 'correct' answer to this question. Whilst you may choose any retail sector it is sometimes more interesting to select a relatively under researched area, for example retail pharmacies, opticians or the duty free sector. You may wish to use the headings of political, economic, social, technological, environmental and legislative (PESTEL) as a guiding framework. As you are aware, each of these headings can be broken down further to help you identify the specific influencing factors. It is important that you avoid developing a 'wish list' of everything that has occurred in the sector over the last decade. The aim of the exercise is to get you to consider in hindsight (which we all know is always an exact science) what the major external influences have been on the sector of your choice. If you are sufficiently critical you may only identify two or three truly influential factors. You then need to ask yourself if you were undertaking this exercise 10 years ago whether you could have identified these factors and predicted the influence they would have. (If you feel you could, there may be a career in retailing beckoning.)

Question 3

Although your answer will be dependent upon the sector you choose one could suggest evidence of the following:

- *Environmental theory*: the broadscale 'environmental' change in social attitudes to waste, conspicuous consumption and the planet has created the 'environment' in which The Body Shop, Body, Face Place and others have prospered.
- *Cyclical theory*: the re-emergence of discount retailing in many sectors may be attributed to existing institutions and retailers 'trading up', leaving an opportunity for operators such as Aldi and Netto to introduce discount/low cost formats.
- *Conflict theory*: the reaction of cash and carry operators, wholesalers in general and even food superstore operators to the 'threat' of conflict with warehouse clubs such as Costco and Price Club.

References

Abernathy, F. H., Dunlop, J. T., Hammond, J. H. and **Weil, D.** (1999) *A Stitch in Time: Lean Retailing and the Transformation of Manufacturing – Lessons from the Apparel and Textile Industries*, New York: Oxford University Press Inc.

ACAS (1994) Absence and Labour Turnover, ACAS Handbook, London.

ACI (1994) The Economic Benefits of Air Transport, Geneva: Air Transport Action Group.

ACI (1998) ACI World Wide and Regional Forecasts, Geneva.

Alexander, N. (1997) *International Retailing*, Oxford: Blackwell.

Alexander, N. and **Akehurst, G.** (1999) *The Emergence of Modern Retailing, 1750–1950*, London: Frank Cass.

Alexander, N., Colgate, M., Freathy, P., Guy, C. and **Reynolds, J.** (2000) *Retailing 2010*, Foresight Retail and Consumer Services Panel, Office of Science and Technology, Department of Trade and Industry, DTI/Pub 5173/3k/12/00/NP URN 00/1276.

Ambrose, G. (1996) *An Investigation of Labour Turnover with Specific Reference to Penny's Supermarkets*, unpublished MBA in Retailing dissertation, University of Stirling.

AMS (1997) AMS Marketing Service AG, Action Alliance (Powerpoint handout).

Ang, S. (2000) 'The influence of physical, beneficial and image properties on responses to parallel imports', *International Marketing Review*, 17(6): 509–24.

Anon (1998) 'What the brokers say', *Daily Telegraph*, 4 April, B2.

Ansoff, I. (1965) *Corporate Strategy*, Harmondsworth: Penguin.

Arndt, J. (1972) 'Temporal lags in comparative retailing, *Journal of Marketing*, 36(1): 40–5.

Association for Payment Clearing Services (2001) Payments markets briefing, London.

Backman, J. (1957) 'Characteristics of retail trade employment', *Journal of Retailing*, Summer: 79–92.

Bagozzi, R.P. (1975) 'Marketing as exchange', *Journal of Marketing*, 39(4), 32–9.

Baker, M.J. (1985) *Marketing Strategy and Management*, Basingstoke: Macmillan.

Barke, M., Braidford, P., Houston, M., Hunt, A., Lincoln, I., Morphet, C., Stone, I. and Walker, A. (2000) *Students in The Labour Market: Nature, Extent and Implications of Term-time Employment among University of Northumbria Undergraduates*, Research Brief No 215, London: Department for Education and Employment.

Bentham, J. (1907) *An introduction to the Principles of Morals and Legislation*, Oxford: Oxford University Press.

Bingman, C. (1996) 'Airports as retail malls? What are the criteria for a successful airport retail mall?', paper presented at Airports: a major trading opportunity, Airports Council International Conference, Marseille.

Bowlby, R. (2000) *Carried Away: The invention of Modern Shopping*, London: Faber & Faber.

Bowman, E. and Asch, D. (1987) *Strategic Management*, London: Macmillan.

Bridle, R. (1998) *The Implications of Labour Turnover within a Retail Organisation*, unpublished MBA in Retailing Dissertation, University of Stirling.

Broadbridge, A. (1991) 'Images and goods: women in retailing', in N. Redclift and M.T. Sinclair (eds), *Working Women: International Perspectives on Labour and Gender Ideology*, London: Routledge.

Broadbridge, A. (1995) 'Female and male earnings differentials in retailing', *The Service Industries Journal*, 15(1) 14–34.

Broadbridge, A. (1996) 'Female and male managers: equal progression?' *The International Review of Retail, Distribution and Consumer Research*, 6(3): 259–79.

Broadbridge, A. (1997) 'Why earnings differentials are different for men and women in retailing', *The Service Industries Journal*, 17(2): 221–36.

Broadbridge, A. (1998) 'Barriers in the career progression of retail managers', *The International Review of Retail, Distribution and Consumer Research*, 8(1): 53–78.

Broadbridge, A. (1999) 'Retail managers: stress and the work–family relationship', *International Journal of Retail and Distribution Management*, 27(9): 374–82.

Broadbridge, A. (2001a) 'Retail managers: their work stresses and coping strategies, *Journal of Retailing and Consumer Services*, 9(3): 173–83.

Broadbridge, A. (2001b) 'Graduate careers: is retailing a serious option?' *Institute for Retail Studies Working Paper 0101*, University of Stirling.

Broadbridge, A. (2001c) 'Industry urged to improve image of retailing as a career', *Retail Week*, 15 June: 39.

Broadbridge, A. and Swanson, V. (2001) 'The impact of part-time employment on students' adjustment to university life', *Department of Marketing Working Paper 0201*, University of Stirling.

Brockway, G. (1993) 'Limited paternalism and the salesperson: a reconsideration', *Journal of Business Ethics*, 12: 275–9.

Brown, J.R., Lusch, R.F. and Muehling, D.D. (1983) 'Conflict and power–dependence relations in retailer–supplier channels', *Journal of Retailing*, 59(4) 53–81.

Brown, S. (1987) 'Institutional change in retailing: a review and synthesis', *European Journal of Marketing*, 21(6) 5–36.

Bubb, N. (1992) 'Retailing and the City', in D. Ricketts (ed.), *Risk and Opportunities in Retailing in the 1990s*, London: Newman Books.

Burnett, J.J. (1996) 'What service marketers need to know about the mobility-disabled consumer', *Journal of Services Marketing*, 10(3) 3–20.

Burt, S. (1986) 'The Carrefour Group: the first 25 years', *International Journal of Retailing*, 1(3) 54–78.

Burt, S. and Sparks, L. (2002) 'Corporate branding, retailing and retail internationalisation', *Corporate Reputation Review*, 5(2/3): 194–212.

Cadman, D. and Topping, R. (1995) *Property Development*, London: E and F&N Spon.

CACI (2000) CACI Geographical Information Systems Database, London: CACI.

Carter, C.R. and Ellram, L.M. (1998) 'Reverse logistics: a review of the literature and framework for future investigation', *Journal of Business Logistics*, 19(1): 85–102.

Ceccini, P. (1988) 1992: *The European Challenge*, Aldershot: Wildwood House.

Central Statistical Office (1996) *Business Monitor, SDA25, Distributive and Service Trades, 1994 Retailing*, London: Business Statistics Office, HMSO.

Chandler, A. (1962) *Strategy and Structure*, Cambridge, MA: MIT Press.

Channon, D.K. (1973) *The Strategy and Structure of British Enterprise*, London: Macmillan.

Christopher, M. (1998) *Logistics and Supply Chain Management*, London: FT/Prentice Hall.

CIES (2002) Food Marketing Newsletter, January – special supplement.

Competition Commission (2000) *Supermarkets*, Stationery Office, Norwich, Cm 4842.

Cooper, C.L. and Lewis, S. (1993) *The Workplace Revolution: Managing Today's Dual-Career Families*, London: Kogan Page.

Cooper, J., Browne, M. and Peters, M. (1991) *European Logistics*. Oxford: Blackwell.

Coopers & Lybrand (1996) 'European value chain analysis study: final report', ECR Europe, Utrecht.

Cordero, R.A. (1988) 'Aristotle and fair deals', *Journal of Business Ethics*, 7: 681–90.

Corporate Intelligence (1998) *UK Retail Report*, London: Corporate Intelligence.

Craven, N. (2001) 'Next extends sourcing activity to North Africa', *Drapers Record*, 15 September: 12–13.

Credit Card Research Group (2001) *Pocket Statistics*, London: CCRG.

Cully, M. and **Woodland, S.** (1998) 'Trade union membership and recognition 1996–97: an analysis of data from the Certification Officer and the LFS,' *Labour Market Trends* 106(7): 353–64.

Cunningham, S. (1998a) 'Criticism acts as a spur to chief as Next loses fashionable tag', *The Times – Business News*, 28 March.

Cunningham, S. (1998b) 'Next star wanes in wake of profit warning', *The Times – Business News*, 27 March.

Cyert, R. and **March, J.** (1963) *A Behavioural Theory of the Firm*, New York: Prentice Hall.

Dandy, J. (1996) 'The ethical route to service quality at John Lewis Partnership', *Managing Service Quality*, 5(5): 17–19.

Davidson, W.R., Sweeney, D.J. and **Stampfl, R.W.** (1988) *Retailing Management*, 6th edn, New York: Wiley.

Davies, G. (1996) 'Supply-chain relationships', in F. Buttle (ed.), *Relationship Marketing – Theory and Practice*, London: Paul Chapman.

Davies, G. (1998) 'Retail brands and the theft of identity', *International Journal of Retail & Distribution Management*, 26(4): 140–6.

Davies, R. (1995) *Retail Planning Policies in Western Europe*, London: Routledge.

Dawson, J. (1995) 'Retail change in the European Community', in R. Davies (ed.), *Retail Planning Policies in Western Europe*, London: Routledge.

Dawson, J. (2000a) *Future Patterns of Retailing in Scotland*, Edinburgh: Scottish Executive Central Research Unit.

Dawson, J. (2000b) 'Retailing at century end: some challenges for management and research', *International Review of Retail, Distribution and Consumer Research*, 10: 119–48.

Dawson, J. and **Burt, S.** (1998) 'European retailing: dynamics, restructuring and development issues', in D. Pinder (ed.), *The New Europe: Economy, Society and Environment*, Chichester: Wiley.

Department of the Environment (1993) Planning Policy Guidance note 13: Transport, London: HMSO.

Dickins, I. and **Ford, A.** (1996) 'The economics of pedestrianisation', *Town & Country Planning*, March: 92–3.

Doganis, R. (1992) *The Airport Business*, London: Routledge.

Doganis, R. (1995) 'Economic issues in airport management', paper presented at the Airport Economics and Finance Symposium, Department of Air Transport, Cranfield University.

Doherty, N. F., Ellis-Chadwick, F. and **Hart, C. H.** (1999) 'Cyber retailing in the UK: the potential of the Internet as a retail channel', *International Journal of Retail & Distribution Management*, 27(1): 22–36.

Drucker, P.G. (1968) *The Practice of Management*, London: Pan.

Eagle, J., Joseph, E. and **Lempres, E.** (2000) 'From products to ecosystems: retail 2010', *The McKinsey Quarterly*, 4: 108–15.

Easey, M. (1995) *Fashion Marketing*, Oxford: Blackwell.

Ebejer, J.M. and **Morden, M.J.** (1988) 'Paternalism in the marketplace: should a salesman be his buyers' keeper?' *Journal of Business Ethics*, 7: 337–9.

Energis (2001) *European e-tail confidence report*, http://195.92.252.136/newsroom /E-tail_confidence.pdf

Faber, R.J. and **O'Guinn, T.C.** (1988) 'Compulsive consumption and credit abuse', *Journal of Consumer Policy*, 11(1): 97–109.

Faber, R.J. and **O'Guinn, T.C.** (1992) 'A clinical screener for compulsive buying', *Journal of Consumer Research*, 19: 459–69.

Fearne, A. and **Hughes, D.** (1999) 'Success factors in the fresh produce supply chain: insights from the UK', *Supply Chain Management*, 4(3): 120–8.

Fernie, J. (1995) 'The coming of the fourth wave: new forms of retail out-of-town development', *International Journal of Retail and Distribution Management*, 23(1): 4–11.

Fernie, J. (1998) 'Relationships in the supply chain', in J. Fernie and L. Sparks (eds), *Logistics and Supply Chain Management*, London: Kogan Page.

Fernie, J. and **Fernie, S.I.** (1997) 'The development of a US retail format in Europe: the case of factory outlet centres', *International Journal of Retail and Distribution Management*, 25: 342–50.

Fernie, J. and **Sparks, L.** (1998) *Logistics and Retail Management*, London: Kogan Page.

Foresight Retail Logistics Task Force (2000) *@ Your Service: Future Models of Retail Logistics*. London: DTI.

Foresight Retail Logistics Task Force (2001) *@ Your Home: New Markets for Customer Service and Delivery*, DTI: London.

Freathy, P. (2002) 'An introduction to the strategy process', MBA distance learning module: Managing the Strategic Environment, Institute for Retail Studies, University of Stirling.

Freathy, P. and **O'Connell, F.** (1998) *European Airport Retailing*, Basingstoke: Macmillan.

Freathy, P. and **Sparks, L.** (1993a) *Sunday Working in the Retail Trade*, Institute for Retail Studies, Stirling.

Freathy, P. and **Sparks, L.** (1993b) 'Sunday working in the retail trade', *International Journal of Retail & Distribution Management*, 21(7): 3–9.

Freedman, L. (2001) 'Heeding the lessons while continuing to lure shoppers online', *European Retail Digest*, 30: 18–20.

Gardner, C. and Sheppard J. (1989) *Consuming Passion: The Rise of Retail Culture* London: Unwin Hyman.

Gist, R. (1968) *Retailing: Concepts and Decisions*, New York: Wiley.

Gold, J.R. and Ward, S.V. (1994) *Place Promotion*, Chichester: Wiley.

Goldman, A. (2001) 'The transfer of retail formats into developing economies: the example of China', *Journal of Retailing*, 77: 221–41.

Goldman, A., Krider, R. and Ramaswami, S. (1999) 'The persistent competitive advantage of traditional food retailers in Asia: wet markets' continued dominance in Hong Kong', *Journal of Macromarketing*, 19(2): 126–39.

Gray, F. (1994) 'Trends in airport retail property: consequences for space allocation, new development and values', Henry Stewart Conference studies airport associated property.

Greater Manchester City Council and Roger Tym & Partners (1986) 'Greater Manchester and the coming of the third wave', in A. West (ed.), *Handbook of Retailing*, Aldershot: Gower.

Guy, C.M. (1994a) *The Retail Development Process*, London: Routledge.

Guy, C.M. (1994b) 'Whatever happened to regional shopping centres?' *Geography*, 79: 293–312.

Guy, C.M. (1995) 'Retail store development at the margin', *Journal of Retailing and Consumer Services*, 2: 25–32.

Guy, C.M. (1997) 'Fixed assets or sunk costs? An examination of retailers' land and property investment in the United Kingdom', *Environment and Planning A*, 29: 1449–64.

Guy, C.M. (1998a) 'Controlling new retail spaces: the impress of planning policies in Western Europe', *Urban Studies*, 35: 953–79.

Guy, C.M. (1998b) 'Alternative-use valuation, open A1 consent, and the development of retail parks', *Environment and Planning A*, 30: 37–47.

Guy, C.M. (1998c) 'Classifications of retail stores and shopping centres: some methodological issues', *GeoJournal*, 45: 255–64.

Guy, C.M. (1999) 'Exit strategies and sunk costs: the implications for multiple retailers', *International Journal of Retail and Distribution Management*, 27: 237–45.

Guy, C.M. (2000) 'From crinkly sheds to fashion parks: the role of financial investment in the transformation of retail parks', *International Review of Retail, Distribution and Consumer Research*, 10: 389–400.

Guy, C.M. (2001) 'Internationalisation of large-format retailers and leisure providers in Western Europe: planning and property impacts', *International Journal of Retail and Distribution Management*, 29: 451–61.

Guy, C. and Lord, D. (1993) 'Transformation and the city centre', in R. Bromley and C. Thomas (eds), *Retail Change*, London: UCL Press.

Harrington, J.M. (1994) 'Shift work and health: a critical review of the literature on working hours', *Annals Academy of Medicine*, 23(5): 699–705.

Harvey, M. (2000) 'Innovation and competition in UK supermarkets', *Supply Chain Management*, 5(1): 15–21.

Hewitt, P. (1993) *About Time: The Revolution in Work and Family Life*, London: Institute for Public Policy Research and the Rivers Oram Press.

Hines, T. and Bruce, M. (2001) *Fashion Marketing: Contemporary Issues*, London: Butterworth Heinemann.

Hogarth, T. and Barth, M.C. (1991) *Age works: A Case Study of B&Q's Use of Older Workers*, University of Warwick: Institute for Employment Research.

Hogarth-Scott, S. (1999) 'Retailer–supplier partnerships: hostages to fortune or the way forward for the new millennium?', *British Food Journal*, 101(9): 668–82.

Hollander, S. (1966) 'Notes on the retail accordion', *Journal of Retailing*, 42: 29–40, 54.

Hollander, S. (1970) *Multinational Retailing*, Michigan State University Press, East Lancing, MI.

Horne, S. and Maddrell, A. (2002) *Charity Shops*, London: Routledge.

Humphries, G. (1996) 'The future of airport retailing: opportunities and threats in a global market', Financial Times Management Report, London.

Huxley, A. (1932) *Brave New World*, London: Chatto & Windus.

Income Data Services Report (1997) 'More full-time students join the workforce', IDS Report No. 749: November.

Income Data Services Report (2000) 'Developing a strategy to reduce staff turnover', IDS report No. 823: 14–15.

Income Data Services Study (2000) 'Labour turnover statistics', IDS Study 692: 21–3.

IGD (2002) *European Grocery Retailing 2002*, Letchmore Heath: Institute for Grocery Distribution.

IRS (1997) 'An assessment of the impact of the abolition of intra-EU duty and tax free allowances', Confidential Report, Institute for Retail Studies, University of Stirling.

Jackson, E. (1991) 'Shopping and leisure: implications of WEM for leisure and for leisure research', *Canadian Geographer*: 280–7.

Johnson, G. and Scholes, K. (1999) *Exploring Corporate Strategy: Text and Cases*, 5th edn, London: Prentice Hall.

Johnson, G. and Scholes, K. (2002) *Exploring Corporate Strategy: Text and Cases*, 6th edn, London: Prentice Hall.

Jones, D.T. (2001) 'Tesco.com: delivering home shopping', *ECR Journal*, 1(1): 37–43.

Jones, J. (2000) *UK Organic Food: Product Brief*, United States Department of Agriculture (USDA), 6 March.

Jones, P. and Hillier, D. (2000) 'Changing the balance: the "ins and outs" of retail development', *Property Management* 18(2): 114–26.

Kaufmann, P.J., Smith, N.C. and Ortmeyer, G.K. (1994) 'Deception in retailer high–low pricing: a rule of reason approach', *Journal of Retailing*, 70(2): 115–38.

Keogh, D. (1994) 'An airport authority with a difference: the Irish experience', *Commercial Airport 1994/95*, London: Stirling Publications.

Kirby, D.A. (1993) 'Working conditions and the trading week' in R. Bromley and C. Thomas (eds), *Retail Change: Contemporary Issues*, London: UCL Press.

Kirkup, M. and Carrigan, M. (2000) 'Video surveillance research in retailing: ethical issues', *International Journal of Retail & Distribution Management*, 28(11): 470–80.

Klapper, S. (1995) 'Innovative use of mobile sales units', paper presented at 4th World Airport Trading Conference, London.

Klein, N. (1999) *No Logo*, New York: Picador.

Koehn, D. (1992) 'Toward an ethic of exchange', *Business Ethics Quarterly*, 2: 341–55.

Kotler, P. (1984) *Principles of Marketing*, 2nd edn, Englewood Cliffs: NJ: Prentice-Hall.

Kotler, P., Armstrong, G., Armstrong, G., Saunders, J. and Wong, V. (1996) *Principles of Marketing*, London: Prentice Hall.

Kotler, P., Armstrong, G., Saunders, J. and Wong, V. (2001) *Principles of Marketing* (3rd edn), London: Prentice Hall.

Kotzab, H. (1999) 'Improving supply chain performance by efficient consumer response? A critical comparison of existing ECR approaches', *Journal of Business and Industrial Marketing*, 14(5/6): 364–77.

KPMG Consulting (2001) *The Quiet Revolution: A Report on the State of eBusiness in the UK*, London: Confederation of British Industry/KPMG Consulting.

Kumar, N. (1996) 'The power of trust in manufacturer–retailer relationships', *Harvard Business Review*, 74: 92–106.

Labour Force Survey (2000) *Labour Markets Trends*, London: HMSO.

Labour Market Trends (1999) 'Students and graduates', *Labour Market Trends*, 107(3): 92.

Larke, R. (1994) *Japanese Retailing*, London: Routledge.

Laseter, T., Houston, P., Ching, A., Byrne, S., Turner, M. and Devendran, A. (2000) 'The last mile to nowhere', *Strategy & Business*, September: 20.

Levitt, T. (1986) *The Marketing Imagination*, New York: The Free Press.

Levy, M. and Weitz, B. (2001) *Retailing Management*, 4th edn, Boston, MA: McGraw Hill Irwin.

Levy, S.J. (1959) 'Symbols for sale', *Harvard Business Review* 37(4): 117–24.

Lewison, D.M. and DeLozier, M.W. (1986) *Retailing: Principles and Practices*, Columbus, OH: Merrill.

Liff, S. and Turner, S. (1999) 'Working in a corner shop: are employee relations changing in response to competitive pressures?', *Employee Relations*, 21(4): 418–29.

Liu, H. and McGoldrick, P. (1995) 'International sourcing: patterns and trends', in P. McGoldrick and G. Davies (eds), *International Retailing: Trends and Strategies*, London: Pitman.

Longstreth, R. (1997) *City Center to Regional Mall*, Cambridge, MA: MIT Press.

Longstreth, R. (1999) *The Drive-In, the Supermarket and the Transformation of Commercial Space in Los Angeles 1914–1941*, Cambridge, MA: MIT Press.

Lord, D., Moran, W., Parker, T. and Sparks, L. (1988) 'Retailing on three continents: the discount food store operations of Albert Gubay', *International Journal of Retailing*, 3(3): 3–53.

Lowe, M (1991) 'Trading places: retailing and local economic development at Merry Hill, West Midlands', *East Midlands Geographer* 14(1): 31–48.

Luffman, G.A., Sanderson, S., Lea, E. and Kenny, B. (1987) *Business Policy: An Analytical Introduction*, Oxford: Blackwell.

McDonald's (2001) Our Environment, company information leaflet.

McKechnie, J., Hobbs, S. and Lindsay, S. (1998) 'The nature and extent of student employment at the University of Paisley', in P. Kelly, (ed.), *Working In 2 Worlds: Students and Part-Time Employment*, Glasgow: Scottish Low Pay Unit.

McKinnon, A.C. (1996) 'The development of retail logistics in the UK: a position paper', *Technology Foresight: Retail and Distribution Panel*, Edinburgh: Heriot-Watt University.

McKinnon, A.C. and Tallam, D. (2002) *New Crime Threats from E-tailing: Theft in the Home Delivery Channel*, London: Foresight Programme, Department of Trade and Industry.

McKinsey Global Institute (1998) *Driving Productivity and Growth in the UK Economy*, London: McKinsey.

McLean, M. and Moore, C. (1997) 'UK retailers and AIDS: an exploratory study', *International Journal of Retail & Distribution Management*, 25(1): 22–8.

McNair, M. (1958) 'Significant trends and developments in the post-war period', in A. Smith (ed.), *Competitive Distribution in a Free High Level Economy and its implications for the University*, Pittsburg PA: University of Pittsburg Press.

Mahler, D. (2000) 'An American century of retailing', *Chain Store Age, Retail Supplement*, April: 44–51.

Mandeville, L. (1995) *Prospects for Home Shopping in Europe*, FT Management Report, London: Pearson.

Mees, M.D. (2000) 'The place of the food industry in the global e-commerce universe: Aholds' experience', paper presented to the CIES Conference on Supply Chain for E-commerce and Home Delivery in the Food Industry, Berlin.

Miller, J., Kim, S. and **Scholfield-Tomschin, S.** (1998) 'The effects of activity and ageing on rural community living and consuming', *The Journal of Consumer Affairs*, 32(2): 343–68.

Millington, A.F. (2000) *Property Development*, London: Estates Gazette.

Mintel (2002) *The UK Retail Rankings*, London: Mintel.

Mockford, D. (1996) *An Investigation of Labour Turnover and Employee Retention within CRS Food Division*, unpublished MBA in Retailing Dissertation, University of Stirling.

Morganosky, M. A. (1997) 'Retailing and the Internet: a perspective on the top 100 US retailers', Research note, *International Journal of Retail & Distribution Management*, 25(11): 372–7.

Morganosky, M. A. and **Cude, B. J.** (2000) 'Consumer response to online grocery shopping', *International Journal of Retail & Distribution Management*, 28(1): 17–26.

Morganosky, M. A. and **Fernie, J.** (1999) 'Mail order direct marketing in the United States and the United Kingdom: responses to changing market conditions', *Journal of Business Research*, 45: 275–9.

MTI (1998) *Retail Employment in the UK*, London: Retail Week.

National Assembly for Wales (2002) *Planning Policy Wales*, Cardiff: National Assembly.

National Statistics (2001) 'Households with Internet access 1998/99, 1999/2000 and 2000/01', *Regional Trends 37*, http://www.statistics.gov.uk/StatBase/ssdataset.asp?vlnk=6016&More=Y

Negroponte, N. (1998) http://www.media.mit.edu/people/nicholas/Wired/WIRED6-07.html

Netherlands Economic Institute (1989) *The Impact of Abolishing Duty and Tax Free Allowances in the European Community*, Rotterdam: Department for Society and Policy.

Next (1998) *Next Factfile 2*, Leicester: Next PLC.

Next (2001) Next 2001 – Interim Statement, www.next.co.uk.

Nockold, C. (2001) 'Identifying the real costs of home delivery', *Logistics & Transport Focus*, 3(10): 70–1.

O'Connell, F. (1993) 'An Aer Rianta response to aspects of change in the micro, task and organisation environments', unpublished mimeo, Dublin: Aer Rianta.

Office for National Statistics (1990) *New Earnings Survey*, London: HMSO.

Office for National Statistics (1995) *New Earnings Survey*, London: HMSO.

Office for National Statistics (2000) *New Earnings Survey 2000, Part D: Analyses by Occupation*, London: HMSO.

Office for National Statistics (2002a) *Labour Market Trends*, 110(10): S26.

Office for National Statistics (2002b) *Labour Market Trends*, 110(11): S72, S75.

OFTEL (2002) 'Consumers use of Internet', Q10, August 2002, http://www.oftel.gov.uk/publications/research/2002/q10intr1002.htm.

O'Malley, L., Patterson, M. and **Evans, M.** (1997) 'Retailer use of geodemographic and other data sources: an empirical investigation', *International Journal of Retail & Distribution Management*, 25(6): 188–96.

Orwell, G. (1949) *Nineteen Eighty-Four*, London: Secker & Warburg.

O'Toole, K. (1997) 'European lead: Europe's hubs begin to face up to the new commercialism', *Flight International*, 151(4572): 34.

Owen, D., Reza, B., Green, A., Maguire, M. and **Pitcher, J.** (2000) 'Patterns of labour market participation in ethnic minority groups', *Labour Market Trends*, 108 (11): 505–10.

Page, S.J. and **Hardyman, R.** (1996) 'Place marketing and town centre management', *Cities*, 13(3): 153–64.

Patten, S. (2001) 'Scion of top UK retail dynasty picks up the reins with aplomb', *The Times*, 15 September, B5.

Peters, T.J. and **Austin, N.K.** (1985) *A Passion for Excellence: The Leadership Difference*, Glasgow: Collins.

Piacentini, M., MacFadyen, L. and **Eadie, D.** (2000) 'Corporate social responsibility in food retailing', *International Journal of Retail & Distribution Management*, 28(11): 459–69.

Planet Retail (2002) *Grocery Retailing in Europe*, London: M+M Planet Retail.

Punakivi, M. and **Saranen, J.** (2001) 'Identifying the success factors in e-grocery home delivery', *International Journal of Retail & Distribution Management*, 29(4): 427–39.

Punakivi, M. and **Tanskanen, K.** (2002) 'Increasing the cost efficiency of e-fulfilment using shared reception boxes', *International Journal of Retail & Distribution Management*, 30: 498–507.

Punakivi, M., Yrjola, H. and **Holmstrom, J.** (2001) 'Solving the last mile issue: reception box or delivery box', *International Journal of Physical Distribution and Logistics Management*, 31(6): 427–39.

Quinn, F. (1990) *Crowning the Customer*, Dublin: O'Brien Press.

Rankine, K. (1998) 'Next plunges as fashions fail to shift', *Daily Telegraph – Business News*, 27 March.

Ratcliffe, J. and **Stubbs, M.** (1996) *Urban Planning and Real Estate Development*, London: UCL Press.

Rawls, J. (1972) *A Theory of Justice*, Oxford: Clarendon Press.

Reda, S. (2001) 'After 15 years and ownership changes, merchandising software still draws retail fans', *Stores*, May: 28–30.

Retail Intelligence (1992) *The UK Retail Rankings*, London: Corporate Intelligence Group.

Retail Review (1996) 'Next excels yet again: annual results, *Retail Review*, CWS: Manchester.

Retail Week (1996) 'Is there a recruiting crisis?', *Retail Week*, 13 September, 10–16.

Retail Week (2002) 'Making the media work for you', 27 September, 16–21.

Reynolds, J. (1993) 'The proliferation of the planned shopping centre', in R. Bromley and C. Thomas (eds), *Retail Change: Contemporary Issues*, London: UCL Press.

Reynolds, J. (2000) 'eCommerce: a critical review', *International Journal of Retail and Distribution Management*, 28: 414–44.

Reynolds, J. (2001) 'The new etail landscape: the view from the beach', *European Retail Digest*, 30: 6–8.

RI (1992) 'Market research report and recommendations', London: Research International.

Ring, L. and **Tigert, D.** (2001) 'Viewpoint: the decline and fall of Internet grocery retailers', *International Journal of Retail & Distribution Management*, 29(6): 266–73.

Robinson, O. and **Wallace, J.** (1974) 'Part-time employment and low pay in retail distribution in Britain', *Industrial Relations Journal*, 5(1): 38–51.

Rowlands, P. (2001) 'Why access is the key', *elogistics Magazine*, 15: Nov/Dec.

Ruston, P. (1999) *Out-of-town Shopping: the future of retailing*, London: The British Library.

Salmon, W. J. and **Tordjman, A.** (1989) 'The internationalisation of retailing', *International Journal of Retailing*, 4(2): 3–16.

Savage, G.C. (1997) *An Investigation into the Causes of Labour Turnover within Farmfoods Limited*, unpublished MBA in Retailing Dissertation, University of Stirling.

Schilling, M. and **Hill, C.** (1998) 'Managing the new product development process: strategic imperatives', *The Academy of Management Executive*, 12(3): 67–81.

Schmidt, R.A. and **Corbett, M.** (1994) 'The image of retailing as a graduate career', Marketing Education Group Annual Conference: Marketing: Unity in Diversity, University of Ulster, 4–6 July: 813–22.

Schon, D. (1969) *Beyond the Stable State*, New York: Penguin.

Seth, A. and **Randall, G.** (1999) *The Grocers: The Rise and Rise of the Supermarket Chains*, London: Kogan Page.

Seth, A. and **Randall, G.** (2001) *The Grocers: The Rise and Rise of the Supermarket Chains*, 2nd edn, London: Kogan Page.

Sewell-Rutter, C. (1995) 'Experiences of privatisation', paper presented at the Airport Economics and Finance Symposium, University of Westminster/Cranfield University.

Smith, C. (1994) 'Airport industry structure: the trend towards commercialisation', report prepared by Coopers & Lybrand, London.

Smith, N.C. (1990) *Morality and the Market: Consumer Pressure for Corporate Accountability*, London: Routledge.

Sneade, A. (2001) 'Trade union membership 1999–2000: an analysis of data from the Certification Officer and the Labour Force Survey', *Labour Market Trends*, 109(9): 433–44.

Sparks, L. (1991) 'Employment in DIY superstores', *Service Industries Journal*, 11(3): 304–23.

Sparks, L. (1998) 'The retail logistics transformation', in J. Fernie and L. Sparks (eds), *Logistics and Retail Management*, London: Kogan Page.

Sparks, L. and Findlay, A. (2000) *The Future of Shopping*, London: Royal Institute of Chartered Surveyors.

Stern, A.L. (1990) 'Sorrell Ridge: slotting allowances', *Harvard Business School Case* N9-590-112, Boston, MA: Harvard University.

Stewart, J.B. (1959) 'Functional features in product strategy', *Harvard Business Review*, March: 89–93.

Stredwick, J. and Ellis, S. (1998) *Flexible Working Practices: Techniques and Innovations*, London: Institute of Personnel and Development.

Swindley, D. (1992) 'Retail buying in the United Kingdom', *Service Industries Journal*, 12(4): 3–15.

Symons, Travers, Morgan (1997) 'Assessment of the impact of the abolition of intra-EU duty and tax free allowances on low cost airlines', London.

Taylor, E. (2002) 'Swiss online grocer LeShop thrives thanks to low costs', *Wall Street Journal*, 15 February.

Thomas, M. (1987) 'Customer care: the ultimate marketing tool', in R. Wensley (ed.), *Marketing Proceedings*, Warwick University, Marketing Education Group, 20th Annual Conference – Reviewing Effective Research and Good Practice.

Thompson, J.L. (1993) 'Employment in retailing', *International Journal of Retail and Distribution Management*, 21(2): 23–31.

Times Books (1998) *The Times 1000, 1998: The Definitive Reference to Business Today*, London: Times Books.

TMS (1992) 'Menswear presentation to Next Retail Ltd', London: The TMS Partnership.

Tordjman, A. (1988) 'The French hypermarket: could it be developed in the States?', *Retail and Distribution Management*, 16(4): 14–16.

Treadgold, A. (1990) 'The emerging internationalisation of retailing: present status and future strategies', *Irish Marketing Review*, 5(2): 11–27.

Tulip, S. (2002) 'E-fulfilment: a tall order', *Logistics Europe*, 10(3): 29–32.

Twomey, B. (2001) 'Labour market participation of ethnic groups', *Labour Market Trends*, 109 (1): 29–42.

UCLA (2001) 'Surveying the digital future: year two', The UCLA Internet Report 2001, http://ccp.ucla.edu/pdf/UCLA-Internet-Report-2001.pdf.

Underhill, P. (1999) *Why We Buy: The Science of Shopping*, London: Orion.

Verdict (1994) *Retail Fashion Images*, London: Verdict Research Limited.

Verdict (2000) *Electronic Shopping, UK*, London: Verdict Research Limited.

Walters, K.S. (1989) 'Limited paternalism and the Pontius Pilate plight', *Journal of Business Ethics*, 8: 955–62.

Ward, P., **Sturrock, F.**, and **Schmidt, R.A.** (1998) 'To shop or to deshop: that is the question', in *Proceedings of the 1998 Annual Conference of the Academy of Marketing*, Sheffield Hallam University: 474–7.

Welling, H. (2000) 'Unveiling AIMs store of the Future: Part I,' *Apparel Industry Magazine*, 61(2): 24–31.

White, G. (1999) 'Pay structures of the low-paid and the national minimum wage', *Labour Market Trends*, 107(3): 129–35.

White, H. (2000) 'Buyer–supplier relationships in the UK fresh produce industry', *British Food Journal*, 102(1): 6–17.

Whitefield, E. (2001) 'Vertical inclination', *Drapers Record*, 4 August: 43–44.

Whysall, P.T. (1999) 'Finding the right location: a case study of the ethics of retail location', in M. Dupuis and J. Dawson (eds), *European Cases in Retailing*, Oxford: Blackwell.

Whysall, P.T. (2000a) 'Addressing ethical issues in retailing: a stakeholder perspective', *International Review of Retail, Distribution and Consumer Research*, 10(3): 305–18.

Whysall, P.T. (2000b) 'Retailing and the Internet: a review of ethical issues', *International Journal of Retail & Distribution Management*, 28(11): 481–90.

Wilkinson, D. (1998) 'Who are the low-paid?', *Labour Market Trends*, 106(12): 617–22.

Williams, A. (1981) *Financial Times*, 25 February.

Wills, J. (1999) *Merchandising and Buying Strategies*, London: Financial Times Retail and the Consumer.

Wilson, N. (1996) 'The supply chains of perishable products in northern Europe', *British Food Journal*, 98(6): 9–15.

Wilson-Jeanselme, M. (2001) 'Grocery retailing on the Internet: the leaking bucket theory', *European Retail Digest*, 30: 9–12.

Winger, A. (2001) 'Elements of change, stability and uncertainty in the retail real estate market', *Real Estate Issues*, 25(4): 54–60.

Worthington, S. (1988) 'Credit Cards in the United Kingdom: where the power lies in the battle between the banks and the retailers', *Journal of Marketing Management*, 4(1): 61–70.

Worthington, S. (1994) 'Marks & Spencer Financial Services: where do they go from here?', in P. McGoldrick, (ed.), *Cases in Retail Management*, London: Pitman.

Worthington, S. (1998) 'The card centric distribution of financial services: a comparison of Japan and the UK', *International Journal of Bank Marketing*, 16(5): 211–20.

Worthington, S. (2000) 'A classic example of a misnomer: the loyalty card', *Journal of Targeting, Measurement and Analysis for Marketing*, 8(3): 222–34.

Worthington, S. (2001) 'Affinity credit cards: a critical review', *International Journal of Retail and Distribution Management*, 29(11): 485–508.

Worthington, S. and Edwards, V. (2000) 'Changes in payments markets, past, present and future: a comparison between Australia and the UK', *International Journal of Bank Marketing*, 18(5): 212–21.

Wrigley, N. (1998) 'Understanding store development programmes in post-property crisis UK food retailing', *Environment and Planning A*, 30: 15–35.

Wrigley, N. (2002) 'The landscape of pan-European food retail consolidation', *International Journal of Retail and Distribution Management*, 30(2): 89–91.

Wycherley, I. (2002) 'Managing relationships in the UK organic food sector', *Journal of Marketing Management*, 18: 673–92.

Yrjola, M., Tanskanen, K. and Holmstron, J. (2002) 'The way to profitable Internet grocery retailing: 6 lessons learned', *International Journal of Retail & Distribution Management*, 30(4): 169–78.

Zola, E. (1883) *The Ladies Paradise*, trans. B. Nelson, published 1995, Oxford: Oxford University Press.

Glossary[1]

Automatic replenishment (AR): once the right systems are in place, such as bar coding, EPOS terminals, advanced ship notices, shipper container markings and electronic data interchange, certain merchandise (usually those with little volatility) can be replenished automatically once sold. This demand information will also drive production schedules.

Advanced Ship Notices (ASN): a notice provided in electronic data interchange format and sent from the manufacturer to the retailer with precise and detailed information on the contents of the shipment as it leaves the plant.

B2B: business to business has come to signify businesses purchasing goods and products from each other via the Internet.

B2C: business to customer has come to mean businesses selling products to customers via the Internet.

B+B2C: business plus business to customer has come to be known as an 'e-marketplace', where the manufacturer and retailer work together to meet the needs of their customer.

Barcode technology: an automatic identification technology in which a laser or incandescent beam of light sweeps across a series of precisely defined bars and spaces. The lines are solid black and the spaces bright white. The scanning beam hits the white and black surfaces and the scanner photo detector, which turns them into electrical impulses, senses the resulting reflections. The impulses are relayed to a computer, which translates or encodes the information.

Central business district: often referred to as 'downtown' in the United States. This is the area of a city where there is the highest concentration of offices and businesses.

Collaborative Planning Forecasting and Replenishment (CPFR): an Internet-based sales forecasting process. CPFR allows retailers to share sales forecast data with selected vendors over the Internet in a process that is designed to substantially reduce inventory levels.

---

[1]   I am particularly indebted to Susan Fiorito for her help in compiling this Glossary.

Cross docking: the process that immediately forwards pallets of merchandise to the retailer without taking the product into warehouse inventory. Also referred to as flow through distribution, it serves as a consolidation service, such that product or goods are taken off the manufacturers' truck at the distribution centre, separated by store destination and placed immediately on to a truck for each store (not to be confused with cross dressing).

Customer relationship management (CRM): these schemes are normally built around communication with customers in order to become more competitive in the marketplace. Through CRM retailers are trying to build greater customer loyalty and retention and develop methods of creating longer-term and continuous relationships.

Data warehousing: huge central repositories of information organized by subject and residing on dedicated computers. It offers the tools to understand and satisfy customers' growing needs for merchandise. It is a means of accessing detailed customer, inventory and financial information on a continuous basis.

Data mining: the automated discovery of 'interesting' non-obvious patterns hidden in a database that have a high potential for contributing to the bottom line. It encompasses 'confirmation' or the testing of relationships revealed through the discovery process.

Disintermediation: refers to removing the middleman. The term is used to describe many Internet-based businesses that use the World Wide Web to sell products directly to customers rather than going through traditional retail channels. By eliminating the middlemen companies can sell their products more cheaply and quickly.

E-commerce: the use of computers and electronic communications in business transactions. E-commerce may include the use of electronic data interchange, electronic money exchange, Internet advertising, web sites and online databases.

Efficient consumer response (ECR): using this strategy retailers make store-level changes in four key areas: (1) ordering, (2) receiving, (3) merchandising and (4) labour scheduling and incentives. Retailers and suppliers reduce total operating costs through the use of automatic reordering, cross docking, barcodes, PC software for front and back office efficiencies, and keep constant lines of communications open between themselves.

Electronic data interchange (EDI): information technology that replaces the paper documents, such as purchase orders and invoices, which usually accompany business transactions. This is achieved through the use of electronic transmissions of information from one computer to another.

European article numbering (EAN): this classification system uses a 13-digit numbering system. The code structure, like that of the UPC, must uniquely identify every product line to prevent confusion and pricing errors. The first two digits represent the issuing organisation. Digits 3–7 represent the manufacturer or company marketing the product, digits 8–12 identify the product and digit 13 is a check digit to ensure the code has been entered correctly.

E-cash: consists of smart card systems that can be used over the Internet or in the same way as cash or debit cards with retailers whose stores are equipped with special card readers. Funds must be deposited into the card, which is then debited every time it is used.

Electronic point of sale (EPOS): a stock control and computerised till software system that uses a scanning system to record transaction data. It ensures the retailer charges accurate prices, enables the checkout staff to work more efficiently and the retailer to accurately gauge sales demand. EPOS may be linked to sales-based ordering (see below).

Electronic shelf labels (ESL): digital pricing labels that accurately and instantaneously reflect point-of-sale data as it changes, using radio frequency technology.

Extranet (Web EDI): a private network that uses Internet protocols and the public telecommunication system to securely share part of a business's information or operations with suppliers, vendor partners, customers or other businesses. It has been used by vendors to access the inventory tracking system of retailers through dedicated networks to view point-of-sale data on their products at the retailer level.

Full-time equivalent: employment figures are expressed as full-time equivalent employment, a computed statistic representing the number of full-time employees that could have been employed if the reported number of hours worked by part-time employees had been worked by full-time employees. This statistic is calculated by dividing the 'part-time hours paid' by the standard number of hours for full-time employees and then adding the resulting quotient to the number of full-time employees.

Geographic information systems (GIS): a computerised database management system for the capture, storage, retrieval, analysis and display of spatial (locationally defined) data.

Gross margin: this is usually defined as a percentage. Gross margin is calculated for a given period of time and must be large enough to cover operating expenses and allow for a reasonable profit. It is expressed as:

$$\frac{\text{Sales} - \text{cost of goods sold}}{\text{sales}} \times 100.$$

Gross profit: the difference between retail sales and the cost of the goods sold. Gross profit is usually expressed in monetary terms. It is defined as:

$$\text{Gross profit} = \text{sales} - \text{cost of goods sold}.$$

Intranet: a formal system permitting the electronic exchange of business data and information within an organisation. This exchange can be between all levels of employees. The information included on the Intranet may be employee benefits, policies, procedures and company news. Some software applications may only be available to senior executives who may need to access a range of software to create or amend text.

Internet: an open, worldwide computer network, linking together by fast data communication many thousands of computers owned by governments, education institutions, commercial organisations and others. The Internet is a set of protocols governing how data are presented by individuals and organisations.

Inventory turnover: the number of times, on average, that inventories 'roll over' or 'cycle through' the department during a year. For example, jeans are delivered to the store through the loading dock in the back, spend some time in the store on the racks, and then are sold and go out of the front door. The faster this process the higher the inventory turnover. There are two methods of calculating inventory turnover, and either should result in the same answer. Here are both ratios:

Inventory turnover at cost = Cost of goods sold/Average inventory at cost,

or

Inventory turnover at retail = Net sales/Average inventory at retail.

Just-in-time (JIT): the underlying principle of JIT is to keep raw or semi-finished goods' inventories as low as possible, maintaining no stock except what is needed for immediate production. Raw materials or semi-finished goods are supplied to the JIT finished-goods' manufacturer frequently and at short notice. Thus the inventory investment necessary when using JIT is close to zero.

Kiosk: also called customer access terminal, this is a multi-media device that relies on a combination of computer and telecommunication technology. Two common uses of kiosks are: (1) to provide a broader selection of product than is typically in a store and (2) to provide information and give customers and employees access to product specifications.

Messaging technology: radio frequency wireless transmissions will be used to transmit messages such as retail advertising, notifications of e-mail messages, weather or stock reports from web sites that the consumer has set up for themselves. These messages will be sent constantly over the mobile phone or other small portable devices.

Loyalty cards: a retail strategy that allows the company to keep track of a customer's purchases and then offers the card holder benefits through reduced prices on goods, pre-notification of sales, cash back or other benefits.

Magnetic stripe technology: currently most credit, debit and loyalty cards have a small amount of information about the card holder that is coded on the reverse of the card using magnetic stripe technology. Specialist devices called card-swipe machines can decode this information.

Merchandise turns: (see inventory turnover).

National minimum wage: the national minimum wage in the United Kingdom is aimed at providing employees with decent minimum standards and fairness in the workplace. It applies to nearly all workers and sets hourly rates below which pay must not fall. The rates set are based on the recommendations of the independent Low Pay Commission. In December 2002 the main (adult) rate for workers aged 22 and over was £4.20 per hour and the development rate for workers aged 18–21 inclusive was £3.60 per hour.

Net margin: is usually expressed as a percentage of sales revenue and is defined as:

$$\text{Net margin} = \frac{\text{net profit}}{\text{sales}} \times 100.$$

Net profit: the difference between the gross profit less other expenses (heat, light, rates, wages, etc. – these are sometimes referred to as overheads or revenue expenditure). Net profit is usually expressed in monetary terms and may be defined as:

$$\text{Net profit} = \text{gross profit} - \text{overheads.}$$

Permission marketing: a retail company asks consumers if they would like to receive notices about sales, product updates, etc. On the Internet, and web sites, this typically would mean an e-mail notice from the company, but customers can indicate they want future communications from the company by post or other delivery methods.

Personal data assistant (PDA): an electronic device that lets the consumer, whilst shopping, scan items to check prices or purchase information. It can also act as a debit card and be used to purchase products. Another feature is its ability to be an electronic diary, which would also store PINs and possibly health and insurance information.

Point of sale (POS): the place where the exchange process takes place – usually where goods and services are purchased by the consumer from the retailer.

Quick response (QR): this strategy involves online electronic communication of sales data from retailers to merchandise vendors, with the vendors promptly supplying retailers the merchandise needed to return the inventory in stores to levels previously determined cooperatively by the retailer and the vendor.

Radio frequency (RF): a non-optical automatic identification device that uses radio waves to transmit data. It is also a generic term referring to the technology used in cable television and broadband networks. It uses electromagnetic wave forms usually in the megahertz (MHz) range of transmission.

Recycling: the return of product for destruction and then incorporation in new products, either or the same or different composition and function.

Resource reduction: the minimisation of waste, which results in more efficient forward and reverse distribution processes.

Reuse: the process that enables an activity to be carried our repeatedly with no additional investment in the infrastructure of that activity.

Reverse logistics/Reverse distribution: the return of packing and handling material 'upstream' for recycling/reuse or disposal.

Sales-based ordering: replenishment based on actual customer demand (via EPoS) to eliminate the labour intensive process of manual reordering.

Shipping container marking (SCM): bar-coded labels permanently attached to containers when they leave the manufacturing plant. They specify what items or goods are in that container and its destination. This eliminates the need to break open packages at the retail distribution centre to check merchandise before it is shipped to each store.

Smart cards (SC): these cards look like credit or debit cards, but rather than storing information on a magnetic stripe all pertinent user information and cash value of the transaction is stored on a microprocessor chip that is embedded in the plastic card. The SC will be more secure than conventional cards and will be able to carry a vast amount of information.

Stock keeping units (SKUs): the unit of measure in which an item is stocked. The SKU is the smallest unit of measure applied to an item when it is issued from or returned to a warehouse.

Stock-outs: the temporary unavailability of products on retailers' shelves, leading to potential lost sales for both retailer and manufacturer.

Universal product code (UPC): a classification system in which each product is assigned a 12-digit number. The Uniform Code Council (UCC) assigns the first five digits to the manufacturer of the product. The next five digits identify the product, its size, colour, fabric, style, etc. The other two digits include a zero added at the front of the number in order to be compatible with the EAN and a final digit that is a check digit used to make sure that the scanner reads the code properly. The numbers are pre-marked on the package by the manufacturer in the form of a bar code.

Web TV: interactive television that is connected to the World Wide Web. An example of how this can be used is that a person watching a television show, such as *Friends*, would be able to purchase an actor's clothing, accessories or even furniture by using a remote mouse-like devise. The television viewer would simply point at an item of clothing and immediately in the corner of the television screen a web site would open up informing the individual of the brand, size, price, etc. of that item and where and how to purchase it.

Wireless area protocol (WAP): basically this means people will be able to access the Internet via a cell phone or another device such as a palm pilot. Information will be divided into smaller applications. There will also be a migration away from PCs to customised devices.

Index